9/11 in European Literature

Svenja Frank
Editor

9/11 in European Literature

Negotiating Identities Against the Attacks and What Followed

Editor
Svenja Frank
Promotionsprogramm
 Textwissenschaften
Georg-August-Universität Göttingen
Göttingen, Germany

ISBN 978-3-319-64208-6   ISBN 978-3-319-64209-3 (eBook)
DOI 10.1007/978-3-319-64209-3

Library of Congress Control Number: 2017949457

© The Editor(s) (if applicable) and The Author(s) 2017
This work is subject to copyright. All rights are solely and exclusively licensed by the Publisher, whether the whole or part of the material is concerned, specifically the rights of translation, reprinting, reuse of illustrations, recitation, broadcasting, reproduction on microfilms or in any other physical way, and transmission or information storage and retrieval, electronic adaptation, computer software, or by similar or dissimilar methodology now known or hereafter developed.
The use of general descriptive names, registered names, trademarks, service marks, etc. in this publication does not imply, even in the absence of a specific statement, that such names are exempt from the relevant protective laws and regulations and therefore free for general use.
The publisher, the authors and the editors are safe to assume that the advice and information in this book are believed to be true and accurate at the date of publication. Neither the publisher nor the authors or the editors give a warranty, express or implied, with respect to the material contained herein or for any errors or omissions that may have been made. The publisher remains neutral with regard to jurisdictional claims in published maps and institutional affiliations.

Cover illustration © Ran Shauli

Printed on acid-free paper

This Palgrave Macmillan imprint is published by Springer Nature
The registered company is Springer International Publishing AG
The registered company address is: Gewerbestrasse 11, 6330 Cham, Switzerland

Contents

Introduction: 9/11 in European Literature   1
Svenja Frank

Part I   September 11 Seen Through European Media and Semiotic Theory

9/11: The Interpretation of Disaster as Disaster
of Interpretation—An American Catastrophe Reflected
in American and European Discourses   37
Rolf G. Renner

The Wind of the Hudson. Gerhard Richter's *September*
(2005) and the European Perception of Catastrophe   61
Ulrich Kinzel

'Burning from the Inside Out': *Let the Great
World Spin* (2009)   83
Eoin Flannery

Part II Literary Translations of September 11 into Europe's National Contexts

Seeing Is Disbelieving: The Contested Visibility of 9/11 in France   105
Jean-Philippe Mathy

Cultural and Historical Memory in English and German Discursive Responses to 9/11   131
Sandra Singer

The Post-9/11 World in Three Polish Responses: Zagajewski, Skolimowski, Tochman   159
Ewa Kowal

The Islamic World as Other in Oriana Fallaci's "Trilogy"   181
Charles Burdett

Part III Negotiating European Identity After September 11 Through the Double Other of the US and Islam

National Identity and Literary Culture After 9/11: Pro- and Anti-Americanism in Frédéric Beigbeder's *Windows on the World* (2003) and Thomas Hettche's *Woraus wir gemacht sind* (2006)   207
Birte Christ

The Mimicry of Dialogue: Thomas Lehr's *September. Fata Morgana* (2010)   253
Svenja Frank

Europe and Its Discontents: Intra-European Violence in Dutch Literature After 9/11   283
Maria Boletsi

Tourist/Terrorist: Narrating Uncertainty in Early European Literature on Guantánamo 323
Philipp Hubmann

Appendix: Extract from Giovanna Capucci's
Twin Towers: poesie, **with translations by Gillian Ania** 357

References 381

Index 383

About the Editor

Svenja Frank is a member of the Ph.D. programme "Text Studies" at Göttingen University, Germany, and works on the reflection of literary criticism in fictional texts. After completing her studies in European Culture, English and German Literature, she has taught Modern and Contemporary German literature at Freiburg University, the University of Latvia and Oxford University. Among her research interests are German and comparative contemporary literature, intermediality and literary theory.

List of Figures

Introduction: 9/11 in European Literature
Fig. 1   Paolo Sorrentino: *La grande bellezza* — 2
Fig. 2   Richard Drew: *The Falling Man* — 3

9/11: The Interpretation of Disaster as Disaster of Interpretation—An American Catastrophe Reflected in American and European Discourses
Fig. 1   Thomas Hoepker: *Young People on the Brooklyn Waterfront on Sept. 11* — 50

The Wind of the Hudson. Gerhard Richter's *September* (2005) and the European Perception of Catastrophe
Fig. 1   Gerhard Richter: *September* — 74
Fig. 2   Gerhard Richter: *25. Febr. 01* — 76

Introduction: 9/11 in European Literature

Svenja Frank

Loud music, people dancing, performance art interludes: Rome's high society is celebrating the city, life, and, above all, itself. In Paolo Sorrentino's film, *La grande bellezza* (2013) [The Great Beauty], the viewer follows the ageing writer Jep Gambardella to the parties of Italy's jet set who, just like the film, subordinates everything to sensual pleasure. This portrayal of Rome's decadent beauty, in many ways a cinematic homage to Fellini, turns the 'eternal city' into one eternal party.

For a few seconds during one of these debauched feasts, amidst the hustle and bustle of the partying people, a work of art in the host's house catches the viewer's gaze, containing a reference to 9/11, a reference that because of its clever subtlety and the fleetingness of the shot has not yet yielded any commentary. In comic-like abstraction, the painting shows a figure in a pose identical to *The Falling Man* in the picture of the same title by US photographer Richard Drew, falling, however, not in front of the World Trade Center's North Tower in New York, but in front of the Colosseum in Rome (Figs. 1 and 2).

Using the analogy of the Roman Empire and the US superpower, with the locus of *panem et circenses* as the very symbol of decadence,

---

S. Frank (✉)
Promotionsprogramm "Textwissenschaften", Georg-August-Universität Göttingen, Göttingen, Germany

Fig. 1 Paolo Sorrentino: *La grande bellezza*

the painting draws a line from classical antiquity to the Western lifestyle which is hypertrophically represented in the film—it is this decadence against which the al-Qaida attacks on September 11 were allegedly directed. Further, this displacement of the "Falling Man" also conjures up, in an uncomfortable way, a connection between entertainment and spectacle (from gladiatorial contests to mock sea battles, for which the amphitheatre had originally been built) to the iconic images of September 11 broadcast to the global TV viewer through an almost simultaneous coverage of the catastrophe. At the same time, the inconspicuous and clever nature of Sorrentino's reference absorbs the terrorist attacks into the aesthetic surface of his cinematic language. As an intarsia transferred into the European context, 9/11 is also dehistoricized, put at the same level as Rome's major tourist attraction and reduced to a pop-art icon.

Sorrentino's *La grande bellezza* exemplifies the versatile and productive reception of the September 11 attacks in the European context, even in unexpected detail. With the geographical distance from the catastrophe, Europe's creative production and intellectual discourse from the beginning disposed of the tragic event with much wider artistic leeway than its proclaimed ally under attack, leading to infamous descriptions of the tragedy as the act of "performance artists"[1] by British Indian writer

---

[1] Rushdie, "Step Across This Line," 375. The greater artistic leeway in Europe becomes evident, for example, if one compares Frédéric Beigbeder's early 9/11 novel *Windows on the World* (2003) with its English translation (2005). In his portrayal of the attacks from the inside of the eponymous restaurant of the World Trade Center North Tower, he likens the growing heat and evolving smoke to the Nazi gas chambers and crematoria, and in a boldly decadent move has a couple, faced with imminent death, engage in intercourse.

Fig. 2 Richard Drew: *The Falling Man*

Both the Holocaust comparisons and the sex scene were removed from the English translation (2005), indicating that four years after the catastrophe, one still assumed a different tolerance level in European and US audiences.

Salman Rushdie, and "the greatest work of art"[2] by German composer Karlheinz Stockhausen. Such comments were surpassed only by French philosopher Baudrillard's claim that "By the grace of terrorism, the World Trade Center has become the World's most beautiful building—the eighth wonder of the world!" Such conceptualizations of the deaths of thousands of people are highly morally questionable. The immediacy and abundance of these reactions showed that 9/11 also spurred one line of reception that is very specific to continental Europe. The footage of the Twin Towers attacks was absorbed into this perceptual framework of European philosophy, semiotics and media theory, and read as a real as well as a symbolic confirmation of postmodernism's major postulates that had been put forward for several decades, such as the indistinguishability of fiction and reality and the intrinsic self-referentiality of language and sign systems in general. This specific European way of conceptualizing reality and culture in the tradition of French poststructuralism was also applied to the US catastrophe as Verso's trio of works by Baudrillard, Virilio and Žižek,[3] published on the first anniversary of the attacks, exemplifies.

While these cultural-semiotic interpretations have become a frequent point of reference in the 9/11 literary canon and build a backdrop to its scholarship, the fictional and literary reception of the terrorist attacks and the following wars in European literatures and languages has not yet gained much attention. This is surprising, given a wealth and variety of European 9/11 literature which prompted literary critic Kristiaan Versluys to dub 9/11 metaphorically also a "European event."[4] *9/11 in European Literature* sets out to shed light on major tendencies among this prolific literary engagement with the attacks.

Despite its global effects the attacks were very much received as a US national tragedy and mourned as such. On September 11, 2001, the United States found itself subject to an unprecedented enemy attack which hit the nation's economic as well as its military heart. Though the World Trade Center epitomized a global economy, of the 2977 victims (excluding the 19 hijackers) in the three airplane attacks and the

---

[2] Hänggi, "Stockhausen at Ground Zero."

[3] The theoretical debate has been summarized from various angles; for a particularly succinct synopsis, see the article by Emma Wilson with the telling title "Europe's 9/11."

[4] Versluys, "9/11 as a European Event."

one attempted, only 372 people were foreigners. Despite its reception as first and foremost a national tragedy, with its far-reaching global consequences, September 11 and the War on Terror, however, also marked a new phase in US-European relations. The rekindled importance of the transatlantic foil for European identity construction after 9/11 and the fact that literature is claimed to be a key vehicle to identity formation certainly account for some of the interest in the historic event among European writers. Further, the al-Qaida attacks on European major capitals spurred the (not only literary) imagination of a terrorist strike of a scale similar to 9/11—as demonstrated by the opening cinematic example. Finally, wartime Europe is employed in both US and European literature as a framework to understand what has happened. The apparent inutterability was transferred to the token discourse of Europe's terror and disaster.[5] As the classic zone of conflict throughout the twentieth century it serves to integrate the September attacks and the wars to follow in the American as well as the European imaginary. Consequently, the texts analysed in this volume reflect the US attacks within their own national and European *longue durée* of violent conflict. Confirming Appadurai's concept of mediascape, the corpus shows how the medial representations of a globally shared event are received in very specific culturally, socially and individually determined frames of interpretation.[6]

European 9/11 literature, similar to other 'outsider' perspectives in literature,[7] tends to incorporate the September attacks and its military retaliation within a broader context of migration, cultural discrimination and global capitalism. In order to draw attention to these extended contexts, the corpus is not restricted to 9/11 literature with a focus on the attacks but extends to the wider field of 9/11-related or post-9/11 literature. Ranging from the depiction of the attacks themselves, through explorations of the wars in Afghanistan and Iraq, to post-9/11 representation of terrorism, such as the Bali bombings, to the experience of Guantánamo detainees, and including Muslim immigration in Europe, *9/11 in European Literature* exemplifies the

---

[5] See., for example, the 9/11 novels: *Extremely Loud and Incredibly Close* by Jonathan Safran Foer, *Windows on the World* by Frédéric Beigbeder, and *September. Fata Morgana* by Thomas Lehr.

[6] Appadurai, "Disjuncture and Difference in the Global Cultural Economy," 296, 307.

[7] The first study to purposefully concentrate on the non-US corpus was Cilano (ed.), *From Solidarity to Schisms: 9/11 and After in Fiction and Film from Outside the US.*

thematic and aesthetic breadth of European 9/11 literature. The chapters analyse British, Dutch, French, German, Italian, Anglo-Irish and Polish texts, but despite the diversity of these cultural-literary contexts, they share the use of 9/11 as a marked backdrop to re-negotiations of European, national and personal identities. Ongoing and overarching questions and themes led to the volume's threefold structure. The texts under consideration deal with 9/11 in a specific way in that: (1) they perceive the event through the lens of existing continental media and semiotic theory and often employ forms of metaization in their literary responses; (2) they incorporate the terror attacks into national, historical and literary memory and are concerned with its significance for national identity construction; and (3) they negotiate national as well as European identity against the double Other of the US nation, on the one side, and a cultural-ethnic idea of Muslim communities, on the other.

THE CORPUS OF EUROPEAN 9/11 LITERATURE

In the wake of September 11, various texts of the European canon, from Greek epic and tragedy, right through to Cervantes, Shakespeare and Virginia Woolf have been reread and largely forgotten European novels have been rediscovered.[8] This provides ample evidence that many texts can be productively related to the attacks, even if reference can be ruled out completely as they came into existence long before 9/11. Even though the volume purposefully refrains from such anachronistic interpretations and concentrates on texts where the themes of 9/11 and its aftermath are clearly discernible, it aims at contextualizing its interpretations in wider European discursive contexts. The volume thus refrains from establishing a clear distinction between specific 9/11 literature and more general post-9/11

---

[8] See Véguez, "*Don Quijote* and 9–11: The Clash of Civilizations and the Birth of the Modern Novel" and Brooks, Biberman, and Lupton (eds.), *Shakespeare After 9/11: How a Social Trauma Reshapes Interpretation*. Aimee Pozorski shows how Ian McEwan's 9/11 novel *Saturday* lets us reread Virginia Woolf's description of airplanes in her novel *Mrs Dalloway* (1925), see Pozorski, *Falling After 9/11: Crisis in American Art and Literature*, x–xi, for the various adaptations of the Greek poem "Waiting for the Barbarians" (1904) by Constantine Peter Cavafy after 9/11 see Boletsi, "Still Waiting for Barbarians after 9/11? Cavafy's Reluctant Irony and the Language of the Future".

literature and does not attempt to define a genre beyond this thematic realm.⁹

Croatian writer Dubravka Ugresic asks in one of her essays: "What is European about European Literature?," and rightly so.¹⁰ Neither Europe nor European literature are stable categories. Political scientists Ulrich Beck and Edgar Grande even go so far as to claim that "Europe as such does not exist, only *Europeanization* in the sense of an institutionalized process of permanent change."¹¹ "Europe" is seen as a perpetual work in progress, a concept that is continuously redefined and reimagined.¹² These uncertainties are also reflected in the unclear usage of the terms "Europe" and the "European Union" in public debate. The question of a European identity remains poignant for the definition of the territorial borders of the EU and is employed, for example, in the debate on Turkey's application process. The texts under discussion here exclusively originate from EU member states and thus offer a further focus on EU integration—but broader definitions of European literature are just as legitimate. The definition of European literature reflects and informs what we understand by "Europe." This is especially true in times of crisis such as the European Union is currently undergoing. Historically, times of war and violence have repeatedly initiated reflections on the practice of comparative literary studies as well as definitions of world literature.¹³

In addition to the question whether to base the definition of European literature on a geo-political territory, historical or cultural categories, the European descent of the authors by no means necessarily implies a European perspective of their texts. In contrast, the European literary canon has become common property and serves as a

---

⁹ See the term "ground zero fiction" which more restrictively denotes texts with explicit references to the September attacks, see Däwes' comprehensive study of the American 9/11 novel *Ground Zero Fiction*.

¹⁰ See Crosetti who stresses the difficulties of defining European literature: "Paradoxically, the task of establishing a concrete European literary geography seems to be an exercise in futility for a number of complex reasons." Crosetti, "Europeanization, Nationalism and Cosmopolitanism," 154. The fact that there cannot be a straightforward definition of European literature is also problematized by Baumbach, "Rooting 'New European Literature'," 55f.

¹¹ Grande and Beck, *Cosmopolitan Europe*, 6.

¹² Buescu, "Europe between Old and New," 11.

¹³ Ibid., 17.

major intertextual foil to world literature in general.[14] The various intertextual relations between literatures further contribute to an increased "internationality of national literatures," according to Udo Schöning. Globalization means that authors, too, live and write in different cultural contexts, even languages, during their career. As a consequence, the borders of national literatures are increasingly blurred, a development which is also reflected in new departmental divisions in universities. In the light of the difficulties in defining a European corpus, this volume deliberately focuses on a selection of texts which take a national or Europe-specific perspective on the 9/11 attacks and the War on Terror. This focus on textual aspects of the corpus follows the definition of a "new European literature" without, however, taking it so far as to include literature which is not written in Europe or by Europeans.[15] The volume's focus on European literature is seen as an additional operational viewpoint complementing 9/11 research conducted within national philologies, on the one hand, and comparative literature, on the other, which might also further the understanding of Europe.[16]

TRANSATLANTIC RELATIONS AND EUROPEAN IDENTITY FORMATION

The construction of the USA from outside has always been crucial for European identity formation and European anti-Americanism has existed as long as the nation against which it is directed.[17] 9/11 marks a decisive point in this transatlantic relationship. Initially, the event provoked an avowal of sympathy, famously expressed by *Le Monde*'s declaration

---

[14] For this discussion, see also Baumbach, "Rooting 'New European Literature'," who questions the use of the delineation of European literature considering the "intrinsic cosmopolitan quality of literature," 56.

[15] For such a wide predominantly text-based definition of (new) European literature, see especially Baumbach, "Rooting 'New European Literature'," 59f. Hence, the volume's scope does not include novels with a distinct European focus by non-European authors, such as Ben Lerner's novel *Leaving the Atocha Station* on the Madrid train attacks.

[16] Simonsen, "Towards a New Europe?," 133.

[17] See Markovits' contention that "Anti-Americanism in Europe has for the first time become a tangible political force on the mass level beyond the elite antipathy and resentment that has been a staple of European culture since at least July 5, 1776," Markovits, "Anti-Americanism in Europe," 207. See also Gulddal, *Anti-Americanism in European Literature*, 2.

"Nous sommes tous Américains" two days after the event, and the affirmation of a united West fighting for the liberal values of freedom and democracy against any fundamentalist perpetrators. In the face of actual military retaliation, this was, however, soon modified. Directed against the imminent Iraq invasion, the 15th of February 2003 saw the largest anti-war demonstration since the Second World War.[18] Jürgen Habermas and Jacques Derrida prominently claimed this collective outcry the "Rebirth of Europe," endowing it with a new unity and identity. This is even more striking given that the demonstrations were a world-wide phenomenon including mass protests in New York and Washington.[19] It demonstrates the widened chasm between the US and several European member states in the post-9/11 world where the terrorist attacks and the following wars initiated reflections on a common European identity that more likely events did not spark in the same way. The fall of the Berlin Wall or the collapse of the Soviet bloc might have more obviously called for a unifying re-definition.[20]

Overcoming the rift in Europe was not a priority when Habermas and Derrida set out to define "Kerneuropa" ("core Europe"), which they reserved for those countries who share the values of the secular state, the Enlightenment and social-democratic traditions. The complementary US neo-conservative coinage of "New Europe," introduced by Donald Rumsfeld for those European countries who supported the Iraq War, drives a deeper wedge between the "coalition of the willing" and its opponents. On 30 January 2003, with the Czech Republic, Denmark, Hungary, Italy, Poland, Portugal, Spain and the United Kingdom, eight of fifteen EU member states signed "The letter of the eight" expressing their support for the US endeavour of the regime change in Iraq, thus jeopardizing an integrative Common European Foreign and Security Policy.

In Eastern Europe, the division over the Iraq involvement carried its own specific implications. After the collapse of the Soviet bloc,

---

[18] Levy, Pensky, and Torpey, "Editors' Introduction," xiii.

[19] Voices critical of Habermas point to the fact that the anti-war demonstrations were not a European phenomenon but a worldwide one which lays bare the ambivalences of such identity constructions, see Levy, Pensky, and Torpey, "Editors' Introduction," xxiii.

[20] Or vice versa: As Serfaty observes, the transatlantic gap did not – as one would have expected – widen so much with the end of the Cold War as with 9/11, because the War on Terror caused strategic differences due to the different previous experiences of war, Serfaty, "Anti-Europeanism in America and Anti-Americanism in Europe," 15f.

Atlanticism played a crucial role in the Eastern European states as a means to distance themselves from Russia. Russia's support of the War against Terror thus led to irritations in the process of national identity formation, as the former Soviet bloc states were now caught in the ambiguity between an Atlanticism which would bring these states closer to Russia and a Europeanism of the anti-Iraq War league.

In addition to the chasm over military intervention, the challenges of the European Eastern enlargements in 2004, 2007 and 2013, the European debt crisis, making inner-European economic rifts drastically visible, and more recently the diverging approaches to the refugee crisis all have raised questions about the Free Movement rule, a fundamental premise of the European idea. Thus, the conceived need for a common European identity has become ever more palpable and the European construction of the US plays a crucial role in this process. The growing European anti-Americanism[21] after 9/11 is certainly also a reflection of this attempt to draft a European "core" identity.[22] Political scientist Andrei Markovits observes a change in this European anti-Americanism, in that it became a mass phenomenon after 9/11. While previously, European elites fostered anti-Americanism—incidentally, in a way prejudice would never be tolerable against any other nation—the masses joined them and the aversion become politically significant in an unprecedented manner.[23] The European construction of the US as a military and imperialist aggressor allows the social-liberal Europe to self-fashion itself as a pacifist continent, a phenomenon in which Robert Kagan's transatlantic comparison of Venus and Mars[24] played so well.

The chapters in this volume explore the changed transatlantic relation as reflected in European literature, uncovering further binaries which put Europe in a positive light, such as conjuring the welfare state against a merciless American capitalism or cultural variety against the globalizing

---

[21] Following Jesper Gulddal's definition, I understand anti-Americanism here not as political criticism but as a chauvinistic ideology that repudiates an essentialized American identity, Gulddal, *Anti-Americanism in European Literature*, 4–6.

[22] See similarly the statement by Levy, Pensky, and Torpey: "References to the US often seem to serve the role of Europe's new—constitutive other," in "Editors' Introduction," xxiv.

[23] Markovits, "Anti-Americanism in Europe: From Elite Disdain to Political Force," 201–203.

[24] Kagan, *Of Paradise and Power: America and Europe in the New World Order*.

pull of US market imperialism. While fictional literature takes a vital role in perpetuating such imaginary identities, several texts discussed in this volume demonstrate how these transatlantic binaries are also undermined in a self-critical way. In this respect, the volume also forms part of the rising scholarship on the transatlantic relationship in post-9/11 culture.[25]

Islamic Terrorism and Populist Construction of the Muslim Other in Europe

Al-Qaida attacks on European major capitals, the 2004 Madrid train bombings, the 2005 London bombings and the 2015 Paris shooting in the offices of the satirical weekly *Charlie Hebdo*, as well as the Islamic State attacks on various Paris entertainment spots later the same year, spurred fear and thus the imagination of Islamic terrorism in Europe. These diffuse fears of the Muslim Other are mirrored by conjuring up inner unity: After 9/11, the need for a strong European identity as well as a coherent immigration and foreign policy on a European, not just a national, level was voiced in Europe.[26] As exemplified by the European restaging of the World Trade Center attacks in Sorrentino's *La grande bellezza*, the idea that an attack of a similar scale could happen in Europe is a present one and the Islamic attacks frequently prompted the use of the catch phrase "Europe's 9/11" in the media.

These diffuse fears of Islamic terrorism also changed the perception of the Muslim population in Europe. Since 9/11 and the subsequent terror attacks in Europe, the tensions between the majority society in Western

---

[25] Miller (ed.), *Transatlantic Literature and Culture After 9/11*. Within this field, special attention has been given to the Anglo-American relationship, particularly on its gendered presentation: Britain's decreasing influence in world politics was constructed as a process of effemination, and the decision to support the Iraq War was thus seen as paramount for a British identity construction. See the representation of US military power as masculine virility and an effeminate Blair, in Carpenter, "September 11, Masculinity, and the British-American Relationship in David Hare's *Stuff Happens* and Ian McEwan's *Saturday*," 143–160. For the gendered representation, see also Araújo, *Transatlantic Fictions of 9/11 and the War on Terror*, 28. Other than the suggestion of her book's title, in *Transatlantic Fictions of 9/11 and the War on Terror*, the transatlantic relationship is less a focus in itself but rather points to her comparative approach, including the analysis of several European texts, for example, Portuguese and Spanish ones.

[26] See explicitly Flood, "Some European Thoughts in the Wake of 9/11," especially 60–62.

European countries with a high Muslim population and the socially marginalized Muslim migrant population have become increasingly strong. European right-wing agitation uses the terrorist attacks to vigorously campaign against Muslim immigrants, thus aggravating the situation for a community already suffering from social marginalization and disappointed hopes of economic improvement.[27]

The rising nationalist parties across Europe[28] hinder integration processes by fuelling irrational fears that the growing Muslim population poses a threat to Christian values and also in a physical sense. In Western Europe's imagination, Islam might soon take on the diffuse fears that used to be concentrated in the Communist threat during the Cold War and which was thereafter handed down to the Balkans as the crisis area within Europe.

The caution of "Eurabia," a term coined by British author Gisèle Littman to describe a dystopian Europe under an Islamic foreign rule, has been expressed not only by conservative populism but also in the literary-intellectual debate. Michel Houellebecq's novel *Soumission* (2015) [Submission] is a prominent example of the Islamic-Fascist scenarios envisioned by European novels. Here the *enfant terrible* of French contemporary literature draws a provocative portrayal of France in 2022, turned into an Islamic state under the rule of Mohammed Ben Abbes of the fictional Muslim Fraternity. Hungarian Nobel Laureate Imre Kertész expresses similar fears in a non-fictional text. Several highly controversial passages in his autofiction *A végső kocsma* (2014) [The Last Refuge] caution against a Muslim invasion in Europe.[29] This is symptomatic of growing European anti-Muslim agitation and shows that the taboo against Islamophobia is rapidly decreasing, even within intellectual circles.

---

[27] Majid, "The Failure of Postcolonial Theory After 9/11," 4.

[28] See for the rise of European right-wing parties, also Todorov, *The Fear of Barbarians*, 9.

[29] Mathias Schnitzler in his review, for example, stresses similarities between these passages condemning Europe's "suicidal liberalism" and the agitation of Germany's right nationalist party NPD as well as the anti-Muslim organization Pegida, see Schnitzler, "Das Leben ist ein Irrtum." Kertész's anti-Muslim warnings in this semi-fictional text can be traced back to his diary entries published in 2013 where he laments Europe's decay. To Kertész, Europe's cowardice and inability to defend itself against Islamic invasions form a *longue durée* from the Persian wars to the capitulation before what he calls the "most disgraceful Eastern power," the Palestinians, see the diary entry for the 3rd of February 2006; Kertész, *Letzte Einkehr. Tagebücher 2001–2009*, 361.

Though Islamophobia and racial profiling have been on the rise in the US since the September 11 attacks, the situation in Europe differs in so far as Islam constitutes the second largest religion after Christianity and is expected to grow much faster than the non-Muslim population. In the US, by comparison, it ranks fourth after Buddhism and Judaism. Though the twelve to twenty million European Muslims do not form a unified community, the non-Muslim public is scarcely aware of the differences and conceives it to be a monolithic block. The chapters in this volume reflect the range of how European literature constructs the Muslim Other, from populist stigmatization to complex self-criticism, unveiling the subtle violence underlying the enlightened tolerance tradition to which Europe lays claim.

THE STRUCTURE OF THIS BOOK

European 9/11 Literature and 9/11 Scholarship

The complexities of post-9/11 Europe have been analyzed from political, sociological and intellectual-philosophical perspectives. Those disciplines have identified the attacks and their consequences as a pivotal point in European identity formation. However, in literary studies, this subject has received surprisingly little attention despite the growing research on non-American 9/11-related literary texts[30] and the public interest in the outside perspective, as demonstrated by a number of English translations, such as collections of Arabic literature on wartime Iraq.[31] The volume builds on

---

[30] See in particular, Cilano (ed.), *From Solidarity to Schisms: 9/11 and After in Fiction and Film from Outside the US*. In contrast to our aim here, it, however, takes a broader cultural perspective and is not concerned with culturally specific reception. Studies on distinct cultural or national contexts, including the Anglo-South-Asian (Liao, '*Post*'-*9/11 South Asian Diasporic Fiction: Uncanny Terror*), the Anglo-Indian (Bharat, *In the Shadow of Terror: Terrorism and the Contemporary Indian Novel in English*) or the German (Reinhäckel, *Traumatische Texturen*) shed further light on non-US 9/11 fiction. Keniston and Quinn (eds), *Literature after 9/11* is a truly exhaustive comparative collection in terms of corpus as well as research questions addressed. However, though the chapters also fruitfully address aesthetic questions, such as literary tradition, no particular focus on culturally specific reception is aimed at. Among the first publications which focus on such cross-cultural comparisons is Hennigfeld's collection of essays, *Poetiken des Terrors*.

[31] See, for example, the English translation *The Corpse Exhibition: And Other Stories of Iraq* (2014) of a collection of short stories by Iraqi-born Hassan Blasim or the anthology *An Arab Mirror: Images of America in Arabic Travel Literature, 1668 to 9/11 and Beyond* (2000) by Kamal Abdel-Malek and Mouna El Kahla.

this interest in tackling an under-researched corpus from the approach of national and post-national identity formation in Europe.

While several publications assume a broad cultural studies perspective and look at a range of media,[32] this volume assumes that a focus on one medium, texts, invites a closer comparison between the modes of representation as a major concern of European literature. It represents a varied literary corpus including fiction, such as novels, poetry and drama, as well as highly rhetorically grafted political writing and conspiracy theories, which could be said to be fictional or factual accounts, depending on personal standpoints.

In this concern for formal aspects, the volume can build upon 9/11 scholarship predominantly conducted in American studies, which, next to the vast research on thematic aspects and plot structure, also includes analyses of narrative techniques and genre traditions. Given that, for most people, 9/11 does not constitute a personal experience but a global media event, it is not surprising that aspects of textual intermediality, particularly the narrative simulation of audio-visual representation, has become one focus.[33] More generally, research has tackled the question of how the texts self-reflexively convey their status as representation which can never fully capture reality,[34] for instance, through unreliable narration.[35]

Other studies concentrated on the play with genre traditions, arguing that it revealed the constructedness of the ideology behind official narratives of 9/11 and the War on Terror.[36] Along similar lines, alternate histories and counterfactual fiction have been on the rise in US literature since

---

[32] See, for example, the collected volumes, Cilano (ed.), *From Solidarity to Schisms: 9/11 and After in Fiction and Film from Outside the US*. Lorenz (ed.), *Narrative des Entsetzens. Künstlerische, mediale und intellektuelle Deutungen des 11. September 2001*; Irsigler and Jürgensen (eds), *Nine eleven: Ästhetische Verarbeitungen des 11. September 2001*; Poppe, Schüller, and Seiler (eds), *9/11 als kulturelle Zäsur*. See for film and television, Dixon (ed.), *Film and Television After 9/11*, and for music, Helms and Phleps (eds), *9/11: The World's All Out of Tune. Populäre Musik nach dem 11. September.*

[33] See, for example, the interrelation of static and dynamic images in Foer's *Extremely Loud and Incredibly Close*—the photograph "Falling Man" and the narrator-protagonist Oscar's flip-book which allows him to reverse the fall from the tower; Huehls, "Foer, Spiegelman, and 9/11's Timely Traumas," 42–59; see also Frost, "Still Life. 9/11's Falling Bodies," 180–206.

[34] Banita, *Plotting Justice*, 42.

[35] Ibid., 127.

[36] In relation to Chuck Palahniuk's use of horror genre in *Lullaby*, see Rothberg, "Seeing Terror, Feeling Art: Public and Private in Post-9/11 Literature," 123–142.

9/11.³⁷ The discontinuous and unfocused narratives have been said to express the state surveillance culture with its amassing unstructured data.³⁸

Further analogies between the attacks' psychological effects (shock, trauma, incomprehensibility) and formal aspects have been established; narrative gaps and disrupted chronology in 9/11 fiction, for example, have been read as symbolic coping mechanisms and the expression of traumatic experiences.³⁹ The use of "meta-narratives, disrupted temporality, multiple viewpoints" demonstrates that rather than triggering formal innovation, the attacks prompted literature to resume Modernism's formal complexity.⁴⁰

Not only with respect to formal analysis, however, but also in the representation of the cultural Other, can the volume build on existing scholarship. Frequently, textual analysis in 9/11 scholarship is interwoven with a political-philosophical agenda. It has thus been argued that literature in the realm of September 11 opens a "new transnational era."⁴¹ Even post-9/11 texts without direct references to the attacks and the War on Terror display an increased interest in the cultural Other. In this context it has been shown—especially with regard to the US context—that they display a "profoundly ethical anxiety"⁴² working against the us-versus-them dichotomy often found in political agitation and media discussion.⁴³ The self-critical questioning of European values and

---

³⁷ For a comprehensive analysis, see, for example, Otten, *Zeit/Geschichte: Amerikanische Alternate Histories nach 9/11*.

³⁸ Banita, *Plotting Justice*, 254f.

³⁹ On temporality, see Gourley, *Terrorism and Temporality in the Works of Thomas Pynchon and Don DeLillo*; on memory and chronology, see Li, "'Sometimes things disappear'. Absence and Mutability in Colson Whitehead's *The Colossus of New York*," 82–98; see also Glejzer on trauma in "Witnessing 9/11: Art Spiegelman and the Persistence of Trauma," 99–119.

⁴⁰ James Gourley argues that the experience of time and temporality in Pynchon and DeLillo shifted after 9/11. He argues that canonical US authors such as the two mentioned increasingly turn to modernist literature, film and art in their post-9/11 texts, see *Terrorism and Temporality in the Works of Thomas Pynchon and Don DeLillo*. Other characteristics of 9/11 plotlines such as cyclical and double structures also seem to point to this modernist tradition, see Däwes, *Ground Zero Fiction*, 406.

⁴¹ Banita, *Plotting Justice*.

⁴² Ibid., 16. Further Banita identifies values such as freedom, (individual) security, justice and empathy as recurrent issues in 9/11-related literature.

⁴³ Däwes, *Ground Zero Fiction*, 411. See also Rothberg, who shows through the example of US poetry how 9/11 literature undermines these binaries and thus creates a key to understanding the War on Terror, "Seeing Terror, Feeling Art: Public and Private in Post-9/11 Literature," 123–142.

appropriations which several chapters in this volume reveal demonstrates continuities between US and European literary representations.

Part I: September 11 Seen Through European Media and Semiotic Theory

The book's division into three parts is intended to represent three major aspects of European 9/11 literature. Part I hence concentrates on how European 9/11 literature transforms a medially over-represented event into texts and how it reflects on this representation through different forms of metaization. European philosophers and cultural theorists heavily influenced by poststructuralist and deconstructivist French media and semiotic theory abstracted from the calamity very early on and perceived the terrorist attacks, first and foremost the images of the Twin Towers, through a framework of aesthetic reflections.

The detached intellectualization displayed in the early theoretical accounts stand in opposition to tendencies in early US 9/11 literature, such as the attempts to overcome trauma[44] or the revival of the nineteenth-century sentimental novel.[45] The European preoccupation with questions of representation in the theoretical reception of 9/11 is also evident in the literary texts. In a provocative exploitation of artistic

---

[44] See Keniston and Quinn's argument for a "sequence of genres," according to which the initial shorter forms, personal reflections, essays and poems responded in a more direct and emotional way, while novels with their evident incubation are allegedly more nuanced, see *Literature after 9/11*, 3. Hence, much early 9/11 scholarship turned to trauma and memory studies as a methodological framework. Kaplan (*Trauma Culture: The Politics of Terror and Loss in Media and Literature*) and Greenberg (*Trauma at Home: After 9/11*) have dealt with the reception of 9/11 in literature and the arts, adopting trauma theory as their methodological springboard. Kristiaan Versluys in *Out of the Blue: September 11 and the Novel* analyses four 9/11 novels seen through the spectrum of trauma theory. In his monograph, *After the Fall*, Richard Gray sketches the change from innocence to experience, "the fall," as a recurrent theme of US literature but sees a new element to the crisis narrative through American 9/11 narratives: the invalidation of language. See also Glejzer, "Witnessing 9/11: Art Spiegelman and the Persistence of Trauma," 99–119.

[45] For the early (2003–2006) US 9/11 novels' indebtedness to the nineteenth-century US sentimental novel, especially the reuse of plot schemes, character types, topoi and motifs from the domestic novel, see Werkmeister, *Domestic Nation* or Chandler, *Pursuing Unhappiness: City, Space, and Sentimentalism in Post Cold-War American Literature*. The revival of the genre stands in the context of a more general "withdrawal into the domestic" in the US 9/11 novel, see Gray, *After the Fall*, 17.

leeway, Frédéric Beigbeder in his novel *Windows on the World* (2003), for example, stresses the catastrophe's inherent dramaturgic quality, thus stripping the real event of its dramatic consequences and reducing it to its potential as a commercial cultural product. With his laconic phrase: "Ils ont souffert 102 min—la durée moyenne d'un film hollywoodien." ("They suffered for 102 minutes, the average running time of a Hollywood film."[46]), he points to the convenient correspondence between the duration of the real event from the attack on the first tower until the collapse of the second and the narrative time of conventional cinema.

The undeniable resemblance of the iconic images of two airplanes hitting the World Trade Center to blockbuster cinema blurs the boundaries between 9/11 as a "Hollywood disaster movie" and the "raw Real of a catastrophe" (as Žižek dubbed it),[47] thus stressing the historical event's seeming fictionality.

Many fictional texts selected for this volume demonstrate—well beyond Part I—how narrative strategies are employed to cross-fade fictional and factual modes, in particular through their striking affinity to forms of metaization and self-reflexive elements.[48] Through focussing on how the representational and media theoretical questions raised in 9/11 discourse influenced literary texts in Europe, Part I serves as an introduction and a backdrop to European literary texts in general.

The application of French continental theory to the tragedy, in itself part of Western Europe's elite self-fashioning, caves in as Rolf Renner's panoramic opening chapter demonstrates. Taking a broad political-historical perspective while locating the 9/11 footage through visual analogies and associations in a *longue durée* of European art history, he shows in chapter "9/11: The Interpretation of Disaster as Disaster of Interpretation—An American Catastrophe Reflected in American and European Discourses" that the European public debate on 9/11 and its

---

[46] Beigbeder, *Windows on the World*, 83. Taken from the English translation by Frank Wynne, Frédéric Beigbeder, *Windows on the World* (New York: Miramax Books/Hyperion, 2004), 61.

[47] Žižek, "Welcome to the Desert of the Real," 16. See also Baudrillard, "The Spirit of Terrorism."

[48] See Mergenthaler, "Warum die Frage, 'Wie reagieren Schriftsteller auf die Terroranschläge?' auf dem Feld der deutschsprachigen Literatur die falsche Frage ist?".

aftermath is precisely not governed by the rational Enlightenment tradition to which it lays claim, and that its anti-Americanism is not based on analysis or reflection. Renner argues that the previously meaningful role of the public intellectual has been replaced by a visual culture much more open to manipulation, thereby further blurring the line between the real and the imaginary. He closes by applying these media theoretical and political reflections to literary representations of 9/11.

Ulrich Kinzel takes up this intermedial approach in chapter "The Wind of the Hudson. Gerhard Richter's *September* (2005) and the European Perception of Catastrophe", by exploring the sublime so often exercised in connection with 9/11, through placing it within the history of European art and philosophy, thus, like Renner, stressing continuities rather than kindling the caesura discourse surrounding September 11. Drawing together the self-reflective aspects of contemporary German poetry engaging with 9/11 and Gerhard Richter's painting *September*, Kinzel analyses how media theory is interwoven with moral self-reflection by integrating the beholder into the piece of art. His focus on the shipwreck as the topos of human catastrophe frequently employed in 9/11 creative production underpins this connection.

Eoin Flannery follows a similar ethical perspective in chapter "'Burning from the Inside Out': *Let the Great World Spin* (2009)", in his analysis of the novel *Let the Great World Spin* (2009) by Irish writer Colum McCann, moving from the reflection of the medial conditions of literature to their function. Addressing the 9/11 theme through indirect reference, Philipp Petit's (1974) wire walk between the Twin Towers becomes the novel's poetological metaphor and an image of literature and the power of art and imagination in general. Set against and above the inhuman dimensions of urban space, this act contrasts sharply with the terrorists' plot while uncomfortably mirroring the idea of performance art detected in the World Trade Center attacks. It becomes clear how McCann employs the attacks to show how an apparently purely aesthetic act takes on a political message through exactly that and opens the narrative to hope and redemption.

Part II: Literary Translations of September 11 into Europe's National Contexts

After the focus on questions of representation, Part II turns to the literary reception of the attacks and the wider consequences in specific national contexts. Existing studies of 9/11 literature in individual European national literatures—particularly France, Germany and Spain[49]—already indicate that this is a worthwhile field of investigation. In concentrating on the incorporation of 9/11 into national literatures, histories and current sociopolitical circumstances, this section displays that cultural heterogeneity does not only pose a major challenge to forging a shared identity but that it is in itself also a source of European self-understanding. Returning to a long-standing topos, this historical, cultural and linguistic diversity is employed to distinguish Europe from the supposed US monoculture against whose global spread it must be protected.

The texts analysed in this section explore analogies between 9/11 and events in national histories as they are represented in literary texts. As the chapters demonstrate, the national perspective and history are still a major influence on literary identity formation.[50] It is a reflection of the fact that Europe, despite the ongoing Europeanization process, has not gone and is not going unidirectionally from national to postnational status. However, this national-specific reception does not necessarily have to be seen in contradiction to a European identity. Tzvetan Todorov, for example, stresses the importance of pluralism as a value in itself for European self-understanding, which he traces back to the Enlightenment.[51] The both/and principle of the national, transnational and the supranational instead has been identified as the key to understanding the European mind set.[52] Surveys have led to the assumption that a form of "cultural schizophrenia" is characteristic of Europeans; the respondents

---

[49] See for the German context, especially, Reinhäckel, *Traumatische Texturen* and König, "'Alles wird anders' – Der 11. September in deutscher Literatur." For the French approach, see, for example, Porra, "Risse in der Mimesis – Bemerkungen zur romanesken Darstellung des 11. Septembers 2001 in der französischen Literatur" and Stratenschulte, "Die Aufarbeitung des 11-M im spanischen Roman und Comic am Beispiel von *El Corrector* und *11-M: La Novela Gráfica*," for the Spanish approach.

[50] Buescu, "Europe between Old and New," 24.

[51] Todorov, *The Fear of Barbarians*, 170. He further claims that it is Europeans' attitude to diversity which unites them, Todorov, *The Fear of Barbarians*, 174, see also 191.

[52] Domínguez, "Local Rooms with a Cosmopolitan View?," 34f.

stated both that Europeans have a lot in common culturally and that there is no common European culture. Nevertheless, there is also a clear indication that the idea of a European culture is far stronger than a much more general idea of a global Western culture.[53]

In post-9/11 US, wartime Europe served as a historical point of reference in an attempt to understand what happened on American soil. The Ground Zero footage, showing a large Western city in a state of war, chaos and destruction is strongly reminiscent of the air raids during World War II. The bombing of European cities thus seems a likely foil in the deeply felt post-9/11 necessity to reinvent US national identity[54] and was perhaps most prominently used in Jonathan Safran Foer's evocation of Dresden in his 9/11 novel *Extremely Loud and Incredibly Close* (2005).

The September 11 attacks are very much perceived as a caesura in US history[55] and the recourse to Europe as a foil gives an idea of how much the event is seen as unprecedented. This marks a visible contrast to the European reception of 9/11 where the attacks were integrated into national histories. It seems that terror attacks are more perceived as part of a *longue durée* of violence and human suffering. Personal accounts

---

[53] Ibid., 27.

[54] Margulies, *What Changed When Everything Changed: 9/11 and the Making of National Identity*.

[55] At first, the caesura discourse prevailed with reference to world history in general before it was increasingly modified. Amy Reynolds and Brooke Barnett's media analysis "'America under Attack': CNN's Verbal and Visual Framing of September 11," for instance, notes the use of the word "unprecedented" in political discourse and the media alike, 86. See also Jacques Derrida, "Autoimmunity: Real and Symbolic Suicides: A Dialogue with Jacques Derrida," 85f., 90. The caesura discourse is also questioned by scholarship that found it more to be a discursive than an actual caesura. See, for example, Butter, Christ, and Keller, *9/11. Kein Tag, der die Welt veränderte*.

As 9/11 constituted a much more marked caesura for Americans, it has been argued that the US and Europe have since been operating on two different timelines. See Serfaty's observation: "Now, unlike 1947, and perhaps more like 1919, America and Europe live in two different time zones – one that began with the collapse of the Berlin Wall on November 1989 and ended Europe's century of total wars, and the other that was born with the outrageous attacks against New York City and Washington and started America's wars against global terrorism." Serfaty, "Anti-Europeanism in America and Anti-Americanism in Europe," 14.

of the 7 July 2005 London bombings, for example, state that people reacted with Blitz-like strategies.[56]

Besides the recourse to historical reference points, the anticipation of "Europe's 9/11" is a recurrent subject matter in European fictions. The introductory example of Sorrentino's "Falling Man" in front of the Colosseum visualizes one of these relocations. Most famously perhaps, Frédéric Beigbeder's *alter ego* in *Windows on the World* imagines the World Trade Center attacks in an analogous European setting. The fictional author writes his 9/11 novel in the restaurant of Paris' highest office tower, the Tour Montparnasse, in order to fuel his literary imagination. Scottish science fiction writer Ken McLeod in his counterfactual novel *The Execution Channel* (2007), next to relocating September 11 to Boston and Philadelphia, depicts a terrorist attack on the small town of Rosyth on the Firth of Forth in Scotland—while the narrator in Pauls Bankovskis' Latvian novel *Eiroremonts* (2005) [Euro renovation] contends in contrast that Riga would never be a favoured terrorist target.

Besides these fictional scenarios restaging the events in Europe, September 11 and the following wars develop their own new meanings already, just by being inserted into specific linguistic and historical contexts. In *11 septembre mon amour* (2003), Luc Lang turned the name of the American President into George "Double V. Bouche," employing the pun on the French word for "mouth" to criticize the US government for the hypocrisy of its official propaganda. The mere import of the English word "checkpoint" in the German novel *September. Fata Morgana* (2010) by Thomas Lehr carries a particular connotation. At the same time as referring to the checkpoints in Iraq after the US invasion, it here resonates with "Checkpoint Charlie," the major Berlin Wall crossing point. By invoking the Cold War situation, the English word in the German text invites ambivalent associations between the Iraqi context and both the German Fascist terror regime that led to German partition and the Communist one that resulted from it.

---

[56] As in Elleke Boehmer's and Stephen Morton's accounts of London during and after the bombings, who, by a curious coincindence, had planned to meet and talk that day about "Terror and the Postcolonial" in Bloomsbury's Senate House in central London, see Boehmer and Morton, *Terror and the Postcolonial*, 1–5, especially 4. See also the personal account by the film scholar and Professor of English, E. Ann Kaplan, who reports how 9/11 brought back her traumatic memories of World War II in the UK; Kaplan, *Trauma Culture*, here especially 3–9.

Such dehistoricization of 9/11 can take bizarre turns, such as in the disturbing encounter which the essay "USA Nails" in the collection *Nikog nema doma* [Nobody's Home][57] reports. Croatian writer Dubravka Ugrešić, living in Amsterdam and the US, relates a conversation with a taxi driver in post-9/11 New York who praises Slobodan Milošević—in reference to the genocide against the Muslim population in Bosnia and Herzegovina during the Bosnian War that occurred under his rule—as the first representative of the fight against Islamic fundamentalism. Ugrešić's narration thus seems to draw a line from Europe's violent ethnic conflicts to the War on Terror and the increase of Islamophobia in societies with a large Muslim migrant influx.

Amidst this range, the chapters in Part II bring together examples from Britain, France, Italy, Germany and Poland to represent the specific reception in national literary and historical identities. It opens with a comprehensive study of French conspiracy theories explaining their mass-psychological function and political significance while drawing comparisons to a similar situation in Germany, as France's major EU partner. Jean-Philippe Mathy elaborates in chapter "Seeing is Disbelieving: The Contested Visibility of 9/11 in France" how the inconsistencies of the official discourse have produced a genre whose status as fiction is at the discretion of the individual reader. In the same way as fiction fills epistemological gaps when representing the victims' or perpetrators' experience, conspiracy theories claim to fill informational gaps and to provide insights which are deliberately withheld from the public. A decisive number of Europeans took those accounts or parts of them at face value and Mathy suggests a link between their striking popularity in France and Germany and the fact that those two countries displayed the strongest anti-war attitudes in Europe. Not only is this popularity indicative of an anti-Americanism that does not put it past the US government to kill its own citizens, but also it is indicative of how much the US is interwoven with Hollywood in the French-German imaginary, the dream factory capable of fabricating as gigantic an illusion as 9/11.

Moving from these directly politically charged texts, Sandra Singer's comparison in chapter "Cultural and Historical Memory in English and German Discursive Responses to 9/11" of a British and a German

---

[57] First published under this title by Fabrika Knijga (in Belgrade) and Devedeset Stupnjeva (in Zagreb), with the English translation by Ellen Elias-Bursác, Dubravka Ugrešić *Nobody's Home: Essays* (London: Telegram, 2007); for the essay, see 153–162.

novel, Ian McEwan's *Saturday* (2005) and Bernhard Schlink's *Das Wochenende* (2008) [The Weekend], focuses on the more indirect impact of 9/11 on the European psyche. The chapter reveals the various confusions between actual and perceived threats in European fiction. Tracing McEwan's references to Britain's mid-nineteenth-century imperial past, the Cold War threat and the Soviets' support of the IRA, as well as Schlink's incorporation of 9/11 into Germany's Nazi past and 1970s left-wing Red Army Faction terrorism, Singer shows how both texts' reception of the attacks and the fear of terrorists are deeply rooted in previous national experiences of violence. Denying the possibility of a perfunctory victim-perpetrator binary, both texts draw together the issues of terrorism and social inequality. *Saturday* thereby exhibits a class consciousness which has been identified as a particularly British concern, which also forms an opposition to the US and its promise of the American dream.[58] *Das Wochenende* also challenges the guilt question when it brings up the political debate about the pardon of former Red Army Faction terrorists, which overlapped with the novel's time of writing and publication, thus linking Islamic terrorism with economic conditions in a more extreme way.

The association of the 9/11 terrorists with historic movements for radical social change can also be seen in the Polish context, which invites subtle comparisons between historic Polish freedom fighters and contemporary terrorists. In her discussion of the novel *Córeńka* (2005) [Dearest Little Daughter] by the acclaimed journalist Wojciech Tochman, in chapter "The Post-9/11 World in Three Polish Responses: Zagajewski, Skolimowski, Tochman," Ewa Kowal considers this wider context of the Polish 9/11-related cultural production. *Córeńka* is the author's attempt to come to terms with his search for his fellow journalist, Beata Pawlak, who was killed in the al-Qaida Bali bombings in 2002. This interlacing of fact and fiction continues the questions of representation from the volume's Part I, which Kowal, however, situates in a specific national tradition, the "Polish School of Reportage." The genre's socio-critical impetus is palpable in this very personal victim narrative. Though not directly criticizing Poland's support of the Iraq War, Kowal's contextualization of the novel in more explicit cinematic examples points to the latency of such critique.

---

[58] Holloway, *9/11 and the War on Terror*, 125.

National history is also a crucial foundation for the best-selling anti-Islamic *La Trilogia di Oriana Fallaci* (2001–2004) by the Italian journalist of the same name. In a populist fashion, she caters to the diffuse fears of an Islamification of the continent by likening it to European totalitarianism in the 1920s and 1930s. In chapter "The Islamic World as Other in Oriana Fallaci's 'Trilogy'," Charles Burdett lays bare the rhetorical sophistication through which Fallaci gives her accounts an aura of factual writing and analyses how she engineers moral credibility as a secular martyr. Resorting to her family history of opposing fascism, she places herself in a *longue durée* of Italian intellectuals—going back to the fourteenth-century mathematician and scientist Cecco d'Ascoli, who died at the hands of the Inquisition —who were prepared to give their life to speak the truth. The chapter uncovers the eschatological structure of Fallaci's own argument, somewhat ironically mirroring the totalitarian discourse she claims to criticize. This construction of an overpowering Other threatening the very essence of Italy's identity closes the section on national paradigms while raising questions that come into focus in Part III of the book.

Part III: Negotiating European Identity After September 11 Through the Double Other of the US and Islam

These negotiations of identity in the literary reception of 9/11 on a national level are paralleled at the supranational level. Twenty-first-century European novels have repeatedly dealt with the issue of European identity and the idea of supranational government. The texts presented in Part III do this in a distinctly post-9/11 context. As the individual chapters demonstrate, this quest for a common European identity significantly rests upon the construction of two pronounced Others: the US and Muslim societies.

If the fall of the Berlin Wall epitomized the collapse of the Eastern Bloc and the end of the Cold War's bipolar world, the two airplanes hijacked by Islamist terrorists crashing into the very symbols of the Western world could be read as a real-world manifestation of Huntington's clash of civilizations. Alternatively, one might interpret the hijacked American Airlines carrying the enemy as 'double Trojan horses,' as a symbol of the 'stranger within,' thus, instead of constructing essentialized cultures revealing inner-cultural contradictions. Several of the texts discussed in Part III show a tendency towards the latter, employing textual ambivalence to challenge the perception of cultures as homogeneous entities in opposition to each other and inviting a multitude of hermeneutical interpretations to encourage the analogous rehearsal of multitude ways to understand the Other.

The selected texts thus continue the ideas of personal and cultural identities as constantly changing imaginaries which postcolonial theory put forward under the influence of poststructuralism. In the wake of 9/11, however, these concepts have been subject to increasing criticism. With a global identity crisis, stressing the uniqueness of each culture gained importance and an imaginary stable identity began to seem preferable over inner heterogeneity.[59] In their meandering construction of European identity, the texts illustrate this spectrum.

In this context, European literature uses fiction to make the Muslim Other accessible to the European majority reader or give an illusion thereof. The manner in which this is done varies widely: British novelist Martin Amis' literary revenge on the 9/11 leading hijacker in his story *The Last Days of Muhammad Atta* (2006), posthumously debasing the perpetrator and imputing vulgar thoughts to him, stands next to examples such as Sherko Fatah's German novel *Das dunkle Schiff* (2008) [The Dark Ship], which uses psychological realism to explain religious radicalization. Along similarly empathetic lines to Fatah, the perspective of an Iraqi refugee on his trail to London is related in the novelistic approach *Ulysses from Baghdad* (2008) by French-Belgian author, Éric-Emmanuel Schmitt.

The US constitutes the second crucial Other for European identity formation in literary representations of September 11 and its consequences. While ethnic-religious stereotyping such as Islamophobic views used to be much more of a taboo, certainly in the light of Europe's history of racism and ethnic cleansing, anti-Americanism, however, is a standing European attitude, expressed freely especially among left-wing intellectuals in Western Europe. It is therefore not surprising that anti-Americanism is also a historic constant in European literature and directly correlates with the need for European identity formation.[60]

---

[59] See Majid, "The Failure of Postcolonial Theory After 9/11," Margulies, *What Changed When Everything Changed: 9/11 and the Making of National Identity*; Balis and Serfaty, *Visions of America and Europe: September 11, Iraq, and Transatlantic Relations*.

[60] Gulddal, *Anti-Americanism in European Literature*, 8. For the severe identity crisis that pertained to all areas on a public as well as an individual level in post-9/11 Europe, see Chitwood, "Five ways a Swedish novel can help us navigate religious, ethnic, tension.".

In their construction of the US, the texts under consideration in this Part continue the ambivalences of the transatlantic relationship.[61] The examples clearly demonstrate that literary engagements with 9/11 and the War on Terror do not write on a unilateral image of the West. Tendentious accounts draw a favourable image of Europe, for example, by asserting that the US answer to multiculturalism is ultimately inferior to Europe's.[62]

As far as popular opinion is concerned, post-9/11 anti-Americanism meant reversing the construction of the US from a desirable model into its opposite. Western Europe's former example whose pop culture, music and film industry, as well as technical innovations were devoured by the majority population, was shattered in 9/11's military aftermath.[63] Several texts in this section reflect this flip from Americanophile to anti-American attitudes as a mass phenomenon. Playing with and undermining topoi, such as the US as "a place of cultural monotony and moral corruption,"[64] they reveal how representations of the US War on Terror in general and the highly controversial Guantánamo detentions in particular serve to construct Western Europe's moral and cultural superiority.

Besides open stereotyping of both the Muslim and the American Other, the chapters also uncover subtler forms of intercultural aggression. Several representations of supposedly desirable intercultural encounters are shown to be less based on mutual understanding than on European appropriation processes. This self-critical strand mirrors the views Todorov put forward in *The Fear of Barbarians*, where he shows that the

---

[61] Gulddal claims that "it is often in works of literature that we find the most clear-cut and radical examples of anti-American resentment," but then adds that many examples also undermine this negative image in complex ways, Gulddal, *Anti-Americanism in European Literature*, 9f.

[62] Patterson, "A Kinder, Gentler Europe? Islam, Christianity, and the Divergent Multiculturalisms of the New West."

[63] This phenomenon was especially clear and present in Dutch cultural response, for instance. Koojiman emphasizes the loss of an imaginary US which is emulated in the construction of identity. He confirms, however, that, less a caesura, 9/11 should be seen as a catalyst for an ongoing debate of national identity in the Netherlands that has been further fuelled by the assassinations of the right-wing politician Pim Fortuyn in 2002 and the filmmaker Theo van Gogh in 2004, "Are We All Americans? 9/11 and Discourses of Multiculturalism in the Netherlands," 182–189.

[64] Gulddal, *Anti-Americanism in European Literature*, 1.

emphasis on tolerance in the tradition of European Enlightenment reinforces power relations, putting the cultural Other at the mercy of a generously acceptable dominant majority. Several literary examples discussed in this section take up this critical self-reflection, questioning the idea of essentalized cultures and their traditions as unchanging entities to which one grants tolerance and which can be studied from a distance.[65]

Chapters "National Identity and Literary Culture after 9/11: Pro- and Anti-Americanism in Frédéric Beigbeder's *Windows on the World* (2003) and Thomas Hettche's *Woraus wir gemacht sind* (2006)" by Birte Christ and "Europe and Its Discontents: Intra-European Violence in Dutch Literature after 9/11" by Maria Boletsi, in particular, concentrate on this self-critical strand of European 9/11 literature. Continuing from the previous Part II, Birte Christ's in-depth comparative study of Frédéric Beigbeder's *Windows on the World* and the German "America novel," *Woraus wir gemacht sind* (2006) [What We Are Made Of] by Thomas Hettche unveils strong national perspectives. At the same time, the two novels exemplify an overarching European self-understanding in their flickering between anti-American and Americanophile self-constructions. Christ unveils Beigbeder's positive image of the US as deferred national narcissism and shows in Hettche's case, how an apparently Americanophile embracing of US superficiality serves the German protagonist as a replacement for a deeply troubled German cultural memory in his post-9/11 personal quest for identity.

The colonization of the Other, analogous to Beigbeder's Frenchifying of all things good in America, can be found in the German lyrical novel *September. Fata Morgana* (2010), which, despite the formal-aesthetic difference to *Windows on the World*, displays a similar doubling of plotlines and settings with its dioptric view of the New York attacks and the war in Baghdad. Chapter "The Mimicry of Dialogue: Thomas Lehr's *September. Fata Morgana* (2010)" by Svenja Frank argues that the novel deconstructs its apparent dialogue between the West and the East and instead reveals the cultured reader's Eurocentric gaze in which the identification with the Iraqi protagonist is based on the subordination of the religious and cultural Other to an unquestioned European value system.

Developments in the contemporary Dutch novel tackling the post-9/11 situation in Belgium and the Netherlands, the focus of Maria Boletsi's chapter "Europe and Its Discontents: Intra-European Violence

---

[65] See Weber, *Violence and Gender in the "New" Europe: Islam in German Culture*, 8f.

in Dutch Literature after 9/11", continue this literary self-critical analysis. Her analysis reveals a tendency to represent violence as an intra-European phenomenon and to draw attention away from the 'Other' as a violent agent and instead underscore Europe itself as a space that generates violence. This could be seen as a form of critical response to a public rhetoric in Europe after 9/11, in which violence is usually associated with Europe's 'Others' despite events such as the killings by Norwegian right-wing extremist and Islamophobic terrorist Anders Behring Breivik in Oslo and the nearby island Utøya, targeting Norway's social-democrats youth organization. Instead of directly representing such historic events, the selected texts point to far subtler, yet all-infiltrating power discourses which are intrinsic to core European values as Boletsi reveals.

A comparison of British and German representations of Guantánamo rounds off the volume. In chapter "Tourist/Terrorist. Narrating Uncertainty in Early European Literature on Guantánamo", Philipp Hubmann analyzes the novel *Guantánamo* (2004) by German writer Dorothea Dieckmann and the British play *Guantánamo. Honor Bound to Defend Freedom*, co-written by Victoria Brittain and Gillian Slovo against the background of Giorgio Agamben's study *State of Exception* (2005). The chapter shows how the self-alienating detention practice leads to perceptions of the self as its absolute Other on an individual psychological level and traces the roots of this approach to Western ideas of subjectivity and the existential crisis of Modernity. In kindling empathy for the Muslim suspect, the texts invert the culturally ascribed roles of victim and perpetrators in the 9/11 attacks. The texts openly reject the undemocratic status quo in Guantánamo Bay and blame the US as overpowering aggressor, whose motivations for military engagement is imperialistic. As in Agamben's account, Guantánamo and the Holocaust become co-extensive terms, the two texts exemplify the importance of this critique for European identity construction as the Other's evil doing apparently distracts from German guilt and the atrocities on European territory.

The Appendix to *9/11 in European Literature* provides an English translation of the Italian poetry collection *Twin Towers: poesie* (2001) by Giovanna Capucci. The translator's, Gillian Ania's, introduction shows that despite later anti-American sentiments discussed in this volume, the more immediate reactions demonstrate a great Western continuity. In loose narration of the September 11 chronology, the poems erect a vivid memory to the victims who perished in the World Trade Center attacks, as a collective and as individuals.

References

Appadurai, Arjun. "Disjuncture and Difference in the Global Cultural Economy," *Theory Culture Society*, vol. 7, no. 2/3 (1990), 295–310.

Araújo, Susana. *Transatlantic Fictions of 9/11 and the War on Terror: Images of Insecurity, Narratives of Captivity* (London: Bloomsbury Academic, 2015).

Balis, Christina V., and Simon Serfaty (eds.). *Visions of America and Europe. September 11, Iraq, and Transatlantic Relations* (Washington, D.C.: CSIS Press, 2004).

Baudrillard, Jean. "The Spirit of Terrorism," in Jean Baudrillard, *The Spirit of Terrorism and Other Essays*, transl. by Chris Turner (London/New York: Verso, 2002), 1–34.

Baumbach, Sibylle. "Rooting 'New European Literature': A Reconsideration of the European Myth of the Postnational and Cynical Cosmopolitanism," in César Domínguez and Theo D'haen (eds.), *Cosmopolitanism and the Postnational: Literature and the New Europe* (Leiden/Boston: Brill Rodopi, 2015), 55–74.

Beck, Ulrich, and Edgar Grande. *Cosmopolitan Europe* (Cambridge: Polity Press, 2007).

Beigbeder, Frédéric. *Windows on the World* (Paris: Gallimard, 2003).

Bharat, Meenakshi. *In the Shadow of Terror: Terrorism and the Contemporary Indian Novel in English* (New Delhi: Nehru Memorial Museum and Library, 2014).

Boehmer, Elleke, and Stephen Morton. *Terror and the Postcolonial* (Malden, Mass.: Wiley-Blackwell, 2010).

Boletsi, Maria. "Still Waiting for the Barbarians After 9/11? Cavafy's Reluctant Irony and the Language of the Future." *Journal of Modern Greek Studies*, vol. 32, no. 1 (2014), 55–80.

Borradori, Giovanna. *Philosophy in a Time of Terror. Dialogues with Jürgen Habermas and Jacques Derrida* (Chicago/London: Chicago University Press, 2003).

Brooks, Douglas A., Matthew Biberman, and Julia Reinhard Lupton (eds.). *Shakespeare After 9/11: How a Social Trauma Reshapes Interpretation* (Lewiston, N.Y.: Mellen, 2011).

Buescu, Helena. "Europe between Old and New: Cosmopolitanism Reconsidered," in César Domínguez and Theo D'haen (eds.), *Cosmopolitanism and the Postnational: Literature and the New Europe* (Leiden/Boston: Brill Rodopi, 2015), 11–25.

Butter, Michael, Birte Christ, and Patrick Keller. *9/11. Kein Tag, der die Welt veränderte* (Paderborn: Schöningh, 2011).

Carpenter, Rebecca. "'We're Not a Friggin' Girl Band': September 11, Masculinity, and the British-American Relationship in David Hare's *Stuff Happens* and Ian McEwan's *Saturday*," in Ann Keniston and Jeanne Follansbee Quinn (eds.), *Literature after 9/11* (New York/London: Routledge, 2008), 143–160.

Chandler, Aaron. *Pursuing Unhappiness: City, Space, and Sentimentalism in Post Cold-War American Literature*, dissertation published online under https://libres.uncg.edu/ir/uncg/f/Chandler_uncg_0154D_10126.pdf, 2009 (accessed 1.12.2016).

Chitwood, Ken. "Five ways a Swedish novel can help us navigate religious, ethnic, tension," *Houston Chronicle*, http://blog.chron.com/sacredduty/2015/01/five-ways-a-swedish-novel-can-help-us-navigate-religious-ethnic-tension/, January 8, 2015 (accessed 7.5.2015).

Cilano, Cara (ed.). *From Solidarity to Schisms: 9/11 and After in Fiction and Film from Outside the US* (Amsterdam/New York: Rodopi, 2009).

Crosetti, John. "Europeanization, Nationalism and Cosmopolitanism: Cases in the Crime Fiction of Poe, Gadda and Simenon," in César Domínguez and Theo D'haen (eds.), *Cosmopolitanism and the Postnational: Literature and the New Europe* (Leiden/Boston: Brill Rodopi, 2015), 153–175.

Däwes, Birgit. *Ground Zero Fiction. History, Memory, and Representation in the American 9/11 Novel* (Heidelberg: Universitätsverlag Winter, 2011).

Derrida, Jacques, and Giovanna Borradori. "Autoimmunity. Real and Symbolic Suicides. A Dialogue with Jacques Derrida," in Giovanna Borradori, *Philosophy in a Time of Terror* (Chicago/London: Chicago University Press, 2003).

Dixon, Wheeler Winston. *Film and Television After 9/11* (Carbondale: Southern Illinois University Press, 2004).

Domínguez, César. "Local Rooms with a Cosmopolitan View? Novels in/on the Limits of European Convergence," in César Domínguez and Theo D'haen (eds.), *Cosmopolitanism and the Postnational: Literature and the New Europe* (Leiden/Boston: Brill Rodopi, 2015), 27–53.

Flood, Christopher. "Some European Thoughts in the Wake of 9/11," *South Central Review*, vol. 19 (2002), 50–63.

Frost, Laura. "Still Life. 9/11's Falling Bodies," in Ann Keniston and Jeanne Follansbee Quinn (eds.), *Literature after 9/11* (New York/London: Routledge, 2008), 180–206.

Glejzer, Richard. "Witnessing 9/11. Art Spiegelman and the Persistence of Trauma," in Ann Keniston and Jeanne Follansbee Quinn (eds.), *Literature after 9/11* (New York/London: Routledge, 2008), 99–119.

Gourley, James. *Terrorism and Temporality in the Works of Thomas Pynchon and Don DeLillo* (New York/London: Bloomsbury, 2013).

Gray, Richard. *After the Fall: American Literature Since 9/11* (Chichester: Wiley-Blackwell, 2011).

Greenberg, Judith. *Trauma at Home: After 9/11* (Lincoln/London: University of Nebraska Press, 2003).

Gulddal, Jesper. *Anti-Americanism in European Literature* (Basingstoke: Palgrave Macmillan, 2011).

Hänggi, Christian. "Stockhausen at Ground Zero," *Fillip.ca*, vol. 15 (2011), available at http://fillip.ca/content/stockhausen-at-ground-zero (accessed 18.5.2015).
Helms, Dietrich, and Thomas Phleps (eds.). *9/11—The world's all out of tune. Populäre Musik nach dem 11. September* (Bielefeld: transcript, 2004).
Hennigfeld, Ursula (ed.). *Poetiken des Terrors. Narrative des 11. September 2001 im interkulturellen Vergleich* (Heidelberg: Universitätsverlag Winter, 2014).
Holloway, David. *9/11 and the War on Terror* (Edinburgh: Edinburgh University Press, 2008).
Huehls, Mitchum. "Foer, Spiegelman, and 9/11's Timely Traumas," in Ann Keniston and Jeanne Follansbee Quinn (eds.), *Literature after 9/11* (New York/London: Routledge, 2008), 42–59.
Irsigler, Ingo, and Christoph Jürgensen (eds.), *Nine Eleven – Ästhetische Verarbeitungen des 11. September 2001* (Heidelberg: Universitätsverlag Winter, 2008).
Kagan, Robert. *Of Paradise and Power: America and Europe in the New World Order* (New York: Knopf, 2003).
Kaplan, E. Ann. *Trauma Culture: The Politics of Terror and Loss in Media and Literature* (London/New Jersey: Rutgers University Press, 2005).
Keniston, Ann, and Jeanne Follansbee Quinn (eds.), *Literature after 9/11* (New York/London: Routledge, 2008).
Kertész, Imre. *Letzte Einkehr. Tagebücher 2001–2009. Mit einem Prosafragment*, trans. Kristin Schwamm (Reinbek: Rowohlt, 2013).
König, Michael. "Alles wird anders" – Der 11. September in deutscher Literatur," *Die Welt nach 9/11. Sonderheft der Zeitschrift für Außen- und Sicherheitspolitik*, 2012, 819–841.
Kooijman, Jaap. "Are We All Americans? 9/11 and Discourses of Multiculturalism in the Netherlands," in Derek Rubin and Jaap Verheul, *American Multiculturalism after 9/11. Transatlantic Perspectives* (Amsterdam: Amsterdam University Press, 2009), 181–190.
Levy, Daniel, Max Pensky, and John Torpey. "Editors' Introduction," in Daniel Levy, Max Pensky, and John Torpey (eds.), *Old Europe, New Europe, Core Europe: Transatlantic Relations After the Iraq War* (London: Verso, 2005), xi–xxix.
Li, Stephanie. "'Sometimes things disappear': Absence and Mutability in Colson Whitehead's *The Colossus of New York*," in Ann Keniston and Jeanne Follansbee Quinn (eds.), *Literature after 9/11* (New York/London: Routledge, 2008), 82–98.
Lorenz, Matthias N. (ed.), *Narrative des Entsetzens. Künstlerische, mediale und intellektuelle Deutungen des 11. September 2001* (Würzburg: Königshausen und Neumann, 2004).

Markovits, Andrei S. "Anti-Americanism in Europe: From Elite Disdain to Political Force," in Daniel Levy, Max Pensky, and John Torpey (eds.), *Old Europe, New Europe, Core Europe. Transatlantic Relations After the Iraq War* (London: Verso, 2005), 198–207.

Margulies, Joseph. *What Changed When Everything Changed. 9/11 and the Making of National Identity* (New Haven/London: Yale University Press, 2013).

Majid, Anouar. "The Failure of Postcolonial Theory After 9/11," *Chronicle of Higher Education*, vol. 49, no. 10 (2002), B11-B12.

Mergenthaler, Volker. "Warum die Frage, 'Wie reagieren Schriftsteller auf die Terroranschläge?' auf dem Feld der deutschsprachigen Literatur die falsche Frage ist?," in Ursula Hennigfeld (ed.), *Poetiken des Terrors. Narrative des 11. September 2001 im interkulturellen Vergleich* (Heidelberg: Universitätsverlag Winter, 2014), 179–197.

Miller, Kristine A. (ed.). *Transatlantic Literature and Culture After 9/11. The Wrong Side of Paradise* (Basingstoke: Palgrave Macmillan, 2014).

Otten, Birte. *Zeit/Geschichte: Amerikanische Alternate Histories nach 9/11*, dissertation published online under http://ediss.uni-goettingen.de/bitstream/handle/11858/00-1735-0000-0028-8697-, 2012 (accessed 1.8. 2016).

Patterson, Patrick Hyder. "A Kinder, Gentler Europe? Islam, Christianity, and the Divergent Multiculturalisms of the New West," in Derek Rubin and Jaap Verheul (eds.), *American Multiculturalism after 9/11: Transatlantic Perspectives* (Amsterdam: Amsterdam University Press, 2009), 147–164.

Poppe, Sandra, Thorsten Schüller, and Sascha Seiler (eds.), *9/11 als kulturelle Zäsur. Repräsentationen des 11. September 2001 in kulturellen Diskursen, Literatur und visuellen Medien* (Bielefeld: transcript, 2009), 163–181.

Porra, Véronique. "Risse in der Mimesis – Bemerkungen zur romanesken Darstellung des 11. Septembers 2001 in der französischen Literatur," in Sandra Poppe, Thorsten Schüller, and Sascha Seiler (eds.), *9/11 als kulturelle Zäsur. Repräsentationen des 11. September 2001 in kulturellen Diskursen, Literatur und visuellen Medien* (Bielefeld: transcript, 2009), 163–181.

Pozorski. Aimee. *Falling After 9/11: Crisis in American Art and Literature* (New York/London: Bloomsbury, 2014).

Reinhäckel, Heide. *Traumatische Texturen. Der 11. September in der deutschen Gegenwartsliteratur* (Bielefeld: transcript, 2012).

Reiter, Margit, and Helga Embacher (eds.), *Europa und der 11. September* (Wien: Böhlau, 2011).

Reynolds, Amy, and Brooke Barnett. "'America under Attack': CNN's Verbal and Visual Framing of September 11," in Steven Chermak, Frankie Y. Bailey, and Michelle Brown (eds.), *Media Representations of September 11* (London: Praeger, 2003), 85–101.

Rothberg, Michael. "Seeing Terror, Feeling Art: Public and Private in Post-9/11 Literature," in Ann Keniston and Jeanne Follansbee Quinn (eds.), *Literature after 9/11* (New York/London: Routledge, 2008), 123–142.

Rushdie, Salman. "Step Across This Line," (Part I and II) in Salman Rushdie, *Step Across This Line. Collected Non-fiction, 1992–2002* (London: Jonathan Cape, 2002), 347–381.

Schnitzler, Mathias. "Das Leben ist ein Irrtum," in *deutschlandfunk.de*, 22.5.2015, http://www.deutschlandfunk.de/imre-kertesz-letzte-einkehr-das-leben-ist-ein-irrtum.700.de.html?dram:article_id=320652, (accessed 20.2.2016).

Serfaty, Simon. "Anti-Europeanism in America and Anti-Americanism in Europe," in Christina V. Balis and Simon Serfaty (eds.), *Visions of America and Europe. September 11, Iraq, and Transatlantic Relations* (Washington, D.C: CSIS Press, 2004), 3–20.

Simonsen, Karen-Margrethe. "Towards a New Europe? On Emergent and Transcultural Literary Histories," in César Domínguez and Theo D'haen (eds.), *Cosmopolitanism and the Postnational: Literature and the New Europe* (Leiden/Boston: Brill Rodopi, 2015), 131–151.

Stratenschulte, Fabian. "Die Aufarbeitung des 11-M im spanischen Roman und Comic am Beispiel von *El Corrector* und *11-M: La Novela Gráfica*" in Ursula Hennigfeld (ed.), *Poetiken des Terrors. Narrative des 11. September 2001 im interkulturellen Vergleich* (Heidelberg: Universitätsverlag Winter, 2014), 229–245.

Todorov, Tzvetan. *The Fear of Barbarians. Beyond The Clash of Civilizations*, transl. by Andrew Brown (Cambridge: Polity Press, 2010).

Véguez, Roberto A. "*Don Quijote* and 9-11: The Clash of Civilizations and the Birth of the Modern Novel," *Hispania*, vol. 88, no. 1 (2005), 101–113.

Versluys, Kristiaan. "9/11 as a European Event: the Novels," in *European Review*, vol. 15, no. 1, 65–79 (2007).

———. *Out of the Blue: September 11 and the Novel* (New York: Columbia University Press, 2009).

Weber, Beverly M.. *Violence and Gender in the "New" Europe. Islam in German Culture* (New York: Palgrave Macmillan, 2013).

Wilson, Emma. "Europe's 9/11," *Paragraph. A Journal of Modern Critical Theory*, vol. 23 (2004), 100–112.

Werkmeister, Till. *Domestic Nation. Der sentimentale Diskurs US-amerikanischer Romane zum elften September 2001* (Berlin: LitVerlag, 2013).

Žižek, Slavoj. *Welcome to the Desert of the Real* (London/New York: Verso, 2002).

Author Biography

Svenja Frank is a member of the Ph.D. programme "Text Studies" at Göttingen University, Germany, and works on the reflection of literary criticism in fictional texts. After completing her studies in European Culture, English and German Literature, she has taught Modern and Contemporary German literature at Freiburg University, the University of Latvia and Oxford University. Among her research interests are German and comparative contemporary literature, intermediality and literary theory.

PART I

September 11 Seen Through European Media and Semiotic Theory

9/11: The Interpretation of Disaster as Disaster of Interpretation—An American Catastrophe Reflected in American and European Discourses

Rolf G. Renner

Preliminaries

The killing of Osama bin Laden almost exactly ten years after the attack on the Twin Towers was viewed by the US government as an important step in the War on Terror. For others, it was an occasion for melancholy musings. One commentary spoke of "ten lost years" for politics and political discourse, and, for many, the intentional killing appeared to be confirmation that Western society has lost its moral compass as a result of this war.[1]

The simultaneously emphatic and irritatingly different comments concerning the terrorist attacks on 9/11 that dominated both the public

---

[1] Cf. Minkmar, "Die Welt nach 9/11. Ein verlorenes Jahrzehnt".

R.G. Renner (✉)
Freiburg, Germany

and the scholarly discourses, confirm this assessment. At the same time as the central themes of the predominantly political discourses were being mobilized, the incompatibility of theoretically grounded understandings of the world, on the one hand, and immediate experience, on the other, became apparent, just like the difficulties in the transferral of theoretical discourse into political discourse and vice versa. In the end, nothing was certain any longer—the multiplicity of interpretations and evaluations revealed a severe lack of orientation among the Western intelligentsia, who nonetheless were reluctant to give up their claim to provide definitive interpretations. The disaster of the terrorist attack led to a disaster of interpretation among the scientific community and social intellectuals. This change in the discourse that was brought about by 9/11 looks like a satirical sideshow that accompanied the breakdown of solidarity between the US and the countries that Donald Rumsfeld, using a phrase taken from Karl Marx, referred to as "Old Europe." Indeed, it became apparent that the opposing opinions about the conflict were not only based on differences between the European and US-American evaluation of terrorism, but primarily on diverging interpretations in the European founding countries and in the new, mainly Eastern European states. The specific social and historical experiences in these countries prevailed over the demand for an overall European solidarity, thus 9/11 also became a challenge for the European idea as such. In addition to the differing political comments, there were also from the very outset ideas inspired by media theory and the aesthetics of media that ran in an entirely different direction. It can be observed that at the same time a specifically European discourse gains importance. All these approaches emphasized the autonomy of the way the media work against the facticity of the event and thereby offended public opinion, which was dominated by stereotypical forms of argumentation and strategies for expressing outrage.

Artists were the first provocateurs, but the public excitement that they consciously provoked quickly subsided. When German avant-garde composer Karlheinz Stockhausen characterized the events of 9/11 immediately afterwards as the "größte Kunstwerk, das auf der Welt existiert" [the greatest work of art that exists anywhere in the entire cosmos],[2]

---

[2] Karlheinz Stockhausen made this statement at a press conference on September 16, 2001, which then made the national news, as cited in Collenberg, "'Vorstellung des Terrors'—9/11, RAF, and the Sublime".

there was still a great deal of disapproval since Germany had just promised the United States not only their sympathy, but even their support. Ten years and many commentaries and images later, Anselm Kiefer, who belongs to the group of contemporary German artists of international standing—like Gerhard Richter, whose creative engagement with 9/11 is explored in this volume—compared the events of September 11 in the Collège de France to the "strong and simple beauty" of Genet's poetry and stated that Osama bin Laden had thereby "created the most perfect images that we have seen since we saw the steps of the first man on the moon." His thesis that bin Laden was not interested in a terrorist act, but above all in the production of symbolically powerful images was greeted by the audience composed of the educated bourgeoisie in France with only polite applause.[3] Maybe it reminded them of Marcel Proust's descriptions of the First World War in the text of *À la recherche du temps perdu,* which present the German bombing of Paris[4] as an aesthetic event comparable to Ernst Jünger's aesthetic celebration of a bombing attack on Paris in the Second World War.[5] In this respect, the French author's text corresponds to the view of the German author, who wrote one of the most famous German narratives about the First World War, namely, the text *In Stahlgewittern,* which is an authentic war diary rewritten several times. Nevertheless, this French indifference is astounding. It is undoubtedly connected not only to a specific national perspective, but also to ideas from media theory that in this particular case were at work in the public discourse and in the meantime have become popular. From the very outset, this act of terror was also perceived from the perspective of a staged media event. This shows how difficult it has become for a society dominated by the media to separate factual events from their presentation in the media.

---

[3] Cf. Bopp, "Anselm Kiefer am Collège de France. Bin Laden—eine Kunst-Performance?".

[4] Proust, *À la recherche du temps perdu,* 380: "[…] des feux intermittents que, soit de ces aéroplanes, soit de projecteurs de la Tour Eiffel, on savait dirigés par une volonté intelligente […]".

[5] Jünger, *Tagebücher III: Strahlungen II,* 271.

Political Context

George W. Bush's statement that, "This will be a monumental struggle of good versus evil. But good will prevail,"[6] is paralleled by Barack Obama's similarly pathos-filled announcement of bin Laden's death. He did not say anything about an intentional killing nor did he ever provide any details about the circumstances of this death. His comments were rather, "So his demise should be welcomed by all who believe in peace and human dignity" and when he added that "justice has been done," his position was not fundamentally different from Bush's, for whom the "justice" that he swore to pursue had nothing to do with a state committed to the rule of law. Nor has the new president, in the view of many European intellectuals, generally distanced himself from his predecessor's position. Severely disappointed, they criticize him that he has taken it upon himself to continue to pursue the American war against evil in Afghanistan and to continue to deny the prisoners at Guantánamo access to normal legal procedures and trials.

Many European intellectuals attributed Bush's statements to the limited world view of an evangelical fundamentalist at the same time as they expressed an understanding for the resistance of the deposed Sunnis in Iraq and the Afghan Taliban. The German assessment of the US pursuit of the war has been especially strongly characterized by a conspicuously limited recognition of its complexity devoid of any sober political analysis. It is ironic that the German defenders of morality thereby resemble not only the American Neo-cons but also the propagators of radical Islam in the way that they simply invert Bush's schema of good and evil and couch it in the religious Manichean vocabulary of a "holy war" undertaken by "God's warriors" that has been uncritically adopted by the Western media.

The development within the European discourse has been astounding because the stance of the European opponents to the war had very different motivations. This is especially true about the differences between Germany and France, whose politics were based not on comparable moral principles but upon different economic and geopolitical interests and attempts to stake out their particular spheres of influence. At the same time, the Europeans in the purported self-certainty of

---

[6] George W. Bush in a White House press release of 12 November 2001, quoted in Virilio, *Ground Zero*, 36.

their judgments ignored their own historical responsibilities. It was not American, but rather European colonial politics that had established the current borders in the Middle East, including the state of Israel. Already during the First World War the colonial powers, England and France, had outlined their spheres of influence in the Middle East after the expected defeat of the Ottoman Empire with the Sykes-Picot Agreement of 1916. The borders resulting from the following Peace Treaty of Sèvres in 1920 ignored ethnic and religious differences within these regions and gave rise to states such as Syria, Libya or Iraq. These states are currently on the brink of becoming failed states. Also as early as 1917, Britain had determined, with the Balfour Declaration, the borders of the state of Israel in its mandated territory of Palestine.

It is worth noting that the intervention by several NATO countries in Libya was legitimized with the same arguments that one did not want to accept from the Americans for their pursuit of the Iraq and Afghanistan wars. It is not without irony that in the course of the first "Arabellion," France celebrates itself for its military support of democracy in its former sphere of influence—the same France whose Foreign Legion is constantly and without any parliamentary control active in several crisis regions in Africa. There are numerous other contradictions along these lines that could be cited, but I hope these brief references will suffice to illustrate my point.

The Discursive Event

The context for these complex affairs involving political power is one of the reasons for the discursive event that the terrorist attacks generate. The unfolding of this discourse led to a polarization of the political fronts and an oversimplification of complex political and historical issues. Both the Islamists and the Americans could each characterize the other as the enemy, which lent support to reactionary forces on both sides.[7] The fact that the attack on New York was compared to Pearl Harbor or to the Algerian resistance against France, in each case, leading to very different conclusions, illustrates how historical coordinates were intentionally neglected, something which is also demonstrated in numerous

---

[7] Cf. Schmitt, *Der Begriff des Politischen*.

novels. Moreover, the Europeans regarded themselves as referees in a conflict in which they saw themselves neither involved nor threatened.

It seems as if the terrorists who attacked New York had planned precisely this discursive collateral damage, a result that had been prepared theoretically and psychologically by discussions in European and to a lesser extent in American universities and among public intellectuals. This is one of the primary reasons why the conflict became the subject of an interpretation that was directed to the genesis of the terror and attributed it to social injustices, American power interests, and global economic cartels. The moral discourse which originated from the German responsibility for the Holocaust and had dominated Germany prior to the *Wende* in 1989, but had been delegitimized by the complexity of the processes involved in the reunification of completely different political and social value-orders, was now revived.

In intellectual circles within American universities, by contrast, the main arguments offered in "postcolonial studies," which was also undergoing a crisis over its legitimacy, were reanimated, even though the Islamists themselves had shown that they completely rejected a hybrid fusing of cultures. Baudrillard vehemently criticized this interpretation as advanced, for example, by Arundhati Roy, author of the Booker-prize winning novel, *The God of Small Things* (1997) and political activist, who saw the attackers as victims. For Baudrillard, a "thesis that takes hopelessness as its point of departure, is itself hopeless" or an unwitting accomplice of the system.[8]

One assessment that at least at first glance appears much more differentiated and is also concretely political came from Noam Chomsky. He does not assign blame to any one group, but traced the New York attack back to the bitterness and anger that many people feel over American politics in the Arab region.[9] Chomsky's judgment was directed at the specific political actions of the US, undoubtedly among them America's acceptance of the Israeli settlement policies in the "West Bank," which was occupied by Israel during the "Six Days War" in 1967. His criticism is consistent with the basic idea also shared by many European public

---

[8] Jean Baudrillard in *Le Monde*, November 3, 2001, and reprinted in Jean Baudrillard, *The Spirit of Terrorism and Requiem for the Twin Towers*, 77.

[9] Noam Chomsky in a 2001 interview, Chomsky, *The Attack: Hintergründe und Folgen*, 18.

figures that, in principle, all political and cultural differences can be solved by consensus.[10] However, Chomsky does not face up to the inner dialectic of enlightened reason that guides this model of thinking, which simultaneously defines the preconditions of a "just war."

Paul Auster's view that the new cultural confrontation that is becoming apparent in the form of an asymmetric war as a sign for the beginning of the twenty-first century, can be instructive here. For Auster, the historical date did not mark off a temporal era.[11] Rather it metaphorically characterized the new global world order that is distinguished not only by the simultaneity of different temporal orders, but also as a fundamental asymmetry of experiential worlds. Both give rise not just to violent conflict but also at the same time to antagonistic explanatory models.

The increasing awareness of this new situation no longer came about just in terms of a rational discourse, but was rather mediated above all through the medium of images.[12] Neither the neoconservative acceptance of a "clash of cultures," i.e., a conflict between progress and reactionary forces in the field of politics, nor the postcolonial interpretation in terms of military and terroristic conflicts, takes sufficient account of the way these political oppositions and their consequences are presented through the media. That is why old models of discourse that were no longer adequate for this new conflict and the current historical situation continued to be employed.

In the confrontation between the West and the Islamic world, the morally grounded acceptance of alterity was seen as the necessary answer to the blameworthiness of the European colonial powers and Germany's historical blameworthiness for fascism. What the Germans forgot in the discussion is above all the fact that the change in their own attitude towards the war in the Balkans and the change in the leading political discourse had been brought about through manipulation of the way these events were portrayed in the media. Faced with the pictures of the Serbian camps broadcast on television, the Foreign Secretary replaced

---

[10] Cf. Habermas and Derrida, *Philosophie in Zeiten des Terrors. Zwei Gespräche, geführt, eingeleitet und kommentiert von Giovanna Borradori.*

[11] Cf. Auster, "Jetzt beginnt das 21. Jahrhundert. Wir alle wussten, dass dies geschehen könnte. Nun ist es viel schlimmer." Cf. also Schami, *Mit fremden Augen. Tagebuch über den 11. September, den Palästinakonflikt und die arabische Welt*, 17.

[12] Cf. the general tenor of the volume edited by Butter, Christ, and Keller, *9/11. Kein Tag, der die Welt veränderte*, 6–12 and 15–46.

the previously dominant motto in Germany "Never again war" with "Never again concentration camps."

Accordingly, the German, the European, and the American discussion of 9/11 all make use of an arsenal of metaphorical formulae that, in the interplay of images and public discourse, unfolded in contradictory ways. What was not considered is the fact that in the course of the loss of legitimacy of the "grands récits," that was decoded by François Lyotard, this arsenal of formulae had already long since lost its original basis. Baudrillard recognizes in the resulting "neutralization of values" at the same time a loss of legitimacy of reality itself through the media.[13] He could have added that this "neutralization of values" also leads to the loss of legitimacy for the public intellectuals' discourse as well. Even the political discourse is interspersed with lacunae in understanding. They are now replaced by the new power of images. But just those images which seem to promise unambiguity open up opportunities for manipulations on an entirely new scale.

The triumph of images has long been the topic of analyses in media history. Representatives of critical theory and Vilém Flusser, among others, have pointed to the political consequences of this development.[14] It has become apparent that the media not only facilitate an awareness "that people no longer (really) talk to each other, and that 'spectacles' and the so-called hyperreality of the media come to substitute for genuine social activity,"[15] and thereby this leads to deformations in the laws by which the social systems operate.[16] Images do not merely replace discursive formations; they become goods—they achieve their effect by their exchange values, not by adequately reproducing actual states of affairs.

This becomes particularly significant with regard to intercultural communication, in which alterity itself becomes a media construct. Arjun Appadurai emphasizes how, in a global community that is subject to the law of "modernity at large," genuine traditional political, moral, and cultural orders dissolve. They are replaced by images that now produce

---

[13] Cf. Baudrillard, "The Spirit of Terrorism," 51.

[14] Cf. Debord, *La société du Spectacle*, 7.

[15] Ibid.

[16] Luhmann (ed.), *Ökologische Kommunikation: Kann die Gesellschaft sich auf ökologische Gefährdungen einstellen?* 269.

mere imaginary communicative communities and imaginary worlds. The epochal signature of a simultaneity of what is not simultaneous corresponds to the simultaneity of imagination and relation to reality that is communicated by the media. The media do not therefore lead to a new experience of reality or to a correction of inappropriate assessments. Rather they make it possible for different groups that live in a global diaspora to tailor everything to their own imaginations. For Appadurai, imagination itself becomes a "social fact and a primary component of the new global order." Under the influence of the media, what emerges are "ethnoscapes," "mediascapes," and "ideoscapes." These are constructions of virtual identity, which are based on ethnic or self-identifying stereotypes transmitted by mass media. They provide the new patterns for orientation that refer to the original orientations but vary and transform them in fundamental ways.

Mediated Staging and Media Presentations of Terror

Shortly after the events of 9/11, Jean Baudrillard told *Le Monde* that, out of all of the different weapons that the terrorists took from the system that they were attacking, the most useful had been the authenticity of the pictures and their immediate world-wide transmission.[17] He shares German philosopher's Jürgen Habermas' view that the meaning of September 11 resulted not from the event itself, but rather from the particular form of its communicative mediation.[18] Both of them agree that the audience's view that is communicated through the media produces a different view compared to the view produced by immediate experience.[19]

Jacques Derrida added a semiotic note to these ideas from media and communication theory. In the temporal formula "September 11," he decodes a language without referential function. It conjures up and names something that cannot be adequately expressed linguistically.[20] The merely deictic naming points to the traumatic effects of an event for

---

[17] Cf. Jean Baudrillard in *Le Monde,* November 3, 2001, quoting in accordance with the English translation in Baudrillard, "The Spirit of Terrorism," 27.
[18] Cf. Borradori, "Die Rekonstruktion des Terrorismusbegriffs nach Habermas," 75.
[19] Cf. ibid., 52f.
[20] Cf. ibid., 368.

which there is no "horizon of anticipation, knowledge, naming," that would allow for its "identification, determination, and interpretation."[21]

In an earlier essay, Baudrillard had insisted that only death can escape the social laws of exchange that he decodes and identifies as the basic form of contemporary society. Corresponding to this way of thinking, he also constructs a theory of the media from the perspective of his theory of the *simulacrum*.[22] He characterizes the attack on the Twin Towers as an "absolute event" that cannot be captured by any historical classification simply because it is comparable to the infinite cinematic fictions and therefore to events that have never actually happened.[23] Only through the association with the fictional and the imaginary can the real terror attack unfold the symbolic power that is the basis for its actual effect.[24] Indeed, the images, metaphors, and collective memories that were set loose in this interaction developed a unique dynamic of their own in the journalistic and intellectual discourses that are responsible for what I earlier called the "disaster of interpretation," the failure to be able to come to any final and rational judgments about these events.[25]

In a manner similar to Slavoj Žižek, Baudrillard connects this symbolic effect of the event with unconscious processes. In his view, the terrorist act just realizes "that terrorist imagination that dwells in all of us,"[26] and its effect is based on a "deep, unconscious complicity,"[27] because its final meaning results in the end from the fact that the terrorists in their strategy precisely calculated that they could count on this complicity that cannot ever be acknowledged.[28] "The catastrophe film of Manhattan" unites "the white light of an image" and the "black light of

---

[21] Cf. ibid., 123.
[22] Baudrillard, *Simulacra and Simulation*, 1–43 and 87–95.
[23] Cf. Baudrillard, "Der Geist des Terrorismus," 42.
[24] Cf. ibid., 74.
[25] Ibid.
[26] Ibid., 12.
[27] Ibid., 13.
[28] Ibid., cf. Schmitt, "Die weiße Magie des Kinos und die schwarze Magie des Terrorismus. Gedanken zum 11. September 2001," indication of Waitz, "Die Frage der Bilder. 9/11 als filmisch Abwesendes," 228.

terrorism,"[29] but in the end what alone dominates is the "view of the images" that for Baudrillard represent nothing other than "our primordial scene (*Urszene*)."[30] The event of terror thereby also shatters society's character as a system of exchanges.[31]

Baudrillard's and Žižek's psychological interpretation, along with Derrida's semiotic argument, can all be traced back to an idea from Kant. An event, Kant concludes, with regard to the perception of the French Revolution in Germany, becomes a "historical sign" above all through the way that it is perceived by the public. It then displays, in addition to its referential power as a "*signum demonstrativum*," a twofold temporality: as a "*signum demonstrativum*," it recalls the past, as a "*signum prognosticon*," it simultaneously points to the future.[32] One explanation for the different contextualizations of the same images that are presented over and over by the media could be that the Europeans, Americans, and Islamists in their "enthusiastischen" ("enthusiastic")[33] perceptions each stress a different temporal structure of the events that are experienced as "historical signs." If that is true, then the differences among the discursive appropriations that are associated with them result from a metonymy of the meanings that are only purportedly intercultural.

Truth and Lies in Images and Texts

Almost every inhabitant of the global public sphere witnessed the events without being there themselves.[34] The transmission of the images, almost in real time, suggested the authenticity of a documentary. However, the images were by no means reliable. The still photos distributed on the internet competed with the blurred pictures taken by smartphones that claimed to be authentic, but as a rule declined to provide decoded details. These were accompanied by film sequences that showed a series of events that were repeated in endless loops. This overlay of

---

[29] Baudrillard, "Der Geist des Terrorismus," 75.

[30] Ibid., 72.

[31] Cf. ibid., 57.

[32] Kant, *Der Streit der Fakultäten*, 357. I would like to thank Kaspar Renner for pointing this out.

[33] Ibid., 357.

[34] Cf. Deupmann, "Ausnahmezustand des Erzählens. Zeit und Ereignis in Ulrich Peltzers Erzählung *Bryant Park* und anderen Texten über den 11. September 2001," 17.

different image formats blurred the difference between analytical and empathic reactions in a fundamental way.

In spite of their authenticity as cool media, which, according to Marshall McLuhan's media theory, are more open and less clearly defined than writing, all of the images turned out to have limited effective power.[35] They only became "historical signs" once they were presented in various cultural codes. These codes were oriented, on the one hand, to the images of catastrophes that were already present in the European cultural memory, such as the images of Napoleon's Battle of Berezina on the retreat from Moscow, the German defeat of Stalingrad in the Second World War, or the motif of the shipwreck in Greek or Roman literature.[36] On the other hand, these codes gain autonomy as images, which structure the predominant political, cultural, and aesthetic discourses and which are nearly all presented by means of the mass media. This interplay of actual and cultural transmissions of the images also influences the conception of the reconstruction of the Ground Zero site.[37] Whereas the terrorist act itself can be comprehended as the culmination point of structure developments,[38] its very character as an event consisted in its transmission through the media and the reactions that followed. This also holds for the self-portrayals of the combatants that were instrumentalized in the war of images that was waged on the internet. Bin Laden presented himself as Jesus or a prophet; Hillary Clinton, by contrast, was reduced to a typically American gesture of horror by a manipulation of the images as she witnessed him being killed. In the first picture of the presidential war room we see Hillary Clinton together with Barack Obama and several military personnel watching the live

---

[35] McLuhan, *Understanding Media*, 22, 25.

[36] Cf. Ulrich Kinzel's chapter "The Wind of the Hudson. Gerhard Richter's *September* (2005) and the European Perception of Catastrophe" in this volume.

[37] Cf. Kolter, "Architecture Criente: Nine Eleven zwischen Katastrophenästhetik, biblischem Strafgericht und Dekonstruktivismus," 349; cf. Reudenbach, *G. B. Piranesi. Architektur als Bild. Der Wandel der Architekturauffassung des achtzehnten Jahrhunderts*, 358.

[38] Cf. Lethen, "Bildarchiv und Traumaphilie. Schrecksekunden der Kulturwissenschaften nach dem 11.9.2001," 3. Niels Werber comes to a similar conclusion with regard to German 'pop literature,' cf. "Der Teppich des Sterbens. Gewalt und Terror in der neuesten Popliteratur." Cf. Mergenthaler, "'Weiter schreiben' nach dem 11. September—Barbara Bongartz, Alban Nikolai Herbsts und Norbert Wehrs '*Inzest* oder *Die Entstehung der Welt*'," 40.

images of the special forces attack, in the second picture, only Clinton can be seen as an observer while only the opened laptops on the table remind us of the digitally deleted persons.

For the 9/11 attack itself, it makes sense to analyse three images with which a visual connection between the factual event and images of cultural memory can be established. These images have served as models not only for the public perceptions, but also for literary and scholarly descriptions. They can also be read as abbreviations for perceptual states.

Ruins of Progress

Baudrillard's thesis that the architecture of the Twin Towers was a symbolic construction explains not only why they became targets for the terrorists, it can also serve as a model for the public as well as the scholarly discourse. At first the current perceptions were related to the cultural memory of images.[39] The steel skeletons of the collapsed towers to which Art Spiegelman's comic strip directly refers, seemed to make reference to Romantic images, whose broken-down monumental ruins with their columns and thresholds recall the architectural plans on which they were based. This overlay of signs of construction and destruction has become a metaphor for the beginning and the failures of the modern world ever since the Romantic-Surreal architectural etchings by the Italian artist Giovanni Battista. They also remind us of the Tower of Babel that has become part of the stereotypical canon of European painting and that, as the background scene to Vienna in the masterpiece of cinematic expressionism *Das Cabinet des Dr. Caligari* (1920) [The Cabinet of Dr. Caligari] has served as the signature of modernity, which is associated with the eruption of that which is alien and impossible to rationalize.[40] It is thus also not surprising how many literary accounts of 9/11 use the Biblical motif.

In the public discourse, by contrast, these pictorial cultural recollections are actualized and recoded. The besieged towers no longer appear as the representation of mutual understanding in a globalized economy,

---

[39] Cf. Kolter, "Architecture Criente," 349–351.

[40] Cf. Pieter Brueghel the Elder, *The Tower of Babel* (1565), Kunsthistorisches Museum, Vienna.

Fig. 1 Thomas Hoepker: *Young People on the Brooklyn Waterfront on Sept. 11*

on the one hand, and American claims to domination, on the other.[41] The cultural critiques in Europe view the attacks above all as directed towards the United States as the epicenter of globalization and secularization, and thereby bestowed special significance on the event that served as confirmation of greatness in its decline.[42]

It is interesting that it is precisely in literary studies that one can see the fatal consequences of the internal dynamics of the metaphors that were unleashed by these images. From the perspective of one feminist scholar, the images of the catastrophe are read against the backdrop of "iconographically assured allegorization" that are supposed to let us see the World Trade Center either as a double phallus or as the female body, symbolizing the modern metropolis as it is being penetrated by the

---

[41] Cf. basically Bongartz and Herbst, "*Inzest* oder *Die Entstehung der Welt*. Der Anfang eines Romanes in Briefen".

[42] Cf. Virilio, *Guerre et cinéma*, 101.

phallic airliners.⁴³ In a literary discussion between the German writers Barbara Bongartz and Alban Nikolai Herbst, the image of the attack on the Twin Towers is therefore set in parallel to Courbet's picture of *The Origin of the World*.⁴⁴ This is a rather embarrassingly awkward paraphrase of Jünger's above-mentioned description of the bombing of Paris as a poetic begetting scene, which for his modern readers shows that all sense of reality has disappeared in the face of scholarship and literature.⁴⁵

Shipwreck With the Audience

Against the background of the catastrophe, Thomas Hoepker's *Young People on the Brooklyn Waterfront on Sept. 11* (Fig. 1), shows a scene with people who are watching the event. By making the observation itself the theme and the observers into the figures who set the perspective, the image can be related to a central configuration of historical memory. In antiquity, it is the "shipwreck with an audience" who take on the perils of sea travel that can lead to catastrophe that is contrasted with the self-contained limitations of those who stay behind on land.⁴⁶ In Romanticism, this is the perspective of those who gaze upon the sublime, that which cannot be grasped by mere understanding, who are both attracted and abhorred by what they see.⁴⁷ Modernity, by contrast, creates an observer which Ernst Jünger called a "cool persona," who in the face of horror transforms the experience of terror into an aesthetic image.⁴⁸

---

⁴³Cf. Elisabeth Bronfen, quoting Klaus Theweleit, *Der Knall: 11. September, das Verschwinden der Realität und ein Kriegsmodell*, 142.

⁴⁴Bongartz and Herbst, "*Inzest* oder *Die Entstehung der Welt*," 59f. Cf. Savatier, *L'origine du monde. Histoire d' un tableau de Gustave Courbet*.

⁴⁵Cf. Mergenthaler, "'Weiter schreiben' nach dem 11. September," 45; Mergenthaler refers here to the interpretation of Courbet by Metken, cf. ibid., 55.

⁴⁶For the thematic history, cf. Blumenberg, *Schiffbruch mit Zuschauer—Paradigma einer Daseinsmetapher*.

⁴⁷Heinrich von Kleist, Clemens Brentano and Achim von Arnim, "Empfindungen vor Friedrichs Seelandschaft," 327f.

⁴⁸After a round undertaken through the historical experience, Ernst Jünger points out that "dieses Zweite und kältere Bewußtsein" [this second and colder consciousness, my translation] of the technically controlled perception replaces the pain, which alone is competent to enable the humans to support the world of nihilism. Jünger, "Über den Schmerz," 181f.

None of this is determined by the image alone. First of all, this is merely a paraphrase of the classic metaphor of a shipwreck. The observer, who is watching from somewhere in Brooklyn that seems to stand outside the laws of globalization, is watching the downfall of the capitalistic enterprise in Manhattan. Moreover, the modern observer demonstrates an almost monstrous indifference to what he sees. The actually perceived catastrophe appears far away, reduced to a mere image that is consumed in just the same way as the images of the catastrophe that are transmitted through various media and can immediately be posted. At the same time, however, the construction of the image also reveals a contradiction that refutes the purported security of viewing from a distance. It thereby reproduces the irritation that the Romantic images once produced, but in a different way. For, in the construction of the image, the viewer as an observer becomes himself the object who can be viewed by others. Without knowing it, the observers are subject to the colonizing gaze that a media society allows everybody, and with which it, at the same time, robs all of them of their unique and distinct experiences.

THE FALLING MAN

This picture sheds light not only on the event but also on the laws of a media society itself that is fixated on images.[49] It was surprising here that the attempts to identify the man who was falling in order to be able to decode this image as an authentic document were intentionally stopped. (The Photograph "The Falling Man" by Richard Drew See Fig. 2 on P. 000). For this very reason, it can be related to the cultural encodings such as medieval court scenes, the Tarot in Marseille, or the pictures from Sandro Chia that all aim to subvert the normal view through the inversion of natural bodies.[50] This picture of the falling man also turns a documentation into a subversion. For it is the result of a selection, one of twelve pictures that were taken as a series. The selection of this image follows a strategy of aesthetization that presupposes the cold view of a Jüngerian *désinvolture*. This is the only picture in which the limbs of the falling body are parallel to the architecture

---

[49] For the detailed history of the painting and his references, cf. Martin Raspe, "The Falling Man. Der 11. September in der Momentaufnahme," in Irsigler and Jürgensen, *Nine Eleven. Ästhetische Bearbeitungen des 11. Septembers 2001*, 369.

[50] Ibid., 380.

lines of the building, it is the only one in which the movement downward seems to be captured effortlessly in the snap moment of the photograph. This opens up a parallel to Antonioni's demonstrations of the interaction between photograph and film in *Blow Up*.[51] In that film, the different medial conditionings of visual perception are paradigmatically exemplified by a murder case. It argues that a single photograph that is selected from a series of photos can show a decisive moment and a detail more precisely than a cinematic sequence of images. In this respect Antonioni's film can be related to Roland Barthes' theory of photography presented in *La Chambre claire*. It distinguishes between "*studium*"—the documentary character of the photograph—and "*punctum*"—the special meaning which can be opened up for the beholder by a special detail in the image. The cinematic presentation in Antonioni's case and in this picture by Drew evokes the perception of detail by means of a merely suggestive staging of the horror.[52] The *punctum* in this picture opens up a further perspective because the aesthetic presentation based on a selection can also be plausibly compared to the purportedly authentic picture of the "Falling Soldier" from the Spanish Civil War, that in the meantime has been unmasked as a fake produced by the US-Hungarian war photographer Robert Capa.[53]

In the tension between documentation and aesthetic production, the image of *The Falling Man* documents a two-fold reduction of the human subject. As the target of a terrorist attack, humans are the objects of a strategy of destruction and elimination as a body without any regard to the specific person. As the object of an aesthetic selection, the falling man is also reduced to a mere body that only through its transformation takes on meaning as an aesthetic sign.

The philosophical conception of "*homo sacer*" by the philosopher Giorgio Agamben, which plays a central role in social systems and is systematically reduced by violence and terror to its mere corporality (as further explored in Philipp Hubmann's analysis of the literary representation of Guantánamo in chapter Tourist/Terrorist: Narrating Uncertainty in Early European Literature in this volume),[54] thereby

---

[51] Cf. Renner, "Das Auge der Erinnerung. Fotografie in Texten der klassischen Moderne und im Film von Michelangelo Antonioni," 198–211.

[52] Cf. Barthes, *La Chambre claire. Note sur la photographie*, 86, 102 and Sontag, *Über Fotografie*, 24.

[53] Cf. Raspe, "The Falling Man. Der 11. September in der Momentaufnahme," 369.

[54] Cf. Agamben, *Homo Sacer. Die souveräne Macht und das nackte Leben*.

takes on a new meaning that translates a basic tendency from the history of totalitarianism into a basic formula for the age of media. The falling man is not only rendered a mere object through the actual terrorist violence that he suffers, but also through the aesthetic manipulations of the media to which he is subjected even after his life is over.

This pattern is reproduced and transformed for a number of reasons in literature as well. First of all, language must try to defend its status against the images that are transmitted by the media and thereby precede it. It is also the case that the narrative finds itself in a state of emergency[55] because it is confronted with a horror that reveals the limits of ordinary language up until now, as the German philosopher Theodor W. Adorno and the author Jean Améry noted in the face of the very different catastrophe of the Holocaust.[56]

Most of the literary accounts from eye-witnesses[57] attempted to reconstruct the suddenness of the event, or, if they were not able to be direct participants in it,[58] to make up for this deficit through various narrative devices. It turned out to be very difficult to establish direct participation as a sufficient basis for the reliability of the narrator.[59] In closing, I would like to point to two texts that successfully overcame this problem.

In the novel *Bryant Park* (2002) by German writer Ulrich Peltzer, the event of 9/11 itself is interjected almost marginally into three different narrative levels, that are embedded within each other and upon which constantly changing images from different contexts are overlain. The result is a high-visible density that connects the settings where the actions take place, namely, Berlin, New York, and Italy to each other in

---

[55] Cf. Deupmann, "Ausnahmezustand des Erzählens," 19.

[56] Cf. Améry, "An den Grenzen des Geistes".

[57] Cf. Foer, *Extremely Loud and Incredibly Close*; cf. Röggla, *really ground zero. 11. september und folgendes.*

[58] Cf. Deupmann, "Ausnahmezustand des Erzählens," 19.

[59] Cf. Derrida, *Eine gewisse unmögliche Möglichkeit, vom Ereignis zu sprechen*, 60. In contrast to this, cf. Buschheuer, *Das New York Tagebuch*, 160 (Diary entry of 12 September 2001, 1:25 New York time): "Ich war zu weit weg zum Sterben, zu nah zum Weiterleben. So fühlt sich das an. Drei Kilometer; gestern hat sich mir das Herz zusammengekrampft, wie nah es doch war, als ich abends zur Unglückstelle ging. Wie knapp." [I was too far away to die, too close, to live. That is how it feels like. Three kilometres; yesterday my heart cramped, how close it was after all, when I went to the destruction site. How close. My translation].

a manner that recalls cinematic superimpositions. The story thereby produces a simultaneity of different temporal levels with very different catastrophes because the transition from one to another level of events often takes place in the same sentence. This narrative continuity is conspicuously interrupted by the event of the terrorist attack. At first, the suddenness of the event and the reaction to it are conveyed only through the media—through film images, telephone calls, and emails.[60] The event itself, however, neither significantly changes the flow of the narrative nor does it disrupt the narrative order through its suddenness. Rather the uniqueness of the event is controlled by its "own unique time" (*Eigenzeit*) of the narration and is finally made to disappear. Against the violence of the actual attack, the self-empowerment of the subject asserts itself in the unmistakable language of its own narration, so that in the end language triumphs over the images. At the same time, the act of narration becomes a psychological self-empowerment that corrects the decentralization produced by the media. In the own unique time of the narration, the narrating itself constitutes itself as noticeably untouched.

Don Delillo's *Falling Man*, by contrast, is determined in every section of the narrative by the event of the terror attacks. All of the different family and relationship histories begin with it and all of them lead up to it. The text thereby develops a temporal structure of its own that comes about in the interaction between stretching out and accelerating the series of events that are described in visually vivid ways. The text thus constantly reproduces the selection within a series of photographs, just as the photographer Drew does with his *Falling Man*. One of the central passages in the text makes a reference to this image and connects it with the story of one of the protagonists.[61] This also occurs across several temporal levels. The fall of the *Falling Man* is perceived during the attempt to escape the North Tower repeatedly and with different levels of accuracy.[62]

This also corresponds to the central motif in the text, namely, the repeated enactments of a falling man presented by a performance artist who simulates a suicide, a fall onto the train tracks or a street over and over, whereby each time he is rescued at the last second by a rope from

---

[60] Cf. Peltzer, *Bryant Park*, 134–145.
[61] Cf. DeLillo, *Falling Man*, 253.
[62] Cf. ibid., 284.

which he ends up hanging upside down. This reduction of the event to a sign is placed in ever new contexts by the audience in different situations and at different moments. This results in an "own unique time" of perception. The fall that is reduced to a mere sign reveals different strategies for coping and creates new forms of interaction with the memory of the authentic events. This is what the phrase "She was the photograph" refers to in the passage where a woman relates the performance of *Falling Man* to a suicide which she now recalls again.[63]

The opposite holds as well, the simulated fall decontextualizes and subverts everyday orders as well, that which is otherwise taken for granted, the context in which the audience is involved. This includes the fact that it leads to unconscious reactions that the audience cannot control, and it becomes clear that many of the horrified spectators are not just expecting, but even hoping for a real calamity.[64] The text illustrates in multiple ways the idea from media theory that the terror attack only achieves its full effect through the audience, the way that it provokes emotional and unconscious as well as intellectual reactions.

At the same time DeLillo's text describes various patterns of reaction whose common trait consists in the tension between linguistic denotation and connotation. On the one hand, the actual, the remembered, and the signitively imitated fall are associated for most of the protagonists with turning points in their lives,[65] that are related to a loss of their ability to communicate due to an illness or trauma[66] that finds its expression in *Ersatz*-actions[67] or images.[68]

On the other hand, the text presents linguistic strategies beyond conceptual language with which the alien becomes tellable and controllable. It is reminiscent of the language of the Innuit, that manifests a different temporal structure as a language made up of syllables rather than a language made up of letters, and it names at great length the private language of children that is analogous to myth, in which the threatening

---

[63] Cf. ibid., 255.
[64] Cf. ibid., 192.
[65] Cf. ibid., 32.
[66] Cf. ibid., 22.
[67] Cf. ibid., 114.
[68] Cf. ibid., 238, 240.

alien figure, Osama bin Laden for the adults, is transformed into the figure of "Bill Lawton."[69]

In addition to this presentation of ways of speaking that point back to the historical beginnings of the linguistic appropriation of the world, the text explicates dissonant images of bodies that cross out the physical integrity of the human subject. It does not treat the real body as an aesthetic sign as the photographer Drew does, but rather provides two counter-images to this construction. The first is the new experience of bodily integrity that precisely at the moment of a catastrophe is set free, and the other is the image of the human body as "organic shrapnel,"[70] in which even mere corporality appeared unnatural.

The unique catastrophe in DeLillo's text explicates its particularity not as an event in historical time but as a metaphor for the primordial history of socialization. Narration adopts the authentic pictures and transforms them at the same time by confronting them with other orders. It is precisely in this interplay of different media that a new space is opened up for experience, one that allows new possibilities of perception and experience to arise out of the reconstruction of historical experience, possibilities that escape the grasp of ideological interpretation. In the end, the linguistic play of the literary text overcomes the limitations of the dominant European and American political discourses.

References

Agamben, Giorgio. *Homo Sacer. Die souveräne Macht und das nackte Leben*, transl. by Hubert Thüring (Frankfurt a. M.: Suhrkamp, 2002).

Améry, Jean. "An den Grenzen des Geistes," in Jean Améry, *Jenseits von Schuld und Sühne. Bewältigungsversuche eines Überwältigten*. Essays (Munich: Szcesny, 1966).

Auster, Paul. "Jetzt beginnt das 21. Jahrhundert. Wir alle wussten, dass dies geschehen könnte. Nun ist es viel schlimmer," in Toni Morrison, Paul Auster and Colum McCann (eds.), *Dienstag, 11. September 2001* (Reinbek: Rowohlt, ²2001), 13–15.

Barthes, Roland. *La Chambre claire. Note sur la photographie* (Paris: Gallimard, 1980).

---

[69] Cf. ibid., 5–97.
[70] Ibid., 19.

Baudrillard, Jean. *The Spirit of Terrorism and Requiem for the Twin Towers*, transl. by Chris Turner (New York/London: Verso, 2002).

Baudrillard, Jean. *Simulacra and Simulation*, transl. by Sheila Faria Glaser (Michigan: University of Michigan Press, 1994).

Baudrillard, Jean. "Requiem für die Medien," in Jean Baudrillard, *Kool Killer oder Der Aufstand der Zeichen*, transl. by Hans-Joachim Metzger (Berlin: Merve, 1978), 83–118.

Blumenberg, Hans. *Schiffbruch mit Zuschauer—Paradigma einer Daseinsmetapher* (Frankfurt a. M.: Suhrkamp, 1997).

Bongartz, Barbara, and Alban Nikolai Herbst, "*Inzest* oder *Die Entstehung der Welt*. Der Anfang eines Romanes in Briefen," *Schreibheft. Zeitschrift für Literatur*, vol. 53 (2002), 1–164.

Bopp, Lena. "Anselm Kiefer am Collège de France. Bin Ladin—eine Kunst-Performance?," *Frankfurter Allgemeine Zeitung*, February 3, 2011.

Borradori, Giovanna. "Die Rekonstruktion des Terrorismusbegriffs nach Habermas," in Giovanna Borradori, Jürgen Habermas, and Jacques Derrida, *Philosophie in Zeiten des Terrors*, transl. by Ulrich Müller-Schöll (Darmstadt: Wissenschaftliche Buchgesellschaft, 2004).

Buschheuer, Else. *Das New York Tagebuch* (Cologne: Kiepenheuer & Witsch, 2002).

Butter, Michael, Birte Christ and Patrick Keller. *9/11. Kein Tag, der die Welt veränderte* (Paderborn: Schöningh, 2011).

Chomsky, Noam. *The Attack. Hintergründe und Folgen*, transl. by Michael Haupt (Hamburg/Vienna: Europa, ^{4}2003).

Collenberg, Carrie. "'Vorstellung des Terrors'—9/11, RAF, and the Sublime," in Christer Petersen and Jeanne Riou (eds.), *Zeichen des Krieges in Literatur, Film und den Medien. Terror*, vol. 3, (Kiel: Verlag Ludwig, 2008), 97–121.

Debord, Guy. *La société du Spectacle* (Paris: Buchet/Chastel, 1967).

DeLillo, Don. *Falling Man*, transl. by Frank Heibert (Cologne: Kiepenheuer und Witsch, 2007).

Derrida, Jacques. *Eine gewisse unmögliche Möglichkeit, vom Ereignis zu sprechen*, transl. by Susanne Lüdemann (Berlin: Merve, 2003).

Deupmann, Christoph. "Ausnahmezustand des Erzählens. Zeit und Ereignis in Ulrich Peltzers Erzählung *Bryant Park* und anderen Texten über den 11. September 2001" in Ingo Irsigler and Christoph Jürgensen (eds.), *Nine Eleven. Ästhetische Bearbeitungen des 11. Septembers 2001* (Heidelberg: Winter, 2011).

Foer, Jonathan Safran. *Extremely Loud and Incredibly Close* (London: Penguin Books, 2006).

Habermas, Jürgen, and Jacques Derrida. *Philosophie in Zeiten des Terrors. Zwei Gespräche, geführt, eingeleitet und kommentiert von Giovanna Borradori* (Berlin/Vienna: Philo, 2004).

Jünger, Ernst. *Tagebücher III: Strahlungen II*, in Ernst Jünger, *Sämtliche Werke*, 1978–2003, 22 vols., vol. 3 (Stuttgart: Klett-Cotta, 1979).

Kant, Immanuel. *Der Streit der Fakultäten*, in Immanuel Kant, *Werke in zwölf Bänden*, ed. by Wilhelm Weischedel, 12 vols., vol. 6, Schriften zur Anthropologie, Geschichtsphilosophie. Politik und Pädagogik 1 (Frankfurt a. M.: Insel, 1964), 261–393.

Kleist, Heinrich von, Clemens Brentano and Achim von Arnim. "Empfindungen vor Friedrichs Seelandschaft," in Heinrich von Kleist, *Sämtliche Werke und Briefe*, 2 vols., vol. 2., extended and completely revised edition, ed. by Helmut Sembdner (Munich: Hanser, 1961), 327–328.

Kolter, Susanne H. "Architecture Criente: Nine Eleven zwischen Katastrophenästhetik, biblischem Strafgericht und Dekonstruktivismus" in Ingo Irsigler and Christoph Jürgensen (eds.), *Nine eleven—Ästhetische Verarbeitungen des 11. September 2001* (Heidelberg: Universitätsverlag, 2008), 345–367.

Lethen, Helmut. "Bildarchiv und Traumaphilie. Schrecksekunden der Kulturwissenschaften nach dem 11.9.2001," in Klaus R. Scherpe and Thomas Weitin (eds.), *Eskalationen. Die Gewalt von Kultur, Recht und Politik* (Tübingen/Basel: Francke, 2003), 3–14.

Luhmann, Niklas. *Ökologische Kommunikation: Kann die Gesellschaft sich auf ökologische Gefährdungen einstellen?* (Opladen: Westdeutscher Verlag, 1990).

McLuhan, Marshall. *Understanding Media* (London: Routledge & Paul, 1964).

Mergenthaler, Volker. "'Weiter schreiben' nach dem 11. September—Barbara Bongartz', Alban Nikolai Herbsts und Norbert Wehrs '*Inzest* oder *Die Entstehung der Welt*'," in Ingo Irsigler and Christoph Jürgensen (eds.), *Nine eleven—Ästhetische Verarbeitungen des 11. September 2001* (Heidelberg: Universitätsverlag, 2008), 29–48.

Minkmar, Nils. "Die Welt nach 9/11. Ein verlorenes Jahrzehnt," *Frankfurter Allgemeine Zeitung*, July 4, 2011.

Peltzer, Ulrich. *Bryant Park*, Erzählung (Berlin: Berliner Taschenbuchverlag, 2004).

Proust, Marcel. *À la recherche du temps perdu*, ed. by Jean-Yves Tadié in cooperation with Yves Baudelle et al., vol. IV (Paris: Gallimard, 1989).

Raspe, Martin. "The Falling Man. Der 11. September in der Momentaufnahme," in Ingo Irsigler and Christoph Jürgensen (eds.), *Nine Eleven—Ästhetische Verarbeitungen des 11. September 2001* (Heidelberg: Universitätsverlag, 2008), 369–382.

Renner, Rolf G. "Das Auge der Erinnerung. Fotografie in Texten der klassischen Moderne und im Film von Michelangelo Antonioni," in Sabina Becker and Barbara Korte (eds.), *Visuelle Evidenz. Photographie im Reflex von Literatur und Film* (Berlin: De Gruyter, 2011), 198–211.

Reudenbach, Bruno. *G. B. Piranesi. Architektur als Bild. Der Wandel der Architekturauffassung des achtzehnten Jahrhunderts* (Munich: Prestel-Verlag, 1979).

Röggla, Kathrin. *really ground zero. 11. september und folgendes* (Frankfurt a. M.: Fischer Taschenbuch-Verlag, 2004).
Savatier, Thierry. *L'origine du monde. Histoire d' un tableau de Gustave Courbet* (Paris: Bartillat, 2006).
Schami, Rafik. *Mit fremden Augen. Tagebuch über den 11. September, den Palästinakonflikt und die arabische Welt* (Munich: dtv, 2004).
Schmitt, Axel. "Die weiße Magie des Kinos und die schwarze Magie des Terrorismus. Gedanken zum 11. September 2001," *literaturkritik.de*, no. 10 (2002), available at http://www.lteratukritik.de/public/rezension.phb?rez_id=5336 (accessed 14.1.2015).
Schmitt, Carl. *Der Begriff des Politischen* (Berlin: Duncker & Humblot, 1962).
Sontag, Susan. *Über Fotografie*, transl. by Mark W. Rien and Gertrud Baruch (Frankfurt a. M.: Fischer Taschenbuch-Verlag, 1999).
Theweleit, Klaus. *Der Knall: 11. September, das Verschwinden der Realität und ein Kriegsmodell* (Frankfurt a. M./Basel: Stroemfeld/Roter Stern, 2002).
Virilio, Paul. *Ground Zero* (New York/London: Verso, 2002).
Virilio, Paul. *Guerre et cinéma*, vol. 1, *Logique de la perception* (Paris: Seuil, 1984).
Waitz, Thomas. "Die Frage der Bilder. 9/11 als filmisch Abwesendes," in Sascha Seiler, Sandra Poppe, and Thorsten Schüller (eds.), *9/11 als kulturelle Zäsur* (Bielefeld: Transcript, 2008).
Werber, Niels. "Der Teppich des Sterbens. Gewalt und Terror in der neuesten Popliteratur," *Weimarer Beiträge*, vol. 49, no. 1 (2003), 55–69.

Author Biography

Rolf G. Renner is Professor emeritus for Modern German Literature and former Director of the Frankreich-Zentrum at the University of Freiburg/Germany. He is also profesor honorario at the Universidad de Guadalajara/Mexico and has held several visiting professorships in Europe, the USA, South America and Australia. His main teaching and research interests are: 20th century literature, literary and media theory. He is the author of Georg Lukács (1976), Thomas Mann (1985, 1987), Peter Handke (1985), Postmodernism (1988), Edward Hopper (1990), Proust (1992), and has published about 120 articles in academic books and journals. He is also editor of four volumes on the history of European thought (1991–1992), an encyclopedia of works in literary theory (1994), an anthology of texts on contemporary literary theory (1995), an anthology of German novels in the 20th century (2004) and a collection of essays on Modern German Literature (2017).

The Wind of the Hudson. Gerhard Richter's *September* (2005) and the European Perception of Catastrophe

Ulrich Kinzel

Much of the 9/11 experience is about seeing. Lianne and Martin, characters from Don DeLillo's novel *Falling Man* (2007), look at *Natura Morta* (1956), a still life by the Italian modernist Giorgio Morandi, in her mother's New York apartment.

> 'What do you see?' he said.
> She saw what he saw. She saw the towers.[1]

Morandi's still life shows eight kitchen objects removed from their original function and arranged in front of monocoloured backgrounds. Two of these objects, dark, long-necked bottles, are taken for the twin

---

[1] DeLillo, *Falling Man*, 49.

U. Kinzel (✉)
CAU Kiel Institut für Neuere deutsche Literatur und Medien,
Kiel, Germany

towers by the novel's two beholders. This reaction is clearly marked as resulting from disorientation and shock. In the immediate aftermath of the destruction of the towers on September 11, the original concept of the still life is suspended. Forcing the beholder to a long and sustained engagement with the reduced landscape of objects, the still life is meant to induce tranquillity, or, to put it in the words of the traditional aesthetics that Lianne's mother Nina, an art historian, represents, "comfort and composure."[2] Lianne's and Martin's projection of the twin towers onto the long-necked bottles floods the painting with the very emotional tumult that the noiseless, pensive representation of objects aims at negating. Yet, there is a sphere in which the traumatized souls of the novel and the moral program of the painting can meet—inwardness. Looking at the painting for the first time, Lianne notices "The irregular edges of vases and jars, some reconnoiter inward, human and obscure [...]."[3] The clearest statement of inwardness as a traumatic reaction to the shock of terror is made in connection with Lianne's formerly hard-boiled husband, Keith:

> It was Keith as well who was going slow, easing inward. He used to want to fly out of self-awareness, day and night, a body in raw motion. Now he finds himself drifting into spells of reflection, thinking not in clear units, hard and linked, but only what comes, drawing things out of time and memory and into some dim space that bears his collected experience.[4]

DeLillo's narrative moral reflection is centred around subjectivity. Particularly in Keith's case, a man who appears to have been tough—he "had once owned a pit bull [...], an American breed, developed originally to fight and kill"[5]—now gives into his trauma and loses his existential orientation. This forms a stark contrast to the moral reflection which is sketched out *ex negativo* by the eminent contemporary German poet Durs Grünbein in his *September-Elegien* (2002) [September Elegies]:

---

[2] Ibid., 42.

[3] Ibid., 12. Keith Neudecker's reaction is only one instance of melencholia which pervades the novel and haunts its characters. Cf. Versluys, "American Melencholia: Don DeLillo's *Falling Man*," 19–48.

[4] Ibid., 66.

[5] DeLillo, *Falling Man*, 44.

kein Stoiker ist hier. Palavernd vor Schwellen und Türen,
Von Terminen und Schulden geplagt, durcheilt man die
Stadt.
Wer hat schon Zeit gehabt, etwas wie Seelenruhe zu
destillieren
Aus der Gewißheit des Todes, und daß alles ein Ende hat?[6]

In a moral reflection referring to a model of ethical experience which is historically prior to subjectivity and inwardness, the fall of the towers is only another example of the fleeting nature of things which should cause us to remain tranquil and composed. This contrast between traumatic inwardness and (the unrealized possibility of) Stoic heroism is further accompanied by a difference in which the question of seeing is addressed. For Lianne and Martin, it is a question of what is or can be seen. For Grünbein's lyrical voice, the reflection of how terror affects people touches upon the medium and thus the possibility of seeing as such:

Er [der Terror] nimmt dir die Lust am Kino, an Bildern

explodierender Autos,
Brennende Wolkenkratzer, in die ein Passagierflugzeug

stürzt.
Er schmiert einen Film über Fensterfronten, schminkt die

Gesichter,
Die sich vor Auslagen spiegeln aschgrau, wie plötzlich

gealtert.[7]

It seems as if inwardness and subjectivity represent an American pattern of reaction, in any case, a mode of reaction of people directly

---

[6] Grünbein, *September-Elegien, Erklärte Nacht*, 50. "There is no stoic here. Palavering in front of thresholds and doors / Pestered by dates and debts, you rush through the city. / Who has had time to distill something like tranquillity / From the certainty of death, and that / everything will come to an end." (My translation).

[7] Grünbein, *Kopie in Zement, Strophen für übermorgen*, 156. "It [terror] takes your appetite away for cinema, images of exploding cars, / Burning skyscrapers in which a passenger plane crashes. / It puts a skin on window fronts, makes up the faces / Which are reflected in shop windows, ashgrey, like suddenly aged." (My translation).

affected by the 9/11 events, whereas Grünbein's reference to Stoicism cites the example of a reflection with extensive roots in the European cultural tradition. The intention of the following is to reconstruct a genealogy of this mode of reflection, which—rather than exclusively focussing on medial representation—combines seeing with moral contemplation. By moving from German poet Thomas Kling's eminent lyrical reflections of the Ground Zero catastrophe back to Stoic meditations on human catastrophes in European marine painting, the way will be paved for the contemplation of one of the most stunning, yet inconspicuous 'representations' of 9/11—Gerhard Richter's painting *September* (2005) which, according to Robert Storr, arrests "'the decisive moment' of September 11, 2001 [...] in perpetual suspension but refuses to embody it."[8]

I

Of the literary reactions in Germany to the September 11 events *Manhattan Mundraum Zwei* [Manhattan Mouthspace Two][9] published in 2001 by Thomas Kling, probably the most significant and influential of Germany's postmodern lyrical voices, is certainly one which follows the fundamental idea that the importance of seeing (or not seeing) is related to the medium which makes things appear (or disappear) rather than to emotional responses of individual beholders. As the title betrays, it refers to a precursor, his poem "Manhattan Mouthspace," which appeared four years earlier in the collection *morsch* (1996).[10] This first Manhattan poem, the overture to the volume, opens with the lines:

>   die stadt ist der mund
>   raum. die zunge, textus
>
>   (v. 1–2)
>
>   [the city is the mouth
>   space. the tongue, textus][11]

---

[8] Storr, *September, A History Painting by Gerhard Richter*, 8.

[9] *manuskripte*, 3–7; then Thomas Kling, *Sondagen. Gedichte*, 7–17. English translation by Michael Hofmann, available at http://www.poetry.internationalweb.net/pi/site/poem/item/2369, accessed 1.5.2015.

[10] In Kling, *morsch*, 7–12.

[11] My translation.

The city, according to these lines, does not primarily consist of buildings, but of texts, or rather: voices—it is "polylingual" (v. 25) and the poem is the writing which does not simply represent this multiplicity of voices; it rather tries to dismantle the layers of this complicated network of spoken or written urban traces. The word "tomographie" (v. 22) mentioned here is thus a clear hint at the poem's method—like an x-ray or ultrasound examination uncovers the layers of the body, the poem tries to excavate and lay bare the folded layers of discourse. The expression "manhattantextus" (v. 73) clearly denotes the idea of the city as text; furthermore, it also implies that Manhattan resembles the space of a mouth: first, because its long, drawn-out expanse is shaped like a tongue; second, because Manhattan's streets lined by skyscrapers form a kind of canyon and thus resemble the oral cavity. And it is this mouth space which resonates with discourses.

Kling's poetry is a mixture of oral discourse and writing.[12] Fixed and deliberately placed on the page, Kling's writing (*Schrift*) is staged as recorded discourse (*Mitschrift*) rather than *écriture*. Kling reminds us of the fact that at its historical origin writing had an administrative function ("Staatsschrift"[13]) while poetry from Homer to the schools of rhetoric was understood as orally transmitted text. Important for our context is the connection that Kling builds between urbanity and lyrical orality. Of prime significance is the multitude of voices which the city streets unfold and which the modern poem, abandoning the ideal of subjectivity and autonomy, should try to capture. This cacophony of the street emerged, for instance, in slang in the fast-growing American cities around 1850, at the same time, Kling hastens to add, when the modern poem and the urban attitude of the modern poet were born.[14] Speech—the material of the modern poem—for Kling is a multitudinous phenomenon emerging from and inhabiting urban space. Another quality is the fact that it travels long distances; thus signs are "Hermen," "Wegmarken"[15] (signposts) testifying to the hermetic nature of poetry. The poem, consequently, is

---

[12] On Kling's poetics cf. Grätz, "Ton, Bild, Schnitt. Thomas Klings intermediale Sprachinstallationen," *literatur für leser*, 127–145.
[13] Kling, *Botenstoffe*, 140.
[14] See Kling, *Itinerar*, 41.
[15] Ibid., 54.

"Botenstoff"[16] transmitting signs which then build "Sprach-Räume,"[17] linguistic urban space: like the Manhattan Mouthspace.

Four years after its publication, Kling returns to his Manhattan poem, but the playful metaphor which bridges urban space and mouth space, now, in light of the September events, receives dramatic intensity, as the oral/urban cavity filled with rubble is plunged into darkness and desperation. What—among other things—becomes more important in the second Manhattan poem is the practice of looking. The "stetig das loopende auge" (v. 4) [continually looping eye] picks up the theme of the previous poem and travels through the new poem as a leitmotif. At the beginning, this eye looks into a "toter trakt" (v. 1) [dead alley],[18] where everything is coated in breadcrumbs, but this "flour," or rather its particles, starts performing a *danse macabre*; at the same time these particles—of which the art critic Robert Storr later said that they are also "the precipitate of some two thousand seven hundred and fifty-two lives"[19]—are part of a writing that fails to record what happened until at last the voice is suffocated:

> zungen die in schlünde sinken in erstickter schlucht
>
> (v. 73/4)
> [tongues sinking in gullets in gurgling gulches]

What the eyes see is the "augn-zerrschrift" [eye-caricature], a defaced, blurred writing that is not able to make anything visible:

> nullsicht. hatten nullsicht
> [zero visibility. we had zero visibility]
>
> (v. 41/42)

The catastrophe of the attack on the 11th of September 2001 is both the catastrophe as such, and the fact that nothing of it can be made visible by the media (even though visual technology is plunged into the event). The desolate cataract Manhattan has become is filled with

---

[16] Ibid., "messenger or neurotransmitter," my translation.

[17] Ibid., 59.

[18] My translation; Hofmann has "dead land".

[19] Storr, *September*, 49. Thomas Lehr in his novel *September. Fata Morgana*, 143, 306 has his observers Seymour and Martin describe a similar experience.

the wind of the Hudson covering up clear vision as it fills the space of the city indiscriminately with layers of faceless and lifeless particles. As (poetic) breath, the same wind blows the particles of fragmented discourse through the mouthspace of the text, keeping the poem's representational power at a low level until the voices vanish in the bleak hissing noise of the transmitting medium:

>   dies bittere mehl, darüber wind geht,
>
>   leiser algorithmen wind
>
>   der wind von
>
>   manhattan
>   (v. 81–84)
>
>   [this bitter flour the wind blows over,
>   soft algorhythm wind
>
>   the wind of
>
>   manhattan]
>
>   (v. 80–83)

The poem does not allow any grand scenes to appear and strips the historical catastrophe of any association with the sublime.[20] What is left instead is a silent, no less scary breeze of death and mourning.

In Kling's concept of poetry, the poet is not somebody who expresses his subjectivity but a nodal point in a network of voices transmitted by media, layers of speech, and discourse that he tries to excavate like an archaeologist. This method of memorizing and literally unfolding discourse could be called historical tomography. And like a DJ, the poet samples decontextualized particles of once-transmitted experience. Kling has no problems with fusing historical experience with current media. In

---

[20] It is interesting to note that for Kling modern lyrical polyphony goes together with a refusal of the sublime (cf. Kling, *Itinerar*, 41–42). A similar intention can be seen in Brigitte Olschewski's laconic 9/11 poem, *Über*: "Über / die aus den Fenstern stürzenden Kommas, klein / wie Menschen, keins –" ["On / the commas falling out of the window, small / like human beings—none"] (Olschewski, *Geisterströmung. Gedichte*, 53. (My translation).

the literature on Kling, his phrase "CNN Verdun,"[21] from his long poem on the First World War, has become a standard quotation. In *Manhattan Mundraum Zwei*, we hear sentences spoken on mobile phones by people obviously trapped in the Twin Towers:

> konnten nicht weiter und saßen fünf
> die lagen auf mir drauf ich ruf wieder an
>
> [couldn't stir and there were five sat
> lying on top of me I will call again][22]
>
> (v. 33–34)

and we hear the voice of Psalm 137:

> wir lagen an den wassern des hudson
> und weineten
>
> (v. 38–39)
>
> [we lay by the waters of the hudson
> and cried]
>
> (v. 38–39)
>
> An den Wassern zu babel sassen wir
> Vnd weineten (Luther)[23]
>
> [By the rivers of Babylon, there we sat down,
> yea, we wept (King James Version)][24]

Despite Kling's strictly anti-subjective concept of poetry "Manhattan Mundraum Zwei" is pervaded by an emotional tone. This expression of mourning breaks through the tightly knit fabric of mediated discourse and lends earnestness to the poem. One instance in which this expression

---

[21] Quoted in Lehmkuhl, "Gedächtnisspeicher: Zu Thomas Klings Zyklus 'Der Erste Weltkrieg'," 48.

[22] Translation modified.

[23] Martin Luther, *Biblia*, 1084.

[24] *The Holy Bible*, 612. The Babylon motif is also taken up in Lehr, *September* 130, 213, 258, 337f. and 397.

becomes audible is the quotation from the Psalm, in particular, the antiquated wording of "weineten"; another is the "Ach" (v. 59, 85), which appears twice, the second time at the end of the poem:

> ach! vom hudson wehend
> kommt der wind
> (v. 85–86)

> [oh! The wind coming
> off the hudson]
> (v. 84–85)

If we follow the trace Kling has laid out to the Psalm, we will find a concept of poetic speech which will lead us further into the question of poetry and existence. In his introduction to the Psalms, Martin Luther connects the challenge of earnest poetic speech with the experience of wild storms:

> WAS ist aber das meiste im Psalter /denn solch ernstlich reden /in allerley solchen Sturmwinden?[25]

> [What occurs most in the Psalms is such serious speech about some such tempests[26]]

Luther uses the storm as a metaphor of anxiety ("furcht vnd sorge"[27]) and compares the human heart with a ship on a wild sea which is tossed by the winds from the four directions. Such tempests, says Luther, teach us to speak with seriousness; they open the heart and raise fundamental questions. Kling's poem on Manhattan invokes the wind from the Hudson as an allegory of the human condition which demands serious speech, a speech which addresses human existence. Kling's poetry is able to let this existential dimension ring through the fragmented text composed of intertextual references and diverse discourses.

Luther praises the Psalms because they paint the Holy Church in vivid colours. If you want to see the Church "in einem kleinen Bilde gefasset" [captured in a small picture], pick up the Psalms; they are a "fine, bright and pure mirror" which shows you what Christianity is. And then Luther makes this little addition:

---

[25] Luther, *Biblia*, 966.
[26] My translation.
[27] Ibid., "fear and melancholy".

> Ja du wirst auch dich selbs drinnen /vnd das rechte Gnotiseauton finden.[28]
>
> [Yeah, you will find yourself in it and find the right gnotiseauton][29]

In other words, the Psalms are small pictures which enable the reader to know himself by listening to a discourse which is serious as it speaks of fundamental questions, of current and future goods and accidents. As Luther's use of the phrase "gnotiseauton" already signifies the way in which he structures the question of how a subject should relate to and reflect fundamental experiences, in particular accidents, is not altogether Christian, it is also antique or Stoic, to be precise. A little later, the Dutch philologist Justus Lipsius merged Christian belief with Stoic principles. This Neostoicism was very influential, particularly on Baroque culture and also helped to create a new type of moral reflection through painting—through "small pictures."

II

In this tradition, little pictures serve as media of self-reflection or self-practice. An example of this is Dutch marine artist Jan Porcellis' *Stormy Sea* (1629), which belongs to a group of monochrome, grisaille paintings that pioneered the seventeenth-century Dutch seascape. The picture shows waves that are whipped up by a storm at sea and merge with the dark and cloudy sky. In the background, ships are battling their course through the storm; the ship in the left foreground is about to capsize. In the context of the realistic conventions of Dutch marine painting, the elimination of topographical detail and ship types reinforces a symbolic meaning of the kind that was depicted and articulated by the older emblem tradition.[30] This is further supported by the trompe-l'œil-effect of the window frame. It suggests that we are looking through (some) window on the world, a world as rough as the storm at sea. The frame thus serves as a medium not only of representation but of meditation. It invites the beholding subject to reflect on its relationship to adverse circumstances. In a similar way, the Elizabethan poet Geoffrey Whitney in

---

[28] Luther, *Biblia*, vol. 2, 967.

[29] My translation.

[30] Cf. Russell, *Visions of the Sea. Hendrik C. Vroom and the Origins of Dutch Marine Painting*, 80.

his emblem "Constantia comes victoriae" depicts and describes a storm-tossed ship and adds the moral comment that they who sail "theire wordly seas" will by keeping their "course direct" win "the wished port" of lasting joy.[31] The German Baroque poet, and editor of the poetic and aesthetic works of his contemporaries, Julius Wilhelm Zincgref in his emblem "Tempestate probatur" puts forth the message that "Beständigkeit /Erscheint in Wiederwärtigkeit" [constancy appears in adversity].[32] If we accept these comments as sound readings of Porcellis' symbolic seascape,[33] then its moral context is clearly that of Stoicism. The furious waters and the changing wind (symbolized by the goddess Fortuna, in particular, the Fortuna di Mare with sail and rudder)[34] thus can be read as a metaphor for the roughness and fickleness of life against which humans have to struggle—persevering in adversity is the Stoic formula. To exclude and battle such contingency—which also comprises the tumults of history—is a process at the end of which the subject reaches a timeless, secure, unchangeable place (symbolized by the harbour).

III

Shipwreck remains *the* human catastrophe, and in the history of marine painting we can observe that painters were trying to increase its intensity by painting spectacular examples.[35] One of these painters is the Frenchman Claude Joseph Vernet (1714–1789). His *Shipwreck* (1772) shows a tempest that drives the high waves against a rocky shore; overhanging cliffs and dark clouds arch over the scene of the shipwreck and create a menacing atmosphere. At the centre of the scene, we see the sinking ship. The pending mast from which crew members or passengers rescue themselves by gliding down a rope adds suspense to the scene while the already rescued passengers on the plateau convey a sense of hope and security. This clearly is a much more lively, intense scene that also includes people who suffer and are rescued. It also follows a

---

[31] Whitney, *A Choice of Emblems, and Other Devices*, 137, quoted in Goedde, *Tempest and Shipwreck in Dutch and Flemish Art. Convention, Rhetoric, and Interpretation*, 170.
[32] Zincgref, *Emblemata ethico-politica, Gesammelte Schriften*, 132f.
[33] Cf. Goedde, *Tempest and Shipwreck*, 169; 131–140; Russell, *Visions of the Sea*, 81.
[34] Reichert, *Fortuna oder die Beständigkeit des Wechsels*, 24f., see also 50–52.
[35] For the second-order observation photo, cf. Chap. 2 by Rolf G. Renner in this volume.

different mode of experience, namely, that of the sublime, which was described and reflected on by Edmund Burke and Immanuel Kant:

> A level of a vast extent on land is certainly no mean idea; the prospect of such a plain may be as extensive as a prospect of the ocean; but can it ever fill the mind with anything so great as the ocean itself? This is owing to several causes, but it is owing to none more than this, that the ocean is an object of no small terror. Indeed terror is in all cases whatsoever, either more openly or latently the ruling principle of the sublime.[36]

"Whatever," Burke states, "therefore is terrible with regard to sight, is sublime, too."[37] It is quite remarkable that Burke links the experience of terror in the sublime to sight. Kant in his comment on Burke (and Longinus) explains these phenomena such as

> hurricanes with their track of devastation; the boundless ocean in a state of tumult [...] exhibit our faculty of resistance as insignificantly small in comparison with their might. But the sight of them is the more attractive, the more fearful it is, provided only that we are in security; and we willingly call these objects sublime, because they raise the energies of the soul above their accustomed height and discover in us a faculty of resistance of a quite different kind, which gives us courage to measure ourselves against the apparent almightiness of nature.[38]

Compared with the Stoic model of reflection, a shipwreck is no longer regarded as an example of adversity but becomes a fascinating theatre of nature, something that not only incites terror but pleasure as well. While resistance is the element of continuity in this meditative setting, aesthetic pleasure—beyond security—is a new element which is designed to heighten the autonomy of the subject and convey its superiority over nature.

The sublime as a model of experience that promises intensity of feeling (terror/pleasure) and elevates and secures the soul can only work

---

[36] Burke, *A Philosophical Enquiry into the Origins of our Ideas of the Sublime and Beautiful and Other Pre-Revolutionary Writings*, 49–199, 102.

[37] Ibid., 101.

[38] Kant, *Critique of Judgement*, quoted in Levine, "Seascapes of the Sublime: Vernet, Monet, and the Oceanic Feeling," 387.

as long as the subject is safe. Or, in other words, as long as there is a separation, a secure distance between picture and beholder. This distance is achieved by the underlying concept of art as a veil, which, since the Italian quattrocento, has dominated the pictorial tradition. Accordingly, the visibility that a painting allows rests on the fact that the canvas functions like a window or a translucent veil.[39] As such, it enables the beholder to see things and it brings them closer to him; at the same time, it obscures objects and distances them from him. Porcellis, for instance, clearly reflected this distance by including the frame in his picture whereas Vernet's overwhelming view negates the veil; the depicted space completely occupies the canvas. However, this comprehensive visibility of the sublime picture is still constructed as a simulation—a *velo di finzioni* [veil of fiction][40]—which puts the subject in a safe position and allows him to assert himself against his fear. Even though Vernet's picture, as so many others of the traditional type, have covered their mediality, they work unconsciously and unadmittedly according to the poetics of the veil.

The veil is the poetico-epistemological backdrop against which one has to approach another problem of the sublime, the question of how it can be depicted. Burke quotes Milton's portrait of Satan:

> He above the rest
>
> In shape and gesture proudly eminent
> Stood like a tower[41]

and praises it for its sublimity and the dignity it attaches to the figure of evil. This effect is achieved through "a croud of great and confused images"[42] underpinning Burke's assumption that clear representation fails to communicate great ideas whereas "uncertain images have a greater power on the fancy to form the grander passions."[43] It was Lyotard in his re-evaluation of Burke who connected the

---

[39] Cf. with particular reference to Alberti's *De pictura* (1435) Krüger, *Das Bild als Schleier des Unsichtbaren*, 29.

[40] Ibid., 41.

[41] Burke, *Enquiry*, 105. Burke quotes from *Paradise Lost*, ii, 666–669.

[42] Ibid., 106.

[43] Ibid.

Fig. 1 Gerhard Richter: *September*

representational problem of the sublime with the avant-garde problem of representation. If the 'vision' of the sublime needed and implied reduced sight, Barnett Newman, the American Expressionist and protagonist of colour field painting, in his essay "The Sublime is Now" (1948) did away with figurative representation altogether and created a new perspective: the painting could avoid the threat of complete darkness and sightlessness by exposing what enables paintings to make one see (colour, line, etc.), instead of allowing things to be seen. And by doing so, art lets the fact that it can no longer represent reality happen. While, for Newman, the painting itself as an event is of paramount importance, the contemporary Austrian critic, novelist and poet Raoul Schrott in a much later reflection on the sublime, the sequence of poems *Tropen. Über das Erhabene* (1998) framed by his own introduction and epilogue, answers the same aesthetic problem by restoring rhetoric and by charging tropes with an epistemological function: the sublime, according to Schrott, cannot be grasped, let alone depicted; it is an "aesthetic category"[44]; it is style, not mimesis. Schrott finds the essence of the sublime in the "paradoxical analogies"[45] which tropes create to allude to the ungraspable of nature: they are "the vision through the lens of the word onto the focus of the figural. The sublime exists only in the image we are able to create of it."[46] In these reflections, representation is dissolved and the question of the autonomy of the subject has become irrelevant.[47]

IV

In 2005, four years after the attacks on the World Trade Center, Gerhard Richter painted *September* (Fig. 1). Richter's work, which started with grey, blurred photo paintings in the 1960s and is continued with abstractions, overpainted photographs and colour plates, must be seen as an ongoing project to expose the possibilities and limits of the painted image through painting. *September*, small in size as it measures only 52 x 72 cm, was exhibited in 2008 at the Marian Goodman Gallery in Paris. Richter then gave it as a gift to the New York Museum of Modern Art.[48] Robert Storr, the American artist, art critic and curator of an important Richter exhibition in New York in 2002, wrote a remarkable essay on this painting in which he reads *September* as a painting that, as a history painting, counters its tendency to represent "major events in rhetorically big formats with melodramatic effects"[49] and to represent the voice of

---

[44] Schrott, *Tropen. Über das Erhabene* [1998], 207. See also Voigt, *Erhabenheit. Über ein großes Gefühl und seine Opfer*, 21f.

[45] Schrott, *Tropen*, 207.

[46] Ibid., 208.

[47] For other German authors, such as Peter Handke and Botho Strauß, cf. Hoffmann, *Positionen des Erhabenen. Zur Produktivität einer ästhetischen Kategorie in der Literatur des ausgehenden 20. Jahrhunderts (Handke, Ransmayr, Schrott, Strauß)* has shown that a postmodern reflection of the sublime coincides with the assumption of a physical and moral weakening of the subject.

[48] I will ignore here the importance of Richter's RAF cycle, *October 18, 1977* (created in the 1980s) for *September*. The close kinship between Richter's reflection on terrorism in Germany, the travelling of the RAF cycle to America (where it was bought by the MOMA) and the September 11 attacks is analysed comprehensively by Silverman, *Flesh of My Flesh*, 221.

[49] Storr, *September*, 47.

Fig. 2 Gerhard Richter: *25. Febr. 01*

authority. However, the comparatively small size of *September* can also be seen in the tradition of the moral reflection for which painters and poets chose "ein kleines Bildchen" [a little picture], as Luther said. In this context of a moral-aesthetic discourse, my reading of *September* rather tries to work out the relationship of the beholding subject to the depiction of the historical catastrophe.

Richter's *September* shows two main layers, which Storr describes as follows:

> The first is a sheer, semiporous skin of mottled pigment that covers the entire canvas, except where it has been scraped or rubbed off, exposing the white primer underneath and the nap of the linen underneath that.[50]

This is the layer of the primary image, of figural representation.

---

[50] Ibid.

The second layer consists of streaks, smears, and clots of pasty pigments whose tonal range is generally broader than the undercoat and extends from milky grays and blues to creamy anthracites aureoles. These impasto passages traverse the rectangle in opposite directions, going from left to right in the upper half of the picture and from right to left in the lower half.[51]

What happens on this second layer is that a curtain-like veil is attached to the surface of the primary image. This addition of the veil is perhaps the decisive intervention into the underlying figural representation. In order to be able to measure the significance of this gesture, it seems useful to carefully locate the use of the veil in Richter's œuvre. In his early black-and-white photo paintings, the depicted objects are distorted. In *Grey House* (1966), for example, we can just about identify a house, a street, and the sky. The image hovers on the brink of visibility because the outlines of the objects have been blurred. The outcome of the painter's intervention, when a dry brush was drawn across the still wet paint, is a "smooth, equalized surface appearance."[52] In *September*, matters are different: here the distortions do not take place on the object level, they happen on the level of the attached veil. In *Grey House*, the intervention of the painter is concealed in the surface of the painting, whereas in *September* the painter has left the traces of his intervention visible on the canvas. As a consequence, we get two layers: the represented object (the south tower and the crashing airplane) and the veil.

Opposite the smoothly blurred photo paintings are the overpainted photos. Here areas of the photo are covered by abstract paint formations which come down like a curtain (as in *25 Febr. 01*) (Fig. 2), creep into the picture like a growing plant, or rain down on the surface in particles. Botho Strauß, one of the most successful contemporary German dramatists, observed about these works that the painter's intervention revives the deadened moment of the photo.[53] In contrast to this device, whereby the object is concealed, the veil in *September* is translucent; the pictorial arrangement allows us to see through the veil.

In *September* the viewer, then, is confronted with a double surface. And the intervention by the painter—clearly highlighted in the stroke

---

[51] Ibid., 48.
[52] Moorhouse, *Gerhard Richter Portraits*, 64.
[53] Strauß, "Der Maler löst den Bann," 205.

of the brush—is not smoothly soaked up into the depicted objects. This intervention does not—as in the overpainted photos—open a dialogue or game/play between representation and abstraction or invite the viewer "to see double"[54]; it comes forth as a strong, pronounced gesture. It signifies a moral reflection on the relationship between the beholding subject and what it sees.

On the other hand, veil and object are not distinguished; they are connected—by the wind. Storr notices an "animating effect"[55] on the second surface. It looks as if the veil has torn itself free or was torn away from the surface of the picture and now in a feral movement links up again with the firestorm in the picture.

What does that mean for our context? Clearly, *September* has to be seen along the historical line of reflections on the sublime: on the figurative level, as it shows remnants of a sublime object (an elevated tower in distress like a storm-tossed ship),[56] on the level of the painting, as the object is represented in an obscure and distorted manner, and finally, on a moral level, as the frame of the picture indicates a beholder reflecting the scene. The peculiar and outstanding significance of *September*, which like so many other works by Richter is painted discourse, consists of the fact that—in front of our eyes—it unravels this sublime texture. Unlike the aesthetic discourse in *Falling Man*, which (in a more Kantian turn) is centred around the objects of the sublime, i.e. the towers, Richter's work is not focussed on the inward sublime object (eating away at the subject), but, along the lines of Kling's "augn-zerrschrift," on the distortion of sight, the "rift in his field of vision" (to borrow a phrase from DeLillo).[57] Also, Richter does not simply restore rhetoric to underpin a postmodern aestheticism. Nor does he follow the avant-garde line of painting the means of painting. Beyond art's self-reflection, Richter includes the beholding viewer and thus links the moral tradition of the sublime with its tradition of medial reflection. Compared with these modern versions of the sublime, Richter's pictorial comment cuts deeper—it analyzes and

---

[54] Silverman, *Flesh of My Flesh*, 169.

[55] Storr, *September*, 48.

[56] Cf. Lehr, *September*, 141 (my translation): Seymour visualizes "die gesamte Lower East Side wie ein düsteres riesiges Schiff das unter Rauchwolken erstickt" [all of the Lower East Side like a gloomy gigantic ship suffocating under a cloud of smoke].

[57] DeLillo, *Falling Man*, 95. Cf. also Lehr, *September*, 143: "er sah / nichts" [he saw nothing].

exposes the components of pictorial and sublime discourse and in doing so disjoins its poetico-epistemological texture *in actu*. If we remember that the unreflected mediality of figural (sublime) painting guaranteed the security of the beholder, the pronounced addition of the veil to the depicted catastrophe—which to the beholder appears as a dissolution of the veil from the picture's surface—shatters the stability of the order of seeing. Together with the veil, the beholding subject is dragged into the catastrophe it is trying to 'see.' Other than in the tradition of the moral or sublime painting, the beholding subject is no longer outside the horror in some safe area of contemplation or aesthetic pleasure[58]; together with the medium of the veil that was supposed to guarantee visuality, the subject is now, in this (and every) moment (of beholding), tossed and drawn into the unstoppable historical movement. If we remember that the wind of Fortune symbolized contingency, the writing of *September* becomes legible: the wind of an uncontrollable historical moment separates medium and object, the veil and the event of the explosion, and at the same time, it fuses them in an anarchic way and thereby brings the painting to the point of vanishing in the catastrophe it desperately tries to depict. This tempest, in blowing away our securities of seeing, confronts us with the catastrophe of the attack and with our historical traditions:

> Oh! the wind coming
> off the Hudson

References

Burke, Edmund. *A Philosophical Enquiry into the Origins of our Ideas of the Sublime and Beautiful and Other Pre-Revolutionary Writings*, ed. by David Womersley (London: Penguin, 1998).

DeLillo, Don. *Falling Man* (New York [et al.]: Scribner, 2007).

---

[58] A refusal of the sublime in its Romantic form can be seen in Storr's convincing reflection: "To exquisitely paint an indescribably ugly subject is not to glamorize something inherently odious but rather to call attention to it by showing tenderness toward something that has been visited by brutality and to make it harder if not impossible for the viewer to turn away from the image once its subject has been recognized" (Storr, *September*, 52).

Goedde, Lawrence Otto. *Tempest and Shipwreck in Dutch and Flemish Art. Convention, Rhetoric, and Interpretation* (University Park: Pennsylvania State University Press, 1989).
Grätz, Katharina. "Ton, Bild, Schnitt. Thomas Klings intermediale Sprachinstallationen," *literatur für leser*, vol. 2 (2005), 127–145.
Grünbein, Durs. *September-Elegien: Erklärte Nacht* (Frankfurt a. M.: Suhrkamp, 2002).
———. *Kopie in Zement: Strophen für übermorgen* (Frankfurt a. M.: Suhrkamp, 2007).
Hoffmann, Tobias. Konfigurationen des Erhabenen. Zur Produktivität einer ästhetischen Kategorie in der Literatur des ausgehenden 20. Jahrhunderts (Handke, Ransmayr, Schrott, Strauß) (Berlin: De Gruyter, 2006).
Kling, Thomas. *Morsch. Gedichte* (Frankfurt a. M.: Suhrkamp, 1996), 7–12.
———. *Itinerar* (Frankfurt a. M.: Suhrkamp, 1997).
———. *Botenstoffe* (Köln: DuMont, 2001).
———. "Manhattan Mundraum zwei", *manuskripte*, vol. 154 (2001), 3–7.
———. *Sondagen. Gedichte* (Köln: DuMont, 2002),
———. "Manhattan Mouthspace Two", trans. by Michael Hofmann, in Thomas Wohlfahrt, and Tobias Lehmkuhl (eds.), *Mouth to Mouth. Contemporary German Poetry in Translation* (Sidney: Giramondo, 2004).
Krüger, Klaus. *Das Bild als Schleier des Unsichtbaren. Ästhetische Illusion in der Kunst der frühen Neuzeit in Italien* (München: Fink, 2001).
Lehmkuhl, Thomas. "Gedächtnisspeicher: Zu Thomas Klings Zyklus 'Der Erste Weltkrieg'," *Weimarer Beiträge*, vol. 49 (2003), 48.
Lehr, Thomas. *September. Fata Morgana* (München: Hanser, 2010).
Levine, Steven Z. "Seascapes of the Sublime: Vernet, Monet, and the Oceanic Feeling," *New Literary History*, vol. 16 (1984/85).
Luther, Martin. *Biblia: Das ist: Die gantze Heilige Schrifft / Deudsch / Auffs new zugericht* [1545], ed. by Hans Volz, 3 vols., vol. 2 (München: dtv, 1974).
Moorhouse, Paul. *Gerhard Richter Portraits. Painting Appearances* (London: National Portrait Gallery Publications, 2009).
Olschewski, Brigitte. *Geisterströmung. Gedichte* (Köln: DuMont, 2004).
Reichert, Klaus. *Fortuna oder die Beständigkeit des Wechsels* (Frankfurt a. M.: Suhrkamp, 1985).
Russell, Margarita. *Visions of the Sea. Hendrik C. Vroom and the Origins of Dutch Marine Painting* (Leiden: E.J. Brill/Leiden University Press, 1983).
Schrott, Raoul. *Tropen. Über das Erhabene* [1998] (Frankfurt a. M.: Fischer, 2002).
Silverman, Kaja. *Flesh of my Flesh* (Stanford: Stanford University Press, 2009).
Storr, Robert. *September: A History Painting by Gerhard Richter* (London: Tate Publishing, 2010).

Strauß, Botho. "Der Maler löst den Bann," in Markus Heinzelmann (ed.), *Gerhard Richter. Übermalte Fotografie* (Kat. Ostfildern: Hatje Cantz, 2005), 203–207.

The Holy Bible. Authorized King James Version (Oxford: Oxford University Press, n.y.).

Versluys, Kristiaan. *Out of the Blue: September 11 and the Novel* (New York: Columbia University Press, 2009).

Voigt, Stefanie. *Erhabenheit. Über ein großes Gefühl und seine Opfer* (Würzburg: Königshausen & Neumann, 2011).

Zincgref, Julius Wilhelm. *Emblemata ethico-politica, Gesammelte Schriften*, vols. 2, vol. 1–2, ed. Dieter Mertens and Theodor Verweyen (Tübingen: De Gruyter, 1993).

Author Biography

Ulrich Kinzel is Professor for German Literature at the University of Kiel. His books include *Ethische Projekte. Literatur und Selbstgestaltung im Kontext des Regierungsdenkens. Humboldt, Goethe, Stifter, Raabe* (2000), and, as editor, *An den Rändern der Moral. Studien zur literarischen Ethik* (2008). He is currently working on a project on urban space and the visual modernism of the beginning 1960s. Part of this work can be found in a volume on *London. Urban Space and Cultural Experience* (2010).

'Burning from the Inside Out': *Let the Great World Spin* (2009)

Eoin Flannery

9/11: Art and Politics

The encounter between 9/11 and literature brings into focus the triumphs and deformations of language and representation since the acts of criminal terror unfolded more than a decade ago. 9/11 has evolved a symbology and a semiotics all of its own. The term itself has entered linguistic circulation as a universal shorthand for murderous terror and noble resistance to unseen terroristic agencies. But, equally, dissent has arisen about the moralistic mobilizations of 9/11 as a legitimation for surveillance, violent interrogation, and illegal invasion. Heated exchanges have cohered around the ethics of employing 9/11 as a political lodestone and/or as an emotional default in the invocation of national identity in the United States. When we come to consider artistic responses to, or reflections on, 9/11, we enter battle-worn ground on which politics and culture have colluded and competed. And at the epicentre of these debates is language and how it has been

---

E. Flannery (✉)
Department of English Language and Literature, Mary Immaculate College, University of Limerick, Limerick, Ireland

competitively utilized as a means of cultivating jingoistic assent, or, less often, non-partisan critical reflection on 9/11 as an act of terror. This is also the case when matters revolving around the performances of a morally endowed national identity in the US are brought into play. In many respects, instead of provoking lateral constructive argumentation on global relations—political, economic and cultural—institutional responses to 9/11 have, more often, recoiled at the prospect of polyphonic debate in lieu of patriotic consensus. Simply put, and most especially within the American public sphere, there has been a degree of "anti-intellectualism" afoot in the aftermath of the 11 September attacks and the intervening duration of the War on Terror. In contrast to a more sceptical and self-reflexive encounter with 9/11 in continental Europe, in the US, according to the late Susan Sontag, there is:

> "the suspicion of thought, of words," and "hiding behind the humbug that the attack of last September 11th was too horrible, too devastating, too painful, too tragic for words, that words could not possibly do justice to our grief and indignation, our leaders have a perfect excuse to drape themselves in borrowed words devoid of content. To say something might be controversial [...] Not saying anything is best."[1]

There is a passionate political criticism and consciousness to Sontag's diagnosis. But her argument also dovetails with the actions and reactions of writers after the events of 11 September. 9/11 might have been a "mute act" requiring subsequent narrative coding, in Susan Buck-Morss' view.[2] But the dominant narrative patterning of 9/11 has been univocal, by and large, and has striven to quell critical questioning. The popular call for unity from within the US, and that reached across, and was accepted, by the West, is matched and abetted by cultural agents that do not defy, but affirm simplistic, binary thinking on East/West relations—historical and contemporary. Difference and diversity, long mainstays of American popular culture, are now watchwords of new idioms of paranoid and xenophobic legislation and monitoring. Political and cultural differences are not the basis for pluralist or multicultural inclusiveness,

---

[1] Sontag, *At the Same Time: Essays and Speeches*, 121.
[2] Buck-Morss, *Thinking Past Terror: Islamism and Cultural Theory on the Left*, 23.

but are now markers of potential menace. Indeed, it is not an exaggeration to speculate that the political and cultural climate of the West has entered the frames of dystopian literary history for many of its narrative figurations in the years since 9/11.

In this intensified state of political and cultural sensitivity, it is worth posing the following questions, as Daniel Lea does in his piece on literary responses to 9/11. Lea inquires:

> Why are the views of writers, and in particular novelists, deemed so worthy of collation and dissemination? Why, in the aftermath, were novelists sought out to air their opinions on the traumatic character of events? What, in other words, does the novelist have to offer that cannot be provided by reportage or political commentary?[3]

Lea's series of questions centres on the role of the novelist in relation to 9/11 and asks what are the exceptional abilities harboured by the literary artist that might enable them to mediate such shocking events for a general readership. The premium placed on the writer, as opposed to the narrative conventions and content of media and political opinion, is not difficult to explain. There is an assumption that the rhetoric of news coverage and political newspeak are blighted by evasion, slant or outright misinformation, whereas the explanatory fictions of the novelist are deemed to express and to possess truths and consolations for the reader. Clearly, Lea's point coheres with the broader issue of the appetite for narrative and explanation after the 9/11 attacks, but it also touches upon other critical issues. In summoning writers to respond to these catastrophic events, it seems as if there is an explicit acknowledgement of the capacity of the literary artist to provide guidance out of the silence and the clamour attendant on 9/11. Likewise, the possibility that literature itself might be a source of succour or solace is implicit in Lea's speculations. This is not to locate the literary artist as a kind of renovated seer in the light of 11 September, but there has been a renewed weight placed on the literary as a medium of consolation and resolution in many critical interventions since 9/11.

---

[3] Lea, "Aesthetics and Anaesthetics: Anglo-American Writers' Responses to September 11," 4.

L*et the* G*reat* W*orld* S*pin* and 9/11

Again the "narrative" labour and expertise of writers, together with their "imaginative" range, are signalled as a means of fashioning and relating understanding to dazed readers. Returning to Lea, is there an inevitability to the prominence of writerly responses to 9/11, and other such extreme public events of violence and spectacle? McEwan's locations of empathy in the imagination, and his belief that this is where morality begins, centres literature as a primary political agent after 9/11. There was little that was empathetic or imaginative about many institutional political responses to the attacks of 11 September. But it seems from these combined reactions that literature houses utopian possibilities towards political and cultural critique, and towards the cultivation of empathetic feeling beyond the local. Post-9/11 novels and other works of art are not solely concerned with eliciting sympathy or empathy for the victims of the hijacked planes—though this is important—this subgenre of contemporary fiction is also cognizant of the need for narratives that complicate our understandings of the 'other.' These 9/11 fictions can help us to see hope in place of an insistent rhetoric of vilification and retribution; and they can impress the possibilities of redemption through empathy rather than through violent purging. The brachiated and democratic structure of *Let the Great World Spin*, in tandem with the one of its central themes, creative daring, allow McCann to address these questions. McCann's literary intervention is a 9/11 novel, and it attempts to loosen the grip of the 9/11 grief industry, which tries to stage-manage the cultural digestion of 9/11, and in its early American literary incarnations were centred on individual trauma and tended to 'subjectivize' the experiences of the attacks and their legacies. *Let the Great World Spin* is a political and social novel that looks aslant at the attacks of 9/11; McCann suggests that it is an allegory on human suffering, which partially speaks to 11 September. Nevertheless, in a manner akin to Ewa Kowal's reading of Wojciech Tochman's *Córeńka* (2005) in Chapter "The Post-9/11 World in Three Polish Responses: Zagajewski, Skolimowski, Tochman" in this volume, McCann's novel de-monumentalizes the suffering of the victims of 9/11, without denigrating their memory. Instead, McCann showcases the longevity and the breadth of human suffering and resilience across races, classes and nationalities in New York City. It is a novel that is stalked by menace and violence, but one that rises to moments of grace and hopeful anticipation.

Speaking in interview after the publication of *Let the Great World Spin*, McCann admitted to a certain confusion as an author dealing with 9/11, particularly as a resident of New York City. He confessed that he: "began to wonder, Who's going to write about this?" and that as responses of various forms and political persuasions began to proliferate, he remarked that: "every piece was poignant […] And everything had meaning: it was like the whole city was infused with meaning."[4] The everyday is transformed into the sacred, as figuration and suggestion engulf the brute realities of a debris-strewn and ash-thickened atmosphere. As the force of the reality of 9/11 manifested itself, understandings of its 'meaning' only became admissible through figuration—symbols and metaphors were drafted in as explanatory buffers: "You couldn't help thinking that everything had importance. Even the child's painting of the two buildings holding hands was a powerful image."[5] McCann's point reiterates the fact that even this event, perhaps especially this event, cannot escape: "the reach of symbol and metaphor."[6] Whereas many saw recourse to narrative and figuration as routes out of aphasia and grief, towards a semblance of healing, it is equally true that 9/11 became a part of a dominant semiotics in the geopolitical imagination. In other words, 9/11 became a symbolic agent of neo-conservative politics and acted as a guarantor of moral legitimacy for physical and cultural violence across the globe. Its cultivated mythology has seen it conscripted into narrow and heavily politicized commemoration. As Simpson avers: "The event has been and will be made to mark a new epoch, and as such it is already generating a mythology and a set of practices of its own."[7]

The attacks of 11 September were entirely without public warning, and, apparently precedent. Yet as Slavoj Žižek argues, the forms the attacks assumed are familiar features of our visual fantasy worlds.[8] But the sheer spectacular qualities of the World Trade Center attacks take us back to Lea's series of questions: were writers summoned in order to verbalize some meaningful explanation of the silent spectacle of the terror attacks?

---

[4] Colum McCann, "*Let the Great World Spin* Interview," author website: www.colummccann.com/interviews (accessed 15.7.2015).

[5] McCann, "*Let the Great World Spin* Interview".

[6] Versluys, *Out of the Blue: September 11 and the Novel*, 3.

[7] Simpson, *9/11: The Culture of Commemoration*, 16.

[8] See Žižek, *Welcome to the Desert of the Real*.

The mute eloquence of the events can be adjudged to confer a level of uniqueness on 9/11, as Buck-Morss concedes: "The staging of violence as a global spectacle separates September 11 from previous acts of terror."[9] Nevertheless, the lethal visibility of 9/11 reminds us of the relative invisibility of legion other acts of terror, often committed in its wake and on our behalf. But the spectacular nature of the event brings into tension the viewers' sense of what is real and what is fictive; and occasions a blurring between the real and the cinematic. There is, in other words, a clash of communicative or narrative codes, and at the moments of the attacks there is no mediation to untangle this confusion. The perpetrators of the crime well understood not only the symbolism of the Twin Towers, but also the centrality of the visual to the West's cultural economy, and the intimacy of remembrance and images. In differential modes—remembrance; cinema; information—the visual is crucial to understanding 9/11, and is a key motif in McCann's 9/11 novel. To return to one of the early novelist respondents, English author Martin Amis, we see this exact point concisely articulated:

> But no visionary cinematic genius could hope to create the majestic abjection of that double surrender, with the scale of the buildings conferring its own slow motion. It was well understood that an edifice so demonstrably comprised of concrete and steel would also become an unforgettable metaphor. This moment was the apotheosis of the postmodern era—the era of the image and perceptions.[10]

9/11 can be located in a specific set of geographical locations, and the abbreviated nomination indicates the calendar date of the attacks in 2001. Through the labours of policy-makers and media agenda-setters, 9/11 has outgrown any sense of itself as a mere temporal marker; the event has transcended historical time and has entered epochal time. As other literary critical volumes amply illustrate, literature and, in particular, the novel, have responded variously to 9/11, though much of the literary output and pursuant literary criticism has tended to reflect on

---

[9] Buck-Morss, *Thinking Past Terror*, 23.
[10] Amis, "Fear and Loathing".

American legacies and experiences of 9/11.[11] In a recent literary critical survey, Catherine Morley notes a suite of trends in 9/11 fiction:

> While many of the initial reactions to the events of 11th September were notable for their uniquely subjective emphasis, with writers discussing what the attacks meant to them, to their art and to their writing, what many writers have also been integrating into their fiction has been the American response to the attacks.[12]

The current discussion strives to depart from domestic, subjective reactions to 9/11 in literary fiction and essays by looking at the National Book Award-winning title, *Let the Great World Spin*, which deals with 9/11 in an elliptical way. McCann's novel is set, like much of his previous fiction, in New York, but principally unfolds in 1974, and deals with, in figurative fashion, themes of trauma, loss and redemption. *Let the Great World Spin* is initiated by the narration of a high-wire walk between the towers of the World Trade Center on 7 August 1974, and his imaginative performance reverberates forward in time to 11 September 2001, as a utopian act of creation. For the high wire walk, the French acrobat, Philippe Petit fitted a 200-kilogram cable 400 metres above the ground between the World Trade Center towers and used a custom-made 8-metre-long balancing pole. He performed for 45 minutes, making eight passes along the wire, before descending and being arrested. But, rather than re-create a world-historical universe in 1974, McCann prefers to navigate the margins of a profoundly troubled metropolis. *Let the Great World Spin* gestures to the accumulated grief of 9/11 and to the symbolism of the attacks by way of Petit's walk, and McCann spotlights the possibility of redemption and recovery in the recessed spaces of New York's cityscape. Grief is not confined to this date and this event, and neither is hope; the novel is, then, an allegory about all human suffering and how that suffering can be alleviated or endured.

---

[11] See Ann Keniston and Jeanne Follansbee Quinn's *Literature after 9/11*; Kristiaan Versluys' *Out of the Blue: September 11 and the Novel*; Dunja M. Mohr and Sylvia Mayer (eds.), *Zeitschrift für Anglistik und Amerikanistik—A Quarterly of Language, Literature and Culture—Special Issue: 9/11 as Catalyst: American and British Responses*; Daniel Lea, "Aesthetics and Anaesthetics: Anglo-American Writers' Responses to September 11".

[12] Morley, "The End of Innocence: Tales of Terror after 9/11," 83.

Let the Great World Spin cannot but be considered a political and social novel, given its embrace of criminality; destitution; addiction; and class division, and in these respects intersects with Sandra Singer's treatment of Ian McEwan's novel *Saturday* (2005) in Chapter "Cultural and Historical Memory in English and German Discursive Responses to 9/11" in this collection. Set in 1974 in New York, the narrative primarily spans downtown and uptown Manhattan, as well as the South Bronx, with interludes in Ireland and upstate New York. Ireland is a site of origin and of return for the Corrigan brothers; for John Corrigan, it is where his spiritual vocation begins, but also where he realizes the limits of its applicability, given the scale of the country. In this respect, it is local in its scale but a spur to the global for the devout John Corrigan. Similarly for his brother, Ciaran, Ireland is firmly networked into global systems via emigration but also through the possibility of return, as seen in his return migration at the close of the novel. Gathered within its plotlines are characters of different nationalities; races and class locations: the anonymous high wire walker; the Irish monk, John Corrigan and his brother Ciaran; Tillie and Jazzlyn Henderson, mother and daughter prostitutes, who are friends with John Corrigan; a wealthy couple grieving for the son lost in Vietnam maybe foreshadowing the military consequences of 9/11 and their evaluation?, Claire and Solomon Soderberg; and Gloria, who lost three of her sons in the same war; a teenage photographer on the hunt for new subway graffiti; and a young artist, Lara, who is involved in John Corrigan's death and begins a long-term relationship with his brother after that accident. From the outset, *Let the Great World Spin* clamours with cultural and social diversity of characters, and pulses with the tensions and insecurities of its cast. The novel acknowledges both the material and the symbolic as forces within daily life, and traces how, as McCann puts it: "the accidental meets the sacred."[13] And a fraction of its political engagement is, of course, its concern with 9/11 as a material and a symbolic event. McCann accepts the immense symbolic trauma of 9/11, but he is equally keen to stress the lateral material sufferings that nourish, and are often subordinated to the public emphasis on symbolic victimhood or symbolic violence. *Let the Great World Spin* is, in this way, a politically engaged narrative, which speaks from an equivalent critical position to that outlined by Rothberg and Kearney above. It is a forceful,

---

[13] McCann, "*Let the Great World Spin* Interview".

though tangential, artistic-political response to 9/11, but there is more to the work than this neat summary may suggest: "9/11 was the initial impetus for the book [...] But I am aware of the pitfalls of labelling it a '9/11' novel [...] 9/11 is certainly part of the book's construction, but it is not limited to that [...] I really wanted to lift it out of the 9/11 'grief machine'."[14] While he acknowledges the symbolic threads that link *Let the Great World Spin* to 9/11, it would be reductive to define McCann's novel as one that is exclusively trained on these events. It is a novel that responds to 9/11 without ever becoming obsessed by the immediate repercussions in 2001 in any direct way. McCann does not 'enter' the world of 9/11 or post-9/11 in a sustained fashion, nor does he imagine characters or events implicated directly in this contemporary tragedy. Tellingly he implies that 9/11 might actually compromise his work; that 9/11 as a 'cultivated' event could contract the interpretive scope of his narrative. In this, there are echoes of Jacques Derrida's argument that works of literature might themselves become objects within the commemorative industry of 9/11.[15] All of these issues, though, cannot disavow the fact that 9/11 is a thematic and ethical point of departure for *Let the Great World Spin*. But it is equally the case that the novel's visions outstrip the political and cultural agons surrounding the 2001 attacks. As McCann stresses: "It's a novel that tries to uncover joy and hope and a small glimmer of grace [...] a novel about creation, maybe even a novel about healing in the face of all the evidence."[16]

RE-IMAGINING SPACE AND PERFORMING HOPE

Mobility and exile are defining preoccupations of McCann's previous two novels *Dancer* (2003) and *Zoli* (2006); this makes them much more obviously 'spatial' in their concerns. Likewise, McCann's 2013 novel,

---

[14] Ibid.
[15] Jacques Derrida argues: "When you say 'September 11' you are already citing [...] You are inviting me to speak here by recalling, as if in quotation marks, a date or a dating that has taken over our public space and our private lives for five weeks now. Something *fait date*, I would say in a French idiom, something marks a date, a date in history," "AutoImmunity: Real and Symbolic Suicides—A Dialogue with Jacques Derrida," 85.
[16] McCann, "*Let the Great World Spin* Interview".

Transatlantic offers a set of loosely connected and transhistorical narratives that underscore the historical durability and longevity of cultural and economic traffic across the Atlantic. The novel continues McCann's philosophical investment in cultural and interpersonal connectivity, a world view and literary device that also underpin the ethical freight of most of his fictional output. Yet *Let the Great World Spin* asserts the locality of spatial politics; its topographies are, principally, those of New York City, but exile and mobility remain prominent. There are other geographies present: Ireland figures at the outset and at the conclusion; and California enters the narrative via telephonic communication. Allusions are made to Guatemala; Cleveland, Ohio; England; Brussels; Naples; New Orleans; Little Rock, Arkansas, Vietnam; and Genoa, but New York City is the spatial main stage. New York City is the localized global space and it is the endpoint of all of these vectors of travel and displacement. Within the city, and the novel, McCann juxtaposes terrestrial and air-borne spaces, which are figurations of hope and despair, as well as reminders that life at ground level can be as precarious as life on an elevated tightrope: both demand balance that is often threatened and uncertain. And this is one of the possible interpretations of the wire walker's funambulism, as an acrobatic correlative of the fragile precariousness of daily living—matters that are close to Ulrich Kinzel's engagement with Gerhard Richter's *September* and the vanitas motif of shipwreck. At the same time, his act is an outrageous seizure of urban space, an act, apparently, with no constructive end other than the outstanding beauty of the act itself. The Twin Towers and the references to the Vietnam War unfolding at this time are confronted by the vision of the wire walker's spatial creativity. Both the war and the buildings are parts of the same capitalistic continuum and are complicit in the spatial appropriation of the globe. Empire building was, and is, founded on the basic contestation of, and appropriation of, space, and both the towers and the war are internal and external signs of this politics. As Edward Soja summarizes: "The production of ideas (and ideologies) is thus an important component of the production of spatiality but this relationship is rooted in social origins."[17]

---

[17] Soja, "The Spatiality of Social Life: Towards a Transformative Retheorisation," 94.

Though he is never named in the novel, *Let the Great World Spin* opens on the morning of Philip Petit's tightrope walk between the Twin Towers of the World Trade Center on 7 August 1974. Immediately McCann gestures to the agency of the visual as both a universal cultural medium and as a core motif of the novel. Vision, spectacle and sightings provide a link between the opening act of funambulism in *Let the Great World Spin* and the brute spectacular of 9/11. Indeed, the preparation of the "walker," as he is referred to, to step out onto his high wire is met with similar silent awe and trepidation by the congregation of confused viewers on the streets of Manhattan below: "Those who saw him hushed [...] Others figured it might be the perfect city joke—stand around and point upward, until people gathered, tilted their heads, nodded, affirmed, until all were staring upward at nothing at all."[18] The grouped crowds may be witnesses to the "walker's" actions, but there is nothing besides suspicion and uncertainty in the accumulated speculations. There seems to be a disjuncture between vision and comprehension in the presence of this acrobatic feat, yet curiosity persists among the viewers:

> He could only be seen at certain angles so that the watchers had to pause at street corners, find a gap between buildings, or meander from the shadows to get a view unobstructed by cornicework, gargoyles, balustrades, roof edges. [...] It was the dilemma of the watchers: they didn't want to wait around for nothing at all [...] but they didn't want to miss the moment either [...] Around the watchers, the city still made its everyday noises. (*LGWS*, 3)

In this opening set-piece, McCann corrals fantasy, illusion and reality; the expectant silence of the watchers and the commotion of the city morning; and the minute vulnerability of the human body amid the domineering concreted scale of the city. The repetitions, the habits of the everyday are intruded upon by: "a dark toy against the cloudy sky" (*LGWS*, 3)—the "walker."

The build-up to the moment when the "walker" steps off the edge of the tower captures the heteronomy of sounds and sights as the working day in Manhattan commences. McCann's description evokes the mobility,

---

[18] McCann, *Let the Great World Spin*, 3. All further references to *Let the Great World Spin* will appear in parenthesis as (*LGWS*).

even the transience, of the city: "Ferry whistles. The thrum of the subway. The M22 bus pulled in against the sidewalk, sighed down into a pot-hole. A flying chocolate wrapper touched against a fire hydrant. Taxi doors slammed [...] Revolving doors pushed quarters of conversation out into the street" (*LGWS*, 4). Snatches of urban sensuousness form the backdrop to the "walker's" defiant artistic performance high above the street level bustle. Yet the fragmented sensory chaos of Manhattan is somehow nullified by the "walker's" gesture; his presence on the skyline unifies the disparate lives into an integrated audience. His brazen act is received with reverent silence as the watchers mingle and convene in pockets on the pavements: "Doctors. Cleaners. Prep chefs. Diamond merchants. Fish Sellers. Sad-jeaned whores. All of them reassured by the presence of one another" (*LGWS*, 4). The improbability of the sight and the rumours that it generates—"he was some sort of cat burglar, that he'd been taken hostage, he was an Arab, a Cypriot, an IRA man, that he was really just a publicity stunt, a corporate scam" (*LGWS*, 5)—create a tangible level of community between the gathered watchers. In some ways, Petit's performative act of transgressive creativity and the ways in which it is linked here to other acts, and actors, of terror, foreshadow and obliquely allude to the historical impetus of McCann's novel: the 9/11 attacks in New York. The slow, methodical preparations of the "walker" allow time for the pedestrian audience to intrigue about his motivations, but more importantly, this period of silent viewing must be and is filled with expectancy and mystery. For those at street level: "the waiting had been made magical [...] shared. The man above was a word they seemed to know, though they had not heard it before. Out he went' (*LGWS*, 7). Given the historical context in which the novel is set, a period during which New York city was rife with violent crime and drug addiction, as well as facing the prospect of financial bankruptcy, the image of the "walker" perched on the highest building in the world is a signal utopian moment. And the significance of using Petit's daring in this fashion, and in a 9/11 novel, is touched upon in these exact terms by McCann. The moment of physical transcendence became a powerful symbolic act for McCann in the wake of 9/11, what he calls, "a spectacular act of creation."[19] The private sufferings and griefs of ordinary people, which exist side by side with faith in possible recovery, are primary thematics

---

[19] Bret Anthony Johnston, "Interview with Colum McCann".

of the novel, and Petit's walk catalyzes this possibility of redemption. Equally, this emboldened creative act assembles disparate individuals in Manhattan, however briefly, and allows them to share a unique spectacle. In this sense, the "walker's" gesture facilitates an instance of belonging and restores faith in the possibility of solidarity and social equality; it is suggestive of the numinous touching upon the banalities of the everyday. The "walker" is apparitional on the Manhattan skyline, a spectre on the horizons of visible and of the possible. But he is, most importantly, an agent of hope in the allegorical structure of the novel. His decision to step out onto the high wire is the ultimate act of faith: faith in oneself. And it is an inspirational, generous act offered to those who stop, wait and watch his sky-borne performance.

The wire walker's feat is an imaginative re-calibration of spatiality; it is an unforeseen subversion of the logic of capitalist space. The hubris and the rational architecture of the World Trade Center are challenged by the wire walker's re-casting of the Twin Towers as objects of acrobatic beauty. And the implications of the wire walker's actions are consummately expressed in the novel by the grieving Claire Soderberg: "And an attempt at beauty. The intersection of a man with the city, the abruptly reformed, the newly appropriated public space, the city art. Walk up there and make it new. Making it a different space" (*LGWS*, 103). Claire's description has implicit references to Ezra Pound's Modernist injunction "to make new," and to Karl Heinz Stockhausen's provocative statement that the World Trade Center attacks were pieces of high art. Her reaction on hearing of the wire walker combines space as art; the redefinition of urban utility; and the aesthetics of violence, in particular in relation to 9/11. In this emotional processing of the wire walk, McCann touches upon: 9/11; the pursuit of arresting innovation in art; and the rousing utopian dynamism of the spatial re-conceptualization of iconic capitalist edifices. The Twin Towers were the concreted and glazed embodiment of a set of economic, political and cultural abstractions, and there is no gainsaying the symbolic violence of their destruction. But rather than dwell on the destructive levelling of the towers in 2001 as an act of incommensurable violence, McCann urges us to appreciate the imaginative spatial assault on the towers in 1974. The wire walk is, of course, a temporary performance, but no less affective for its brevity; it is a jolting act of faith and creativity. And the achievement, with its possibilities, are apprehended by Claire's husband, Solomon, who is the judge assigned to try and to sentence the wire walker after his arrest. For Solomon Soderberg:

> The tightrope walker was such a stroke of genius. A monument in himself. He had made himself into a statue, but a perfect New York one, a temporary one, up in the air, high above the city [...] He had gone to the World Trade Center and had strung his rope across the biggest towers in the world. The Two Towers. Of all places. So brash. So glassy. So forward-looking [...] The glass reflected the sky, the night, the colors: progress, beauty, capitalism. (*LGWS*, 248)

The wire walker not only stills and silences the gathered urban crowds, but he carves a monument out of thin air. The spectacle of the walker undermining rationality, as he draws his audience skyward, re-imagines the potential use of the Twin Towers. These other monuments, to financial functionalism, are alternatively deployed by the wire walker's performance. His act and his art are highly impractical, and they are, in fact, treated as criminal. But the brazen creativity displayed infects the lives of those who witness the walk first-hand, and those who hear of it subsequently. The walk may not change the ways in which spatiality is conceived of and produced in New York City, and it does not alter the spatial employment of the Twin Towers. But the wire walker's gesture opposes 9/11 in pre-emptive fashion with an act of daring creation. The tightrope walk defies belief, but is equally driven by the belief and the faith of the walker, and, again, flags the roles of faith and belief in the overall narrative. The wire walker, then, performs a utopian spatial act that strikes one of the thematic keynotes of *Let the Great World Spin*.

CREATING THE FUTURE

Though the wire walker's aerial performance is a singular act, as a metaphor it is an act of union with the tightrope stitching the Twin Towers to each other. As we have seen, it is a radical spatial re-imagining as it utilizes the air space between the buildings as a bridge rather than as a boundary. The wire walker, then, imagines a link out of nothingness and enacts a precocious feat of courage and balance. Such a resounding figuration necessarily carries throughout the novel, and another of the strands in which the motifs of boundaries and balance materialize is in the braided stories of Claire Soderberg; Gloria; and Jazzlyn's orphaned daughters. Claire and Gloria are members of a group of women who meet regularly as a support network for those who have suffered loss in the Vietnam War. The intrusion of geographical and military aggression in this local context, again, hints at the parallels being drawn by McCann between this historical period and the contemporary moment. The women are from different backgrounds, but none seem further apart than Claire, the Jewish wife of a Manhattan judge, and Gloria, a Southern-born, working-class, single mother of three deceased sons. Their respective geographical locations on Park Avenue and in the South Bronx confirm the social distance between the women, and reinforce the social fragmentation of New York's urban tapestry along class and ethnic markers. Yet their relationship, though pock-marked by difference, is a testimony to the agency of the redemptive solidarity that underpins the politics of the novel.

Claire's material wealth does little to compensate for the loss of her only son, Joshua, and her husband, Solomon, is routinely diffident about Joshua's death. And in the context of her support group, this wealth and apparent privilege are further barriers to genuine and unequivocal acceptance by the remainder of the women. On the day that the wire walker performs in downtown Manhattan, Claire hosts a meeting of the support group at her uptown apartment. At the close of this meeting a potentially irredeemable exchange occurs between Claire and Gloria. Claire pleads with Gloria to stay a while longer, but conflates her desire for company with an earlier thought that she might pay Gloria as a housekeeper, and offers Gloria money to stay. The exchange sets Gloria off on a prolonged walk from Park Avenue to Harlem and back to Claire's apartment. She returns after being mugged, and her decision to return to the scene of social embarrassment is instinctive rather than rational, but it enables a valuable reconciliation. The larger unit of the support group had been a means of talking over the past and of resurrecting the memories of dead children. But on Gloria's return to Park Avenue, she intuitively resists dwelling exclusively on her deceased sons. When Claire inquires about her boys, Gloria thinks: "I didn't want to think about my boys anymore. In a strange way, all I wanted was to be surrounded by another, to be a part of somebody else's room [...] I guess I wanted another sort of question altogether" (*LGWS*, 312). Without neglecting the memory of her sons, Gloria understands the burden of a melancholic fixation with the past. Levelling social, racial and geographical borders, the companionship that is shared by these two women—across many subsequent years, as we learn—is a connection forged despite difference. Their respective lives may have been assailed by the machinations of global politics, but there is the mutual recognition of humanity in their supportive relationship. The novel's insistent metaphor of the tightrope walk asserts the notion of connection. And despite the fractured structure of the narrative, connection is always possible, though not without difficulty, through imagination and acts of faith.

At the end of this day, 7 August 1974, as Claire drops Gloria at her building in the South Bronx, social workers are escorting Jaslyn and Janice, Jazzlyn's daughters, out of the same building. Throughout her time residing in this environment, Gloria has resolutely ignored the lives of squalor that thrived around her. But Jazzlyn's orphaned girls suddenly enter her life, a life that has been renewed with her new friendship with Claire. Symbolically, she is given a chance to save two lives after seeing three lives taken from her through warfare. Gloria alights from the car and "saw them come out, two darling little girls coming through the globes of lamplight" (*LGWS*, 321). The luminescence prompts her memories of these girls and their deceased mother:

> I knew them. I had seen them before. They were the daughters of a hooker who lived two floors above me. I had kept myself away from all that. Years and years. I hadn't let them near my life. I'd see their mother in the doorway, a child herself, pretty and vicious, and I'd stare straight ahead at the buttons. (*LGWS*, 321)

Wrapped in the difficulties of her own life, Gloria had previously abjured intervening in the lives of those in the projects. But at this moment, she chooses to extend herself in an act of unsolicited and selfless grace. The only motivation that she can reason for adopting the girls is that: "It was a deep-down feeling that must've come from long ago" (*LGWS*, 285). Her charity is ineffable, and is, in the end, the culminating act of redemption and hope in *Let the Great World Spin*. The narrative spools forward to 2006, to Jaslyn's brief contemporary narrative. The adult girls now live in post-9/11, post-Hurricane Katrina America, with international wars also ongoing. In temporal terms, McCann reaches past 9/11, framing a temporal link, instead, between 1974 and 2006. In this he urges us, again, to see connections between the possibility for redemption out of tragedies and conflict in the earlier period and similar opportunities in the current time. Symbolically, Jaslyn and Janice pursue "political" occupations: Jaslyn works for a small foundation helping working-class victims of Hurricanes Katrina and Rita with tax forms, while Janice is the U.S. Army. In fact Jaslyn's occupation is an oblique recollection of Corrigan's immersion in the plights of the discarded. And part of her vocation, her attentiveness to the practical bureaucratic needs of these people, allows her to appreciate the vulnerable yet passionate humanity of such forgotten communities. As Jaslyn reflects on her daily tasks, she provides telling summative words on the structure of *Let the Great World Spin*; on the thematic of the potential healing power of relating one's story; and on the intimacy of dignity and self-representation:

> Sometimes it takes them an age just to sign, since they have something else to say – they are off and chatting about the cars they bought, the loves they loved. They have a deep need just to talk, just to tell a story, however small or reckless. Listening to these people is like listening to trees – sooner or later the tree is sliced open and the watermarks reveal their age. (*LGWS*, 337)

The stories that Jaslyn hears may be wildly divergent in form and content, much like the novel itself, but the driving impulses are the needs to share and to connect, and the desire to be heard. From the dizzying summit of the World Trade Center towers to the recessed graffiti of the New York subway system and all spaces in between, there are stories and potential tellers of stories waiting to be heeded.

Art is seen to embody a redemptive moral value system in contradistinction to the destabilizing values of murderous terrorism. Art facilitates a reflective, even temperate, coming to terms with 9/11; again, in contrast to impulses of rage or blind hostility evidenced elsewhere. And this is the context in which we should, finally, read *Let the Great World Spin*. As a work of art, the novel advertises and embodies the durability of human creativity as a utopian resource. This literary fiction is exemplary of what Gilles Deleuze calls: "the realm of the possible."[20] A realm neatly defined by Susheila Nasta and Elleke Boehmer as: "the visionary territory of the imagination, a world situated between the political and cultural borderlines of national/international struggles, a realm where it is the artist's imperative to keep speaking, to keep writing, to keep interrogating, to keep making art even in the face of terror itself, counter-insurgent or otherwise."[21] It is a multivocal, democratic text that braids diverse narratives and lives together in varying patterns

---

[20] Boehmer and Nasta, "Editorial 'Cultures of Terror,'" 1.
[21] Ibid.

of unity and empathetic understanding. To the dominant U.S.-centric narratives of post-9/11, McCann tenders a disjunctive counter-narrative that expands the horizons of what can be labelled as 9/11 literary fiction. In the context of this collection, McCann's novel is a fraction of a broader body of work by writers who are less concerned with narrating the indigenous and isolated traumas of the 9/11 attacks. Though a dual citizen of Ireland and the US, McCann's work, though more often than not sited within American society, should not be stabled within the corpus of American literary responses to 9/11. The geographical oscillations and national variety evident in *Let The Great World Spin* allow us to read McCann's 9/11 novel within broader historical and cultural contexts, in particular in relation to what have been less visible European literary and cultural mediations of the terror attacks in September 2001.

REFERENCES

Amis, Martin. "Fear and Loathing," *The Guardian*, September 18, 2001, available online http://www.guardian.co.uk/world/2001/sep/18/september11.politicsphilosophyandsociety (accessed 15.7.2015).

Boehmer, Elleke, and Susheila Nasta. "Editorial 'Cultures of Terror'," *Wasafiri—Special Issue on 'Cultures of Terror'*, vol. 22, no. 2 (2007), 1–3.

Buck-Morss, Susan. *Thinking Past Terror: Islamism and Cultural Theory on the Left* (London: Verso, 2003).

Derrida, Jacques, and Giovanna Borradori. "AutoImmunity: Real and Symbolic Suicides—A Dialogue with Jacques Derrida," Giovanna Borradori (ed.), *Philosophy in a Time of Terror* (London/Chicago: University of Chicago Press, 2003), 85–136.

Johnston, Bret Anthony. "Interview with Colum McCann," *National Book Award Website*, http://www.nationalbook.org/nba2009_f_mccann_interv.html (accessed 15.7.2015).

Keniston, Ann, and Jeanne Follansbee Quinn (eds.), *Literature after 9/11*. (New York: Routledge, 2010).

Lea, Daniel. "Aesthetics and Anaesthetics: Anglo-American Writers' Responses to September 11," *Symbiosis: A Journal of Anglo-American Literary Relations*, vol. 11, no. 2 (2007), 3–26.

McCann, Colum. "*Let the Great World Spin* Interview," Author website: www.colummccann.com/interviews (accessed 15.7.2015).

———. *Let the Great World Spin* (London: Bloomsbury, 2009).

Mohr, Dunja M., and Sylvia Mayer (eds.), *Zeitschrift fur Anglistik und Amerikanistik—A Quarterly of Language, Literature and Culture—Special Issue: 9/11 as Catalyst: American and British Responses*, vol. 58, no. 1 (2010).

Morley, Catherine. "The End of Innocence: Tales of Terror after 9/11," *Review of International American Studies*, vol. 3, no. 3 (2008) and vol. 4, no. 1 (2009), 81–99.

Simpson, David. *9/11: The Culture of Commemoration* (Chicago: University of Chicago Press, 2006).

Sontag, Susan. *At the Same Time: Essays and Speeches* (London: Hamish Hamilton, 2007).

Soja, Edward. "The Spatiality of Social Life: Towards a Transformative Retheorisation," in Derek Gregory and John Urry (eds.), *Social Relations and Spatial Structures* (Basingstoke: Macmillan, 1985), 90–127.

Versluys, Kristiaan. *Out of the Blue: September 11 and the Novel* (New York: Columbia University Press, 2009).

Žižek, Slavoj. *Welcome to the Desert of the Real* (London: Verso, 2002).

Author Biography

Eoin Flannery is a Lecturer in the Department of English Language and Literature at Mary Immaculate College, University of Limerick, Ireland. He is the author of four books: most recently, *Ireland and Ecocriticism: Literature, History, and Environmental Justice* (2016), and also, *Colum McCann and the Aesthetics of Redemption* (2011); *Ireland and Postcolonial Studies: Theory, Discourse, Utopia* (2009); *Versions of Ireland: Empire, Modernity and Resistance in Irish Culture* (2006). His edited publications include: *Enemies of Empire: New Perspectives on Literature, History and Imperialism* (2007); *Ireland in Focus: Film, Photography and Popular Culture* (2009), and *This Side of Brightness: Essays on the Fiction of Colum McCann* (2012). He has also edited special issues of *The Journal of Ecocriticism* on 'Ireland and Ecocriticism' (2013) and *Postcolonial Text* on 'Ireland and Empire' (2007). He is currently completing a book on *Debt, Guilt and Aesthetic Forms in Post-Celtic Tiger Ireland*.

PART II

Literary Translations of September 11 into Europe's National Contexts

Seeing Is Disbelieving: The Contested Visibility of 9/11 in France

Jean-Philippe Mathy

9/11 has been caught up from the very start in a web of competing interpretations. The official version almost immediately provided by the American government and media was soon followed by rival, and sometimes counter, narratives produced by supporters and opponents of the United States, and by authorized or self-appointed commentators both inside and outside the country, including countless bloggers on the Internet. The shocking, unpredicted nature of the attacks, the fact that their images were broadcast almost immediately all around the world, the geopolitical stakes of the event and its momentous consequences (we are still living in a world that is largely shaped by them, as the 2015 and 2016 attacks in Paris and Nice, to stay within the French context, make patently clear) explain why considerations about the meaning, authenticity and credibility of 9/11 have loomed large in ideological debates from the start.

The proliferating theories and counter-theories we have been subjected to since that fateful day in 2001 have attempted to provide a symbolic articulation (a "making sense") of what remains for many an

J.-P. Mathy (✉)
Champaign, USA

"unbelievable" event, in both senses of the word (a disaster of tremendous proportions, and one devoid of any plausibility). The fact that the event had global consequences while only a handful of people actually witnessed it placed 9/11 at the centre of a web of controversies born of the ambiguous relationship between image-making and truth-telling in a "postmodern" world informed by the logic of virtual reality. The widespread diffusion of conspiracy theories based on the dialectics of credibility and visibility was a signal that for large segments of the world's public opinion, "seeing was not believing."

The growing invisibility of the war on terrorism ("we aren't allowed to see what we are supposed to believe") contributed to the growth of scepticism regarding the truth about 9/11 ("we should not believe the filtered information we are given to see"). It is not surprising that one of the first books questioning the truth of 9/11 was published in France to considerable success, given the long history of anti-Americanism present in the country's intellectual and political circles since the end of the eighteenth century. Many among the French have rejected the "American Way of Life" on a variety of grounds, often regardless of their political persuasion. In the 1930s and 1940s, for example, and again during the Cold War and the Vietnam War, both the Right and the Left have emphasized the threat American hegemony posed to the survival of the high culture and national independence of European countries.

My reading of the reactions to 9/11 will examine two different sets of responses to the official version given by the US government and shared by the vast majority of the American people in the months following the attacks (the hegemonic narrative). I will look for interpretive commonalities between critical assessments by philosophers and cultural critics writing as public intellectuals, on the one hand, and one literary account of the tragedy on the other, Frédéric Beigbeder's novel, *Windows on the World* (2003). The philosophical deconstruction of the dominant, consensual versions of the event, because it focuses on the interplay of the real, the imaginary and the symbolic, raises representational issues which are also present in fictional accounts, including the various conspiracy theories that have questioned the dominant interpretation of 9/11, and continue to do so. The contested ontological nature of the event (did it "really" happen the way we saw it happen?) and the disputed epistemological status of its discursive constructions (did it really happen the way we were told it happened?) may well justify the inclusion of conspiracy theories in a volume dedicated to literary accounts of 9/11. Regardless of the validity of their claims, conspiracy theories are signifying practices. As such, they raise issues pertaining to the relationship between words and things, being and appearance, and signs and their referents, and can be subjected to protocols of reading, interpretation, criticism, and formal analysis applicable to other texts, whether literary, filmic, or philosophical. When they are fiction, they belong in the same category as myths, legends, and rumours and can be examined as such.

The images of the planes hitting the World Trade Center were played again and again to viewers in shocked disbelief glued to their television set or personal computer. For several hours following the tragedy, the obsessive broadcasting of the same few available shots taken by "amateur" filmmakers was only matched by the compulsive consumption of the same visual material by millions of people all over the globe. Philosopher and cultural critic Slavoj Žižek has described in psychoanalytical (Lacanian) terms the visual repetition of the trauma involved in the early structuration of the reaction to 9/11, as follows:

> And so, during the days that followed September 11, 2001, our gaze fascinated by these images of the planes striking the towers, we were forced to experience the compulsion to repeat and enjoyment (*jouissance*) beyond the pleasure principle. The same shots were shown ad nauseam, we wanted to see them incessantly, and the strange satisfaction they gave us was pure *jouissance*.[1]

9/11 became almost instantaneously a local, a national, and a transnational event, but it soon became clear that the geographical distance between those three spaces of reception would make all the difference in the world, so to speak, upon the way diversely located people attempted to make sense of the tragedy. Carol Gluck, a historian living in Manhattan and teaching at Columbia University, suggested New York City residents and visitors who had witnessed the event and/or its aftermath "for real," without technological mediation, enjoyed the privilege of authenticity over the millions who had only seen it via the distancing prism of television images already caught up in the commentaries of professional broadcasters:

---

[1] Žižek, "Passion du réel, passion du semblant" 45 [all translations from the French are mine].

While I embark on an ethnographical essay on the media to analyze the construction of television narratives of the war on terrorism, my reflection cannot but be affected by the fact that I reside in New York. What others only saw on screens, we lived in full force: we saw it with our very eyes, we breathed the noxious air, we felt that New York, and not America, had been attacked, New Yorkers and their mayor faced the crisis and not Americans and their president. The fact that so many commentaries following the attack did not make any distinction between New York and America was irritating, as if we were all transformed immediately into stupid flag-waving patriots. Thucydides wrote for Athens, he came to his city's defense, and that's what I did for mine.[2]

The very short time that elapsed between the first impact at 8.46 a.m. EST and the first live shot shown on CNN at 8.49 a.m., as a result of the speed of satellite transmissions, means that the viewing of the event was almost "live," a striking development in terms of the timing between a traumatic event and its symbolic inscription within an individual or collective psychic economy. While the first time lapse occurred between the actual event and its initial visual representation, the second one separated the initial newsbreak from the first politically significant discursive articulation by George W. Bush's Chief of Staff who informs the President at 9.05 a.m. that "a second plane hit the second tower. America is under attack." The first hit could have been an accident, the second one confirmed an intentional, i.e. politically meaningful, act.[3]

In his controversial analysis of 9/11,[4] French theorist Jean Baudrillard focused on the instant that preceded its symbolization, the gap filled with what Gluck calls the "raw images and information" that were put forward before anybody knew what was going on, before narrative forms had started to appear.[5] Jean Baudrillard was a prominent cultural critic

---

[2] Gluck, "11 Septembre. Guerre et Télévision au XXIe siècle," 136.

[3] In his novel about 9/11, *Windows on the World*, French novelist Frédéric Beigbeder plays on the immediate, "live" quality of the reporting of the event, and its minute-by-minute unfolding in the very structure of his text, made up of short chapters corresponding to an instant in time. His novel starts at 8.30 (a.m.) and ends at 10.29 that same morning.

[4] Baudrillard, *La violence du Monde*. Baudrillard himself contributed to the century-old intertext of French interpretations of the United States in his much-discussed 1986 essay, *Amérique*.

[5] "During the [early] special news breaks, when nobody really knew what had happened, raw images and information filled the screens because there was not any 'narrative' yet,

and public intellectual, author of several influential books on consumerism and post-Marxist political economy in the 1970s, before becoming one of the leading theorists of postmodernity. He made headlines in 1991 when he claimed, paraphrasing Clausewitz, that the first Gulf War was not "the continuation of politics by other means," but rather "the continuation of the absence of politics by other means." Moving from the absence of politics to the non-existence of the war itself, Baudrillard provocatively entitled his reflections of the military campaign against Saddam Hussein, *The Gulf War Did Not Take Place*.[6]

In his equally iconoclastic and paradoxical account of 9/11, Baudrillard wrote that the attacks eluded any attempt to symbolize them in any narrative form:

> Everything is in the first instant. [...] If one gets rid of this moment of stupefaction, of admiration – immoral, no doubt, but where one finds condensed, through the immorality of the image, the stupefying intuition of the event – if one repudiates this very moment, one loses any chance of understanding. If the first thought is to say: this is horrendous, that is unacceptable, then all the intensity, all the impact of the event gets lost in political and moral considerations. All discourses take us irrevocably further from the event and we will no longer be able to get close to it, not any more than to the Big Bang.[7]

Baudrillard's "first instant" does not refer to the moment in time when the tragedy actually happened, since it took some time to unfold, the first plane having struck at 8.46 a.m. and the second at 9.03,[8] but to the instant when viewers first saw the live shot of the first plane hitting the first tower, as if the "truth" of 9/11 occurred not in reality (what the New Yorkers and tourists who were *there* witnessed) but in the virtual space of the media. Which allows Baudrillard to claim that "the image

---

or any control of the facts" (Gluck, "11 Septembre. Guerre et Télévision au XXIe siècle", 136).

[6] Baudrillard, *The Gulf War Did Not Take Place*.

[7] Baudrillard, *La violence du Monde*, 20.

[8] Flight 77 hit the Pentagon at 9.37:46. For a minute-by-minute (and sometimes second-by-second!) account, see http://en.wikipedia.org/wiki/Timeline_for_the_day_of_theSeptember_11_attacks (accessed 12.4.2015).

and the event are there first [while] usually, in our media world, the image takes the place of the event."⁹ Contrary to what usually happens in our visually driven culture where the imaginary serves as a refuge against the impact of any traumatic event, in the case of September 11 the image itself became the event, it was inseparable from the shocking realization it signified. In Baudrillard's account, this "visibility of substitution" usually associated with the image does not apply in the case of 9/11, since the "fusion between the real and the fictional" means that "there is no loss of reality" through the fiction of the image. The fascination is first and foremost that of the image, to which is added the "chill of the real": "Not only is it terrifying, but on top of it, it is real."[10]

In the case of 9/11, there is a long list of "moral and political considerations" that answered the collective need for understanding the "unbelievable" and assuaging the anxieties it triggered. The "unimaginable, unrepresentable, pure event" soon disappeared under the sheer mass of its interpretations, ruining what Baudrillard calls the "silent efficiency we try of course to dilute in all the commentaries that are like its metastases."[11] The Bush administration's official version denied all historical responsibility in the attacks on the part of the United States, framing it from the start in a moral and religious rather than political register; the patriotic "heroic narrative" (Gluck) provided by the media and the political class rested on the victimization of innocent individuals and, beyond, of the entire American people, by the pathological hatred of democracy, freedom, and modernity shared by a group of fanatics; Al-Qaeda's supporters (including the highly coded "Arab street," as journalists are fond to say) denounced the neo-imperialism of the US and "the West" in South-western and Central Asia, mixing religious arguments (occupation of the holy sites of Islam) with political (diplomatic and military support of Israel and of autocratic regimes in the Arab world) and economic ones (America's national interests require the control of energy resources in the region as a result of the competition with Europe and China, who need access to oil reserves); meanwhile, competing and contradictory, paranoid theories soon saw behind the attacks the secret hand of Saddam

---

[9] Baudrillard, *La violence du Monde*, 21.
[10] Ibid., 24.
[11] Ibid., *La violence du Monde*, 23.

Hussein, and other members of "the axis of evil" (Bush's version) or the secret hand of the CIA (anti-Bush version).

Baudrillard is highly critical of any "historical-political explanation" that ends up erasing "the singularity of the event," whether these accounts provide a plethora of often incompatible reasons for the attacks or whether they find no reason at all behind what is described as a senseless, purely nihilistic acting out. The only tenable position, therefore, would be to provide no explanation at all in order to preserve the pure hyperreal nature of what happened. Our critical theorist nevertheless fulfils his professional *raison d'être*, answering in his own way the demand for meaning he finds so objectionable in others. He delivers his own version of the event, a version based unsurprisingly, for those familiar with his work, on the relationship between death and the logic of symbolic exchange, and more specifically the escalation of symbolic violence (*défi symbolique, symbolic challenge*): "Terrorism has no meaning, no goal, and cannot be measured in terms of its real consequences, whether political or historical."[12]

The paradoxical meaningless meaning of September 11 is understandable, but not explicable, at least not by a set of conventional "reasons." Baudrillard's own interpretation enables him to steer clear of both the theories grounded on political, psychological or economic principles, and the views of those who refuse to see any logic in a purely gratuitous destructive act. Since it is impossible to win against the system on the level of reality, what is required, from the terrorists' point of view, is

> to transfer the fight to the sphere of the symbolic, where the rule is one of challenge, reversion, and escalation (*surenchère*). So that death can only be answered by an equal or superior form of death. To challenge the system by a gift to which it cannot respond, if not by its own collapse and death. The terrorist hypothesis is that the system itself will commit suicide as an answer to the multiple challenge of death and suicide. For neither the system nor power can escape the symbolic obligation: that of responding in order not to lose face. [...] The tactic of the terrorist model is to bring on an excess of reality.[13]

The interplay between the real, the fictional, and the imaginary has become one of the dominant frameworks for interpreting the meaning

---

[12] Ibid., 34.
[13] Ibid., 35.

of 9/11, and has understandably been very attractive to fiction writers. Frédéric Beigbeder wrote one of the most often referenced French novels on 9/11 (*Windows on the World*), together with Luc Lang's *11 septembre mon amour* (2003) and Didier Goupil's *Le jour de mon retour sur terre* (2006) [The Day I Returned to Earth]. Beigbeder's text is made up of two distinct narrative lines. On the one hand, we have the fictional eyewitness account of a middle-aged Texan who finds himself trapped with his two sons in "Windows on the World," the restaurant on top of one of the World Trade Center towers. Woven into the description of the growing terror and horror experienced by the victims trapped in the burning restaurant, are the retrospective reflections of a narrator called Frédéric Beigbeder, who is having breakfast on top of the highest building in Paris, the Montparnasse Tower, two years later.

The paradoxical nature of the event as both unreal and hyperreal, unrepresentable and yet the object of endless representation, whether visual or linguistic, is a leitmotif of the book. In the first few pages, the French narrator declares that

> Since September 11, 2001, reality has not only outstripped fiction, it's destroying it. It's impossible to write about this subject, and yet impossible to write about anything else. Nothing else touches us. […] This thing happened, and it is impossible to relate. (*WoW*, 8f.)[14]

Echoing this statement, the American narrator, Carthew Yorston, makes near the end of the book, which coincides with the end of his own life (he jumps out of the window of the 107th floor of the towering inferno with his son) that "I wanted to live in a virtual world; I'm dying in a real one" (*WoW*, 248).

The elusive play of being and its appearances so often associated with 9/11 naturally led to considerations on the dialectics of visibility and invisibility, since theories of perception are central to the validation of knowledge in the Western philosophical tradition, as the role accorded to the senses in classical debates between empiricists, sceptics, and rationalists amply demonstrates. The notion of "the spectral" as an ambiguous zone between reality and fantasy has enjoyed much favour in some

---

[14] In the following in-text quotations indicated by the abbreviation "*WoW*" refer to the English translation of the novel, Frédéric Beigbeder, *Windows on the World*, trans. by Frank Wynne (London: Fourth Estate, 2004), 8f.

philosophical circles following the publication of Jacques Derrida's influential *Specters of Marx*.[15] It is not surprising, therefore, that Slavoj Žižek, for example, would resort to the notion of spectrality in his analysis of September 11.[16] The "screen fantasmatic apparition" of obsessively repeated images that keep haunting the viewers' memories has a ghostly quality to it, while the anxiety of terrorism and virtual warfare implies the silent, uncontrollable threat of immaterial weapons of mass destruction such as chemical and biological substances invisible to the eye. As Žižek pointed out, what we did not see was more important than what we saw about the catastrophe. More than the shockingly visible, there was the uncanny, disturbing invisible: "And the same 'derealization' of the horror went on after the WTC bombings: while the number of 6000 victims is repeated all the time, it is surprising how little of the actual carnage we see—no dismembered bodies, no blood, no desperate faces of the dying people."[17]

In *Windows on the World* the spectral takes the form of a sign written in French (*Crédit Lyonnais*) that has remained on a New York building where the narrator used to work long after the bank that employed him has left the premises, haunting the neighbourhood, as it were, with the narrator's ghostly personal memories of his own American past: "I'm evicted by my past. My past wants nothing to do with me. My past accompanies me through the revolving door" (*WoW*, 236). Walking through the streets of New York two years after the attacks, Beigbeder's fictional double sees his reflection in the tinted windows of glass towers, "a tall, stooped silhouette in a black coat, a heron with glasses walking in enormous strides. Fleeing the image, I walk faster, but it follows me like a bird of prey" (*WoW*, 235). Unable to shake off the ghastly, uncanny presence of his double, the narrator compares art to a "window on the world" and describes his own predilection for auto-fiction as an attempt not to reveal himself, but to melt away, presumably like the Twin Towers themselves. "A novel is a two-way mirror," the narrator writes, "behind which I hide so I can see and not be seen" (*WoW*, 236).

---

[15] See Derrida, *Specters of Marx: The State of the Debt, the Work of Mourning and the New International*. Derrida coined the term "hauntology" to point to the ambiguous status of spectrality, neither ideal nor material.

[16] Žižek, *Welcome to the Desert of the Real*.

[17] Ibid., 3.

Several temporal dimensions are present in Beigbeder's reading of 9/11. While instantaneity marks the relationship between the event and its global broadcasting, its subsequent memorialization in written, visual and monumental/architectural form implies the long term of historical time. In Beigbeder's text, the victims of 9/11 are said to continue to haunt the site of the attacks long after their death, ensuring that they will never be forgotten, that the work of memorialization represented by the video archives of the tragedy and the spatial absence that is Ground Zero will go on forever. "I'm starting to see things differently," says the American narrator. "As if they're not happening now, as if they're already memories […] The world is so much more beautiful when you're no longer really a part of it. I know that I'll remember even when I no longer have a memory. Because, even after death, others will remember us" (*WoW*, 265).

The continued remembrance, whether within living or deceased subjects, that contrasts with the fleeting quality of the event itself, reinforces the survivors' duty to recollect traumatic events of great proportions. That is the way in which the Shoah can be said to haunt Beigbeder's text. The French narrator explicitly equates the two catastrophes, despite the staggering disproportion in the number of their victims, and quotes documentary filmmaker Claude Lanzmann, author of the monumental filmic memorial *Shoah* (1985), as saying that "the Shoah is a mystery: September 11 is too" (*WoW*, 263) and "The Windows on the World was a high-class gas chamber. The customers were gassed, burned and reduced to ash. To them, as to many others, we owe a duty of memory" (*WoW*, 274).

As Slavoj Žižek mentioned in the passage quoted above, despite the continuous screen presence of the planes hitting the towers long after the event, the subsequent "war on terrorism" was largely kept out of view, especially in the American media. The lesson of Vietnam was that the broadcasting of combat footage, shots of burning villages, and images of "body bags" on their way back home had been largely responsible for the rise of the anti-war movement and the shift of public opinion against "the dirty war." The proper conduct of the wars in Afghanistan and Iraq implied both government censorship and media self-censorship as to how much visual and written information would be offered to the public. As speech took over image, and the discursive framing of 9/11 and its afterlives replaced the haunting, eerily disturbing graphic forms of the smoking towers, the aftermath of 9/11 became selectively visible.

According to Carol Gluck, the Pentagon bought all the satellite pictures available on the market in order to erase all traces of what was going on in the air and on the ground. As for the "mainstream media," they accepted, somewhat reluctantly, the government's request that Bin Laden's second videotape not be made public, officially for fear that it might contain coded messages for his men. In Carol Gluck's words:

> The war in Afghanistan had at the beginning no precise narrative structure; and, more importantly, no image was available: neither the typical Vietnam war scenes (helicopters landing on grassy areas, running soldiers, thick smoke from an explosion on the horizon), nor the high tech images of Scud missiles and "smart bombs" provided by the Pentagon during the Gulf War. It was a television war that the viewers could not "see".[18]

And thus, not only because of the strategic and political imperatives of secrecy, but because of the kind of military campaign it was, a "dematerialized" war waged with night raids, invisible strikes from above, and covert operations with undercover elite troops on the ground.

Frédéric Beigbeder also refers to the invisibility of the victims' bodies in what he calls one of the greatest post-war campaigns of media disinformation ever perpetrated. "Don't show the blood, I can't bear to look at it," he writes. "When a building collapses, feel free to repeat the footage endlessly. But whatever you do, don't show what was inside: our bodies" (*WoW*, 262). Rendering suffering invisible contributes to its dematerialization, and Beigbeder echoes Žižek's comments on "the derealization of the horror" performed by the absence of any visual representations of the victims' death. In Beigbeder's words,

> I think that if you hide your suffering, it disappears. And it's true, in a sense: it is invisible, and therefore it does not exist, since we live in a world that worships what is visible, demonstrable, material. My suffering is not material; it is hidden. I am my own revisionist (*WoW*, 29).

As opposed to the visual censorship performed by television coverage, the privilege of literature, according to the narrator, is to show the invisible, to speak the unspeakable: "It may be impossible, but it is [fiction's] raison d'être. Literature is a *Mission: Impossible*. [...] Nowadays, books

---

[18] Gluck, "11 Septembre. Guerre et Télévision au XXIe siècle," 150.

must go where television does not" (*WoW*, 295). Beigbeder can then claim that the only way of knowing what happened in the restaurant located on the 107th floor of the World Trade Center, on September 11, 2001, between 8.30 and 10.29 a.m., is to invent it. In this view, fiction is the only substitute for the lack of imagination that lies at the core of our inability to believe that the towers could collapse:

> "Singular lack of imagination. Confidence in the supremacy of reality over fiction. It's like being inside a chimney," says one of the firefighters in [...] *The Towering Inferno* (released in 1974, the year the World Trade Center was inaugurated). The fact that they didn't attempt an air rescue is probably because the cops had seen the movie in which police drop cables from a helicopter in an attempt to save people trapped by a fire on the top floor of a skyscraper. In the film, the chopper crashes onto the roof. At 9:14, the police probably didn't want to imitate art. (*WoW*, 144)

The French original of the last sentence literally reads: "The police probably didn't want to lend any reason to fiction," which makes the point more cogently.

Art or fiction in this case refers to film through the allusion to *The Towering Inferno*, and Beigbeder here repeats one of the most ubiquitous clichés on 9/11, namely that the attacks look like the standard fare offered by countless Hollywood disaster films. Beigbeder's perhaps more original point is that visual fiction (as opposed to literature) has a profound impact on the way the police and rescuers as witnesses chose to act in the wake of the catastrophe. The novel quotes a non-fictional individual, Mehdi Dadgarian, presented as a survivor from the 72nd floor, as having told the media: "I couldn't stop thinking: it's not real, it's a film. It can't be real" (*WoW*, 271). In Beigbeder's view, the superimposition of fictional images over what was really happening framed the bystanders' interpretation of what they were witnessing, thereby orienting their responses to the spectacle of disaster and possibly endangering their own lives.

> The "killer cloud," a tornado of rubble, 100-foot steel girders like train tracks falling from the sky [...] is an image lifted from disaster movies: we've seen the same scene in *The Blob*, *Godzilla*, *Independence Day*, *Armageddon*, in *Die Hard 2* and in *Deep Impact*: that morning, reality contented itself with imitating special effects. Some bystanders didn't

run for cover, so convinced were they that they'd seen it all before. (*WoW*, 266)

Beigbeder's repeated references to film in relation to the believability of 9/11, both during and after the event, lead him to considerations about the cinematographic nature of American culture found in other French depictions of life in the United States.[19] Beigbeder claims that

> "in the United States, life is like a movie, since all movies are shot on location. All Americans are actors, and their houses, their cars, and their desires all seem artificial. Truth is reinvented every morning in America. It's a country that has decided to look like something on celluloid" (*WoW*, 21) and "In America, dreams come true not because Americans want their dreams to come true, but simply because they dream. Dream without thinking of the consequences" (*WoW*, 210).

Literature, as opposed to film, is in Beigbeder's view, the only medium where the invisibility of suffering can actually stimulate the reader's imagination, rather than stifle it, because the evocative power of the written word, as distinct from the seduction of the image, does not provide the crippling illusion of reality. "From here," the French author/narrator says at the end of the book, which describes the final agony of those trapped in the restaurant,

> we can penetrate the unspeakable, the inexpressible. Please excuse our misuse of ellipsis. I have cut out the awful descriptions. I have not done so out of propriety, nor out of respect for the victims, because I believe that describing their slow agonies, their ordeal, is also a mark of respect. I cut them because, in my opinion, it is more appalling still to allow you to imagine what became of them (*WoW*, 272).

The censorship of many aspects of the official versions and media coverage of 9/11 could not but give rise to doubts as to the nature of its reality. Within six hours of the attacks, a discussion on an Internet chat room suggested that the collapse of the towers looked like an act of

---

[19] See, for example, Jean Baudrillard: "It is not the least of America's charm that even outside the movie theatres the whole country is cinematic [...] the American city seems to have stepped right out of the movies" (*America*, 56).

controlled demolition.[20] One week later, *Le Monde* mentioned the existence of individuals and groups that viewed the attacks as the result of an "inside job" by the US government. Interestingly enough, the same newspaper addressed the tenth anniversary by regretting the spread of rumours regarding 9/11.[21] According to the article, among the factors explaining the phenomenon are the need to reduce anxiety, the excessive coverage of rumours by the media in an attempt to disprove them, and the spread of "cognitive relativism" among intellectuals and the educated elites. The latter, ironically, make up most of *Le Monde*'s readership. I take the charge of "cognitive relativism" here to mean the usual complaint that the postmodernists' questioning of the validity of truth claims by science makes all truth claims, whether regarding culture, religion, or politics, socially constructed and therefore relative to a particular place and time. This generalized scepticism about the foundation of truth, and the lack of simple, direct equation between language and reality, words and things, would prevent any value judgement being passed on any belief or practice. This is precisely what is at stake in current discussions about the spread of "fake news" in the era of "post-truth."

In fact, the notion of "conspiracy theory" itself harbours a plurality of meanings and is used in different contexts to perform different ideological functions. As in the case of *Le Monde*'s article, the term is often used negatively to discredit views that seem impossible to document in a convincing manner. Adepts of conspiracy theories are described as either deluded or dishonest, or both, and their assertions as motivated by bad faith, resentment, or propagandistic motives. Disgruntled individuals or groups are said to react to political and socio-economic decisions that affect them adversely by giving into well-known psychological mechanisms such as denial, wishful thinking, or even self-fulfilling prophecy.[22]

But not all suspicions, rumours or secret plots are a figment of the imagination, an exercise in bad faith, or an attempt to manipulate public opinion. Some of them eventually prove to be true. To stay within the orbit of post-9/11 developments, the claim that Saddam Hussein

---

[20] Summers and Swan, *The Eleventh Day: The Full Story of 9/11 and Osama bin Laden*, 93.

[21] *Le Monde*, September 11, 2011.

[22] For two recent studies of conspiracy theories in the context of American history and foreign policy in South-west Asia, see Butter and Reinkowski (eds.), *Conspiracy Theories in the United States and the Middle East*, and Butter, *Plots, Designs, and Schemes: American Conspiracy Theories from the Puritans to the Present*.

did not possess the famous weapons of mass destruction seemed at first a wild allegation motivated by political agendas ranging from pacifism and anti-imperialism to a desire to spare the Iraqi dictatorship a likely military defeat. Today, most people would agree that there were no weapons of mass destruction on Iraqi soil, and that Saddam Hussein had maintained the fiction of their existence as a deterrent against his enemies, both inside and outside the country. Conspiracy theories, then, can be viewed either as phantasmatic imaginings or as reasonable suspicions that defy conventional wisdom and deserve further investigation. In the remaining pages, I will refer to both uses of the term, in part because I am less interested in the validity of these claims than in what they reveal about our increasing inability to agree on the truth of an event such as 9/11.

In February 2002, French activist and essayist Thierry Meyssan published a book-length refutation of the official version of 9/11 entitled *L'effroyable imposture* [The Horrifying Deception], weakly translated in the English edition as "The Big Lie."[23] A former Catholic conservative turned left-wing militant, Meyssan was known in media circles for revealing damaging information about the French extreme right, the traditionalist Catholic organization Opus Dei, and corruption in the Vatican. Meyssan later became a fierce critic of George W. Bush and American neo-conservative foreign policy, continuing to publish on 9/11 several years after the fact. He subsequently moved to Syria, worked for the Russian media, and claimed in 2011 that US agents had tried to assassinate him while he was in Tripoli reporting on the war in Libya. In *The Big Lie*, Meyssan claimed that no plane had crashed into the Pentagon, a thesis partly based on the absence of any visible remnants of a large airline carrier in the first photos taken after the crash. The issue of photographic evidence is characteristic of the role played in controversies about 9/11 by electronic artefacts such as pictures, films, and videotapes, because of our growing capacity to alter and duplicate the physical world.

Although the book focused primarily on the attack on the Pentagon, and did not address the collapse of the Twin Towers at any length, the argument laid the foundation of what would become key elements of 9/11 conspiracy theories: the puzzling fact that the North American Air Defense Command and the US Air Force were unable to intercept the hijacked planes; the presence in the Bush Administration of politicians

---

[23] Meyssan, *9/11: The Big Lie*.

and advisers closely connected to oil business interests, making the invasion of Afghanistan, and later of Iraq, a classic case of a neo-colonial attempt to control the flow of oil from the Caspian Sea to the Red Sea; and the publication in the years preceding 9/11 of position papers and policy memos from influential figures in the American President's neo-conservative entourage. These position papers advocated the reformulation of American foreign policy after the Cold War, especially in relation to the Arab and/or Muslim world and to what would soon be known as the "Greater Middle East," from Mauritania to Pakistan.

The publication of Meyssan's book sparked a storm in French media and among opinion-makers, gave rise to a series of TV documentaries, talk shows, articles and books denouncing his thesis as fabrication, rumour-mongering or outright propaganda, and recast traditional French anti-Americanism in new ways, more adapted to the new geopolitical environment created by 9/11 itself. But the phenomenon was hardly limited to France, traditionally the most unreliable ally of the United States. In 2003, two books questioning the official version of the event appeared in Germany, one by Socialist politician and former Secretary of Defence Andreas Von Bülow, and the other by journalist Gherard Wiznewsky. It is significant that the most elaborate theories appeared in France and Germany, the two countries whose political elites and public opinion alike most vehemently opposed the invasion of Iraq. By 2004, the worldwide coalition of intellectuals, politicians, artists, journalists, scientists, bloggers, and militants known as "the 9/11 Truth Movement" had members in the United States as well, in part because the inability of the US military to find weapons of mass destruction after the collapse of Saddam Hussein's regime confirmed earlier suspicions that the American government had been involved in the 2001 attacks.

The immediate response to 9/11 in France had been a public expression of support for the victims' families and the American people: on September 12, *Le Monde* stated "Today, we are all Americans."[24] This early show of solidarity gave way to familiar forms of opposition to US foreign policy soon thereafter. Some 150,000 copies of *L'effroyable imposture* were sold in France in the year following its publication, the

---

[24] On the emergence of a similar universal and global subject identified with the victims of terrorism, see the recent example of the ubiquitous statement "Je suis Charlie" [I am Charlie] as a response to the attacks on the French magazine *Charlie-Hebdo* in January 2015.

book was subsequently translated into more than twenty languages, and a sequel, entitled *Le Pentagate* (2002), soon followed. As a best-selling author, Meyssan could not escape public scrutiny and he quickly became a very controversial figure himself. After the publication of *The Big Lie*, he faced growing opposition from some members of his own alternative media group, the Voltaire Network. Books and articles questioned the validity of his assertions, and critics denounced his frequent trips to Iran and Syria to talk with authorities, as well as the presence of Holocaust deniers among his close collaborators. The fictional status of the book in the eyes of its critics raises issues linked to the broader field of fictional and non-fictional textual and filmic accounts of 9/11. The attention the book called upon itself divided the French media, brought about unexpected alliances and realignments among the intelligentsia, and played a role in the constitution of a post-9/11 "anti-anti-Americanism."

The Great Burning of Rome in 64 CE is the archetype of the catastrophic event generating unconfirmed rumours and resentment towards the sovereign, either for its incompetence or for its cynicism, or for both. According to Tacitus, Nero returned to the city as soon as he heard the news, and made several buildings accessible to the homeless, including his own Gardens. However, he was blamed for his lack of empathy, and, in the historian's words, rumours quickly spread that "while the city was burning, [the Emperor] had gone on his private stage and, comparing modern calamities with ancient, had sung of the destruction of Troy."[25] As the fire raged on for several days, conspiracy theories emerged, imputing sinister plans to the Emperor, including the deliberate destruction of the city to found a new one named after himself. In order to regain the favour of his public opinion, Nero famously blamed the Christians, and made peace with the Roman people by throwing many of the former to the lions.

Even though what the secret services call "false flag proposals" obviously go back to ancient times, our contemporary societies are particularly prone to distrust the powers that be. Transparency on the part of any authority, a guiding principle of democratic dynamics, and the multiplication of alternative, uncontrollable sources of information force governments, business corporations and other institutions to become increasingly secretive regarding their goals and their decisions. It was

---

[25] Tacitus, *The Annals of Imperial Rome*.

much easier to convince the citizenry of the inevitability of war or economic austerity fifty years ago, even in liberal societies, than it is now. What Noam Chomsky called in the 1960s the manufacture of consent is increasingly difficult to achieve. The example of WikiLeaks is a case in point.

As a result, corporate bodies from British Petroleum to the Catholic Church try to restrict the media's and the public's access to information, in turn fuelling suspicions that something is going on that they do not want you to know. And it cannot be good, otherwise why would they want to hide it from you? Contrary to the birthers, who claimed that Barack Obama was not an American citizen, those who oppose the official version of 9/11, known in the blogosphere as "the truthers," did not simply deny evidence. They produced counter-evidence of their own, and a large part of it rested on claims of scientific legitimacy. One of the most interesting aspects of the 9/11 debate is that it gave rise to a series of disputes among professional scientists as to the validity of the opposing camp's claims to the rational explanation of the facts. One of the first rebuttals of the accepted version to emerge after the event was the so-called "controlled demolition" thesis. According to it, the impact of the planes was not sufficient to explain the collapse of the buildings. Some physical cause of another nature must have been at work, most likely the use of explosives detonated at the same time as the attack from the skies.

Such a seemingly incredible allegation with such far-reaching political consequences led to a scientific debate involving experts from a variety of fields, from physics, chemistry, and astronomy to computer science and architectural engineering. The participants were not militants, propagandists and bloggers, but credentialled researchers from highly ranked universities in the United States and abroad, including Purdue University, Brigham Young University and the University of Copenhagen. The discussion of nanothermite composites and the burning temperature of jet fuel raged on in the columns of professional journals with names such as *The Open Chemical Physics Journal* and in magazines with a wider circulation such as *Popular Mechanics* and *Scientific American*.[26]

A similar, if less wide-ranging, dispute also took place regarding the Pentagon site, following Meyssan's and others' assertion that the impact

---

[26] See, for example, Dean, "Physicist says heat substance felled WTC"; Harrit et al., "Active Thermitic Material Discovered in Dust from the 9/11 World Trade Center Catastrophe"; "Debunking the 9/11 Myths: Special Report", *Popular Mechanics*, March

on the façade of the building was not large enough to have been made by a Boeing 757, but was the result of a missile launched from a fighter jet.[27] Again, civil engineers weighed in on the debate, mostly to rebuke the missile theory, and every single television show on the topic brought in its own aeronautical expert, airline crash site investigator or long-distance air carrier pilot to discuss empirical evidence contained in the plane's flight data recorders or the debris found on the ground. The dispute involved respected government agencies such as the National Institute of Standards and Technology, who backed the official version, and each camp ended up questioning the professional competence of the other. What had started as a highly charged emotional event was being adjudicated in the supposedly neutral, objective, dispassionate court of scientific knowledge, but to no avail.

What are we to make of the fact that the researchers did not agree, that the protocols of rational inquiry failed to deliver on their promise to settle the matter once and for all? Tweeters, militants and TV commentators are expected to be biased, but why would a professor of civil engineering lend credence to supposedly unfounded claims of conspiracy, unless he was convinced of the validity of his or her claim? If experts armed with the methods of the physical sciences cannot agree on the material "facts" of 9/11, how will anyone ever be able to find out what really happened? If science cannot settle the dispute by firmly establishing what went on, then are we not thrown back to the infinite regress of interpretation that feeds conspiracy theories? Theorists as paranoids can never be convinced, since every piece of evidence put forward to discredit their views is immediately questioned as having been manufactured by their enemies, and every eyewitness testimony is disqualified as having been coerced or bought.

Many organizations in the 9/11 Truth Movement demand the creation of a non-partisan, unbiased international investigation into the matter. But who would lead such a fact-finding mission? How would the members of the investigative team be selected? Wouldn't those whose expectations were not met by the results of the investigation call foul

---

2005. The *Popular Mechanics* issue was later expanded into a book, cf. Dunbar and Reagan (eds.), *Debunking 9/11 Myths: Why Conspiracy Theories Can't Stand Up to the Facts*.

[27] See Novitski, "Pentagon Battered but Firm".

play? The 9/11 Commission was supposed to be one of these objective truth-finding entities. Not only did its findings fail to convince most sceptics, they themselves became in their critics' eyes part and parcel of the plot to hide the truth, together with the scientific reports of the National Institute of Standards and Technology or Barack Obama's June 2009 speech to the Muslim World. The capacity of technology to produce virtual simulacra can only add to the ontological instability that is central to the world of cyber-reality. One of the most radical theses regarding 9/11 was that no plane actually hit the World Trade Center, but that the videos of the burning towers were later doctored with the help of holographic images that made missiles look like airplanes. Since the whole thing resembled a Hollywood terror movie anyway, why not assume that the video footage was just as much the product of special effects as *Star Wars* or *Avatar*? The questioning of the indexical status of images equally applies to the still pictures of the Pentagon crash site as to the videos of Osama bin Laden the Bush administration used after their release by Al-Jazeera to prove once and for all that Al-Qaeda was responsible for the attacks. The claim that the bin Laden tapes are fake rests both on visual data (it's not really him on the tapes, but a look-alike) and oral clues (the translation of the Arabic soundtrack into English is said to be either inaccurate or the brainchild of the US secret services). Some have argued that the speaker not only was physically slightly different from bin Laden, but that he could not have been a Muslim, since he was wearing a gold ring, which is strictly forbidden by Islamic faith.[28]

The thesis of the doctored tapes was not only popular among supporters of Al-Qaeda, as would be expected, but among growing numbers of "truthers" in the West. Once again, academic expertise was brought to bear on the issue as a way of legitimizing counter-narratives. A German television documentary on the "Jalalabad tape" released in December 2001 included interviews with two independent translators and a scholar who called into question the reliability of the soundtrack. Gernot Rotter, a professor of Islamic and Arabic Studies at the Asia-Africa Institute at the University of Hamburg, was quoted in the broadcast as saying that "The American translators who listened to the tapes and transcribed them apparently wrote a lot of things in that they wanted to hear but that cannot be heard on the tape no matter how many times you listen

---

[28] See Morris, "U.S. urged to detail origin of tape".

to it."²⁹ The insistence by the speaker on several of the tapes that Al-Qaeda bore the sole responsibility for 9/11 could only raise the suspicion that bin Laden's avatar was overdoing it simply to discredit the thesis that he had not acted alone but in concert with the CIA, his former employer during the war between the Soviets and the Taliban in Afghanistan. In a further twist of the spiralling out of control of interpretations, the government of Iran, in its desire to establish that Shiite terrorists are the only true enemies of America, has used the thesis of the collusion between bin Laden and the US secret services to minimize the role played by a Sunni organization such as Al-Qaeda in the war against the United States and its allies. In other words, Sunni terrorist groups should not take credit for having brought the evil empire to its knees, since they could not have pulled it off without the help of the American government itself.

The complex network of narratives surrounding September 11 not only includes contemporary developments, it reaches backwards to other defining moments in time, many of them also engulfed in the culture of conspiracy. Suspicions of government involvement and stonewalling have been raised after every single terrorist act in the past twenty years, including the Oklahoma City bombing of 1995, the 2004 and 2005 terrorist attacks in Madrid and London, and, of course, the assassination of bin Laden himself in 2011, which was immediately framed as a major plot to accredit the official version of 9/11. Is America's number one enemy really dead, or was the whole operation a hoax? Why did the White House refuse to publish pictures of bin Laden's dead body? Why were the remains not brought back to American soil instead of being dropped in the ocean, thereby erasing all evidence? Unsurprisingly, the Obama administration's set of responses, i.e., to avoid offending Muslims because of the lack of proper burial, further antagonizing terrorists and their supporters, and turning the slain leader of Al-Qaeda into a martyr for the cause, failed to convince a lot of people, and the controversy machine was once again up and running, humming beautifully.

I mentioned earlier that Tacitus' account of the Great Fire in Rome contained an explicit reference to the destruction of Troy. Similarly, 9/11 has been caught up in an extensive web of interrelated memories

---

²⁹ "Bin-Laden-Video: Falschübersetzung als Beweismittel?" WDR, Das Erste, *MONITOR*, no. 485, December 20, 2001; see also "Osama Tape Appears Fake, Experts Conclude," *Looking Glass News*, June 1, 2006. http://www.lookingglassnews.org/viewstory.php?storyid=6233 (accessed 12.4.2015).

connecting it to previous events that are also said to have profoundly altered the course of history and produced significant cultural changes, such as the Japanese bombings of Pearl Harbor, the assassination of John F. Kennedy, and the fall of the Berlin Wall. One measure of the impact of some of these world-historical events on the collective psyche is the extent to which they found their way in the narratives of individual lives, as in the answer to the questions: "Where were you when Kennedy was shot?," "What were you doing when the towers collapsed?" Most people remember, as collective and individual times collided. Because these events were televised, they have become part of the archival memory of entire generations, regularly broadcast anew in the media, and available at a stroke of the keyboard on the Internet. In the case of November 22, 1963, and September 11, 2001, the tragedies took place on American soil and were in large part the consequence of national political dynamics, but they immediately took on a global character, becoming part and parcel of world history, affecting the life of people everywhere. The Fall of the Berlin Wall also became an iconic visual moment, whose impact far exceeded the limits of German domestic politics.

Thierry Meyssan's *The Big Lie* was one of the first attempts to explicitly link 9/11 to the Kennedy assassination. The core of Meyssan's argument was based on a comparison between the CIA's "Operation Northwoods" in the early 1960s and the planned invasion of Iraq. The documents pertaining to this covert operation aimed at ending Fidel Castro's regime after the failure of the Bay of Pigs invasion in 1961 were declassified by the Clinton administration in the early 1990s, at a time when Oliver Stone's film *JFK*, released in 1991, had renewed the public's interest in the assassination. According to the documents released to public scrutiny, the aim of Operation Northwoods was "to place the United States in the apparent position of suffering defensible grievances from a rash and irresponsible government of Cuba and to develop an international image of a Cuban threat to peace in the Western Hemisphere."[30] In order to achieve this objective, the project included a series of "false-flag proposals": hijackings, bombings, and the introduction of false evidence incriminating the Cuban government.

---

[30] See http://www.gwu.edu/~nsarchiv/news/20010430/ (accessed 12.4.2015), for the 15-page document entitled "Chairman, Joint Chiefs of Staff, Justification for US Military Intervention in Cuba [includes cover memoranda], March 13, 1962." The quote is on page 5.

One option was to attack the base in Guantánamo (another striking connection with post-9/11 developments), others included the destruction of a US ship in Cuban territorial waters (an incident reminiscent of the deliberate sinking of the *U.S.S. Maine*, which was used as a pretext for the Spanish-American War of 1898), a campaign of terror against Cuban exiles in Miami, the bombing of one of Cuba's neighbours to spread fear of military aggression from Castro, an attack on a civilian air charter on its way to the Caribbean, and even the destruction of a space flight with John Glenn on board to shock international public opinion and convince the world of the threat represented by the Castro regime. Substitute Saddam for the Cuban dictator, and the downing of a civilian plane with the use of a civilian plane as a missile, and the similarities are striking. That is where documented evidence meets unconfirmed speculation, however. Meyssan's account of Operation Northwoods (based on declassified documents) lead him to the yet unproven claim that Kennedy was killed because he refused to go along with extremist anti-communist elements in the government, the secret service, and the military.

The proliferation of connections between September 11 and other culturally defining moments in our recent history might mean that the truth of the event will never be settled in the realm of academic knowledge, whether by aerospace engineers, political scientists, or cultural historians, even if archives are opened up and secret documents are published in the future, as in the case of Operation Northwoods, whose release only fuelled more suspicions regarding Kennedy's assassination. The 1980s "historians' debate" (*Historikerstreit*) in Germany about the historiography of Nazism or the more recent "memory wars" in France opposing militant groups, professional historians, and conservative politicians in a struggle over the legitimate assessment of colonialism and the slave trade clearly show that scientific knowledge today cannot help but being dragged, willy-nilly, into the political passions of the day.

In anticipation of the tenth anniversary of the attacks, an organization called ReOpen911 called for a mass demonstration in Paris in support "of peace and an end to the silence and state-sponsored lies regarding terrorism and illegal wars."[31] The demonstration included the performance of a song called "Barry and Tower 7" (the building next to the

---

[31] http://www.reopen911.info/11-septembre/grande-manifestation-a-paris-le-dimanche-11-septembre/, August 26, 2011 (accessed 4.4.2015).

World Trade Center that also collapsed) by a musical group involved in the Movement for the Truth on 9/11, an exhibition on the attacks, and a presentation on the results of the decade-long investigation of the event. To set the stage for its commemoration of the tenth anniversary, ReOpen911commissioned a French survey from June 6 to June 24, 2011. Some 58% of the individuals polled doubted the official version of September 11. Half of the French respondents did not rule out the fact that the American authorities may have let the attacks happen, while 34% found admissible the claim that the American government might have been actively involved in the attacks in one form or another. A similar poll conducted in Germany in January 2011 concluded that 90% of the German respondents did not believe in the official version.[32] The cycle of controversies, conspiracies and self-fulfilling prophecies regarding 9/11 and subsequent major terrorist attacks still has a bright future ahead.

References

Baudrillard, Jean. *La violence du Monde* (Paris: Le Félin, 2003).
———. *Amérique*, transl. by Chris Turner, *America* (London: Verso, 1988).
———. *The Gulf War Did Not Take Place*, transl. by Paul Patton (Seattle: University of Washington Press, 2012).
Butter, Michael. *Plots, Designs, and Schemes: American Conspiracy Theories from the Puritans to the Present* (Berlin/Boston: de Gruyter, 2014).
Butter, Michael, and Maurus Reinkowski (eds.), *Conspiracy Theories in the United States and the Middle East. A Comparative Approach* (Berlin/Boston: de Gruyter, 2014).
Beigbeder, Frédéric. *Windows on the World*, transl. by Frank Wynne (London: Fourth Estate, 2004).
Dean, Suzanne. "Physicist says heat substance felled WTC," *Desert Morning News*, April 10, 2006.
Derrida, Jacques. *Specters of Marx: The State of the Debt, the Work of Mourning and the New International* (London: Routledge, 2006).

---

[32] http://www.reopen911.info/11-septembre/sondage-h-e-c-pour-reopen911-les-francais-et-le-11-9-11-questions-sur-le-11-septembre/, September 8, 2011 (accessed 4.4.2015). On the German survey, see Kurt Nimmo, "Nearly 90 Percent of Germans Do Not Believe Official 9/11 Fairy Tale," http://www.infowars.com/nearly-90-percent-of-germans-do-not-believe-official-911-fairy-tale/ (accessed 12.4.2015).

Dunbar, David, and Brad Reagan (eds.), *Debunking 9/11 Myths: Why Conspiracy Theories Can't Stand Up to the Facts* (New York: Hearst, 2006).
Gluck, Carol. "11 Septembre. Guerre et Télévision au XXIe siècle," *Annales. Histoire, Sciences sociales*, vol. 1 (2003), 135–162.
Harrit, Niels H., et al., "Active Thermitic Material Discovered in Dust from the 9/11 World Trade Center Catastrophe," *The Open Chemical Physics Journal*, vol. 2, 2009, February 13, 2009.
Meyssan, Thierry. *9/11 The Big Lie* (London: Carnot, 2002).
Morris, Steven. "U.S. urged to detail origin of tape," *The Guardian*, December 15, 2001.
Nimmo, Kurt. "Nearly 90 Percent of Germans Do Not Believe Official 9/11 Fairy Tale," http://www.infowars.com/nearly-90-percent-of-germans-do-not-believe-official-911-fairy-tale/, (accessed 12.4.2015).
Novitski, B. J. "Pentagon Battered but Firm," *Architecture Week*, October 3, 2001.
Summers, Anthony, and Robbyn Swan. *The Eleventh Day: The Full Story of 9/11 and Osama bin Laden* (New York: Ballantine, 2011).
Tacitus, Publius Cornelius. *The Annals of Imperial Rome*, ("The Burning of Rome," 360–368), transl. by Michael Grant (London: Penguin, 1989).
Žižek, Slavoj. *Welcome to the Desert of the Real* (London: Verso, 2002).
———. "Passion du réel, passion du semblant," *Erès. Savoirs et Clinique*, vol. 2 (2003), 39–56.

Author Biography

Jean-Philippe Mathy is Professor of French and Comparative Literature, and Director of the School of Literatures, Cultures and Linguistics at the University of Illinois, Urbana-Champaign. His research interests include French-American cultural relations, contemporary France, and French and European intellectual history. Major publications are *Extrême-Occident: French Intellectuals and America* (University of Chicago Press, 1993), *French Resistance: The French-American Culture Wars* (University of Minnesota Press, 2000) and *Melancholy Politics: Loss, Mourning, and Memory in Late Modern France* (The Pennsylvania State University Press, 2011). He is currently working on a book about the legacy of 9/11 in France.

Cultural and Historical Memory in English and German Discursive Responses to 9/11

Sandra Singer

> Know my habits, way ahead of time
> Listening to me on your satellite
> (The Rolling Stones, "Fingerprint File")

INTRODUCTION

This chapter focuses on comparisons and explorations of the incorporation of 9/11 into the English and German national contexts. Why is 9/11 creatively fused with the critique of the class system in Britain in Ian McEwan's *Saturday* (2005)? What does it mean to compare 9/11 events in the Red Army Faction (RAF) context for Bernhard Schlink in *Das Wochenende* (2008, English translation *The Weekend*, 2010)? The people cast in these two texts anticipate terror, in part on account of

---

S. Singer (✉)
University of Guelph, Guelph, Canada

© The Author(s) 2017
S. Frank (ed.), *9/11 in European Literature*,
DOI 10.1007/978-3-319-64209-3_6

experiencing violence and horror in day-to-day urban life (*Saturday*) or being exposed to political terrorism (*The Weekend*).[1]

By way of symbols, narrative perspectives, and genre history, both novels incorporate their national traumas of violence into the cultural memory of September 11, 2001. 9/11 is configured along an historical timeline stretching back through generations, even centuries. In the case of McEwan's *Saturday*, the timeline reaches all the way back to British imperial warfare of the mid-nineteenth century. Schlink's *Das Wochenende* references Nazi historical memory. These cultural-historical reflections—positioned with respect to post-9/11 transnational media influences—provide evidence for Kristiaan Versluys's claim that "discursive responses" to 9/11 through fiction are capable of parsing ideological, dogmatic arguments fostered through mass media.[2] Seen through the example of these two European novels, the world is more fractious than the pervasive post-9/11 American global military model encouraged through mainstream media networks.[3]

Removed from the US-led media and military war on terrorism, fiction often inside and definitely outside the US potentially engages with the ethical or "universal" (socialist) principles Baudrillard advances, even when truncated notions of democracy, freedom, culture, and human rights bear in his view a "deceptive similarity" to globalization.[4] "What can thwart the system [of integrated technologies, the market, tourism, information]," claims Baudrillard in "The Violence of the Global" is "singularities."[5] McEwan and Schlink offer singular characters—what Lukács may have termed types—with conflicted life histories whose internal and external struggles are fathomed in relationship to 9/11 and subsequent events. Importantly, protagonists Henry in *Saturday* and Jörg in *The Weekend* inhabit a literate cultural milieu. The novels use

---

[1] This chapter ascribes to Schmid, "The Revised Academic Consensus Definition of Terrorism."

[2] Versluys, *Out of the Blue: September 11 and the Novel*, 1–17.

[3] This American military model originated with President George W. Bush's 2001 clarion call for a "War on Terror" including various domestic securitization laws (with extended time limitations wherein the State of Exception lasts beyond a decade) deemed necessary to counter post-9/11 "New Terrorism."

[4] Baudrillard, "The Violence of the Global," 87.

[5] Ibid., 96.

intertextual references productively to engage with ethical principles such as Baudrillard recommends.

American literary critic Stacey Olster succinctly condenses Versluys's categorizing of shared traits of 9/11 novels: there is "the tendency to express the actuality of 9/11 by way of allegory and indirection," such as "the 1945 firebombing of Dresden and atomic bombing of Hiroshima in Jonathan Safran Foer's *Extremely Loud and Incredibly Close* (2005), and the tendency of the imagination to blunt the impact of 9/11 with recuperative measures," such as "the invocation of poetry" steeped in British cultural experience by Matthew Arnold as source for restorative, "transcendent meaning" in McEwan's *Saturday* (2005).[6] The first approach Olster describes narrowly accords with *Das Wochenende*; the second with *Saturday*.

Worthy of comparison in several respects, McEwan's and Schlink's work each registers the impact of the events of 9/11 on the European experience. One of Schlink's characters writes a twenty-plus page fiction about the 9/11 jumpers that is interspersed throughout the larger novel. *Saturday* offers a distanced view of 9/11 mediated through a British lens, even though protagonist Henry discovers that the spatial separation from the sites of initial impact in New York, Pennsylvania, and Washington on September 11, 2001 does not free Europeans such as himself and his family from its implications, especially when the United Kingdom joins the 2003 Iraq War. McEwan's literary approach is comparable to modernist works by E. M. Foster and Virginia Woolf when the text delves into the main character's psychological process. Psychology bears on the structure and themes primarily through the protagonist's interior monologue in the case of McEwan (which Versluys categorizes as "indirection") and various characters' internal focalization in the case of Schlink. Unlike many 9/11 novels where the plot unfolds episodically over a period of months or years, these two texts encapsulate storyworld events in a brief time frame of a day or two, such as Virginia Woolf's *Mrs. Dalloway*. While constructing a plotline framed in hours, both authors find abundant textual space to probe the characters' psychology in depth and to broaden their insights in relation to global news events, as Woolf does in *Mrs. Dalloway* which scrutinizes the fallout of World War I.

---

[6] Olster (ed.), *Don DeLillo: Mao II, Underworld, Falling Man*, 118; Jonathan Safran Foer, *Extremely Loud and Incredibly Close*.

Furthermore, through collapsing the storyworld plot to a matter of days, the 9/11 foundational mythological narrative is recast with less monumental "allegory" of which Versluys is critical. Finally, the novels interpret the impact of 9/11 within British and German national political interests and each nation's distinct cultural, political, and military legacy. The theme of the terrorist as symptomatic outsider within the nation-state is developed in relationship to this history.

ALL IN A DAY: *SATURDAY*

English novelist Ian McEwan has won various major literary prizes including the Man Booker prize for *Amsterdam* (1998) and the James Tait Black Memorial Prize for *Saturday* (2005). His 2001 novel *Atonement* was adapted into a commercially successful film with the same title, which then won many film awards including seven Oscar nominations for the 2008 Academy Awards. McEwan began his career as a novelist writing gothic tales and this delight in the macabre is evident in the salacious climax of *Saturday*. His refined, fluid, and restrained writing style is characteristic of English aristocratic sensibility and modernism.

Saturday reveals post-9/11 England troubled by the unrestrained outsider (terrorist) figure haunting its first-world collective imagination.[7] This post-9/11 novel presents terror in ordinary lived experience in relationship to terrorism, an unrelenting topic of interest since the riveting events of September 2001. *Saturday*'s protagonist, London neurosurgeon Henry Perowne is confused and unable to reconfigure the world in his mind after the 2001 violent attack. His conceptual discontinuities reflect ongoing difficulty with emplotting 9/11 and its aftermath of wars with respect to preceding events. Henry concedes: "he isn't thinking clearly, and just as bad, he senses he isn't thinking independently."[8] Captive of the 24-hour news cycle, his susceptibility "vibrate[s]

---

[7] Earlier IRA terrorist acts in the United Kingdom and elsewhere were coined "The Troubles." The term 'Troubles' invokes a complex understanding wherein objective, troubling news events serve to unbalance and trouble subjective, psychological well-being. For a discussion of the emplotment of terrorist events in *Saturday*, see Singer, "Exploring War Horror's Narrative Punch in Spielberg's *Munich* and *Saving Private Ryan*," especially 62–66.

[8] McEwan, *Saturday*, 181. Further citations from the novel will be noted parenthetically in the text.

obediently with each news 'release'" (*S*, 181), further compromising his capacity to think critically and thereby act reasonably in ways that do not contribute to more violence and destruction. McEwan's novel explores the global unease pervading contemporary existence, which gives urban violence and plane, rail, coach, or bus travel new meaning. Vulnerability and presumed innocence are crucial to the mechanisms of terrorism: "The feeling of innocence, together with vulnerability, form crucial elements in what may be called the 'process of terror' – the process by which violence generates political effects [...] Targets may not be in an objective sense innocent, but they must be in practical terms defenceless ('soft')."[9] Perowne and his family function as a microcosm for distinguishing perceived from actual threats.

Saturday scrutinizes the British response to 9/11 by registering its consequences through an analogy to Britain's own unresolved class politics, evidenced through the aggression of antagonist, working-class Baxter. He assaults Henry twice—once in a side-street near the anti-Iraq War demonstration and later him and his whole family in the Perownes' home. Among British news events, Baxter's gang-land violence resembles in its disturbing effects the widely reported 2011 criminal summer rampage of looting and burning in London. Yet Britain's own history of recent home-grown terrorism—for example, the experience of IRA terrorism—is absent from *Saturday*. The novel starts at 3.40 a.m. when naked Henry opens the shutters to his bedroom windows and is struck by the sight of a large burning plane streaking toward a Heathrow runway. During the night and next day he scours news media for explanation of the events he eye-witnessed and reflects on how he automatically grasped the screaming plane as possibly a terrorist attack.

Dominic Head presumes "readers will identify with Perowne's compulsive habit, [...] to tune into the news, and be 'joined to the generality, to a community of anxiety.' In this false community of the consumer as voyeur, the possibility that 'monstrous and spectacular scenes' might recur is 'one thread that binds the days.'"[10] McEwan compulsively watched news programming with his son on September 11; he says: "my son and I surfed – hungrily, ghoulishly – between CNN, CBC and BBC24. As soon as an expert was called in to pronounce on the politics

---

[9] Townshend, *Terrorism: A Very Short Introduction*, 8.
[10] Head, *Ian McEwan*, 178.

or the symbolism, we moved on. We only wanted to know what was happening."[11] Similarly Henry searches the media with his son Theo for the facts about the burning night flight. His horror-predisposed, melancholic mood contributes to his lack of attention to his driving that results in his disastrous interaction with ruffians in the street and later in his home.

As the plot develops, Londoner Perowne's narrow scientific understanding, on the basis of which his global privilege rests, is disturbed. First it is by the 3.40 a.m. foreign Russian cargo plane, about which his son Theo—having emerged into adult consciousness in a consumer world shadowed by "[i]nternational terror, security cordons, preparations for war" (*S*, 32)—construes: "You think it's jihadists…?" (*S*, 33, ellipsis in original). Calamity is attributed to subaltern "jihadists," while ironically the plane that we learn was having ordinary engine trouble is from Russia—Britain's former Cold War enemy, which covertly sponsored a variety of terrorists including most notably the IRA. While the Soviet Union was an existential threat for North Americans who anguished over potential nuclear annihilation, for Europeans the threat was more immediate. Not only was the enemy geographically closer, but also its weaponry of conscripted armies, tanks, and nuclear devices more omnipresent. Henry's fear of subaltern jihadists is arguably anchored to this previous experience of Cold War terror. McEwan and Perowne share "a clear consciousness" that "current comforts are precarious, sustained by activities that are complicitous in wider processes of despoliation or degradation."[12] Underwritten by global capitalism, the local is inextricable from "wider processes" that it remains nonetheless vulnerable to.

Between Henry's sleep disturbance and the day's street mugging followed by a perverse home attack on his family, the other anxiety-inducing event is the mass mobilization in the anti-Iraq War demonstration. By referencing the Saturday, February 15, 2003 anti-Iraq War demonstrations in the title of his novel, McEwan is promoting an alternate history that identifies February 15 as a day of primary importance, rather than the 911 "emergency" call the acronym 9/11 conjures. The anti-Iraq War march in London was estimated to include up to two million participants, the largest political demonstration ever in England. Other February 15 anti-war marches in many European capitals were similarly

---

[11] McEwan, "Beyond Belief."
[12] Head, *Ian McEwan*, 184.

estimated to include millions. Together these massive protests have been interpreted by Habermas and Derrida among other intellectuals as a significant instance of rising European identity. The United Kingdom's consideration of joining the war in Iraq in 2003 is the significant event being debated in the text, more so than rehashing the attacks against the US from two years earlier. Focus on London neurosurgeon Perowne and the global anti-Iraq War demonstrations reinforces urgency over whether Britain should continue its post-war imperial role of being second to the United States in Iraq.

The novel accounts for Britain's twenty-first-century stance in relationship to previous nineteenth- and twentieth-century wars, when it was the primary imperial world power. McEwan's text makes reference to these earlier English conflicts through literary allusions, such as to Virginia Woolf's novel *Mrs. Dalloway* (1925), and directly to Matthew Arnold's poem "Dover Beach" (1867).[13] In both *Mrs. Dalloway* and *Saturday*, the story is focalized through a controlling figure: the reader positions him/herself at a distance while sympathetically questioning Mrs. Dalloway's and Perowne's assertions and judgements. Intertextual echoes in *Saturday* work to probe the relationship between the individual and society or the centre and the periphery in war conflict. Predictably following the trajectory of Woolf's *Mrs. Dalloway*, in *Saturday*, English balance and propriety are accordingly restored after the calamity of one day: that is, in *Mrs. Dalloway*, after WWI veteran Septimus Warren Smith's suicide[14] and, in *Saturday*, after Perowne processes unsettling post-9/11 London that includes debating with others over the wisdom of waging a preventative war against Iraq. Characters resist allowing terror to undermine what they see as their ethical positions.

The intertextuality of Matthew Arnold's poem in *Saturday* functions to query Perowne's dominant, unexamined assumptions. Included at the end of the paperback edition, "Dover Beach" ends with these memorable lines imagining war: "And we are here as on a darkling plain/Swept with confused alarms of struggle and flight,/Where ignorant armies clash by night." The "ignorant armies" specifies the 1853–1856 Crimean War

---

[13] Woolf, *Mrs. Dalloway*.

[14] The theme of suicide and the 9/11 tower jumpers is taken up much more overtly in *Das Wochenende*.

context of the poem and British colonial wars more generally. During and after the Crimean War, the British public criticized the incompetence of its political and military leadership. The "ignorant" ascription likewise brings to mind English Prime Minister Tony Blair's support for the military campaign in Iraq against vocal opposition to it. When Henry observes Blair's self-contradictory facial expression—during meeting him at the Tate Modern gallery in London and afterwards seeing him on television—he is unconsciously registering his own inner schisms. Henry chooses not to attend the February 15 march; the reader may reflect on Perowne's absence and perhaps chuckle as he tries to drive his car around the march by going the "wrong way" down a one-way street and ends up delayed nonetheless—through the automobile collision involving Baxter.

The multigenerational Perowne family microcosm represented in the Saturday evening rendezvous at Perowne's home that Baxter's break and entry disturbs offers a variety of positions to the debate over what would constitute a gauged and reasonable response to terrorism now understood as having global presence directly impacting Western countries. In the example of domestic terror, Perowne instructed by his son accepts responsibility for having provoked Baxter's vengefulness in the street. During the altercation it is revealed that Baxter has congenital Huntingdon's disease. So later, even after Baxter's vicious threat to his family and Theo and Henry's cracking Baxter's skull by pushing him down a flight of stairs in self-defence, "one small fixed point of conviction holds Henry steady" (*S, 277*) as he employs his capacity as a neurosurgeon to save Baxter's life. The sequence of Perowne's relation to Baxter, where he is threatened by him, gets the upper hand in the street altercation, is terrorized by him in his home, attacks Baxter, and then operates on him, is ethically bizarre for a physician but not for a Western nation describing its military violence in euphemistic terms. In relationship to the West's strategic, *surgical* strike against Saddam Hussein's thuggish regime in Iraq, similar controversy could be stirred by the British record after the invasion of Iraq, resulting in murky military outcomes and the overall deterioration of Iraqi civil society into civil war. The pathological criminal, terrorist or barbarous dictator needing brain surgery presumes national good intentions.[15]

---

[15] The idea that terrorists are clinically crazy has been debunked by the social scientific community. See Silke (ed.), *Terrorists, Victims and Society: Psychological Perspectives on*

The home functions as a metonym for the nation and Perowne in the end grasps the precarious nature of its comforts and security. As the novel was published after Al-Qaeda-inspired attacks had already entered the European mainland during the 2004 Madrid train bombings, this intrusion of terror into Perowne's home embodies the fear that, with entering the Iraq War, terrorist events stemming from the War on Terror could attract further violence in Europe. Furthermore, ethnicity introduced through immigration into the matrix of the English class struggle makes profiling, fingerprinting, and enforcing clear boundaries between inside and outside threats impossible.

Fallible Henry attributes the threat of terror invading the domestic insularity of English elites from outside consistently throughout—whether by way of planes or street ruffians. He equates the domestic space of home and nation when he maps out the theatre of war from his upstairs front window.

> People often drift into the square to act out their dramas. Clearly, a street won't do. Passions need room, the attentive spaciousness of a theatre. On another scale, Perowne considers, [...] this could be the attraction of the Iraqi desert – the flat and supposedly empty landscape approximating a strategist's map on which fury of industrial proportions can be let loose. A desert, it is said, is a military planner's dream. A city square is the private equivalent. (*S*, 60)

On one level the protective view from inside situates him in the enclosed domestic space in which Woolf's Clarissa Dalloway operates as wife and hostess. It is a bounded secured space. 9/11 and the War on Terror are thus linked to the class system, a quintessentially British structure that also shapes Mrs. Dalloway's role. The solid front door to the Perownes' home, equipped with multiple original and high-tech locks, blocks Henry's view of the outside square unless he chooses to gaze down from above through the upstairs window. Yet "the Perownes' own corner, a triumph of congruent proportion; the perfect square laid out by

---

Terrorism and its Consequences. Rather, terrorists function rationally like the average person. Both authors ascribe physiological pathology to their terrorists that does not inhibit the characters' capacity to think rationally—perhaps too rationally as each plot furthers criminal activity.

Robert Adam [...] an eighteenth-century dream" (*S*, 5) is easily made vulnerable. The original locks on Henry's home importantly date back nostalgically to the integrative yet highly structured and hierarchical community of the eighteenth century. Perowne was responding to the deteriorated community when he added electronics to an already elaborate security system. Free indirect discourse discloses the motivation behind Perowne's protections: "Such defences, such mundane embattlement: beware of the city's poor, the drug-addicted, the downright bad" (*S*, 37).

Although resembling Clarissa Dalloway's comfortable 1920s privilege, Perowne's new millennial protections are easily undone when Baxter brandishing a knife challenges Henry's wife Rosalind's entry into their fortified residence. Using the plot elements of a gothic novel, the intrusion of terror into Perowne's home symbolizes the public's fear, here associated with England's participation in the European Union, with relaxed borders, and its entering into the Iraq War, as well as Al-Qaeda entering Europe. With the inevitability of personal and communal attacks strengthening, McEwan through Henry acknowledges the inevitability of a terrorist attack on London. Published before the 2005 London transit bombings, McEwan wrote: "London, [Henry's] small part of it, lies wide open, impossible to defend, waiting for its bomb" (*S*, 276). London waits in terror for the inevitable horror that is foreshadowed by the results following Baxter's easy break-in.

Though defended, ordinary existence has a propensity to unravel and reveal terrifying aspects. Due to freedom of movement and association, Western democracies are especially vulnerable to terrorist attack. Baxter's entry into the Perownes' house by threatening Henry's wife Rosalind's life has resonance after the 2015 *Charlie Hebdo* murders in Paris, in which a mother threatened by Islamist radicals opened the door for gunmen into the guarded magazine headquarters. In both instances, where the female is vulnerable, the response is male force. Once inside Perowne's fortress, Baxter threatens to rape Henry's only daughter, Daisy, in the sitting room in full view of the gathered three-generation family complement. Historically, rape as a military strategy is used to brutally subdue a restive conquered nation. The novel's suspense peaks with Baxter commanding Daisy to disrobe in front of her family sitting on the household sofas. Tellingly, Baxter's conquest needs a public viewing—in a manner of spatial organization where the family is oriented to Baxter's intended rape as if watching television—in order for the impact to be recognized and appreciated.

When Daisy disrobed delivers the short lyrical poem "Dover Beach" by Victorian poet and cultural critic Matthew Arnold, she improbably, though successfully, appeases Baxter's rage that was directed at Henry. The incongruous introduction of "Dover Beach" is appropriate to *Saturday*'s debating Britain's participation in the American-led war, to which Tony Blair agreed—contributing to the growing disapproval towards him. For a reader invested in cultural history, for which Arnold and McEwan advocate, the poem's mid-nineteenth-century humanist lament against the consequences of imperial trade expansion partly suits the early-twenty-first-century obsession with scarcity of global resources, especially oil. Britain, which had cast off its colonies during the latter half of the twentieth century in order to pay its post-war debts to America, complied enthusiastically with the Bush administration's aggressive neo-colonial foreign policy and invasion of Iraq. Provocatively "Dover Beach" works intertextually by inviting contemplation of precisely why its introduction in the novel both seems implausible as a plot event and yet is thematically spot-on in a comparison to the politics of engaging in the 2003 Iraq War.

The two worlds of the private and the public are brought together in the family scene. Baxter and his side-kick Nigel, representative of the criminalized working class, end up ejected from the family of elites who restore order. Initially, Henry believes himself insulated from class and racial threats through his marshalling a narrow repository of unreflexive scientific knowledge. He is not otherwise attentive, so he "only half remembers" (*S*, 220) the poem Daisy reads aloud, though it "is in all the anthologies and used to be taught in every school" (*S*, 232). Further Perowne remains unaware of the cultural importance of Arnold's poem, which privileges inter-subjectivity by foregrounding it against a backdrop of ungodly scientific and mercantile ambition; and also of the relevance of Arnold's polemical arguments about the role of cultural elites in opposing anarchy. By referencing "Dover Beach," *Saturday* is identifying and privileging the twenty-first-century British culture embodied positively in Henry's adult children, Theo and Daisy, respectively working the Blues and poetic forms.

Daisy's and Theo's cultural work—her first poetry collection *My Saucy Bark* and his jazz-blues piece "City Square"—is interpreted. In effect, Theo revisits Perowne's earlier positionality in relationship to the square.

By contrast to Henry's proprietary view of the eighteenth-century square his property looks onto, Theo envisages the square for the twenty-first century as a place of shared inspiration through enabling new meetings. Moved by the "unworldly melody" of Theo's jazz-blues piece about the city square (*S*, 170), Henry then reflects on "mirages for which people are prepared to die and kill" (*S*, 171f.). His own comparison of the city square to an Iraqi battlefield bespeaks his sense of property acquisition *vis-à-vis* the city square in his actual view and the Iraqi desert which he concludes will inevitably be invaded (*S*, 62). However, while both these squares map identical physical territory, their imagined uses are very different. By the process of invoking affective connections, Theo and fellow blues performer Chas's "close, strange harmony" (*S*, 170) rejects given models for which people are prepared to fight—whether "Christ's kingdom on earth, the workers' paradise, [or] the ideal Islamic state" (*S*, 172). For Henry, and similarly Clarissa Dalloway, "only on rare occasions" (*S*, 172) such as this Saturday is "a coherent world [where] everything fits [...] at last" evoked (*S*, 172).

Perowne is invited by Theo minimally to interact responsibly with "the city's poor" (*S*, 37), and by Daisy to entertain the social and cultural consequences of waging war on Iraq. At the beginning of the day at his window, Henry had indulged in the fantasy of the city as a new modern organism: "a success, a brilliant invention, a biological masterpiece – millions [...] nearly everyone wanting it to work" (*S*, 5). He discovers that Baxter has no interest in "wanting it to work" on account of his having limited social means and bearing a defective gene. Perowne has to admit the damaged or defective outsider such as Baxter and the possibility that Britain may be making its own terror delivered by the hands of young people like Baxter who hold no hope for the future: "a man who believes he has no future [...] is therefore free of consequences" (*S*, 210). The notion of the 'Other within' one's midst without hope establishes Baxter as a local source of terror impacting the nation. At the end of *Saturday*, Henry does not stand naked before his bedroom window as he did at its beginning, imagining the threat of terrorists arriving in planes over London. Drawing the cord of his dressing gown protectively around himself, Henry prepares for threats to his family that he can mediate somewhat through direct connections with people like Baxter. Perowne cannot prevent a cataclysm that will shake or crash into the city, but by re-engaging with the society surrounding him, he could come to a fuller recognition of the people living in London. While Henry does not approach Baudrillard's socialist ambitions—instead, he decides like the nineteenth-century middle class to retreat to the suburbs—he does eventually grasp the universalist obligation to provide care and assistance to Baxter: his Hippocratic Oath extends to strangers in his midst. The events of February 15, 2003 oblige him to reflect on what England has become and, in turn, to reconsider who he is as an Englishman and what role he plays in creating a society that jihadists and urban malcontents likewise reject.

Thus *Saturday* bridges the span of time from the eighteenth century until the early twenty-first. Allusions to canonical literary masterpieces such as "Dover Beach" and *Mrs. Dalloway* accentuate continuities and discontinuities within Britain's vision that are framed within its long imperial past. Terror writ large is contextualized in terms of violent conflicts over centuries, and terrorism is understood as but one form of terror in this continuum. Henry Perowne shows that terrorism's real danger is that it tends to produce a state of generalized melancholia and resultant apathy in the body politic. As if etherized, the citizen is incapable of positively and productively engaging with issues and changes to community. Henry takes a recumbent position in the end, but the young reach forward and are outward-looking. As with Elizabeth Dalloway's class differences from her restrictive mother Clarissa, the possibility in the Perowne offspring has only begun to be realized; yet importantly Theo and Daisy find a sense of place and direction through creativity which, like that of their creator Ian McEwan, bears an appreciable interrelationship with the past and its bearings on the future.

SUNDAY, A DAY OF RECKONING IN *DAS WOCHENENDE*

Just as Ian McEwan gained a wider audience by way of the adaptation of his novel *Atonement* into an award winning movie, Bernhard Schlink obtained global recognition for the film adaptation of his 1995 novel *Der Vorleser* (*The Reader*), which garnered five 2008 Academy Award nominations. Kate Winslet won the Academy Award for Best Actress playing the role of Hanna Schmitz, an illiterate concentration camp guard charged under German state law for the murder of several hundred Jews. Schlink's novels fixate on the relationship between ethics and state law, and how the post-war generation is impacted by their parents' Nazi past.

Das Wochenende did not generally receive favourable reviews in the English press.[16] Perhaps the Anglophone world with its raw memory of 9/11 and the subsequent wars was not prepared to consider novels that could be construed as glamourizing terrorists.[17] Further, this unfavourable reaction might be explained by Schlink's change of subject matter from the Nazi heritage to the terrorist Red Army Faction (RAF). Schlink's previous novel *Die Heimkehr* (2006, translated *Homecoming*), which has been dismissively described as a footnote to *Der Vorleser*, topically analyses the mindset of writers like Günter Grass or Paul de Man and their convenient memory loss of their Nazi past, a history only revealed without much risk once the author's reputation was shielded by global fame.

In *Das Wochenende*, there is no storyline of a hidden parental Nazi past needing revelation. By comparison to *Saturday*, although the setting is similarly situated in time—a few years past 9/11- and place—a large residence—Schlink's novel foregrounds the legacy of 1967-and-onwards German groupuscular terrorism. This form of politically inspired terrorism refers to discrete fissiparous cells with a tendency to break apart that proliferated in Western countries in the 1970s. In this historicizing way, *Das Wochenende* subscribes to the first category of texts Versluys depicts that process while deflecting the effects of 9/11 by considering them in relationship to other, seemingly comparable historical markers.[18]

---

[16] German reviewers of *Das Wochenende* were equally unimpressed and "underwhelmed," cf. Preece, *Baader-Meinhof and the Novel*, 23.

[17] In *Baader-Meinhof and the Novel*, Preece speculates on two possible "reasons for the glut of Baader-Meinhof fiction in the 2000s" (3). First, the German "national imaginary" is only now, after a period of peaceful years, able to integrate the shock of the terrorist "years of lead" into its own confident mythology. (Maybe there will be a similar rash of terrorist fiction in the English-speaking world similarly containing detailed sympathetic character portrayals of Islamist terrorists at a later time when the War on Terror has subsided.) Second, Otto Schily and Joschka Fischer, with personal pasts associated with the Red Army Faction, held important positions in the 1998 government coalition of the Social Democrats and the Green Party (Minister of the Interior, and Deputy Chancellor and Foreign Minister, respectively). Curiously Preece does not connect the production of new millennial German works about terrorism to 9/11 and its political aftermath. Consider, for example, that the topical *Baader Meinhof Complex* was nominated in the Best Foreign Language Film category in the same 2008 Academy Awards that Kate Winslet won Best Actress award for *The Reader*.

[18] Versluys, *Out of the Blue*, 14.

Saturday inhabits the second group of texts Versluys categorizes whose characters revisit the cultural archive to construct a recuperative, personal ethical relationship to 9/11 and the subsequent War on Terror.

Das Wochenende takes its historical source material from the 1992 German government pronouncements about the possible release of RAF prisoners. The fictional member names in Schlink's novel—Andreas and Ulrich—recall members of the original, first-generation RAF Baader-Meinhof gang—Andreas Baader and Ulrike Meinhof. The main characters in *Das Wochenende* were leftists in the later 1960s and 1970s who meet together again in the new millennium at a rundown rural estate in the former East Germany. It is similar in purview to the small family reunion in *Saturday*, yet the rationale for the gathering of ex-politicals is the pardon and release of the fictionalized character Jörg, a former German RAF terrorist responsible for the murder of four German citizens. The gathering of Jörg's family and friends orchestrated by his doting sister Christiane aims to help facilitate his reintegration into normative German society. The 2008 publication date of *Das Wochenende* was opportune and the novel topical as it provided a fictional counterpoint to the controversial 2008 parole of former second-generation RAF member Christian Klar (Jones).[19] Granting his release was debated in the German Parliament, including comparison of RAF sentences to light sentences for Nazi war criminals. After over twenty years in prison, protagonist Jörg is suddenly pardoned and released. Thus, Schlink considers three sets of violent perpetrators (Nazi regime, 1970s terrorists, and 9/11), thereby alternating between state violence, paramilitary terrorist groups, and jihadists.

Schlink's text is worthy of consideration for its updating of the German understanding of terrorism beyond the dissolution of the RAF by way of its official communiqué in 1998. Julian Preece contends that *Das Wochenende* "is a 'national-unity closure narrative' because it brings both sides of the formerly divided country together and consigns

---

[19] See "RAF Member out of Jail: Prison Releases German Terrorist Christian Klar," *Spiegel International Online*, December 19, 2008, available at http://www.spiegel.de/international/germany/raf-member-out-of-jail-prison-releases-german-terrorist-christian-klar-a-597511.html (accessed 31.3.2015) and "Germany Frees Last Red Army Faction Activist," *Herald Sun*, June 22, 2011, available at http://www.heraldsun.com.au/news/breaking-news/germany-frees-last-red-army-faction-activist/story-e6frf7jx-1226079621100 (accessed 31.3.2015).

Baader-Meinhof to the past."[20] Rather, in my view, *Das Wochenende* should be interpreted as an open narrative that traces further fissures in German terrorist history beyond the RAF involving a racially diverse German body-politic. Characters share a feeling of living in exile from the RAF dream of the end of capitalism while capitalism's systemic colonial exploitation continues. Another compelling feature of the novel is its sympathetic rendering of an amoral character, terrorist Jörg, by using an Aristotelian form of dramatic tragedy engendering audience catharsis. Moreover, the novel rejects "grand narratives" and instead uses a multi-perspective narrative through internal focalization from a variety of characters' perspectives.

The novel's storyworld comparison of left extremist terrorism of the 1970s and 9/11 introduces subsequent fourth and potentially fifth generational iterations of RAF-inspired terrorism.[21] Fictional author Ilse is Schlink's alter ego trying to get his creative bearings around the transgenerational legacy of totalitarianism and terrorism in Germany in view of 9/11: "Ilse looked at Jörg and thought of Jan."[22] Character Ilse, a striving author, writes fiction about Jan, a former RAF member who committed suicide. In Ilse's metafictional account, the actual group member Jan never died but rather feigned death and later participated in the 2001 attack on the Twin Towers. In her story, Jan fools the police by injecting drugs which cause his deep sleep, wherein his bodily organs slow to a near halt. Jan's strategy resembles the disguise of the 9/11 Hamburg terrorist cell—representing the fourth terrorist iteration—which led the attack orchestrated from afar by Osama bin Laden. The Hamburg cell, including 9/11 terrorist Mohamed Atta, was a sleeper cell, whose agents trained in a foreign country[23] and then returned incognito, mixing amicably among the population only to "awaken" when the mission was initiated. Jan's fictional role in the attack is to take

---

[20] Preece, *Baader-Meinhof and the Novel*, 24.

[21] The well-documented RAF "generations" include the first generation Baader-Meinhof gang of 1967–1975; the second generation of 1975–1980, and the third generation between 1980–1998.

[22] Schlink, *The Weekend*, 2008, trans. Shaun Whiteside, 140. Further citations from the novel will be noted parenthetically in the text.

[23] Baader, Meinhof, Gudrun Ensslin, and Horst Mahler trained with the Popular Front for the Liberation of Palestine (PFLP) and the Palestine Liberation Organization (PLO) in Jordan; Mohamed Atta and the Hamburg cell trained with Al-Qaeda in Afghanistan.

a bag with a radio honing signal to the top of the World Trade Center. The radio honing device delivered to the top of the North Tower, Windows on the World restaurant coatroom leads the plane to its target. The earlier anti-capitalist RAF is thus shown enabling the later Hamburg sleeper cell.

Storyteller Ilse, a German-English art teacher, directs a lesson to the general public through her writing. Through her interior focalization, the reader learns that she is obsessed with the notorious under-reported and under-examined 9/11 jumpers (*W*, 15–17). Her tale about the feigned suicide and reappearance of Jan speaks to the desire for living life in the moment; literally, living on the edge. In Ilse's tale, Jan chooses to stay in the restaurant to experience the hijacked plane smashing into the North Tower and then, as a jumper, to leap and fly from the edge of a burning top floor. Ilse's writing about Jan suggests that the human attraction for committing an act of terrorism consists in its rollercoaster excitement of living in the moment and the feeling of power through choosing one's own and any victims' time of death. Writing after the First World War and envisaging the Second World War, Freud theorized the Death Wish as an inherent human drive. Ilse's conceptualized model terrorist, Jan, perishes as the Death Wish's premier exemplar.

Tellingly, Ilse does not fixate on the falling towers, but rather pursues the haunting image of the iconic Twin Tower jumpers. Her paratextual tale ends with two jumpers. While in the burning North Tower, Jan rescues a female office worker, perhaps representing Ilse herself. The unnamed female trapped in a windowless photocopy room believes Jan has come in the role of a firefighter to rescue her from death—a contemporary knight in protective armour. She quickly comprehends her fate as a victim. Performing her role doubly as the female victim, she first phones home weeping and then, without control, "tumbles out of the window and falls, flails her arms around, pedals with her legs" (*W*, 186). Conversely, Jan chooses his moment "to enjoy the flight" (*W*, 186). His desire to fly mirrors the most filmed moment in RAF history when Baader is freed from jail on May 14, 1970. Baader jumped out of a reading room window followed by journalist Meinhof—who symbolically jumped out of her past, including leaving her children.

Just as German capitalism opposed by Jörg and the RAF continues to thrive, the crash of capitalism symbolized by the fall of the World Trade Center never happened. As an aesthetic event, though, 9/11 jumpers continue to haunt cultural memory in a variety of fictional forms including Ilse's writing.[24] Why do the jumpers still haunt many people's imaginaries? Ilse provides two possible paths for understanding the attraction through her two "jumpers." First, Jan "living on the edge" embodies the courage and nobility of the artistic sublime.[25] Second, as a visualization of the penultimate victim, the female jumper personifies people's feelings of oppression—imaginary or real—whether feeling trapped in a job, yearning for companionship, or struggling in poverty, to name a few everyday examples.

Schlink's line of continuity from RAF terrorist violence of recent memory to its new millennial manifestations includes the younger Marko, who discussed socialist values and goals with Jörg while he was serving time. If Jan is imagined as a fourth generation RAF terrorist reconfigured as a member of the notorious Hamburg cell, then the younger radical, Marko, might be construed as representing a further, potentially fifth German terrorist iteration, the jihadist foreign fighter. Marko intends to co-opt Jörg's history of political radicalism after his release by issuing a defiant missive to the media, including Jörg's name supporting Marko's current cause. Thereby, Marko tries to align the remnants of the European left with Al-Qaeda to form a global revolutionary movement, i.e., a global jihad.[26] Speaking to the collective group, Marko orates: "If we joined forces with our Muslim comrades we could really get things going. They with their power and we with what we know about this country—together we could really strike where it

---

[24] Arguably the jumpers have become an expected figure within the 9/11 novel. See Singer, "Fiction and Historical Memory: Negotiating the Traumatizing Image of the Falling Man," and "The Image of the Falling Man Revisited."

[25] For further discussion of the 9/11 novel and the sublime, see Chaps. 2 and 3 by Rolf Renner and Ulrich Kinzel in this volume.

[26] As of March 2015, it is estimated that approximately twenty thousand foreign fighters have joined the Iraq-Syria conflict "(Number of Foreign Fighters in Syria/Iraq Sets Alarming Record," *United Nations Regional Information Centre for Western Europe*, March 26, 2015, available at http://www.unric.org/en/latest-un-buzz/29708-number-of-foreign-fighters-in-syriairaq-sets-alarming-record [accessed 31.3.2015]). Four thousand foreign fighters came from western Europe (predominantly European nationals ["Number of Foreign Fighters"]), including approximately six hundred foreign fighters from Germany (Daniel H. Heinke and Jan Raudszus, "German Foreign Fighters in Syria and Iraq," Combating Terrorism Center at West Point, January 20, 2015, available at https://www.ctc.usma.edu/posts/german-foreign-fighters-in-syria-and-iraq [accessed 31.3.2015]).

hurts" (*W*, 52). He seeks to convince the legendary Jörg to sign onto his plan during the weekend reunion.[27]

Jörg discovers when he is confronted by Marko's determination that his desire to agitate has weakened—not because of his rehabilitation, nor because of changed beliefs, but because he has aged and is in ill-health. Jörg's medical condition functions as his tragic, fatal flaw; while Baxter in *Saturday* is a somewhat bumbling criminal in the British-American comedic tradition, Jörg is glamourized as an attractive heroic warrior figure. Ilse admits being attracted to Jörg's swagger and political bravado in university. She refers to Jörg as "[t]he boy I'd fallen in love with" (*W*, 11). She wrote to him in prison after reading his request for clemency. In conversation with former lawyer, now writer Henner, she glowingly recites word-for-word Jörg's strident written application for release from prison: "I'm not asking for mercy. I fought against this state, and it has fought against me, and we owe each other nothing. We owe loyalty only to a single cause" (*W*, 11). Jörg remains committed to the heroic political "cause." After corresponding with the younger Marko in prison, upon his release he invites Marko to the reunion so that he can be seen publicly considering Marko's revolutionary communiqué and thus remain a *cause célèbre* among his friends and potentially the wider German society.

Saturday and *Das Wochenende* abound with comparisons beyond their previously mentioned *courte dureé* storyworld timeframe: including their principal "terrorists," Baxter and Jörg, cast with symbolic, pathological medical conditions. Baxter's degenerative neurological condition, Huntington's disease, in part explains his monstrous behaviour towards the Perownes. The reader might conclude on the basis of Perowne's state-institutionalized medical intervention near the end of the story that the terrorist impulse can be contained and controlled, though not completely eliminated within British society. Similarly towards the end of *Das Wochenende*, the reader discovers that Jörg has incurable, late-stage prostate cancer. Jörg's cancerous fatal flaw symbolically recalls his trail of four murders and the general spread of RAF terror. Jörg is confronted by former RAF sympathizer, now dental supplier, Ulrich at the dinner table and needled to retell what it felt like to commit his first murder (*W*, 35).

---

[27] Many jihadist foreign fighters in Iraq and Syria are converts to Islam (18% of Germans who joined are converts, "Number of Foreign Fighters").

Jörg first feigns weariness but later responds by offering a speech that justifies murder for the greater political good. Similarly in Ilse's fiction, with each successive murder, Jan's affective response to his victims diminishes. Perhaps much like Jörg's metastasizing cancer, bodily sensation treated with radiation and drugs is eliminated.

Jörg's cancer proves to be his undoing. In one of the more jarring and humourous scenes in the story, on retiring to bed after Friday supper the revolutionary Jörg rejects the sexual advances of Dorle, Ulrich's teenage daughter. She screams in disbelief. The others rush to the bottom of the staircase to peer upwards to naked Dorle and Jörg in his nightshirt. Jörg is embarrassed though his lack of (revolutionary) verve remains unexplained at this point. Comically, Marko speculates, "Why chuck her out of bed? Does he want to be a Muslim and martyr – on earth, battle and prayer and women only in heaven, an endless supply of virgins?" (*W*, 45). On Saturday Jörg's university-aged son Ferdinand arrives unexpectedly and confronts his father at the dinner table about his heroic anti-capitalist ambitions carried out through murderous actions that damaged many families, including his own. Jörg is unable to respond to his son's accusations as he did on Friday night when he rejected Dorle's advances; he wants to make peace with his son rather than create further strife and he knows, given his medical prognosis, that he has little time.

The heroic figure of Jörg is further queried when it is revealed that, in the 1970s, his over-protective sister provided information to the police regarding his whereabouts so that he could be apprehended and sentenced. His stature is reduced again after Marko delivers his revolutionary communiqué with Jörg's forged signature and the German government feels obliged to respond to the public. In a radio address to the nation, the German President reveals Jörg's 'private' medical condition in order to explain and excuse his supposed endorsement and call for global jihad. At the tale's end unwittingly played and easily sacrificed, Jörg appears like Hamlet, in the tradition of Greek dramatic tragedies such as Sophocles's *Oedipus Rex*. In a chronological retelling of the comparative re-enactment of kingly demise, Jörg before incarceration materializes like King Hamlet, as a mighty presence and heir to German power (if only appearing as a Marxist spectre haunting Europe). Without parents, Jörg curried favour from his only older sister, Christiane. Together they manage the family home and dominate their leftist allies. Jörg's overbearing sister assumes the maternal role of Hamlet's controlling mother, Gertrude. Jörg's patriarchal rival, the German President, is like the opportunistic Claudius who, in Shakespeare's play, murders his own brother, King Hamlet—the rightful king. Just as Hamlet's mother is suspected of falling in with Claudius's plan against King Hamlet, Christiane turned her lionized RAF brother in to the German authorities. She later organizes the weekend to readmit her 'rehabilitated' brother, the diminished Prince Hamlet, into German society. The rejected love interest, Dorle, mirrors spurned Ophelia, while competent Marko resembles Horatio. At the beginning of the play, Horatio, like Marko, envisions the ghost of King Hamlet and, at tale's end, lives on to reimagine and retell the days of terror and glory.

In *Das Wochenende*, harmony is achieved through the words and actions of the older ex-politicals. The gathered community functions productively as a team substituting for *Saturday*'s more insular multigenerational gathering that establishes harmony through the retrenchment of the British family. *Saturday*'s model builds on traditional values of protection and care that are extended to twenty-first-century acceptance of other nationalities and differing cultural perspectives. Schlink's former leftists state they have given up their large-scale dreams but envisage a meaningful life within the reduced purview of close relationships or work. Co-owner with Christiane of the house where the gathering occurs, Margarete thematically describes their present existence as exiles: "'No,' she said, 'no reason for disappointment. We live in exile. What we were and wanted to remain and were perhaps destined to become, we lose. Instead we find something else. Even if we think we've found what we're looking for, in truth it's something else'" (*W*, 145). In positioning themselves as "exiles," the community is able to create distance from dreamers—such as Jörg, Marko, and Ilse. Yet as former leftists, the "exiles" remain alienated from the superfluities of consumer culture and nationalist jingoism.

Exile has diverse connotations referencing a variety of positional markers from the past. Schlink's stories have often concerned Jews who traditionally consider themselves an exiled people forced out of their biblical home. Displaced peoples from war-torn countries seeking asylum are termed exiles. Though East German dissidents followed by the Stasi sought refuge as political exiles in West Germany, it is more difficult to seriously consider Christiane's gathering of prosperous Germans living comfortably in the West as exiles. Perhaps a closer appraisal of the wider meaning of exile as conceived by Margarete comes by way of the title of the classic Rolling Stones double album, *Exile on Main St.* The cover references their perceived role as entertainers exiled to the margins of society.[28] Just as with the Stones, Margarete concedes the 1960s leftist political vision is gone, although some of its radicalizing cultural trappings remain[29]: she suggests, "Perhaps that's what makes a terrorist. He can't bear living in exile. He wants to bomb his way to his dream of home" (*W*, 145).

The nostalgic "dream of home" which is a component of the theme of exile is left purposely ambiguous and open to exploration and interpretation. Literally the "dream of home" might be conceived as the converse of the split/broken family home that children and the other members dream of reuniting. Jörg grew up without a father while his mother died when he was very young (following on the oedipal tragedy meme, Hamlet's father is murdered and his mother poisoned). Ilse lost the security associated with the family farm when her family went bankrupt, while Marko never mentions his family. Figuratively, "home" might reference religious messianism, communism or another political, utopian option. With their collective appreciation for the allure of the "dream of home," the "exile[d]" political activists are better able to sympathetically provide guidance and support to Jörg as he adjusts after his absence in prison to the changed social environment. In conversation over meals, the group discusses social change: what killed the leftist political project—East Germany's disenfranchisement and terrorism—and changes in political discourse that accepts multiple perspectives and serves to query

---

[28] The cover featured numerous black and white postcards of circus entertainers on the front cover and a similar number of portrait photographs of the Rolling Stones on the flip side. As well, the Stones were "tax exiles" and "on the lam" from British authorities given the probability of further drug arrests. More importantly the Rolling Stones exiled themselves from political activism. Mick Jagger no longer advocated for free concerts after the 1969 free concert at Altmont, nor wrote politically charged lyrics like "Street Fighting Man" advocating revolt after attending the violent protest against the Vietnam War in London's Grosvenor Square, nor invited Jean-Luc Godard back to film another revolutionary political treatise after *Sympathy for the Devil*.

[29] There is one politically motivated song on *Exile on Main St.* and each of the next two albums. The song "Sweet Black Angel" protests the trumped-up murder charges against American Black activist Angela Davis. The 1972 album produced in Munich contained the politically motivated song "Fingerprint File" about ever pervasive surveillance. Perhaps they were reflecting on the increased presence of surveillance in West Germany counteracting RAF terrorism. Thus, the Stones maintained some connection to the more politically radical past, and the cultural trappings of 1960s rebellion were not completely forgotten.

Jörg and Marko's strident, implacable views. Henner best models supporting Jörg when he claims to have led the police to Jörg's capture and arrest, though he knows that it was Jörg's sister who betrayed him. Henner seeks to build peace between brother and sister, which is all that Jörg has left of family—except for Ferdinand, his disconsolate, angry son.

Ferdinand accuses his father and his terrorist cohort of selective memory and lack of accountability. Significant violence and consequential terror were meted out by Jörg's cell in the 1970s and by the Nazi fathers of the Red Army Faction cell members. Now grown up, Ferdinand challenges his father in the same way teenaged Jörg and members of his generation recognized convenient tales of denial from parents who were former-SS members. Ferdinand says, "You [Jörg] don't remember whether you shot him or someone else did? [...] and the old men didn't remember either, that they had beaten and shot and gassed the Jews [...] You got worked up about your parents' generation, the generation of the murderers, but you turned out exactly the same" (*W*, 150, 151). Similar to Shakespeare's *Hamlet*, murderous behaviour is "examined" and "condemned" (*W*, 208) with cathartic affective resonance and interpretational value. The oedipal drama involves the next generation when Jörg seeks Ferdinand's understanding (and "forgiveness" is mentioned [*W*, 208]) through his admitting to "hurt[ing] you and your mother" (*W*, 207); he receives his son's address from Christiane so they may correspond afterwards by letter. Prepared to take a menial job in Ulrich's dental lab, Jörg no longer swaggers. His stature diminished, he reflects on his own actions while recognizing familiar traits in his son. During the difficult reunion, Jörg observes Ferdinand's similar hurtful dismissive gestures directed towards himself, the patriarchal figure, and Ferdinand's use of moral categorical imperatives as a defence mechanism to dodge the present circumstance. The meeting of father and son occurs in a broken-down, glass-smashed greenhouse that is symbolic of the context of Jörg's personal despair and collapsed political ambitions.

In a Habermasian sense, through its symptomatic characters, Schlink's fiction recommends reconciling with the past in order to embrace the future in terms of it.[30] The novel emphasizes painful transgenerational legacies such as Habermas probed and elaborated in his psychoanalytic

---

[30] See LaCapra, "Revising the Historians' Debate: Mourning and Genocide," and Habermas, "On Systematically Distorted Communication."

arguments during the German Historians' Debate of the 1980s. In this context of the nation attempting to reconcile with the Nazi past through the popular press, Habermas dismissed historian Ernst Nolte's claim that the Third Reich was an aberration in Germany's history of otherwise greatness represented by its achievements in the nineteenth century. Condensing Habermas's arguments, American trauma theorist Dominick LaCapra warns that

> [a] diminished faculty of memory would [...] increase chances that the secreted [...] aspects of the Nazi past would be passed on to those born later as a disorienting and destabilizing [...] unworked-through heritage that would [...] haunt descendants and possibly create the basis for a renewed fascination with fascism.[31]

In the novel, interpersonal failures in the family are drawn on the Nazi legacy and contribute to terrorist political impulses.

Bishop Karin in her official capacity sermonizes on impediments to messianic goals aligned with church doctrine. Early Sunday morning, she leads a prayer meeting that all attend. In her sermons, Karin talks about the value of truth in relative terms where one must be accepting of another's "life lies" (*W*, 189) when a personal truth is too painful to reveal. Only when a person is emotionally ready and stable should a person choose to confront his/her own "life lies." This way of thinking appears to structure Schlink's narrative about Jörg as he struggles with his demons. Jörg's lawyer interjects that it is sometimes necessary to impose the truth—for example, from parent to child or from outside as with the 1945 Nazi defeat. Karin accepts this conception of constructed truth that is associated with postmodern philosophy:

> Some people turn it around, so that it's not that the truth makes you free, it's that freedom makes things true. In that case there are as many truths as people freely living their lives – that idea scares me; I'd like there to be a single truth. But what does my wish count for! (*W*, 190f.)

In the late 1960s and early 1970s, young German adults were conflicted about the RAF. Terrorist violence was viewed with some sympathy as a causal response to German authoritarian structures, sometimes

---

[31] LaCapra, "Revising the Historians' Debate," 52.

administered by former Nazis, and government policies that supported a plethora of brutal foreign dictatorships through trade—including in military hardware. The ex-politicals attending Jörg's release event indicate German terrorism is now viewed disfavourably with near unanimity. Germans and the English are likely to grasp 9/11 and subsequent terrorism from their own lived and historical experience of terrorism. For England, this experience occurred primarily in the context of nationalist uprisings in the colonies—for instance, encountering the 1951–1954 Mau Mau rebellion in Kenya or, more recently, battling the IRA on home soil. For contemporary Germany, terrorism stretches back to Nazi atrocities and through the German government's lengthy and bloody battle against the RAF. The Hamburg cell targeting the World Trade Center or German ISIL jihadists are further generational iterations.[32]

Both McEwan and Schlink view 9/11 and subsequent Islamist terrorism as part of an historical continuum, not a world-shattering event. They are not invested in 9/11 as a highly emotionally charged, sentimentalized depressant. 9/11 events are used as a catalyst for the reader's relating to a tale about the author's own distinctive national and cultural history. Both texts further minimize the significance of 9/11 by bookending the storyworld to the time frame of a day or two. Both are modelled on culturally recognizable, classic literary texts. Each personifies the major terrorist having a terminal disease. Cast as an outsider, the terrorist is separate from traditional normative family life through which communal harmony is re-envisaged at the novel's end.

While there are similarities between *Saturday* and *Das Wochenende*, many intriguing differences impress. These begin with a differing 9/11 catalyst, the planes striking the towers in *Saturday* and, after the fact, the jumpers' "suicide" in *Das Wochenende*. Subjective effects of 9/11 are diagnosed: whereas McEwan relates anxiety to lack of security, Schlink structures his aesthetic around the sublime victimhood of the jumpers. Divergent historical understandings of terrorism emerge. The English (McEwan's) encounter with terrorism primarily begins outside the home country in the colonies, though Baxter is evidence of Britain's internal class struggle; German terrorism through Schlink's example of the RAF is internal to the national home. Discursively, this distinction explains

---

[32] Michael Wildenhain's 2008 novel, *Dreamers of the Absolute* also draws the connection between the RAF and jihadist attacks in Europe.

Schlink's studied analysis of an actual terrorist rather than McEwan's allegorical analysis of a small-time thug with class aspersions mirroring the devastation of which an imagined terrorist is capable. While the differences mentioned are significant, the texts share a similarity with other European novels fitting into the 9/11 terrorist genre. McEwan's and Schlink's narratives encourage understanding of historical events along a continuum stretching over many decades and modelled according to the national cultural legacy.

References

Baudrillard, Jean. "The Violence of the Global," *The Spirit of Terrorism and Other Essays*, trans. Chris Turner (London: Verso, 2003), 85–105.

Foer, Jonathan Safran. *Extremely Loud and Incredibly Close* (New York: Houghton Mifflin, 2005).

Habermas, Jürgen. "On Systematically Distorted Communication," *Inquiry*, vol. 13, no. 1–4 (1970), 205–218.

Head, Dominic. *Ian McEwan* (Manchester: Manchester University Press, 2007).

LaCapra, Dominick. "Revising the Historians' Debate: Mourning and Genocide," in Dominick LaCapra, *History and Memory After Auschwitz* (Ithaca: Cornell University Press, 1998), 43–72.

McEwan, Ian. *Saturday* (Toronto: Vintage Canada, 2006).

———. "Beyond Belief," *The Guardian*, September 12, 2001, available at http://www.ianmcewan.com/bib/articles/9-11-02.html (accessed 31.3.2015).

Olster, Stacey (ed.). *Don DeLillo: Mao II, Underworld, Falling Man* (London: Continuum, 2011).

Preece, Julian. *Baader-Meinhof and the Novel: Narratives of the Nation/Fantasies of the Revolution, 1970–2010* (New York: Palgrave Macmillan, 2012).

Schlink, Bernhard. *The Weekend*, 2008, trans. Shaun Whiteside (New York: Pantheon, 2010).

Schmid, Alex P. "The Revised Academic Consensus Definition of Terrorism," *Perspectives on Terrorism*, vol. 6, no. 2 (May 2012), 158f.

Silke, Andrew (ed.). *Terrorists, Victims and Society: Psychological Perspectives on Terrorism and its Consequences* (Chichester, UK: Wiley, 2003).

Singer, Sandra. "Exploring War Horror's Narrative Punch in Spielberg's *Munich* and *Saving Private Ryan*," in Douglas A. Cunningham and John C. Nelson (eds.), *A Companion to the War Film* (West Sussex, UK: Wiley Blackwell, 2016), 56–70.

———. "Fiction and Historical Memory: Negotiating the Traumatizing Image of the Falling Man," in Margrét Gunnarsdóttir Champion and Irina Rasmussen Goloubeva (eds.), *Ethics and Poetics: Ethical Recognitions and*

Social Reconfigurations in Modern Narratives (Newcastle upon Tyne: Cambridge Scholars Publishing, 2014), 229–249.

———. "The Image of the Falling Man Revisited," in Leslie Boldt, Corrado Federici and Ernesto Virgulti (eds.), *Silence and the Silenced: Interdisciplinary Perspectives* (New York: Peter Lang, 2013), 127–142.

Townshend, Charles. *Terrorism: A Very Short Introduction*, 2nd ed. (Oxford: Oxford University Press, 2011).

Versluys, Kristiaan. *Out of the Blue: September 11 and the Novel* (New York: Columbia University Press, 2009).

Woolf, Virginia. *Mrs. Dalloway* (Oxford: Oxford University Press, 2000).

Author Biography

Sandra Singer is Associate Professor in the School of English and Theatre Studies, University of Guelph, Ontario, Canada. Her primary scholarship concerns Doris Lessing, in which capacity she co-edited *Doris Lessing Studies* (2003–2014) and two essay collections: *Doris Lessing: Interrogating the Times* (2010, paperback 2015) and *Doris Lessing's* The Golden Notebook *After Fifty* (2015). Current projects concern fiction, trauma and terrorism: she has published, in narrative studies, on works by Kate Chopin, Michael Cunningham and Eden Robinson; in trauma studies, on texts by Clark Blaise, Wayson Choy, J. J. Steinfeld, Aryeh Lev Stollman, Rebecca Wells, Jonathan Wilson and Rose Zwi; and in terrorist fiction, on writing by Don DeLillo, Ghassan Kanafani, Colum McCann, Ian McEwan, Claire Messud, Joseph O'Neill and Bernhard Schlink, among others.

The Post-9/11 World in Three Polish Responses: Zagajewski, Skolimowski, Tochman

Ewa Kowal

ZAGAJEWSKI

"Who could have foreseen the poetic ripples of Sept. 11?" is the opening line of a 2002 *New York Times* article with a surprising juxtaposition in its title "Falls of Towers and the Rise of Polish Poetry."[1] The article's author looks back at the unexpected post-9/11 development (at least) in New York, where suddenly, as previously "[i]nnocent America became a land of experience," "[p]ostwar Polish poetry became eerily pertinent."[2] Inspired by Poland's excessive historical experiences, poems by such authors as Czesław Miłosz, Wisława Szymborska, Zbigniew Herbert and

---

[1] Boxer, "Falls of Towers and the Rise of Polish Poetry."
[2] Ibid.

E. Kowal (✉)
Institute of English Studies, Jagiellonian University, Kraków, Poland

Adam Zagajewski "hit a new American nerve"[3] in late 2001, apparently like no other nation's poetry. While new poems such as "Fotografia z 11 września" ("Photograph from September 11" in the English translation by Clare Cavanagh and Stanisław Barańczak) by Szymborska, "11 września 2001" [September 11, 2001] by Ewa Lipska or "Wieże" [Towers] by Julia Hartwig were yet to be written, in the immediate aftermath of the terrorist attack, it was a poem by Adam Zagajewski that played a very prominent role among the first literary responses to the tragic events, even though it did not address them directly, having been written over a year and a half beforehand.[4] "Try to Praise the Mutilated World"[5] appeared on the back page of the special 9/11 issue of *The New Yorker* (September 24, 2001), with the immediately iconic black on black cover by Art Spiegelman, and it is perhaps easy to see why it struck such a chord with American readers at that difficult time. The poem's dominant imagery of "June's long days, and wild strawberries, drops of wine, the dew" and "gather[ing] acorns in the park in autumn" might seem merely pleasant if rather precious at a different time, but a week after the collapse of the Twin Towers it was exactly such peaceful banality and comforting beauty of small things that was most missed and urgently needed, since for the time being the sense of order and safety which they denote appeared completely lost. What was probably less visible, since it was less appealing to and less sought after by the American readers in September 2001, was the other, parallel kind of imagery to be found in the poem built upon the principle of duality or alternating opposites. Such lines as "The nettles that methodically overgrow / the abandoned homesteads of exiles" and "the refugees heading nowhere," on the one hand, simply correspond to the other negative elements in the poem (and the world), attached to the positive ones like a shadow, as, for example, in the image of "the stylish yachts and ships," one of which "had a long trip ahead of it, / while salty oblivion awaited others." At the same time, however, the images of refugees and abandoned houses, as a clear echo of World War II, in the context of immediately post-9/11

---

[3] Ibid.

[4] O'Rourke, "Famed Polish Poet Adam Zagajewski Reads Tonight Joins David Ferry and Valerie Duff for Lowell Lecture."

[5] Zagajewski, "Try to Praise the Mutilated World," the English translation of the poem, by Clare Cavanagh, can be found online: http://www.poetryfoundation.org/poem/247934 (accessed 28.3.2015).

America are a pre-echo of yet another war, in fact, two wars, which, in retrospect, makes the poem appear strikingly prescient. However, its prescience lies not just in "prefiguring" the consequence of one mutilation of one part of the world as one more mutilation of another part of the world, but in the awareness of the inevitability of this principle and the universality and interconnectedness of "the mutilated world." "[T]he gentle light that strays and vanishes / and returns" that the poem ends with, while encouraging us to praise it, appears to be nothing less than the eternal ebb and flow of history. At once optimistic and pessimistic, depending on one's location in time and space (and perhaps, most simply, depending on chance), it may provide comfort to those who need it (and from this perspective Zagajewski's poem could currently be read in, for instance, Syria or Ukraine), while for the currently lucky ones, it provides an ever valid reminder and warning.

Skolimowski

A similarly poetic and universal, albeit this time direct, response from Poland to the aftermath of 9/11 can be found in the 2010 film *Essential Killing*.[6] Written by husband and wife team of Jerzy Skolimowski and Ewa Piaskowska, and directed by Jerzy Skolimowski, one of Poland's most accomplished screenwriters and directors, the film won numerous prestigious awards, including the Special Jury Prize, and Best Actor (for Vincent Gallo) at the 67th Venice International Film Festival. It is a story of a Muslim man, a supposed terrorist, who, after killing three American soldiers, is captured by US Forces in a desert, which could be in Afghanistan or Iraq, and is then brutally tortured in a secret detention centre. Then, together with other prisoners, the man is transported by a plane to a secret facility in Poland included in the CIA's network of extraordinary renditions.[7] On the way from the military airbase to

---

[6] Jerzy Skolimowski (dir.). *Essential Killing*, screenplay Jerzy Skolimowski and Ewa Piaskowska (2010). Usually, and somewhat misleadingly because insufficiently, the film is labelled a political thriller.

[7] Skolimowski's idea for the film was based on a rumour that such a facility existed near his home in Poland's Masuria region (Bodrog, "Essential Filmmaking: An Interview with Legendary Polish Director Jerzy Skolimowski"). Later the rumour turned out to be true (cf. Traynor, "Poland Admits Role in CIA Rendition Programme") and the fact remains a not fully disclosed and still controversial issue in Polish politics and for Polish society, from

the facility, a road accident takes place, as a result of which the protagonist escapes and continues to be on the run for the rest of the story. The fugitive, just like the refugees from Zagajewski's poem, is "heading nowhere" for most of the eighty-three minutes of the film, which, in terms of the plot, cover four excruciating days and even more dangerous nights in an unfamiliar, hostile landscape in the dead of winter.

Long sections of the film look almost like a wildlife documentary, with the protagonist—who, like all the other characters, is never named in the film, but in the credits is given the name Mohammed—never uttering a single word, but always hiding while being hunted, scavenging for potential food (ants, lichen, rose hips, a stolen fish, and even breast milk from a drunken Polish woman), and encountering—it could even be said *other*—wild animals. As the director said himself, "The political aspects of the situation didn't interest me [...] What is important is that the man who runs away is returning to the state of a wild animal, who has to kill in order to survive."[8] Of course, the same logic, "killing in order to survive," is also what motivates those who hunt for the man whom they see as a terrorist and a threat to their (Western) way of life. Hence the essential nature of killing signalled in the very title. However, the analogy between the man (or all men) and animals widens the scope of this nature and makes killing universal, inevitable and essential to all forms of life.

Animals are perhaps the most symbolic element of Skolimowski and Piaskowska's vision. They also play an important role as agents in the forwarding of the plot. The car accident that—at least to some extent—liberates Mohammed is caused by a herd of wild boars. When Mohammed is caught in a snare, like a wild animal, it is the dog that he rescues from a similar snare that helps him escape other, military working dogs. Another dog wakes the man up at night, thus saving him from freezing to death, and then leads him to the house of the deaf and mute woman (played by Emmanuelle Seigner), who is the only human being who not only helps him (feeds him, cleans his wound, offers him a place

---

whom this element of Polish-American co-operation during the War on Terror period was kept secret.

[8] Quoted, in Dawson, "Polish Director, Writer and Actor Jerzy Skolimowski on New Film *Essential Killing*."

to sleep and warm clothes to wear), but in fact treats him with genuine care and tenderness. Herself treated by the man of the house no better than the dog that is kicked by its drunken master on his way out, the nameless woman (Margaret in the international credits), is wordlessly connected with the stranger in need of help exactly through their shared muteness (also shared with animals) and animal-like disadvantaged status in a world dominated by male aggression, which in the film is represented by both the US Army, the Polish personnel assisting them, and the backward civilian inhabitants of the remote rural Polish area depicted as a vast snow-covered wilderness.[9]

In fact, if it were not for their power over weaker creatures and their speech—albeit usually reduced to drunken mumblings and swearwords—these inhabitants would be animal-like themselves; moreover, their appearance and behaviour, as well as their surroundings, share a timeless quality and could just as well belong to the early twentieth, or even the nineteenth, century. It is possible that the Poles are depicted as such incomprehensible and potentially dangerous savages because this is how Mohammed sees them (as no less strange than the moose or deer he encounters). In fact, his point of view is the perspective of almost the entire film (with the exception of several aerial shots, and the scene in Margaret's house) beginning with an early scene where we see other prisoners in orange jumpsuits through a hole in the bag put on Mohammed's head. However, additionally, such a depiction of the Polish countryside, as if taken from a dark fairy tale, provides an ironic reversal of the usual, stereotypical "Western" representation of "the Other," as in the film "the Other" is both Mohammed—an alien from a different culture in an unknown land—and this land's inhabitants, seen through the eyes of the protagonist, with whom the viewers are made to identify. At the same time, this depiction of rural Poland provides also an ironic contrast between the United States and the greatest military power's "best" ally. Paradoxically, a similar contrast in terms of scale, although not tone, is established in the opening scene of the film where the manhunt begins: the helicopter (a Black Hawk) resembles a huge predatory animal, while the man on the run looks like a helpless insect.

---

[9] The location for this forested area in the film was in fact Norway, where snow was more reliable than in Poland (Dawson, "Polish Director, Writer and Actor Jerzy Skolimowski on New Film *Essential Killing*"). Other winter scenes were filmed in Poland, while the desert scene was shot in Israel.

The barren desert landscape could not be more different from the frozen forested expanse of Poland (and Norway), and yet both places are similar in terms of their inhospitableness; yet they also both (although admittedly to a different extent and in a different capacity) serve as hosts for the US. Thus, upon immediately apparent contrasts the film builds subtle parallels, while problematising seemingly stable and unquestionable associations.

Perhaps the most subtle of the film's parallels appears in its last scene, which is the most symbolic one and which involves yet another animal. The animal is a white horse; Margaret gives it to Mohammed in the morning, having sheltered him for the night after hiding him from two Polish soldiers who came to the house to make inquiries. Mohammed slowly rides away on the white horse in an unknown direction, as the woman sees him off. The tableau of the bearded man on a horse and the woman by the fence of a poor Polish rural homestead (one can easily imagine the nettles from Zagajewski's poem that "methodically overgrow" it later, in the summer) seems to belong to a different era, to several different occasions at once, depicted in numerous Polish historical paintings showing a man departing for a war or stopping by on his way to or from one of the many Polish insurrections. In particular, this Muslim man, bleeding and swooning on a horse, bears a striking resemblance to the image of a Polish freedom fighter in the January Uprising (1863–1865), fought by the Poles against the Russian Empire (which had partitioned Poland together with Prussia and Habsburg Austria in 1772, 1793 and 1795; and in which a Polish pro-independence fighter was a terrorist, although the term was not used at the time). The association with this particular uprising is intensified by the time of the year and the historical fact that defeated Polish insurgents were deported to Siberia, where winters are particularly harsh: Mohammed, sent to Poland in the early twenty-first century, finds himself in similar circumstances. An association with insurgents from an earlier Polish rebellion (the November Uprising, 1830–1831) is created by both the above-mentioned fate of captured insurrectionists and by the protagonist's Romantic aura which he is charged with by means of the enigmatic atmosphere of the film, its oneiric quality (not only owing to the man's hallucinations caused by hunger and exhaustion, but also on account of his displacement, confusion and fear—which perspective is captured well by frequent use of a hand-held camera), and a few actual dream sequences—flashbacks occurring when Mohammed falls asleep or loses consciousness (e.g. as a result of torture)—where he sees a woman in a blue burka, probably his wife, sometimes accompanied by (presumably) his small child. The penultimate image of the film's final scene is made up of several close-ups of snow with the first blades of grass emerging from underneath as signals of the coming spring, followed by an image of the white horse, smeared with blood, but now riderless and drifting aimlessly, with the rider lost somewhere offstage, nameless, grave-less, forgotten, like so many (from their own perspective: heroic) fighters for causes doomed to failure—such as the above-mentioned Polish insurrections. Nonetheless, spring follows winter, just as in Zagajewski's poem, "the gentle light […] strays and vanishes /and returns."

Tochman

Such a relentless and inexorable ebb and flow of history, in addition to widely conceived human nature, is the major theme for a Polish writer who created another, this time, literary, reaction to the September 11, 2001 attacks and their aftermath: other attacks and the War on Terror. To date, in the absence of any purely novelistic Polish response to this subject matter, Wojciech Tochman's *Córeńka* (2005) remains the most prominent *partly* novelistic Polish contribution to the post-9/11 genre.[10] *Córeńka* is an unconventional book in the sense that it is

---

[10] My earlier analysis of *Córeńka* (and of *Windows on the World*, discussed in comparison with Tochman's book later in this chapter) has appeared in my book entitled *The "Image-Event" in the Early Post-9/11 Novel: Literary Representations of Terror After September 11, 2001*. In this comparative study I examine thirteen Western responses (predominantly novels) to the terrorist attacks of 9/11 and/or their aftermath. The books are presented on a scale measuring the distance in time and space between the literary works (i.e. the subjects who act as the sources of the point of view in the texts) and the event of a terrorist attack (predominantly 9/11 but in the case of *Córeńka*—the Bali bombings). The proposed conclusion is a correspondence between a given work's distance from the explosion and the level of its formal conventionality: the closer a work is to the explosion, the more unconventional its form. The discussed works, listed here in four groups presented in order of increasing formal conventionality (and therefore increasing distance from a terrorist attack), are: (1) Frédéric Beigbeder's *Windows on the World* (2003), Art Spiegelman's *In the Shadow of No Towers* (2004), Jonathan Safran Foer's *Extremely Loud and Incredibly Close* (2005), Wojciech Tochman's *Córeńka* (2005); (2) William Gibson's *Pattern Recognition* (2003), Nick McDonell's *The Third Brother* (2005), Don DeLillo's *Falling Man* (2007); (3) Claire Tristram's *After* (2004), Philip Beard's *Dear Zoe* (2005); and (4) Ian McEwan's *Saturday* (2005), Lynne Sharon Schwartz's *The Writing on the Wall* (2005), John Updike's *Terrorist* (2006), and Jay McInerney's *The Good Life* (2006).

impossible to assign it to just one category. Its four parts are a heterogeneous hybrid of fact and fiction: "Trzeci zeszyt" [The third notebook], "Zamach" [The attack], "Tamto" [That] and "Aniołek, potem Imam" [Aniołek,[11] then Imam]. Only the first part is fictitious and can be called a novella. Then a sudden transition takes place to the other parts of the book which belong to the genre of literary reportage.

Because of this purely literary attempt in the first chapter, *Córeńka* is unusual for its author as well, but this exceptionality must stem from the exceptional and particularly personal circumstances which gave rise to it, and which I will address below. To demonstrate the book's special status, it is necessary to put it in the context of the author and his other works. Wojciech Tochman[12] is one of Poland's most respected reporters and non-fiction writers, and a recipient of many prestigious Polish literary and journalism awards. He belongs to the so-called "Polish School of Reportage," whose most celebrated representative was Ryszard Kapuściński, author of such works as *Cesarz* [The Emperor: Downfall of an Autocrat, 1978], *Heban* [The Shadow of the Sun, 1998] or *Podróże z Herodotem* [Travels with Herodotus, 2007], and who was said to have "transformed journalism into literature in his writings about Africa."[13] The same quality of writing which turns reportage into a literary genre can be ascribed to the whole "Polish School of Reportage," whose other members known to English-language readers are Kazimierz Moczarski, author of a series of interviews with a Nazi war criminal, Jürgen Stroop, entitled *Rozmowy z Katem* [Conversations with an Executioner], serialised in 1972–1974, and published in 1977 and 1992 (unabridged version), and Hanna Krall, best known for her 1977 book *Zdążyć przed Panem Bogiem* [Shielding the Flame], an interview with Marek Edelman, the only surviving leader of the 1943 Warsaw Ghetto Uprising. Both Kapuściński and Krall were not only professional role-models for Tochman but also his direct mentors in terms of writing style and the ethics of journalism.[14] It is important to note that even though excellent

---

[11] This is the title (meaning "little angel") of a novel written by the main and eponymous character of *Córeńka*.

[12] All biographical and bibliographical information on the author comes from his official website: http://tochman.eu/en/ (accessed 29.3.2015).

[13] Deedes, "A Good Man in Africa".

[14] Modzelewska, "Wpływ Ryszarda Kapuścińskiego i Hanny Krall na twórczość reporterską Wojciecha Tochmana," 29.

examples of literary reportage can be found in the English language, e.g. in Truman Capote's *In Cold Blood* (1966) in the US and, and in George Orwell's *Down and Out in Paris and London* (1933) or *Homage to Catalonia* (1938) in Britain, the genre is not only much more popular and established in Poland, but also much more critically acclaimed and on a par with fiction genres such as the novel. In addition to Wojciech Tochman, its most contemporary representatives, i.e. the next generation who took over from Kapuściński and Krall, are such authors as Wojciech Jagielski, Mariusz Szczygieł, Katarzyna Surmiak-Domańska and Lidia Ostałowska among others. The next generation is being trained, e.g. in Szczygieł and Tochman's Polish Reportage Institute in Warsaw.

Tochman is the author of eight books, several of which have been translated into a number of foreign languages (English, French, Italian, Dutch, Swedish, Finnish, Russian, Ukrainian, Czech, Slovak, Romanian, Bulgarian and Bosnian):

- three collections of reports on contemporary Polish society: *Schodów się nie pali* [Staircases Don't Burn], 2000; *Wściekły pies* [The Rabid Dog], 2007; and *Bóg zapłać* [God Bless You], 2010;
- *Córenka* [Beloved Daughter], 2005;
- a book about the post-Yugoslavian present—the legacy of the 1992–1995 war: *Jakbyś kamień jadła* (*Like Eating a Stone. Surviving the Past in Bosnia*, English translation by Antonia Lloyd-Jones), 2008;
- a book of reporting on "the scars of the Rwandan genocide that can still be found today"—*Dzisiaj narysujemy śmierć* [Today We're Going to Draw Death], 2010;
- "the story of the unknown Philippines, of the world of the poorest of the poor who have lived for years in the slums and graveyards of Manila"—*Eli, Eli* (with photographs by Grzegorz Wełnicki), 2013;
- a book of reporting on Syrian refugees—*Kontener* [The Container], co-authored by Katarzyna Boni, 2014.

As can be seen, most of Tochman's output has been concerned with issues from outside Poland, namely, the Balkans, and reaching beyond Europe: to Africa and Asia, but always focusing on such topics as poverty, social injustice and war. *Córenka* combines a Polish element with an interest in Asia. The book (whose film rights have been sold in Poland) tells the real story of the author's friend, another Polish journalist, Beata

Pawlak, who was killed in the Bali bombings on 12 October 2002. The terrorist attack took place in and near popular nightclubs in the tourist district of Kuta on the Indonesian island and was perpetrated by a violent Islamist group, Jemaah Islamiyah. The attack claimed 202 lives (mainly from Australia, Indonesia and Britain), and injured a further 209 people. Tochman's book is named after Beata, the only Polish victim: the word "córeńka" is a diminutive form of the word "córka," meaning "daughter." Importantly, "córeńka" is not just a diminutive but one of the *most* diminutive forms of the word "daughter" in the Polish language (which is very productive in diminutives formation), and is used as a term of endearment by the main character's mother. Interestingly, this highly emotionally charged word (which could be translated as "dearest little daughter" or "beloved daughter") denotes also the book itself, conveying the author's personal emotional involvement in its creation as a tribute to someone close who was lost.

The book is a tribute to Beata and her own work,[15] but mainly it is a documentary account of Tochman's search for his colleague and friend when her fate was still uncertain. When news of the bombings arrived and there was no contact with his friend, Tochman travelled to Bali and the site of the terrorist attack hoping to find her alive. Several years later, working on his books on the genocides in Bosnia and in Rwanda, where again Zagajewski's "nettles" "methodically overgr[ew] /the abandoned homesteads of exiles" and "refugees head[ed] nowhere," Tochman would again have an opportunity to witness the work of forensic scientists trying to identify human remains recovered from exhumation sites for surviving family members. In late 2002, the writer himself was in the position of an anxious close friend to a potential victim. However, while none of the bodies had yet been identified as Beata's, and no object with traces of her DNA had been found, there was still hope that she was not among the victims. At this point Tochman even contemplated the possibility that his friend, the imaginative adventurer that she was, might have simulated her own death (*Córeńka*, 112) to start a new life in the exotic setting of Bali (it was well known among her friends that as soon

---

[15] Another tribute to the journalist is an annual prize established in her name in 2003 and awarded on 12 October to authors of accomplished "publications about other cultures, religions and civilisations," available at http://wyborcza.pl/1,75475,12610059,Nominowani_do_Nagrody_im__Beaty_Pawlak.html#ixzz3U5pZuUgj (accessed 29.3.2015).

as she was financially able to do so, Beata wanted to travel the world and was particularly drawn to Asia; in 2002, she reached Indonesia and Bali, which she believed to be paradise, after travelling in Nepal, Thailand and Malaysia—this was meant to be the greatest journey of her life).[16] Unfortunately, this scenario was just a fantastical wish meant to eke out hope. Five days after the attack, her body was identified: she died not knowing that her murderer was a fanatic follower of a warped version of Islam—paradoxically, a religion which had fascinated her.[17] As one of her friends remarked, "In a way, it can be said that she was killed by her passion."[18]

"Beata wrote about Islam like no one else in the Polish press. Masterfully combining knowledge with sensitivity, passion with responsibility and hard work with exceptional determination, she wanted to explain this world," said Ryszard Kapuściński (quoted in Noch 2012). A fellow-reporter and friend added to this: "She perceived terrorism as a social phenomenon, a kind of rebellion. She tried to understand the reasons driving people to reach for such drastic measures" (Bartosz Węglarczyk quoted in Noch 2012). A collection of her articles about the world of Islam (in Algeria, France, Bosnia, Gaza, Israel, Lebanon, Iraq, Kurdistan, Egypt, Poland, and Turkey, as well as about Ali Ağca, the Turkish assassin who wounded John Paul II) entitled *Piekło jest gdzie indziej* [Hell Is Elsewhere] and published posthumously in 2003, conveys her genuine curiosity, openness and empathy in the absence of prejudice and judgement. In his book about her, Tochman himself retains objectivity, but stresses that Beata was "attracted" to terrorism as a subject[19] (*Córeńka*, 118)—she wanted to be *close* to it, and in the end, she found herself all too close to its dangerous interpretation. Beata "[ś]ledziła wszystko, co ukazuje się w polskiej prasie na temat terroryzmu"[20] (*Córeńka*, 117). About her alter ego from the first, fictitious, part of *Córeńka*, Tochman says: "Ekscytowała się śmiercią, jak ekscytują się nią terroryści. I nimi się ekscytowała!"[21] (*Córeńka*, 19).

---

[16] Pytlakowski, "10. rocznica śmierci Beaty Pawlak".

[17] Ibid.

[18] Bartosz Węglarczyk, quoted in Noch, "To już 10 lat od śmierci Beaty Pawlak".

[19] "Pociągał ją terroryzm." All translations into English from *Córeńka* are mine.

[20] "She followed everything that appeared in the Polish press about terrorism."

[21] "She was excited by death the way terrorists are excited by it. And she was excited by them [terrorists]!"

Tochman also tells us that Beata "[c]hciałaby z pewnością porozmawiać z własnym mordercą"[22] (*Córeńka*, 141), because "[z]awsze uważała, że z każdym trzeba poważnie rozmawiać. Z terrorystami szczególnie. Żeby ich zrozumieć"[23] (*Córeńka*, 142). She would have been interested in her murderer's (Imam Samudra's) autobiography, which he wrote in prison, awaiting his execution which was carried out in 2008. "Na pewno chciałaby się dowiedzieć, kto i dlaczego z pubów pełnych śmiechu w sekundę zrobił rzeźnię pełną krwi"[24] (*Córeńka*, 141) The terrorist's bomb turned the clubs into a deathly negative of the discotheque[25]—a symbol of the Western lifestyle in the eyes of the terrorists. Due to this symbolic value, Paddy's Pub and Sari Club in Bali, filled with Western tourists and holiday-makers in their twenties and thirties, were as deliberately chosen as a terrorist target as the Twin Towers. And the carnage that took place in them is at the centre of *Córeńka*. I suggest that it is exactly this fact that collapses a predictable unified structure of a single genre and prevents the book's clear classification as fact or fiction, since this distinction became blurred by the instance of a terrorist attack itself.

Paradoxically, *Córeńka* combines simultaneous closeness to the explosion in reality and distance from it within the text. Since the real-life author went to the site of the terrorist attack shortly after it killed the real-life "main character" of his book, the factual author, Wojciech Tochman, and the factual Beata Pawlak were *in reality* extremely close

---

[22] "She would have certainly wanted to talk to her murderer."

[23] "She always believed that one should talk seriously with everyone. Especially with terrorists. In order to understand them."

[24] "She would have certainly wanted to find out who and why in one second turned pubs full of laughter into a bloody slaughterhouse."

[25] This image: dancing and drinking young foreigners, male and female bodies commingling, loud music and voices, colours in movement, pulsating light—transformed into motionless, lifeless, silent, unidentifiable body parts and blood and rubble must be a black carnival image. The carnival of the West became the carnival (and the same root, meaning meat or flesh, as in the words "carnal" and "carnage" is noticeable here) of the fundamentalist Islamists. It is important to distinguish between "Islamist" from "the more general, and politically neutral, 'Muslim,'" as Salman Rushdie urges us to do in his article, "A war that presents us all with a crisis of faith." In another article, "Let's get back to life," Rushdie specifies: "Such people are against, to offer just a brief list, freedom of speech, a multi-party political system, universal adult suffrage, accountable government, Jews, homosexuals, women's rights, pluralism, secularism, short skirts, dancing, beardlessness, evolution theory, sex. These are tyrants, not Muslims," Rushdie, "Let's get back to life."

(to paraphrase the title of Jonathan Safran Foer's novel *Extremely Loud and Incredibly Close* [2005]) to the event of the terrorist attack—in fact, in the case of the tragically killed journalist, we can say the greatest proximity that is physically possible (which, in turn, renders physical existence impossible). Yet, in a sense, *within the text* Beata is distant from the attack and so is the author. For Beata, this distance is, perforce, silence: because of the actual real-life proximity to the attack, now, as a victim, she cannot tell her own story. In line with German writer Thomas Lehr, the author of *September. Fata Morgana* (2010), Tochman opts for silence instead of using the literary imagination to fill this epistemological gap, unlike Frédéric Beigbeder in his novel *Windows on the World* (2003). Admittedly, there may be an ethical difference between giving a voice to *fictitious* dead characters (as in Beigbeder's *Windows on the World*, and Lehr's *September. Fata Morgana*) and giving it to an actual dead person (Beata Pawlak); another difference is perhaps between giving a fictitious literary voice to a factual victim (Beata Pawlak) and giving it to a factual terrorist/murderer and suicide—which is what Martin Amis did in his short story "The Last Days of Muhammad Atta" (2008).[26] This latter case appears to be more morally acceptable, however, since there is no ethical imperative to respect a disrespected—in fact, morally condemned—murderer: in this instance, giving him a voice is rather an act of deliberate disrespect (as opposed to unintentionally indelicate, which would be the case if a real victim was involved), imposing it on someone whose own original voice would be considered unworthy of honouring. Such ventriloquism may even be an instance of taking control of the story, an ersatz act of recapturing a hijacked narrative, or more than that: substituting the original voice of a terrorist by a Western author may be a symbolic act of retaliation or revenge. In the case of *Córeńka*, however, Tochman includes Beata's voice only by quoting her own writing from the past, trying to put together any pieces left from her life and death. The rest of the text is his own voice, which in the three reportage parts of the book always comes from the position of a reporter. And this is what distances the author from the terrorist attack, the explosion, *within the text*: carefully balanced and reliable professional journalistic language. However, as was mentioned earlier, the form of *Córeńka* is hybrid, and the hybridity consists in the combination of the three reportage parts

---

[26] Amis, "The Last Days of Muhammad Atta."

with the opening novella part. It is in this element that the author, finding himself on the edge of real danger, makes his book balance on the edge of two genres—as well as on the border between reality and fiction.

The first chapter of *Córeńka* is clearly marked as fiction. In fact, "Trzeci zeszyt" [The third notebook] might even be called "fiction squared," as it is an attempt at a fictitious reconstruction of a fictional text which certainly existed, but which was destroyed in the Bali bombings. This is why the author tries to recreate it, or rather create it anew. The explanation of what "Trzeci zeszyt" is can be found in the next part of the book, "Zamach" [The attack], and in fact, part of the explanation *is* the terrorist attack.

Immediately after arriving in Bali, Tochman looks through his friend's possessions left behind in her hotel room, searching for some clues about her possible whereabouts. Among Beata's possessions he finds two green notebooks filled with writing that looks like a draft of a novel. As one of her friends recalled, writing to her friends in Poland from her travels across Asia, Beata mentioned many ideas and plans for several books, including novels.[27] In the draft in the two green notebooks, Tochman read about two main characters, two women: Czajka and Matylda. They are Polish reporters who work together. Czajka was travelleing across Asia and went missing, and consequently Matylda follows her to the countries she visited to look for her friend (*Córeńka*, 108). Tochman adds that the writing in the second notebook ends a month before the bombing. He suspects that there must be a third notebook which Beata most certainly always carried with her (*Córeńka*, 109).

What appears striking here is the later uncanny repetition of Beata Pawlak's fiction in Wojciech Tochman's reality. When Tochman comes to Bali to look for Beata, who is missing like Czajka, Beata's literary creation (and, as it seems, her alter ego), it is as if he takes on the role of Matylda, the other character—looking for her missing friend. Later, he also takes over the role of Beata as the author of her unfinished novel, because realising that the third notebook must have been destroyed with its owner in the terrorist attack, he sets out to reconstruct the inaccessible original in the only way possible: he *invents* it. Notably, this very strategy was also used by Beigbeder, who said: "Le seul moyen de savoir ce qui s'est passé dans le restaurant situé au 107e étage de la Tour Nord

---

[27] Pytlakowski, "10. rocznica śmierci Beaty Pawlak."

du World Trade Center, le 11 septembre 2001, entre 8 h 30 et 10 h 29, c'est de l'inventer."[28] However, the difference between these two cases is that, for Beigbeder, the original was a factual event, and actual lives of real people, which he substituted with his literary creations (including his own alter ego), while, for Tochman, the original was a work of fiction, and fictitious lives of literary characters (including the original author's alter ego), which he substitutes with an alternative work of fiction (including an alternative version of the original author's alter ego). Importantly, Tochman not only writes "Trzeci zeszyt" and tells the story of Czajka and Matylda. What is more, in a way, he also actually acts out his vision of this story about a journalist searching for a missing journalist and friend in south-eastern Asia, since he himself searches for a missing journalist and friend in the same region and records this enactment in the three non-fictitious parts of the book. In contrast, Beigbeder only symbolically "performed" and imagined what he "recreated" or, by his own admission, invented.

To further demonstrate the difference between the two books, it may be helpful to explain what is meant here by Beigbeder's "performance" in more detail. The "performance" was "staged" during the period of writing of *Windows on the World*, approximately from September 2002[29] till March 2003, and the "performance"—which could be seen as an attempt at achieving an "iconicity of experience"—consisted in carrying out whatever was within the author's power to get close to the unreachable original. The first and main symbolic attempt to create affinity between the author and the subject of his book is made by choosing the setting and time for writing the book. Most of the autobiographical sections largely devoted to struggling with the process of writing *Windows on the World* are set in Le Ciel de Paris, the highest restaurant in Europe, located on the 56th floor of Tour Montparnasse, the tallest tower in Paris (*WoW*, 6 [8:32][30]). This is also where most of the fictitious part of the book—set in New York—is said to be written (this is

---

[28] Beigbeder, *Windows on the World*, back cover; English: *Windows on the World*, trans. Frank Wynne. "The only way to know what took place in the restaurant on the 107th Floor of the North Tower, World Trade Center on September 11th, 2001 is to invent it," ibid., 307.

[29] In fact, in an interview, Beigbeder said that he "started taking notes at once," on September 11, 2001 (Géniès, "Sept. 11, the Novel: Possible or Not?").

[30] Chapters of the novel are given in square brackets.

said in the autobiographical part of the book, and as readers we have no way of ascertaining the truth value of these statements; we can only trust them in accordance with the "autobiographical pact"[31]). Significantly, the writing is said to be taking place in the morning (*WoW*, 6 [8:32]), at the same time as the tragedy—and, as we can see, in a similar place of the restaurant "Windows on the World" which was located in one of the Twin Towers. Thus, the place and the time of the Paris plot which deals with the process of writing it, mirror, as much as they can, the place and the time of the parallel second action embedded in the first one (i.e. in Beigbeder's writing) and resulting from it.

Obviously, this attempt to create affinity with September 11 on the part of the author of this autobiographical work is very limited. Still, he does not refrain from carrying them out. He (says that he): walks fifty-six floors downstairs, in a building which has *not* been hit by an airplane, in order to imagine what people *might* have felt like that morning (*WoW*, 112 [9:04]); goes to the roof of Tour Montparnasse; times himself in the lift; goes to three exhibitions devoted to the tragedy (*WoW*, 123 [9:08], 170 [9:24], 194 [9:32]); flies to New York; and, finally, symbolically closes his eyes in the last scene of the book. All these described—and we are led to believe: acted out—gestures of the author hold the key to understanding a simple truth: until the readers make at least a minimum effort and try to *imagine* for themselves what it might have felt like to be on the planes and inside the towers, even the most detailed and reliable information will not help us know more on its own.

Beigbeder's "performance," however, must be contrasted with Tochman's "enactment" of his recreated version of Beata Pawlak's story of Matylda searching for Czajka (the content of "Trzeci zeszyt"), which he unknowingly began even before he found Beata's green notebooks and which the remaining reportage parts of *Córeńka* are devoted to. Although Tochman's writing, being mainly reportage, has some implicit autobiographical dimension, it is not an autobiography. The Polish author is a reporter who never puts himself at the centre of his work: he is a transparent mediator. The parallel between life and writing in which life reflects prior writing and not just the other way round, as is the journalistic norm, is striking but accidental in Tochman's case (who

---

[31] See Philippe Lejeune's *Le Pacte autobiographique* (1975), Lejeune, *Wariacje na temat pewnego paktu. O autobiografii*.

inadvertently enacts somebody else's scenario). In contrast, it is designed and deliberate in Beigbeder's case: the French writer first writes about his intention to fly to New York and then carries out his own plan; he himself decides to walk fifty-six floors downstairs, to go to the roof of Tour Montparnasse, to time himself in the lift there, and then describes the experience, which was carried out in order to be described.

Córeńka and *Windows on the World* are two hybrid literary works which find themselves the closest to the event of a terrorist attack,[32] even though they do so in different ways: the former is the closest to the explosion on a factual level (the protagonist was killed in it, the author went to its site days later), while the latter is the closest on a fictional level (its fictional characters were killed in it, the author imagined being at the site and "performed" this approximate experience—to the extent to which it was accessible to him—two years later). Although they do so in different ways and for different reasons, both books strongly problematise the distinction between reality and fiction, pointing to the mutually formative relationship between the two: it is not only reality that is reflected in or creates fiction, but also fiction becomes reality. In fact, this corresponds with what Jean Baudrillard wrote about the reality of the events of 9/11 themselves: being visually indistinguishable from Hollywood disaster movies, this reality itself became fiction after having absorbed fiction's energy.[33] And since the power of terrorism consists in the fact that it transgresses borderlines, disrupts order, and suspends established conventions,[34] it is only fitting that the authors whose literary works come closest to the explosion created narratives which are fragmentary, as if already "broken," in this way, reflecting the effect of an explosion. They are broken because they come so close to the tragedy, but also, in a circular way, they come so close to the tragedy, because they are broken.

---

[32] Among the thirteen literary works which I have analysed and listed earlier.

[33] Baudrillard, *The Spirit of Terrorism or Requiem for the Twin Towers*, 28.

[34] It does so by blurring distinctions between a number of hitherto separate and stable phenomena, such as "vehicle of air transport" and "weapon," "accident" and "attack," "casualties," "victims" and "heroes," "Americans" and "non-Americans" (the terrorists became American all the better to kill Americans; they also killed themselves). Finally, there is the unreliable, because limitless, nature of the terms "terrorist" and "War on Terror" itself.

It remains to be seen if this effect, the deliberate blurring of fact and fiction and the creation of complex multilevel narratives, is something that 9/11 has brought into terror literature in general and perhaps has become a topos even in literary accounts that do not focus on 9/11 but on the post-9/11 reality, which is all the more likely since the reality at this time happens to be simultaneously the beginning of the global Internet era. The September 11, 2001 terrorist attacks have undoubtedly "forever changed the way we approach architecture and design," not only in the Western world, with safety being the primary concern, gradually addressed by subtle, aesthetically pleasing and environmentally sustainable solutions.[35] Since today, and certainly increasingly so, material, physical places are not the only spaces we inhabit, a corresponding broadening of the concept "reality" appears to be inevitable.

Conclusion

What can be observed about the Polish responses to the aftermath of September 11 which have been discussed above, including Zagajewski's universal poem, which admittedly predated the events but became part of the post-9/11 literary discourse through its reading, is that they offer a wider historical and geographical perspective. The poem, drawing partly upon World War II in the mid-twentieth century, was just as applicable to the wars in Rwanda and the former Yugoslavia at the end of the same century as to the wars in Iraq and Afghanistan in the early twenty-first century, and, unfortunately, it proves and most certainly will continue to prove useful as a source of quotations about current conflicts and conflicts yet to come, which all seem to follow the same pattern (so devastatingly described by Tochman in his *Like Eating a Stone* and *Dzisiaj narysujemy śmierć*). The apparently more topical film by Skolimowski and book by Tochman also share some of the poem's universality, however. Importantly, unlike most early Western responses to the post-9/11 reality, *Essential Killing* and *Córeńka* do not limit themselves to the instance of a terrorist attack and psychological reactions to it. Both formally unconventional, the two works are reluctant to pass judgement, but instead remain open, offering the viewer and the reader space for their own interpretations and conclusions. In the film, hardly

---

[35] Gonzales, "10 Ways 9/11 Changed the Way We Build."

any words are spoken, and not one word that is said is understood by the main character who himself never utters a single word. Such paring down of artistic expression to bare essentials is also typical of the "Polish School of Reportage," and accordingly *Córeńka* also demonstrates its author's characteristic restraint. Above all, the analysed works by Polish authors remind us that the world is everywhere inhabited by people with parallel experiences—as victims or oppressors, depending on circumstances—whose main goal, like that of all living organisms, is to survive, and that consequently, albeit paradoxically, this is why the world is repeatedly, and always in some place(s) at one given time, "mutilated."

REFERENCES

Amis, Martin. "The Last Days of Muhammad Atta" in *The Second Plane. September 11: Terror and Boredom* (New York/Toronto: Alfred A. Knopf, 2008), 93–121.

Baudrillard, Jean. *The Spirit of Terrorism or Requiem for the Twin Towers*, trans. Chris Turner (New York: Verso, 2002).

Beigbeder, Frédéric. *Windows on the World* (Paris: Gallimard, 2005).

———. *Windows on the World*, trans. Frank Wynne (New York: Miramax Books, 2005).

Bodrog, Robert. "Essential Filmmaking: An Interview With Legendary Polish Director Jerzy Skolimowski," Filmfestivals.com, December 22, 2010, available at http://www.filmfestivals.com/blog/robert_bodrog/essential_filmmaking_an_interview_with_legendary_polish_director_jerzy_skolimowski (accessed 30.3.2015).

Boxer, Sarah. "Falls of Towers And the Rise Of Polish Poetry," *The New York Times*, March 16, 2002, available at http://www.nytimes.com/2002/03/16/books/falls-of-towers-and-the-rise-of-polish-poetry.html (accessed 30.3.2015).

Dawson, Tom. "Polish director, writer and actor Jerzy Skolimowski on new film *Essential Killing*," *The List*, March 18, 2011, available at https://film.list.co.uk/article/33344-polish-director-writer-and-actor-jerzy-skolimowski-on-new-film-essential-killing/ (accessed 30.3.2015).

Deedes, W. F. "A good man in Africa," *The Telegraph*, June 15, 2001, available at http://www.telegraph.co.uk/culture/4724092/A-good-man-in-Africa.html (accessed 30.3.2015).

Géniès, Bernard. "Sept.11, the Novel: Possible or Not?" the November issue of *World Press Review*, vol. 50, no. 11 (2003), available at www.worldpress.org/Americas/1583.cfm (accessed 30.3.2015).

Gonzales, Robbie. "10 Ways 9/11 Changed the Way We Build," *Gizmodo*, September 12, 2011, available at http://io9.com/5839066/10-ways-911-changed-the-way-we-build (accessed 29.3.2015).

Kowal, Ewa. *The "Image-Event" in the Early Post-9/11 Novel: Literary Representations of Terror After September 11, 2001* (Kraków: Jagiellonian University Press, 2012).

Lejeune, Philippe. *Wariacje na temat pewnego paktu. O autobiografii*, ed. R. Lubas-Bartoszyńska, trans. Wincenty Grajewski et al. (Kraków: Universitas, 2001).

Modzelewska, Anna. "Wpływ Ryszarda Kapuścińskiego i Hanny Krall na twórczość reporterską Wojciecha Tochmana," *Naukowy Przegląd Dziennikarski / Journalism Research Review Quarterly*, no. 1 (2014), available at http://naukowy-przeglad-dziennikarski.org/nr/1-2014/3.pdf (accessed 30.3.2015).

Noch, Jakub. "To już 10 lat od śmierci Beaty Pawlak," October 12, 2012, available at http://natemat.pl/35241,to-juz-10-lat-od-smierci-beaty-pawlak-weglarczyk-patrzyla-na-terroryzm-jako-zjawisko-spoleczne-rodzaj-buntu (accessed 11.03.2015).

O'Rourke, John. "Famed Polish Poet Adam Zagajewski Reads Tonight Joins David Ferry and Valerie Duff for Lowell Lecture," *BU Today*, September 15, 2010, available at http://www.bu.edu/today/2010/famed-polish-poet-adam-zagajewski-reads-tonight/ (accessed 30.03.2015).

Pytlakowski, Piotr. "10. rocznica śmierci Beaty Pawlak," *Polityka*, October 12, 2012, available at http://www.polityka.pl/tygodnikpolityka/kraj/1531295,1,10-rocznica-smierci-beaty-pawlak.read (accessed 11.03.2015).

Rushdie, Salman. "Let's get back to life." *The Guardian*, October 6, 2001, available at http://www.guardian.co.uk/books/2001/oct/06/fiction.afghanistan (accessed 30.3.2015).

———. "A war that presents us all with a crisis of faith." *The Guardian*, November 3, 2001, available at http://www.guardian.co.uk/books/2001/nov/03/afghanistan.terrorism (accessed 30.3.2015).

Skolimowski, Jerzy (dir). *Essential Killing*, screenplay Jerzy Skolimowski, Ewa Piaskowska (2010).

Tochman, Wojciech. *Córeńka* (Kraków: Znak, 2005).

Traynor, Ian. "Poland admits role in CIA rendition programme," *The Guardian*, February 22, 2010, available at http://www.theguardian.com/world/2010/feb/22/poland-cia-rendition-flights (accessed 30.03.2015).

Zagajewski, Adam. "Try to Praise the Mutilated World," trans. Clare Cavanagh, available at http://www.poetryfoundation.org/poem/247934 (accessed 28.3.2015).

Author Biography

Ewa Kowal is Assistant Professor in the Department of Comparative Studies in Literature and Culture in the Institute of English Studies at the Jagiellonian University, Krakow, Poland. She is the author of the book *The "Image-Event" in the Early Post-9/11 Novel: Literary Representations of Terror after September 11, 2001* (Kraków: Jagiellonian University Press, 2012) and a series of articles devoted to post-9/11 literature. Her research interests concentrate on contemporary literature and film, in particular the most recent responses to the aftermath of (post-)9/11 terror and the current economic crisis. Her general interests are: contemporary literary, cultural and aesthetic theories, feminist criticism and gender studies, as well as the visual arts. She is also a translator and editor.

The Islamic World as Other in Oriana Fallaci's "Trilogy"

Charles Burdett

The first part of what is now generally known as Oriana Fallaci's "trilogy" on the significance of the terrorist attacks on 11 September 2001 was initially published on 29 September 2001 in the pages of the newspaper, the *Corriere della Sera*: it was at the invitation of Ferruccio de Bortoli, the then editor of the paper, that she wrote her reflections on the meaning and the probable ramifications of 9/11. Shortly after the appearance of her extended article in the *Corriere*, a book-length version of her views was published by the publishing house Rizzoli in December 2001 with the title, *La rabbia e l'orgoglio* [The Rage and the Pride].[1]

I would like to thank the AHRC for financing the research on which this chapter is based. The chapter has previously been published in my monograph *Italy, Islam and the Islamic World: Representations and Reflections, from 9/11 to the Arab Uprisings* (Oxford: Peter Lang, 2016) under the same title. I would like to thank the publisher Peter Lang for the permission to reprint this chapter here.

[1] The book, as is noted by Fallaci, is about twice the length of the original article. Rizzoli have published all the texts in the trilogy, cf. Fallaci, *La rabbia e l'orgoglio*, 14.

C. Burdett (✉)
Bristol, UK

The second text of the trilogy was initially intended to be a kind of post-script, written two years after the publication of *La rabbia e l'orgoglio*, but the text expanded into book form and was published as *La forza della ragione* [The Force of Reason] in April 2004. The book explored the expansion of the Islamic world through migration, the responses of various European governments to the question and the likely effects on the development of Western culture in the longer term. The final part of the trilogy, entitled *Oriana Fallaci intervista Oriana Fallaci* [Oriana Fallaci interviews Oriana Fallaci], appeared in September of the same year and was subsequently printed with its post-script, *L'Apocalisse* [The Apocalypse].[2] The book offered further reflections on Italy's relationship with the Muslim world, on the stance of leading politicians or institutions and, as its title suggested, on Fallaci's own views on the current state of Western culture.

There is no doubt that every book in the trilogy represents a publishing phenomenon: within two years of its appearance, *La rabbia e l'orgoglio* had sold over one million copies, while the third book in the series sold over half a million copies on the first day of its publication.[3] Though, clearly, many authoritative commentaries on the events of 11 September 2001 have been printed in Italy and figures of the standing of Umberto Eco (2001), Tiziano Terzani (2002) and Stefano Allievi (2001)[4] have produced powerful and meticulously argued reflections on the wider significance of 9/11, such is the appeal of Fallaci's writing that it has exercised considerably more influence than any other work on the subject. Indeed, many other analyses of global culture in the wake of the attack on the Twin Towers that have been published in Italy have been written as *reactions* to the views that are expressed in the trilogy.[5]

---

[2] The text was subsequently given the title, *Oriana Fallaci intervista sè stessa* [Oriana Fallaci Interviewed by Herself]. All translations from the Italian are my own.

[3] These details are given on the cover of each text. Orsini notes in her analysis of the work's success, that Rizzoli claims that *La rabbia e l'orgoglio* has been the greatest non-fiction best-seller ever in Italy, cf. Orsini, "Cannons and Rubber Boats: Oriana Fallaci and the 'Clash of Civilizations'," 445.

[4] Eco, "Le guerre sante: passione e ragione," Terzani, *Lettere contro la guerra*; Allievi, *La tentazione della guerra. Dopo l'attacco al World Trade Center*.

[5] In addition to the texts already cited, see Belpoliti, "The Fallacies of St. Fallaci," Bosetti, *Cattiva maestra. La rabbia di Oriana Fallaci e il suo contagio*. Within the Anglo-American academy, Orsini, "Cannons and Rubber Boats," and Gatt-Rutter, "The Dummy Interlocutor and Oriana Fallaci's Self-Projection in *La rabbia e l'orgoglio*," have written incisively on the trilogy.

Terzani's *Lettere contro la guerra* [Letters against the War], as its title implies, is a collection of letters that were initially printed—for the most part—in the pages of the *Corriere della Sera* between September 2001 and January 2002. Published in the same newspaper as the first draft of *La rabbia e l'orgoglio*, 29 September 2001, Terzani's letter, dated 4 October 2001, is addressed to "Cara Oriana" [Dear Oriana]. Each of the "letters" is written from a different location and indicates the itinerary that the author follows as he moves from his private residence in Orsigna in northern Tuscany, to Florence and then, as he attempts to gain a clearer view on the War on Terror, to Peshawar, Quetta and Kabul before journeying to Delhi and finally returning to his adoptive home in the Himalayas. In his response to the publication of *La rabbia e l'orgoglio*, an alternative trilogy,[6] Allievi speaks explicitly about the need not only to refute Fallaci's ideas but to do so in a way that is as direct, as personal and as accessible as the trilogy undoubtedly is. Other texts that provide a complex refutation of the thesis that Fallaci expounds have been written by Franco Cardini (2002) and by Khaled Fouad Allam (2011).[7]

It is perhaps not difficult to identify the reasons for the success, at least in terms of its circulation, of Fallaci's trilogy. In the aftermath of 9/11, in the wake, that is, of such an unexpected, devastating and spectacular assault on a collectively constructed and recognized sense of material and conceptual order, the appeal of Fallaci's work was principally, though not exclusively, threefold.[8] First, her texts provided an account of the wider significance of the terrorist atrocities that was written by a figure of very considerable authority. The authority with which she spoke derived from her lengthy career as a journalist and as a writer: she was someone who had witnessed first-hand many of the most important conflicts of the latter part of the twentieth century and who was

---

[6] Allievi, *Niente di personale, Signora Fallaci: Una trilogia alternativa*, 17f.

[7] Cardini, *I cantori della guerra giusta: religioni, fondamentalismi, globalizzazione*; Khaled Fouad Allam, *L'Islam spiegato ai leghisti*.

[8] In the words of Umberto Galimberti (2001), "L'azione terroristica ha incrinato in noi occidentali quella condizione base della vita quotidiana che è la prevedibilità del domani" [The terrorist action has, in we the inhabitants of the West, fractured one of the most basic conditions of everyday life—the predictability of tomorrow], cf. Galimberti, "La condizione dell'angoscia."

familiar with world leaders of the past and the present.⁹ She was someone who had repeatedly asserted her independence and who had always been prepared to risk her personal safety in stating what she believed to be true and in exposing the folly and brutality that people in positions of power were, and are, capable of perpetrating.

The second reason for the success of the trilogy in connecting with an extremely extensive community of readers lies in the style in which the books are written. Rather than relying on a sophisticated mode of expression, the trilogy is written in a demotic style that recreates the rhythms of everyday speech. In the texts, Fallaci continually refers to a Tuscan tradition of plain speaking and she frequently evokes episodes from her family's past when she remembers either her father or her mother standing up for what they believed to be true in the face of Fascist repression: indeed, the notion of her anti-Fascism is central to her identity as a writer and as a journalist and the fight against fascism becomes the most important point of comparison with the present.¹⁰ Stating throughout that her views are expressed in a way that is unencumbered by political correctness or by the niceties of diplomatic discourse, the author suggests that she articulates a basic common sense that others have been too self-seeking or too timorous to voice. From the beginning, she establishes both her authority as a commentator and the nature of the voice that she intends to use: in giving a forthright and uncompromising interpretation of the immediate effects of the terrorist action, its underlying causes and likely consequences, she asserts that she speaks for a large body of public opinion.

The third reason for the tremendous popular appeal of the trilogy is that it gave vent to the feelings of its author. Rather than seeking to exclude every trace of emotion, the trilogy openly and explicitly seeks to go beyond the conventionalities of journalistic or academic discourse and express the intensity of the emotions of outrage, fear and aggression created by the attacks on 11 September 2001. The very title of the first part of the trilogy, *La rabbia e l'orgoglio*, indicates the nature of the writing and this is compounded early on in the text when Fallaci defines

---

⁹On the authority with which Fallaci speaks in the trilogy and her role as "eyewitness to history," see Orsini, "Cannons and Rubber Boats," 446–448.

¹⁰For a longer discussion of the importance of Fascism and the Resistance in Fallaci's formative years, see Gatt-Rutter, *Oriana Fallaci: The Rhetoric of Freedom*, 6–8.

her writing both as a "scream" and as a "sermon."[11] Reflecting on the genesis of her work, she speaks of a compulsive desire to write and of filling page after page in which she had "emptied all her emotions."[12] Any reader of the trilogy, therefore, not only witnesses the elaboration of the thought processes of the author but is drawn into the drama of the representation of her responses to the atrocities of 9/11 and is asked, in a manner that appears to be entirely uncomplicated, to share the emotions that the works convey.

But the books of the trilogy are, of course, anything but straightforward. While they appear simply to deliver information, they are all highly skilled rhetorical exercises which rely for their effectiveness on the exploitation of the characteristics of different styles of writing, on their ability to fuse a certain journalistic sobriety with the evocation of images of extremity, and on their manipulation of an array of events and circumstances from the past. Given the huge circulation figures of Fallaci's work and its consequent impact in shaping the significance of 11 September 2001 within the collective imaginary in Italy, it is clearly important to examine the means by which the trilogy manipulates its readers' perceptions of the past, the present and the future. The trilogy has been exposed to a significant amount of comment, both within academic circles and outside, and the aim of the present chapter is to add to our understanding of some of the most basic mechanisms on which Fallaci relies in order to present a picture of the Islamic world and its relation to the West in the aftermath of 9/11.

The initial section of what follows aims to unravel the complex of theories on culture and identity on which the whole of the trilogy rests. The chapter then seeks to examine how Fallaci builds up an image of the Islamic world, of its geographical and cultural boundaries, and of its likely future development. At the same time, my aim is to look at the way in which that vision is intended to play upon the fears of the works' readership and at how it includes the prediction of the imminent decline of the West. As with all of Fallaci's writing, the way in which the authorial

---

[11] Fallaci, *La rabbia e l'orgoglio*, 36.

[12] Fallaci writes of having covered "metri e metri di carta su cui avevo rovesciato il cuore" [reams and reams of paper on which I had poured out my heart] (*La rabbia e l'orgoglio*, 20) and of writing " appunti convulsi, spesso disordinati, che prendevo per me stessa cioè rivolgendomi a me stessa" [impulsively written, often disordered, notes taken for myself, often addressing myself] (ibid., 18).

persona is constructed is central to the argument, and what follows aims, therefore, also to analyse the texts' presentation of their author. However, the single most important feature of the trilogy as a whole is the apparently simple, yet in reality intensely complicated, portrayal of the Other. The intention of the latter part of the chapter is to explore, with reference to recent critical writing, the range of techniques that are used to construct an image of the Muslim world as implacably hostile to all aspects of Western culture.

The trilogy contains no detailed statement on its theoretical underpinnings. Fallaci implies, mostly through the very directness of her style, that the observations that she makes, since they are based on her lengthy and distinguished experience as a journalist, are self-evidently true and therefore do not need to be supported by a sophisticated theoretical apparatus. Her work contains very few acknowledged references to recent theological, sociological or historical studies and there is little complex discussion of such issues as the way in which culture is moulded by religious belief or how the individual internalizes the dominant trends of the society of which he or she is a part. Though its premises are rarely explored, a theory of the underlying connections between culture, society and religion does, however, operate in her work. A number of critics have referred to her indebtedness to Samuel Huntington's well-known text *The Clash of Civilizations* and, though the writing of Fallaci is framed very differently, there are points of convergence between the arguments that she advances and the paradigm of global politics that Huntington sought to establish at the end of the 1990s.[13]

It is clear that Fallaci shares the assessment that the rivalry between superpowers which dominated world politics for so long has been replaced by conflicts between peoples belonging to different cultural entities: more precisely, she shares Huntington's view that the local conflicts most likely to escalate into broader wars are those between groups and states from different 'civilizations' and this type of conflict will be given a greater impetus by the revitalization of religion across the globe. Though written from a very different perspective, Fallaci's work is concerned with tracing a history of the interaction of different civilizations and, like Huntington, she devotes considerable space to discussing the probable decline of Western power and influence in the face of other

---

[13] See, for example, Orsini, "Cannons and Rubber Boats."

economically or demographically more dynamic civilizations.[14] With her distinctive assertiveness, she discusses the problems that are posed by the possibility of political disunity within the West and the likely effects of cultural, or indeed, moral decline. She endorses Huntington's proposition that the major fault line between the world's seven or eight major civilizations runs between Islam and its neighbours. She shares the contention that, in contrast to other world religions, a concept of non-violence is absent from Muslim doctrine and practice,[15] and, still more notably, she subscribes to the notion that, in Huntington's words, "Islam's borders are bloody, and so are its innards."[16]

Fallaci does, however, develop an interpretation of the Islamic world that has little connection with Huntington's work. The conception of Islam that is present throughout the trilogy and which is set forth explicitly in the preface to *La rabbia e l'orgoglio* is that, as a religion and as a civilization, it represents an unmoving body of thought and belief which structures human identity in such a way that it is relentlessly hostile to the West. She seeks to prove her contention regarding what she considers to be the stasis of Islamic societies by making a series of highly tendentious contrasts between the development of science and technology in the West and in the Islamic world. Her assertion concerning the contrasting pace of technological change is accompanied by a failure to acknowledge the advances in scientific knowledge originating in the Arab world.[17] The apparent slowness of technological innovation in Muslim societies is, she contends, intimately related to a corresponding closure towards a Western discourse of progress that has led to the development of democracy and a largely secular political sphere. As it is represented in the trilogy, Islam is a religion that "produces only religion,"[18] and, in Fallaci's view, the degree to which it supposedly promotes obscurantism over progress is exemplified by attitudes towards women throughout the Muslim world. In *La rabbia e l'orgoglio*, she recounts, from her life as a journalist, her personal experience of discrimination in the Middle East and

---

[14] On this specific point, see Huntington, *The Clash of Civilizations and the Remaking of World Order*, 303–305.

[15] Ibid., 263.

[16] Huntington described this phrase (ibid., 258) as the most controversial of the whole text.

[17] Fallaci, *La rabbia e l'orgoglio*, 86f.

[18] Ibid., 25.

the narration of instances of this kind is supplemented by accounts that she takes from the lives of others.[19]

In Fallaci's definition of the fundamental characteristics of Islam, the idea of stasis is closely aligned to that of violence. Though, as I suggested, she concurs with Huntington's contention that violence is intrinsic to Islam, any comparison between their views is valid only up to a point because she does not develop her thinking through the structures of an academic discourse but through partial reconstructions of history and through the narration of scenes that she has either witnessed firsthand or which she has seen represented in the media. Further, as Žižek points out,[20] her claim was that the ongoing War on Terror was not a clash of civilizations but a clash between civilization and barbarism.[21] In the trilogy, there are many scenes, recounted with a correspondent's eye for drama and detail, which recount the perpetration of violence. Each example that Fallaci provides is distinguished by the anachronistic cruelty of the punishment, its extremity and its status as public spectacle. As it is described, each ritual symbolizes the need of the collectivity to affirm its determination to communicate its power by simultaneously inciting a feeling of terror and mass participation. In *La rabbia e l'orgoglio*, she describes seeing twelve young men executed in the stadium of Dhaka in front of a cheering crowd of 20,000 spectators and witnessing the crowd, after the executions, ritually stamping over the bodies of the dead.[22] Shortly afterwards, she describes in detail a documentary which includes the filming of the public execution of three women in the main square of Kabul.[23]

The pattern of Fallaci's reasoning is to isolate a particular incident and then to claim that it is symptomatic of the whole of the Islamic world.

---

[19] Ibid., 91–99.

[20] Žižek, *Violence*.

[21] In Fallaci's own words, "Contrasto-fra-le-Due-Culture? Bè, se vuoi proprio saperlo, a me dà fastidio perfino parlare di due culture" [Clash of cultures? Well, if you really want to know, I find it irksome even to speak of two cultures] (*La rabbia e l'orgoglio*, 85).

[22] Fallaci, *La rabbia e l'orgoglio*, 93f.

[23] Ibid., 97–99. In the third book of the trilogy, Fallaci writes: "L'Islam avido, strisciante, ambiguo. La sua fame e la sua sete di conquistare, soggiogare. Il suo culto della Morte, la sua voluttà per la Morte" [Islam [is] rapacious, evasive and ambiguous. Its hunger and thirst to conquer and subjugate. Its cult of death, its avidity for death] (*Oriana Fallaci intervista sé stessa*, 152).

This method of reasoning means that she does not think about Islam as a complex that has built up over centuries with a remarkably different series of traditions and forms of adherence; she does not consider differences of social structure, institutions and prevailing values; and, as the journalist Magdi Allam and others have argued, she does not consider the fact that most Islamic countries have lived peaceably for centuries.[24] What the trilogy does, instead, is to argue that extremism is not a separate reality, divorced from the central current of Islam, but the expression of the inner form of the Muslim world. This assertion is explicit and repeated in *La rabbia e l'orgoglio* where she argues that Muslim majority countries are, without exception, victims of one kind or another of theocratic government and that Osama bin Laden and the Taliban are "only the most recent manifestation of a reality that has existed for 1400 years."[25] The refusal to make a distinction between Islam and fundamentalism is essential to the argument that is propounded by the trilogy. While one might have thought that, owing to the nature of Fallaci's past experience, she would have represented a deeply heterogeneous reality, she constructs, instead, an image of the Muslim world as a homogenized totality. The trilogy not only collapses distinctions between different parts of the Muslim world, it also sees every Muslim as the product of a radical version of Islam and, as a consequence, complicit in the furthering of a violent, anti-Western ideology. It is Fallaci's claim, again in *La rabbia e l'orgoglio*, that the mosques that have recently appeared across Italy are brimming with "terrorists or aspiring terrorists."[26]

There is, without doubt, a basic orientalism at the heart of Fallaci's thinking: she creates, in Edward Said's terms (1978), a division between the West and the East, between the familiar and the strange, and she asserts, with uncommon vehemence, the superiority of the former to the latter. But whereas the majority of the writings that Said examined in *Orientalism* set out to produce a vision of the East as a place that legitimated Western imperialism, the notion of colonialism works quite differently in the trilogy. Instead of suggesting that supposedly different levels

---

[24] Allam, *Vincere la paura: la mia via contro il terrorismo islamico e l'inoscienza dell'Occidente*, 174.
[25] Fallaci, *La rabbia e l'orgoglio*, 117.
[26] Ibid., 28.

of civilization necessitate the West's role in the East, the trilogy is devoted to the idea that a reverse form of colonialism is occurring without the West even noticing. It is Fallaci's contention that the Islamic world is essentially violent not only because of its, putative, hostility towards the West and the extremity with which it protects its own system of values but because it is, by its very nature, expansionist.[27]

The second book of the trilogy, *La forza della ragione*, is devoted to the exploration of this notion. It begins with a reconstruction of the spread of Islam—from the death of the Prophet to the height of the Ottoman Empire—that concentrates uniquely on episodes of violence; it thus creates an image of the growth of Islam as a relentless assault on Christian Europe. It is thus not only the geographical proximity of the Islamic world that Fallaci focuses upon, but a particular reading of the past that sees a *longue durée*, supposedly dominated by conflict. The book subsequently moves forwards to the contemporary world where it presents a picture of the development of large Muslim communities in France, Germany and the United Kingdom. Much of the book is, however, concerned with Italy and with instances, such as the building of a mosque in the small Tuscan town of Colle Val d'Elsa, which demonstrate the increasing visibility of Italy's growing Muslim population.[28] What the book argues is that the increase in the numbers of Muslims living in Western Europe is not simply the effect of migratory flows determined mostly by global economic factors but the result of deliberate Islamic expansionism. Drawing on her experience as a journalist working in different parts of the world from the 1960s onwards, Fallaci constructs a theory according to which, under the cover of the Cold War, the 'greatest conspiracy of modern history'[29] was set in motion. Through such movements as the Islamic Revival, she argues, through migration and through the building of mosques and sites of Islamic learning in Europe

---

[27] In order to gain a sense of the crudity of the distinction that Fallaci makes between the West and the supposedly expansionist Islamic world, her notions of inter-cultural contact can be contrasted with the analysis of the West's dealings with their cultures that Jürgen Habermas and Jacques Derrida, interviewed by Giovanna Borradori, explore, cf. Habermas and Derrida, *Philosophy in a Time of Terror: Dialogues with Jürgen Habermas and Jacques Derrida*.

[28] For an analysis of the opposition to the building of mosques in Italy and elsewhere, see Allievi, *La guerra delle moschee: L'europa e la sfida del pluralismo religioso*.

[29] Fallaci, *La forza della ragione*, 151.

and the United States, those in power within the Muslim world have pursued a strategy aimed at undermining the cultural and religious fabric of the West. In support of her theory, she cites her interview with George Habash in the early 1970s in which, as she recalls, he claimed that the whole of the Arab world was engaged in a 'total war' with America and Europe.

In *La forza della ragione*, Fallaci not only claims that Western governments have failed to resist what she sees as the surreptitious Islamification of Europe, she maintains that, blinded by the necessity of importing crude oil, they have connived in the process over decades and that they are therefore guilty of what she terms the sale of Western identity. Like so much of the trilogy, the theory that is advanced is based on very little formal documentation yet it is used to substantiate one of Fallaci's most disturbing propositions. She does not simply maintain, to use Huntington's concept, that there is a 'clash of civilizations' between Islam and the West: her assertion is rather that it is the aim of the Islamic world to undermine and colonize Western societies by changing their demographics and by undermining their systems of value. Thus, in the view that she propounds so forcefully, phenomena as apparently disconnected as migration and the attack on the Twin Towers are in reality part of the same process. The figure of the migrant from a Muslim country is, in other words, in some way connected with that of the terrorist.

Fallaci herself points to the difficulty in defining the literary form that her texts assume: to a degree they can be seen as a series of essays on the social and cultural world; they can also, to use her own definition, be seen as a kind of extended sermon; but they also, without question, expound an eschatological treatise. A large part of the purpose of her texts is, quite clearly, to articulate her fear of the decline and potential demise of Western civilization and to incite, using a whole series of writing styles, a similar fear in her readers. References to impending catastrophic change abound within her work: most obviously, the final text of the trilogy is entitled *L'Apocalisse* but throughout the trilogy, she invokes the notion of a citadel that is under siege and that is likely shortly to succumb. In *La rabbia e l'orgoglio* the trope of the Apocalypse is consistently used to define the meaning of the events of 11 September 2011. The destruction wrought in the centre of New York and the trauma caused to American society by the events of 9/11 prove, for Fallaci, the power of human agency to cause cataclysmic events, but her essential point is that New York is a metonym for the whole of the West and that events there do not represent an end point but an indication of what is to come.

The thesis that she advances is one in which the events of 9/11, though unique in their horror, must be seen as an occurrence within an infinitely greater historical process; a process which, as I outlined above, she sees as leading ultimately to the dissolution of Western identity. In his text of 2005, *Vincere la paura* [Overcomng Fear], the journalist Magdi Allam argued that the overwhelming effect of the terrorist attacks of 11 September 2001 was to create a climate of fear which obstructed rational analysis and he suggested that in Italy the writing of Oriana Fallaci had significantly added to such a climate. Every kind of fear, as Zygmunt Bauman reminds us in his introduction to *Liquid Fear* (2006),[30] involves the perception of a threat to personal or collective identity, but the trilogy presents nothing less than a prediction of the end of the essential features that constitute Western culture. The way in which Fallaci presents her readers with a terrifying picture of the future is to imagine a world in which the collectively recognized frame of reference, the social structure in which ordinary life is led, has been radically subverted and transformed into her sinister characterization of the Muslim world. The future that she imagines is a place where, to quote her directly, churches have been replaced by mosques, where the burkha has become a standard form of feminine dress,[31] where cities like Turin or Genoa closely resemble Dakar, Beirut or Damascus,[32] and where liberty, democracy, and material well-being have all been sacrificed.[33] In the vision of the world that is conjured up, it is not only the destruction of established social structures but the loss, or estrangement from, personal identity that is presented as an object of terror. The notion of the threat to the very idea of a Western model of personhood is conveyed by Fallaci's reiteration of a conquest that is religious or cultural rather than simply territorial. In *La forza della ragione*, she describes a threat

---

[30] Bauman, *Liquid Fear*.

[31] Fallaci, *La rabbia e l'orgoglio*, 83.

[32] Ibid., 125.

[33] Ibid., 133. The notion of a European country being ruled according to Islamic law is the subject of Michel Houellebecq's *Soumission* (Paris: Flammarion) published on 7 January 2015, the day of the *Charlie Hebdo* shooting. As Adam Shatz notes in his review of *Soumission*, in the *London Review of Books*, 9 April 2015, although the book is deeply reactionary, it is not Islamophobic.

to 'il nostro sistema di vita [...] il nostro modo di pensare, di agire, di amare',[34] while in the third book of the trilogy, she writes:

> Oggi la conquista è di tutt'altra natura. È una conquista religiosa, culturale. Più che a occupare il territorio mira ad impadronirsi delle anime con principii che non sono i nostri principii, concetti che non sono i nostri concetti, costumi che non sono i nostri costumi.[35]

Fallaci emphasizes what she regards as the likelihood of her prediction of the future becoming a reality by referring to historical precedent. One of the key rhetorical features of the trilogy is the tendency to draw an analogy between the perception of the present and an interpretation of the past. She asserts that history repeats itself and that what she regards as the danger of the Islamification of Europe is similar to the menace of totalitarianism in the 1920s and 1930s. One of the means by which she incorporates her understanding of the significance of 9/11 into an explicitly Italian historical context is precisely to draw an analogy between the threat posed by Islamist terror and the past experience of the rise of Fascism, its consolidation as a result of people's inaction and its catastrophic effects upon the country. The analogy is intended to increase a feeling of fear: what she is saying, in effect, is that the terrifying happenings of the past will be replicated in the future. But the analogy also highlights the role that Fallaci believes that she fulfils. In the preface to *La rabbia e l'orgoglio*, she compares her warning of the putative threat posed by Islam to Gaetano Salvemini's forewarning, in the 1920s, of the likely development of Fascism.[36] Speaking from a place of voluntary exile, she asserts that she has the courage, like Salvemini, to defend a tradition of national sentiment and name an incipient danger

---

[34] Fallaci, *La forza della ragione*, 285; [Our system of living [...] our ways of thinking, acting, loving.]

[35] Fallaci, *Oriana Fallaci intervista sè stessa*, 201. [Today the conquest is of a completely different nature. It is a religious and cultural conquest. Rather than aiming to occupy territory, it aims to take control over people's minds with principles that are not our principles, concepts that are not our concepts, customs that are not our customs.]

[36] In *La forza della ragione* (15), she quotes a letter to the *New York Post* in which *La rabbia e l'orgoglio* is compared to Winston Churchill's *Step by Step 1936–39* (1939). For a further comparison between the 1920s and 1930s and the present, see the third book of the trilogy (Fallaci, *Oriana Fallaci intervista sé stessa*, 14f.).

that others are reluctant to see but which will become starkly evident in the future.

In addition to drawing comparisons between herself and figures like Salvemini and Churchill, she also suggests that she shares a moral likeness with the fourteenth-century scholar Cecco d'Ascoli who was vilified, persecuted and eventually burned at the stake for pursuing and exposing his ideas. While Fallaci claims that she does no more than speak her mind, her strategy of self-presentation in the trilogy is, in reality, quite complex. By making comparisons between herself and figures from the relatively recent past, she asserts that she is defending a tradition of national sentiment; while her claim that like Mastro Cecco she is prepared to sacrifice herself for her ideas is a way of dramatizing the role that she believes that she performs. Indeed, she accentuates this comparison by, on occasions, assuming the voice of a transhistorical figure who, prepared to speak truth to power, has been persecuted over centuries.[37] By tracing an illustrious genealogy and by assuming the voice of a potential martyr, Fallaci justifies the accusatory tone that she assumes in her imagined dialogues with world leaders, she substantiates her assertion that the West is complicit in its own downfall and she emphasizes the urgency of her call to resist. *La rabbia e l'orgoglio* is a "sermon" not only in its content but in its style of delivery and in the imaginative and emotional journey that it asks its readers to make. In one of her most direct addresses to her readership, Fallaci writes:

> Sveglia, gente, sveglia! Intimiditi come siete dalla paura d'andar contro corrente oppure di apparire razzisti, (parola oltretutto impropria perché il discorso non è su una razza, è su una religione), non capite o non volete capire che qui è in atto una Crociata alla Rovescia [...] non volete capire che qui è in atto una guerra di religione. Voluta e dichiarata da una frangia di quella religione forse. (Forse?) Comunque una guerra di religione.[38]

---

[37] See, for example, the way in which Fallaci writes on the history of the Church in *La rabbia e l'orgoglio* (85f.).

[38] Fallaci, *La rabbia e l'orgoglio*, 78 [Wake up, people, wake up! Intimidated as you are by the fear of seeming to go against the current of opinion or to seem racist (a word that is highly inappropriate because this isn't about race, it is about religion), you don't understand or you don't want to understand that here we are dealing with a reverse kind of crusade [...] you don't want to understand that what is happening is a war of religion. Wanted and declared by a fringe of that religion perhaps (Perhaps?) but nevertheless a war of religion.]

The huge publishing success of the trilogy was due in no small part to the outstanding ability of its author to articulate a series of reactions provoked by the horror of the terrorist attacks on 9/11. The range of feeling that is encompassed by the trilogy spans anger, mourning and aggressiveness, but the dominant feeling that the works express—and which in many ways is inseparable from all the other emotions that they articulate—is, as I have suggested, that of fear.[39] Fallaci communicates a fear of the recurrence of terrorist attacks, of the wider geopolitical reality, of the dissolution of a recognizable model of cultural identity, but she does so not through an abstract academic discourse; she does so through her ability to communicate alarming scenes of the past or the future to her readership.[40] In her work she implies that history follows a cyclical logic; she conjures up the ghost of totalitarian terror, she affirms that the West is subject to an insidious and possibly irreversible kind of colonialism, and she considers 9/11 as the prelude to a sort of apocalypse.

The scenes that Fallaci evokes are not intended simply to be passively surveyed by her readers: they are clearly intended to exercise a much more dynamic function. The trilogy is a remarkable piece of writing in that it presents a picture of the contemporary world seen by an author whose perspective is unapologetically dominated by an intensity of feeling. Fallaci wishes her reader to share her vision of the contemporary world and, equally explicitly, the reactions that it produces. Her sense of impending catastrophe is communicated both by her consistent use of an emotive vocabulary and by her continual reference to extreme states of mind. Her reader is addressed most clearly by injunctions (see above) to share the same sense of rage and preoccupation. The essential point is that the kind of fear with which the trilogy is concerned is double-sided. On the one hand, Fallaci expresses acute unease at the destruction of a familiar paradigm, a sense of diminishing power of action in the face of

---

[39] Among those who have written most persuasively on the collective emotional crisis following the terrorist attacks of 11 September 2001, and on the predominance of a fearful attitude towards the Muslim world, is Magdi Allam in his work of 2005, *Vincere la paura* [Overcoming Fear].

[40] Marc Redfield, in *The Rhetoric of Terror*, 19, reiterates Derrida's point (Derrida, "Autoimmunity: Real and Symbolic Suicides: A Dialogue with Jacques Derrida") that part of the trauma of the attacks on the World Trade Center lay in the fact that they threatened worse to come. For Redfield's analysis of the prevalence of religious motifs in 9/11 discourse, see Redfield, *The Rhetoric of Terror*, 38–41.

an increasing threat, and a feeling of helplessness at the perceived weakness of the very institutions whose role it is to defend a settled order of things. But, on the other hand, the feeling of unease and apprehension that her works record serves to motivate an equally powerful and equally complex set of aggressive responses.

Fallaci's writing presents us with a vision of the cultural world of the West veering towards destruction, but the writing also, of course, presents us with an image of the sinister power which, supposedly, will be responsible for this collapse. Rather than examining in detail those groups within the Islamic world that are explicitly hostile to the West and which promote terrorism, the trilogy constructs a much more generalized figure of the Other; a figure that encompasses the whole of the Islamic world and all Muslim men and women. This figuration is, as I suggested, motivated by a sense of unease, even terror, but it expresses at the same time and at various levels a violent attitude towards the Other.[41]

In her work on violence, mourning and politics in the wake of the terrorist atrocities of 11 September 2001, Judith Butler explores the question of why aggression seems so quickly to follow on from the experience of loss. Developing this theme, she writes on the facility with which those who are seen to be on the other side of a cultural or religious fault line are exposed to a process of de-humanization (2004, 98). In the trilogy, a kind of violence—or, at the very least, a forceful derogation of the Other—is evident in the way in which Muslim men and women are represented. Fallaci's style of presentation is to refer infrequently to individuals and to define the Islamic community as a whole. Thus, the accusations of violence, hostility or cruelty that she makes are not directed simply at one specific group or another but are applied to the whole of the Muslim world, or to use Fallaci's term, at the "sons of Allah." Instead, therefore, of there emerging a variegated and nuanced picture of another religious identity, one is left with a picture of Muslim men and women that seems purposefully to deny them their very humanity; they are simply reduced to a set of stereotypical attributes that accentuate a divide between an "us" and a "them." In the preface to

---

[41] On the dangers inherent in a failure to see the world from the perspective of others, see the works of Nussbaum, *The New Religious Intolerance: Overcoming the Politics of Fear in an Anxious Age* (and Todorov, *The Fear of Barbarians: Beyond the Clash of Civilizations*).

La rabbia e l'orgoglio, the author writes of there being "millions and millions of fanatics" and "millions and millions of extremists" (2001, 24).

If the denial of a commonality of emotions and aspirations denotes a violent attitude towards the Other, that violence of representation is compounded by the many instances within the trilogy when Fallaci unequivocally gives vent to her feelings of aggression towards those who, in her opinion, threaten to undermine Western culture. One of the reasons why the trilogy has proved for its many readers an enthralling piece of work is that it displays a mastery of different modes of address: Fallaci draws her reader into the dynamics of her argument both through a direct and hectoring form of address and by constructing a series of imagined dialogues with institutions and people. In the course of her work, she chastises a whole range of prominent politicians who are, as far as she is concerned, responsible for failing to defend Western interests against what she considers to be an Islamic conspiracy. But she also speaks directly to those whom she perceives to be her antagonists and on such occasions she replicates the belligerence with which she feels that she, as an inhabitant of the West, is addressed. Apostrophizing those forces behind the attacks on the Twin Towers, in the preface to *La rabbia e l'orgoglio*,[42] she embraces the challenge of all-out war; after having described a public execution in the main square of Kabul, she expresses her desire to kill the Taliban's Minister of Justice, Wakil Motawakil[43]; she threatens to burn down a tent erected by Somali migrants in the Piazza del Duomo in Florence.[44]

It is beyond doubt that in the trilogy's representation of the figure of the Muslim various processes coalesce. Within Fallaci's construction of contemporary Islamic identity, those responsible for the terrorist atrocities are equated with all adherents to Islam; the fear that the events of 9/11 are the prelude to something much worse are projected onto the figure of the Muslim; in the prose of the trilogy, the Muslim assumes the attributes of everything that lies outside of Western notions of the rational, the normal or the civilized. In short, the Muslim as he or she appears in the Fallaci's writing is possessed of—to adapt a phrase from

---

[42] Fallaci, *La rabbia e l'orgoglio*, 35.
[43] Ibid., 101.
[44] Ibid., 122.

the writing of Slavoj Žižek[45]—a fantasmatic dimension. Though Fallaci does not, of course, acknowledge this, the fury that she directs against Muslims is not aimed at individuals since she has almost no capacity for describing the lived reality of ordinary people living within Islamic societies. The vehemence of her rhetoric is directed rather against a faceless figure that appears as the embodiment of her most deep-seated fears. Real or imagined dialogues are essential to the way in which Fallaci's thought works within the trilogy, but her work exemplifies a dialectic that Butler sees as typical of reactions to the terrorist attacks of September 2001, namely, the tendency to think of and address others in the way in which we believe that we are imagined and interpellated by them.[46] The dialogue in addressing a spectral figuration which we attempt to quell is at base a distorted mode of reasoning.

In spite of its demotic style, its colloquial use of language and its apparent desire to cut through layers of political correctness and say things as they are, the trilogy is thus a work of considerable complexity which, while it appears to communicate its literal meaning simply, is making a sequence of highly problematic projections and identifications. But any exploration of the work should not just consider the shape of the author's thought and the different levels at which it speaks to its readership but examine also the kinds of reception to which it has been subject. As I began by suggesting, the fact that *La rabbia e l'orgoglio* was initially published in the pages of one of Italy's leading newspapers, that each work within the trilogy has gone through multiple editions, and that the trilogy has excited a great deal of comment all point to its undeniable impact on public debate. Among the other indications of the extent of the works' reception among a wide section of the Italian public are the views of the readers that Fallaci includes within the texts themselves.[47]

But some of the most trenchant arguments concerning the reception of Fallaci's work are made by Stefano Allievi. In his alternative trilogy, he points to the irony of Fallaci's self-figuration as a latter-day Mastro Cecco, when rather than her thoughts being repudiated by a hostile public, they have enjoyed unprecedented popular appeal. Rather than

---

[45] Žižek, *Violence*, 84f.

[46] Butler, *Precarious Life: The Powers of Mourning and Violence*, 128–151.

[47] In the course of her article (2006), Orsini analyses how Fallaci's statements resonate with her readers.

simply indicating the extent of the dissemination of her texts, he refers to the adoption of her views by members of the Lega Nord who distribute free copies of her work at party functions and who proposed that she be elected as a Senator for Life.[48] Orsini notes that Fallaci's assertions on migration are similar to the xenophobic pronouncements of the Lega Nord and that they share the same use of slang and colloquial language.[49] Allievi also describes how the kind of opinion that Fallaci expresses with such fervour, and in particular what he characterizes as the 'poisonous, shameful and unworthy'[50] assertion that there is a connecting line between Islamic fundamentalism and migration to Italy, all too easily translate into acts of violence and discrimination against Italy's Muslim population.[51] In order to demonstrate the pernicious implications of the perspective in which Fallaci interprets reality, Allievi draws an analogy between the stereotyping of the Islamic population in the trilogy and the production and the effects of anti-Semitic literature in earlier decades.[52] He claims that in the view of Fallaci and those who assume a similar stance, the Muslim has now taken over the role as Europe's scapegoat, the figure onto which all conceivable ills are projected.[53]

But the comparison that Allievi makes alerts us to what is perhaps the greatest contradiction within the thesis that the trilogy propounds. In arguing that Italy faces a threat to the core of its identity, Fallaci has to construct a notion of that identity. She does this, to a degree, by referring to the country's Catholic heritage, but the touchstone of her values is to be found more in the secular legacy of the Risorgimento and, above all, in those forces which were most actively engaged in the struggle

---

[48] Allievi, *Niente di personale, Signora Fallaci*, 145.

[49] Orsini, "Cannons and Rubber Boats," 455, 458. For an analysis of the spectrum on perceptions of Islam within Italian political life at the beginning of the twenty-first century, see Allievi, "Sociology of a Newcomer," Guolo, *Xenofobi e xenofili*, and Orsini "Cannons and Rubber Boats," 456–459.

[50] Allievi, *Niente di personale, Signora Fallaci*, 53.

[51] See, in particular, ibid., 85–87. Allievi maintains that Fallaci is responsible for shifting the limit of what is considered acceptable within public discourse.

[52] He makes an explicit comparison between the trilogy and the *Protocols of the Elders of Zion*, cf. Allievi, *Niente di personale, Signora Fallaci*, 75f.

[53] His exact words are: "Il nuovo capro espiatorio, il ributtante contenitore di ogni perversione, la sentina di ogni vizio" [The new scapegoat, the revolting container of every perversion, the symbol of every vice] (ibid., 81).

against Fascism. The movements, therefore, that she sees as absolutely fundamental to the Italian experience in the modern world were predicated on a common model of humanity and were explicitly opposed to the exclusion of one group or another. Thus, the extremity of her hostility towards the Muslim world is alien to the very values that she invokes when seeking to define the history and the meaning of the Italian nation.[54]

It is true, of course, that the importance of Fallaci's trilogy—in common with any other text—resides not only in what it says but how it is, and can be, read. If it is interpreted, at its most literal level, as a treatise on the West's, supposedly inevitable, conflict with the Islamic world, then the work's various commentators are right to point to the dangers of this interpretation of reality and the series of attitudes that it promotes. But the trilogy can also be read as a work that serves to illuminate the ways in which the subjective world of the individual can be altered through the contemplation of acts of terrorist atrocity. In their writing on the trilogy, both Allievi and Allam take this point further by arguing that it is not possible to see the challenge posed by Islamist extremism with any kind of objective distance. Events like the attack on the World Trade Center are so deeply shocking that they necessarily cause a response that is not confined to the purely intellectual sphere; they force us to question our sense of who we are, and to question our knowledge and understanding of our own culture and that of others. Thus, the conflict occurs not simply within the world of objective reality; it occurs also internally in the way in which we allow, or do not allow, the intended consequences of terrorism to define the way in which we think and feel, in the way in which we conceive of ourselves as well as other people.

If we read Fallaci's work both as a commentary on world events and as a dramatization of her own thought processes and emotions, then it is clear that we are in the presence of someone who has allowed themselves to be conditioned by the effects of terrorism. In her analysis of the etymology of terror, Adriana Cavarero suggests that "terror," when understood as the manifestation of total fear, becomes synonymous with

---

[54] Belpoliti points to this contradiction by claiming that despite Fallaci's declared hostility to Fascism, the deepest instincts of *La rabbia e l'orgoglio* lie in its nationalism, xenophobia and chauvinism ("The Fallacies of St. Fallaci," 86).

absolute disorder.[55] While it is not true in any literal sense that Fallaci shows a loss of all control, it is nevertheless the case that some of the most basic structures of rational argument collapse in her work.[56] The tendency to make huge generalizations, to insist on drawing issues together that are clearly disconnected, and to be drawn into making unthinking assertions of superiority are all indications of what Tiziano Terzani[57] has described as the tendency to allow a certain blindness to predominate.

For Terzani, in his *Lettere contro la guerra* (Letters against the War), the real challenge is to avoid the temptation of being guided by an instinctual reaction. For him, as it is for a number of other critics of Fallaci's work, the irony of her response to the terrorist attacks of 11 September 2001 is that, to use Allievi's phrase, it replicates elements of bin Laden's system of thought.[58] In his original critique of Fallaci's work, Magdi Allam, while expressing his appreciation of her attempt to encourage a sense of civic consciousness in the face of the growing threat of extremist terror, was nevertheless highly critical of her tendency to identify a stereotype of the fundamentalist with an idea of all Muslims. He argued that the same assertion that there is only one kind of Muslim and that he or she subscribes uncritically to all the tenets of radical Islamism is exactly what defines the reasoning of her antagonists.[59] On a separate but related point, Allievi argues that the propensity to see one's own religion or culture as right and all others as deviant is exactly what makes Fallaci's reasoning similar in some respects to that of the followers of

---

[55] Cavarero, *Horrorism*, 5.

[56] As Bernardo Valli points out: "Il coraggio non le fa difetto neppure oggi. Quel che ha perduto è l' ironia. E con essa la razionalità" [She certainly does not lack courage, even today. What she has lost is a sense of irony. And with that she has also lost touch with rationality.] ("I profeti dell'odio sono anche in Occidente," *La Repubblica*, 25 July 2005.

[57] Terzani, *Lettere contro la guerra*, 38.

[58] Allievi, *Nienti di personale, Signora Fallaci*.

[59] Allam suggests that both imagine that every Muslim is a kind of clone produced automatically by what claims to be the "absolute, universal and eternal Truth" (*Vincere la paura*, 174). On the trope of the clone within post-9/11 discourse, see the work of W. J. T. Mitchell (*Cloning Terror: The War of Images, 9/11 to the Present*). In his more recent work Allam, now Magdi Cristiano Allam, has come to revise his opinion on Fallaci's work. For an analysis of the development of his thought, see Burdett, "Representing Italy and the Islamic World: Culture, Self and Society in the Works of Magdi Cristiano Allam."

bin Laden.[60] Moreover, in claiming that Italy and the West in general are involved in an inter-civilizational conflict (rather than combating an extreme Islamist faction) and that in this conflict nothing less than the survival of Western culture is at stake, Fallaci mirrors the eschatological reasoning of her adversaries: the world that her texts create is a world that to some extent reflects their vision of an apocalyptic struggle between East and West. There is, finally, an underlying violence in the way in which so many of the arguments of the trilogy are structured.[61] It is evident in the bellicose rhetoric which she deploys, in her wish to trade blows with the perpetrators of Islamist terror, in her construction of a past history of conflict and in her call to the West to resist what she sees as insidious Islamic colonization. But, above all, this conceptual violence is evident in her creation of a stereotype of Muslim identity, in her reliance on a normative notion of the human, and in her consequent reluctance to see a common bond of humanity linking people of different religions and cultures.

References

Allam, Khaled Fouad. *L'Islam spiegato ai leghisti* (Milan: Piemme, 2011).
Allam, Magdi. *Vincere la paura: la mia via contro il terrorismo islamico e l'inoscienza dell'Occidente* (Milan: Mondadori, 2005).
Allievi, Stefano. *La tentazione della guerra. Dopo l'attacco al World Trade Center. A proposito di Occidente, Islam e altri frammenti di conflitto tra culture* (Milan: Zelig, 2001).

---

[60] Allievi, *Niente di personale*, 46f. Equally, Bernardo Valli (2005) writing in *La Repubblica*, drew attention to the degree to which Fallaci's vision of Islam is one that flatters bin Laden. In his words: "La visione di Oriana va a genio a bin Laden, perché così lui, in quanto incarnazione del terrorismo, diventa l'immaginario rappresentante di un Islam che è ben lontano dal controllare" [Oriana's vision suits bin Laden down to the ground, because within it he, as the incarnation of terrorism, becomes the imaginary representation of an Islam that is difficult to control] (Valli, "I profeti dell'odio sono anche in Occidente").

[61] On this point see Bosetti (*Cattiva maestra*, 9) who argues that instead of isolating those who encourage Islamist terror, the trilogy is a catalogue of all the errors that encourage "il risultato opposto, nuovi conflitti più gravi ed estesi, nuova violenza" [the opposite result, new conflicts that are more serious and more extensive, new kinds of violence].

———. "Sociology of a Newcomer: Muslim Migration to Italy. Religious Visibility, Cultural and Political Reactions," *Immigrants and Minorities* in *Historical Studies in Ethnicity, Migration and Diaspora*, vol. 22, iss. 2–3 (2003), 141–54.

———. *Niente di personale, Signora Fallaci: Una trilogia alternativa* (Reggio Emilia: Aliberti, 2006), 17f.

———. *La guerra delle moschee: L'europa e la sfida del pluralismo religioso* (Venice: Marsilio, 2010).

Bauman, Zygmunt. *Liquid Fear* (Cambridge: Polity, 2006).

Belpoliti, Marco. "The Fallacies Of St. Fallaci," *Foreign Policy*, vol. 130, May–June (2002).

Bosetti, Giancarlo. *Cattiva maestra. La rabbia di Oriana Fallaci e il suo contagio* (Venice: Marsilio, 2005).

Burdett, Charles, "Representing Italy and the Islamic World: Culture, Self and Society in the Works of Magdi Cristiano Allam," *Italian Studies*, vol. 65, no. 3 (2010), 398–414.

———. *Italy, Islam and the Islamic World Representations and Reflections, from 9/11 to the Arab Uprisings* (Oxford et al.: Peter Lang, 2016).

Butler, Judith. *Precarious Life: The Powers of Mourning and Violence* (New York: Columbia University Press, 2004).

Cardini, Franco. *I cantori della guerra giusta: religioni, fondamentalismi, globalizzazione* (Rimini: Il Cerchio, 2002).

Cavarero, Adriana. *Horrorism. Naming Contemporary Violence* (New York: Columbia University Press, 2009).

Derrida, Jacques. "Autoimmunity: Real and Symbolic Suicides: A Dialogue with Jacques Derrida," in Jürgen Habermas, Jacques Derrida, Giovanna Borradori, *Philosophy in a Time of Terror. Dialogues with Jürgen Habermas and Jacques Derrida* (Chicago: Chicago University Press, 2003).

Eco, Umberto. "Le guerre sante: passione e ragione," *La Repubblica*, October 12, 2001.

Fallaci, Oriana. *La rabbia e l'orgoglio* (Milan: Rizzoli, 2001).

———. *La forza della ragione* (Milan: Rizzoli, 2004).

———. *Oriana Fallaci intervista sé stessa* (Milan: Rizzoli, 2004).

Galimberti, Umberto. "La condizione dell'angoscia," *La Repubblica*, October 12, 2001.

Gatt-Rutter, John A. *Oriana Fallaci: The Rhetoric of Freedom* (Oxford: Berg, 1996).

———. "The Dummy Interlocutor and Oriana Fallaci's Self-Projection in *La rabbia e l'orgoglio*," in Peter Hainsworth and Martin McLaughlin (eds.), *Biographies and Autobiographies in Modern Italy* (Oxford: Legenda, 2007), 188–204.

Guolo, Renzo. *Xenofobi e xenofili. Gli italiani e l'Islam* (Rome-Bari: Laterza, 2003).

Habermas, Jürgen, Jacques Derrida, and Giovanna Borradori. *Philosophy in a Time of Terror. Dialogues with Jürgen Habermas and Jacques Derrida* (Chicago: Chicago University Press, 2003).
Houellebecq, Michel. *Soumission* (Paris: Flammarion, 2015).
Huntington, Samuel Phillips. *The Clash of Civilizations and the Remaking of World Order* (London: Simon and Schuster, 1997).
Orsini, Francesca. "Cannons and Rubber Boats: Oriana Fallaci and the 'Clash of Civilizations'," *Interventions: International Journal of Postcolonial Studies*, vol. 8, no. 3 (2006), 444–460.
Mitchell, W. J. T. *Cloning Terror: The War of Images, 9/11 to the Present* (Chicago/London: University of Chicago Press, 2011).
Nussbaum, Martha. *The New Religious Intolerance: Overcoming the Politics of Fear in an Anxious Age* (Cambridge, Massachusetts: Harvard University Press, 2012).
Redfield, Marc. *The Rhetoric of Terror: Reflections on 9/11 and the War on Terror* (New York: Fordham University Press, 2009).
Shatz, Adam. "Colombey-les-deux-Mosquées" (Review of Michel Houellebecq: *Soumission*) *London Review of Books*, 9 April 2015.
Terzani, Tiziano. *Lettere contro la guerra* (Milan: TEA, 2010) [2002].
Todorov, Tzvetan. *The Fear of Barbarians: Beyond the Clash of Civilizations*, trans. Andrew Brown (Cambridge: Polity, 2012).
Valli, Bernardo. "I profeti dell'odio sono anche in Occidente," *La Repubblica*, July 25, 2005.
Žižek, Slavoj. *Violence* (London: Profile Books, 2008).

Author Biography

Charles Burdett studied Modern Languages (French and Italian) at Oxford University (BA 1989) where he also studied as a postgraduate, writing his doctoral thesis (awarded 1994) on Italian literary culture between the wars. He taught at Cardiff University (1993-97) and has worked at Bristol since 1997 as Lecturer, Senior Lecturer (2002), Reader in Modern Italian Studies (2009) and Professor of Italian (2012). The principal areas of his research are literary culture under Fascism; Italian colonialism; theories of inter-cultural and transnational contact. His publications include *Journeys Through Fascism: Italian Travel Writing between the Wars* (2007) and *Italy, Islam and the Islamic World: Representations and Reflections from 9/11 to the Arab Uprisings* (2016).

PART III

Negotiating European Identity After September 11 Through the Double Other of the US and Islam

National Identity and Literary Culture After 9/11: Pro- and Anti-Americanism in Frédéric Beigbeder's *Windows on the World* (2003) and Thomas Hettche's *Woraus wir gemacht sind* (2006)

Birte Christ

All references to the novels in the body of the text refer to the original French and German editions, Frédéric Beigbeder, *Windows on the World* (Paris: Gallimard, 2003), tagged as *WW*, and Thomas Hettche, *Woraus wir gemacht sind* (Köln: Kiepenheuer & Witsch, 2006), tagged as *Wwgs*. English translations are provided in the notes; the editions used are Frédéric Beigbeder, *Windows on the World* (trans. Frank Wynne, London: Harper, 2004), tagged as *WW-E* and Thomas Hettche, *What We Are Made Of* (trans. Shaun Whiteside, London: Picador, 2008), tagged as *WWAMO*.

B. Christ (✉)
Institut Für Anglistik, Justus-Liebig-Universität Gießen, Gießen, Germany

Relating to Post-9/11 America: National Identity and Literary Culture

When Jean-Marie Colombani famously entitled his editorial on the front page of *Le Monde* "Nous sommes tous Américains" on September 13, 2001, this identification of the French with the American people was read as an expression of wholehearted solidarity with the United States after the terrorist attacks two days before.[1] The headline also proclaimed an overarching community of Western nations that any member could fall back upon in times of crisis: enemies would not be able to drive a wedge between nations of the West. "Nous sommes tous Américains," however, in stressing France's identity or sameness with America, goes beyond expressing a commonality of interests: it also lays claim to 9/11 as "a European event,"[2] to owning and working through the terrorist attacks as France's very own wound and trauma. Stating that "nous sommes tous Américains," then, can also be read as an identificational move of a speaker who is less concerned with the object of identification than with his or her own identity.

In this chapter, I propose that in treating the attacks of September 11, 2001 and their aftermath, European 9/11 texts similarly engage in identification with—and ultimately also the Othering of—the United States: they do so to negotiate their own national identities and literary cultures. In his essay "9/11 as a European Event," Kristiaan Versluys notes that "9/11 has had the effect of leading to a new stocktaking, a new assessment of the mutual influence" between Europe and the US.[3] I would like to give Versluys's observations on what he calls the 9/11 "novel of the outsider"[4] a slightly different emphasis: in European 9/11 texts, the events of September 11, 2001 and their aftermath also become an

---

[1] The headline, it should be noted, has become an emblem of European solidarity with the US in discussions of US-European relations after 9/11 and, in the process, has been detached from the content of the editorial. While clearly denouncing the terrorists, Colombani does not uncritically embrace the position of the US but also reflects on the role of the United States in creating the structures that eventually led to the attacks.

[2] Verslyus, "9/11 as a European Event: the Novels," 77.

[3] Ibid., 77. Many points of Versluys's essay are reiterated in his later booklength study, *Out of the Blue: September 11 and the Novel*, cf. chapter "'Burning from the Inside Out': *Let the Great World Spin* (2009)", "Exorcising the Ghost."

[4] Versluys, "9/11 as a European Event," 68.

occasion for a more self-centred, *national* "stocktaking." In other words, European 9/11 texts at times say less about issues related to 9/11 or the transatlantic relationship than about French, German, and other European national sensibilities, identities, and, finally, literary cultures. Many aspects of "outsider" representations of 9/11 have been considered in independent essays, monographs, and collections, yet the issue of European texts' delineations of national identity and national boundary-making vis-à-vis the US through an appropriation of 9/11 seems to call for more comprehensive scrutiny.[5]

In the following, I discuss two novels that use 9/11 to reflect on French and German national identity respectively and that, moreover, make this reflection and the re-negotiation of national identity one of their central concerns: Frédéric Beigbeder's *Windows on the World* (2003) and Thomas Hettche's *Woraus wir gemacht sind* (2006). On the surface, both novels appear as fiercely pro-American, yet a closer look shows that they engage in a highly complex meta-discourse on French and German pro- and anti-American sentiment, or Americanophilia and anti-Americanism. By positioning themselves vis-à-vis nationally specific, stereotyped discourses on America, these texts create a new space for post-9/11 versions of French and German national identity.

---

[5] Examples of collections that include discussions of European representations of 9/11 are Bauder-Begerow and Schäfer (eds), *Learning 9/11: Teaching for Key Competences in Literary and Cultural Studies*; Cilano (ed.), *From Solidarity to Schism: 9/11 and After in Fiction and Film from Outside the US*; Hennigfeld (ed.), *Poetiken des Terrors: Narrative des 11. September 2001 im interkulturellen Vergleich*; Irsigler and Jürgensen (eds), *Nine Eleven: Ästhetische Verarbeitungen des 11. September 2001*; Mohr and Mayer (eds), *9/11 as Catalyst: American and British Cultural Responses*, Poppe et al. (eds), *9/11 als kulturelle Zäsur. Repräsentationen des 11. September 2001 in kulturellen Diskursen, Literatur und visuellen Medien*. Focusing on the novel exclusively, Birgit Däwes offers the most comprehensive bibliography of what she calls "international 9/11 and 9/12 novels" to date in *Ground Zero Fiction: History, Memory, and Representation in the American 9/11 Novel*. National specificities of 9/11 literature are discussed in an article by Porra in Poppe et al. (eds), *9/11 als kulturelle Zäsur*, which I draw on later; questions of national identity construction are, to my knowledge, not explicitly discussed in scholarship on representations of 9/11 at all. Jürgen Donnerstag touches on issues of German constructions of national identity in the past decade that are important for my argument yet looks at the way in which national identity is constructed through a specific mode of reception rather than production of (9/11) texts: he focuses on the German reception of Michael Moore's documentaries, including *Fahrenheit 9/11*, "The Documentaries of Michael Moore and Their German Reception: Anti-Americanism and Intercultural Learning," 142–160.

Both Beigbeder and Hettche, moreover, combine their meta-discursive interrogation of attitudes towards the United States with a similar reflection on the possibilities and limits of representation, narration, and the novel. *Windows on the World* and *Woraus wir gemacht sind* are thus also centrally engaged in negotiating French and German national literary cultures.

In the first section, I will briefly introduce the two texts, along with an initial argument about the ways in which *Woraus wir gemacht sind* can ultimately be read as a critical engagement with *Windows on the World*'s attempt at national identity construction through an embrace of the national Other. In the following three sections of this chapter, I will take *Windows on the World* and *Woraus wir gemacht sind* as my points of departure to give an overview of the specific national conditions that shape 9/11 texts. Here I closely follow Véronique Porra who has suggested that French literary representations of 9/11 are shaped, most generally, by three contexts: (1) the presence of a strong Muslim minority within the country; (2) the ingrained anti-Americanism among intellectuals; and (3) the heritage of the national literary tradition.[6] One might surely add other contexts, particularly with other national configurations in mind,[7] but I will demonstrate that these three French factors, in fact, take a similarly important role in shaping German representations of 9/11—yet with nationally specific inflections. It is these nationally specific inflections that these three sections are concerned with. In the final two sections, I return to Beigbeder's and Hettche's uses of pro-Americanism—and thus to their reflections on nationally inflected anti-Americanisms—and explore how these are employed to carve out personal and national identities for their characters and a programme for the French and German novel after September 11, 2001.

---

[6] Porra, "Risse in der Mimesis – Bemerkungen zur romanesken Darstellung des 11. September 2001 in der französischen Literatur."

[7] Ursula Hennigfeld, for instance, suggests that the referencing of intertexts and prior historical caesuras are central aspects of 9/11 texts—in other words, national memory cultures may be another central context. As the contributions to her volume demonstrate, these textual and historical references may be nationally specific, even if texts of what may be called (Western) "world literature" and caesuras that have been attributed global importance may be cited across national literatures, such as Dante's *Inferno* or the Shoa. Cf. Hennigfeld, "Vorwort," 11.

Windows on the World and *Woraus wir gemacht sind*

Since the publication of his best-seller *99 francs* in 2001, Frédéric Beigbeder—born into a privileged life in Neuilly-sur-Seine in 1965—has figured as the *enfant terrible* of the French literary scene. *Windows on the World*, for which Beigbeder won the Prix Interallié, is one of the most popularly successful and most widely discussed European 9/11 novels. Moreover, the novel can be read as a first test case of the "nouveau nouveau roman" which would enter "les endroits interdits afin de décrire ce que nul ne décrit," and whose era Beigbeder announced in a manifesto in 2003, the same year that *Windows on the World* appeared.[8] *Windows on the World* tells the story of the last two hours before the collapse of the North Tower minute-by-minute and alternates between two discrete perspectives: those of Carthew Yorston and his sons in the Windows on the World Restaurant, and that of Beigbeder[9] himself eating breakfast a year later at Le Ciel de Paris, the restaurant on top of the Tour Montparnasse. Through its bipartite structure alone, the novel announces that it engages in what Versluys calls an "assessment of mutual influence."

Critics have repeatedly noted that in *Windows of the World*, Beigbeder revels in unabashed Americanophilia. He states: "J'écris ce livre parce que j'en ai marre de l'anti-américanisme hexagonal" (*WW*, 29).[10]

---

[8] "Pour un nouveau nouveau roman" was first published in *La Règle du jeu*, vol. 23 (2003), 18–22; quoted from Beigbeder, "Pour un nouveau nouveau roman," 48.

[9] Seen from a formal standpoint, this perspective is the perspective of the autodiegetic narrator "Beigbeder" rather than the author Beigbeder, and scholars have generally differentiated between the two, indicating the narrator by the use of quotation marks. When I am not commenting specifically on narrative structure, I conflate "Beigbeder" and Beigbeder in my discussion because I agree with Marie-Christine Clemente that the novel is structured as a panopticon that can be "read as having a central tower inhabited by the author" and that, "hiding behind the mirror of the text," the author can be seen as "infiltrat[ing] the center of the narrative." In other words, it can be argued that most statements made by "Beigbeder" and Carthew and David Yorston can be attributed directly to the author Beigbeder. Cf. Clemente, "Beigbeder's Evil Personae in *Windows on the World*: Authorial Ethics and 9/11," 121 and 123; on the same issue, cf. also Schehr, "*Éffondrements*: Frédéric Beigbeder's *Windows on the World*," 133; for an undifferentiated conflation of the author and narrator Beigbeder, cf. Harper, "Turning to Debris: Ethics of Violence in Wilkomirski's *Fragments* and Beigbeder's *Windows on the World*," 237.

[10] "I am writing this book because I'm sick of bigoted anti-Americanism" (*WW-E*, 16f.). For discussions of this statement on anti-Americanism, see, for instance, Durham, "Daring to Imagine: Frédéric Beigbeder's *Windows on the World* and Slimane Benaïssa's *La Dernière Nuit d'un damné*," here 171f. and Versluys, "9/11 as a European Event," 74.

In doing so, he is seen to radically reverse his anti-liberal position in his previous best-seller *99 francs*,[11] to break a taboo among left-leaning French intellectual circles, and to "picture a joint Western episteme."[12] As I will argue here, however, such a reading of Beigbeder's positioning misses one additional layer of the text. The pro-American stance of *Windows on the World*, I maintain, is a ploy that in fact demonstrates France's cultural superiority over the United States, rescues France from political and economic irrelevance, and thus re-affirms a positive national identity at the expense of the United States. Pro-American sentiment in the novel is taken to an extreme through the author's and "Beigbeder's" narrative merging with the American autodiegetic narrators, Carthew and David Yorston, and thus through the French author's/narrator's "becoming American."[13] Yet, on the reverse, the text even more forcefully engages in what may be called a "Frenchifying" of 9/11 and the United States. It incorporates what it represents as the desirable qualities of America—one of which is the trauma of 9/11 that promises recourse to a deeper understanding of human existence—into an updated identity of a globalized France.

Woraus wir gemacht sind is a novel that created a heated debate among German reviewers in 2006 but, in contrast to *Windows on the World*, has received only little scholarly attention so far.[14] Niklas Kalf, the novel's protagonist, is writing a biography of Eugen Meerkaz, a fictional German Jewish physicist who was forced to emigrate by the Nazi regime.

Both Durham and Versluys take the statement as an indication of the author Beigbeder's straightforward intentions and agree—wrongly to my mind—that the text is "unambiguous" in its "Americanophilia" (Versluys).

[11] Porra, "Risse in der Mimesis," 174.

[12] Versluys, "9/11 as a European Event," 74.

[13] For a detailed analysis of how the voices of "Beigbeder" and Yorston merge to an ever greater degree as the novel progresses, see Clemente, "Beigbeder's Evil Personae," 113–123.

[14] To my knowledge, Kozlowski's brief discussion and Reinhäckel's analyses, one in the context of a broader discussion of space and place in German 9/11 novels, are the only treatments to date, cf. Kozlowski, "Thomas Hettche"; Reinhäckel, *Traumatische Texturen* and "Literarische Schauplätze deutscher 9/11-Romane." A brief comment can be found in König, "Literary Accounts of Terrorism in Recent German Literature: An Attempt at Marginalization?," 163.

When Kalf travels to New York with his pregnant wife Liz to meet his publisher Al Snowe, his wife disappears from their hotel room after they have spent September 11, 2002—in a wilful gesture of avoiding the confrontation with history and reality after 9/11—in bed. The text is intimately concerned with 9/11 and its aftermath: its plot is structured as a parallel to US preparations for the invasion of Iraq between September 12, 2002 and March 17, 2003 and is interspersed with snippets from Bush's decisive speeches. Kalf is informed that his wife has been kidnapped and will be released if Kalf provides Jack Jackson, a film producer in Los Angeles, with sensitive material surrounding Eugen Meerkaz' death. Meerkaz, the novel has it, lost his life in the same explosion that killed the physicist and occultist John Whiteside Parsons in his laboratory on June 17, 1952 under mysterious circumstances. Al Snowe advises Kalf not to go to the police, and Kalf embarks on a trip through the US, searching for the unspecified material that the kidnappers believe is already in his possession and, on another and more important level, searching for his own identity.

The novel can be read in at least two ways: one, as a conspiracy thriller "and, if you are so inclined, as nothing more,"[15] and two, as a complex collage of myths, genres, and texts, as a work that shares with Beigbeder's its grounding in a postmodern "civilisation de la citation"[16] and, like Beigbeder's work, also takes its direction from Bret Easton Ellis.[17] This conjunction of the genre of the thriller, which coheres with the realist mode and is easily accessible, with a highly intellectualized, highly "artificial," non-realist sub- or parallel text of intertextual references, can be read as Hettche's attempt to write a novel that represents what he himself has called a "Relevant Realism," a combination of popular contemporaneity with aesthetic finesse.[18] Much like Beigbeder,

---

[15] Brandt, "Ein Schlaukopf haut rein."

[16] Frances Fortier, quoted in Clemente, "Beigbeder's Evil Personae," 130.

[17] On Beigbeder's affinities with Bret Easton Ellis, cf. Klohs, "Frédéric Beigbeder," 303; see also Beigbeder's mention of Ellis as one of his favourite authors (*WW*, 30), as the author of *Less Than Zero* (*WW*, 213), or his linking of *Windows on the World* to *Glamorama* via the image of confetti (*WW*, 358).

[18] Hettche was one of four German writers who, in 2005, published a much derided because rather full-mouthed manifesto on "What Is the Novel Supposed to Do?" The writer subscribing to "Relevant Realism," they proclaim, "clothes [...] his subject into fiction so skilfully that, when read superficially, this fiction could be taken to be a representation of reality: staged realism." Moreover, the writer engages in a "tightrope walk

Hettche published a manifesto on the future of the novel just a year before *Woraus wir gemacht sind* was published.[19]

In the context of literary treatments of 9/11, one might characterize Hettche's novel as a German counterpiece to Luc Lang's *11 septembre mon amour*. It is a "road novel" in which the protagonist visits the America that he has dreamt of since his childhood, yet in which American imperialism and aggression—which Lang's text rails against—are embraced and admired. I suggest, however, that Hettche's novel can be read more productively against Beigbeder's because, on another level, it critically examines the consequences of its own and Beigbeder's similar attempt at re-affirming European national identity through an appropriation of America from a distinctly German perspective. While in *Windows on the World*, French and American narrator(s) eventually merge on the level of narrative structure, in *Woraus wir gemacht sind*, the German protagonist pursues the same merger on the plot level: he tries to become one with the country, to become American. But this attempt to become American, as well as the attempts of various historical groups of German emigrants to the United States to appropriate an Americanized or even American identity, are shown to be eventually (self-)destructive. Kalf, and by extension Germans as a whole, the novel suggests, cannot derive a sense of self by embracing the national Other. Moreover, the novels lend themselves to comparison because of their explicit negotiations of national literary culture: both Beigbeder and Hettche offer their texts as the first specimens of the new French and the new German novel that they proclaim in their literary manifestos in 2003 and 2005.

---

between what has always been the only appropriate way of narrating from within the midst of lived experience itself and that which has been salvaged of virtuosity from the avant-garde" (Dean et al., "Was soll der Roman?" my translation), a balancing act that Gerrit Bartels has dubbed "contemporaneity plus aesthetic clout" ("Amerika, Blicke. Am Ende aller Gewissheiten und am Anfang der Liebe und der Diskurse: Thomas Hettches Roman *Woraus wir gemacht sind*," my translation). On *Woraus wir gemacht sind* as a "test case of 'Relevant Realism,'" see also Reinhäckel, *Traumatische Texturen*, 138; my translation.

[19] One might also read the novel's insistence on citation—in line with Volker Mergenthaler's recent argument—as a move against the critical demand to subordinate literariness to "authentic speech" after 9/11, cf. Mergenthaler, "Warum die Frage 'Wie reagieren Schriftsteller auf die Terroranschläge?' auf dem Feld der deutschsprachigen Literatur die falsche Frage ist," here especially 186.

Context I: The Cultural-Religious Other: Muslims in France and Germany[20]

Véronique Porra observes that one major factor in shaping French 9/11 literature is the presence of Muslims in French society. Germany is similarly characterized by a comparatively high percentage of Muslims,[21] which manifests itself in German treatments of 9/11. In both *Windows on the World* and *Woraus wir gemacht sind*, however, the presence of Muslims within French and German society is never registered and does not affect the texts' negotiations of French and German cultural identity. Muslims do not populate Beigbeder's Paris, and Niklas Kalf, Hettche's protagonist, is geographically—and in his thoughts even historically—far removed from present-day Germany. Considered against texts that do engage with Muslims as a part of French and German society, this absence becomes significant.

As Porra demonstrates, French writers with Muslim backgrounds used 9/11 as an occasion to dramatize conflicts between the Maghribian minority and the majority population in France as a "clash of civilizations" in Huntington's sense. These texts do not argue for an integration of minorities into French society in the tradition of the "Roman beur," but can be seen as a development of the "littérature de banlieue" in representing the divisions between the two groups.[22] Unlike in France, Muslim writers and film-makers in Germany have not drawn parallels between the "clash of civilizations" supposedly epitomized by the 9/11 attacks and their own position in German society. The presence of Muslims in Germany becomes relevant for treatments of 9/11 in other ways.

First of all, Mohamed Atta, Ramzi Binalshibh, Marwan al Shehhi, and Ziad Jarrah, referred to as the "Hamburg contingent" in the *9/11 Commission Report*,[23] had lived and studied in Germany during the 1990s.

---

[20] This essay was written before the beginning of the so-called refugee crisis in 2015 and thus may no longer reflect the status of Muslim immigrants in France and Germany correctly at the time of publication. Its account remains relevant, however, for the context of the novels discussed.

[21] The presence of Muslims in Germany, however, does not have its roots in a colonial past but is due to the mass hiring of foreign workers from Southern Europe in the 1960s and 1970s; hence the highest percentage of Muslims in Germany has a Turkish and not a Maghribian background.

[22] Porra, "Risse in der Mimesis," 165–167.

[23] *9/11 Commission Report* (National Commission on Terrorist Attacks upon the United States, 2004), 160.

These key players in the 9/11 attacks used Germany as their base in 2001.[24] In consequence, German culture after September 11, 2001 is troubled by the figure of the "sleeper" who infiltrates society and feigns integration in order to launch his attacks on the West. In contrast to the concerns of the "littérature de banlieue," German representations thus do not deal with a lack of social integration of the Muslim minority, but betray a fear of Muslims who appear to be perfectly integrated and use this very integration as a weapon against society. Literature did not immediately take up the issue, but several films came out that dealt with the perceived threat of "sleepers," for example, Elmar Fischer's *Fremder Freund* (released as *The Friend* in the US in 2005), Samir Nasr's *Folgeschäden* [Subsequent Damages] (2004), and Benjamin Heisenberg's *Schläfer* [Sleeper] (2005).[25] Non-German texts that focus on "sleepers" or (potential) terrorists such as Don DeLillo's sections on Hammad in *Falling Man* (2007), John Updike's *Terrorist* (2006), or Mohsin Hamid's *The Reluctant Fundamentalist* (2007) are primarily interested in the question of why and under which circumstances individuals—to be precise: Muslims and, except for Updike's Ahmad, immigrants—turn to fundamentalism and violence. Fischer's, Nasr's, and Heisenberg's films, by contrast, are interested in how the fear of "sleepers," which results in blanket suspicions against all Muslims and even against one's neighbours, friends, and lovers, has transformed German society and relations between majority and minority groups in the aftermath of 9/11.

Other specifically German concerns in this context are the radicalization of converts to Islam, which reached a peak after converts Fritz G. and Daniel S. were arrested in 2007 for planning attacks on US targets; the detention of German Muslims as "unlawful combatants," as in the case of Murat Kurnaz, which became public in 2006; and Germany's own history of terrorism, which received increased attention due to the thirtieth anniversary of the bloody events of the "German Autumn" in 2007. In Christoph Peters's novel *Ein Zimmer im Haus des Krieges* [A Room in the House of War] (2006), for instance, a German diplomat

---

[24] For a concise overview and analysis of the ways in which these individuals were recruited by Al-Qaeda and were involved in planning the attacks from Germany, see Greiner, *9/11. Der Tag, die Angst, die Folgen*, 31–46.

[25] For a discussion of *Fremder Freund*, see Hicks, "My Roommate the Terrorist: The Political Burden of September 11 in Elmar Fischer's *The Friend*," for a discussion of *Schläfer*, see Lehngut, "Sleepers, Informants, and the Everyday: Theorizing Terror and Ambiguity in Benjamin Heisenberg's *Schläfer*."

tries to understand the motivations of a German convert involved in a terrorist attack in Egypt in 1993 and, in the process, has to come to terms with his own sympathies for the actions of the terrorist group Red Army Fraction (RAF) in the 1960s and 1970s.[26] Similarly, in Pia Frankenberg's novel *Nora* (2006), the attacks of September 11 trigger the protagonist's process of dealing with her former membership in the RAF. As Philipp Hubmann shows in chapter "Tourist/Terrorist: Narrating Uncertainty in Early European Literature on Guantánamo" in this volume, Dorothea Dieckmann's novel *Guantánamo* (2004) is concerned with the detention of Rashid, a German with Indian cultural ties.[27]

The fact that Muslim minorities do not play a role in Beigbeder's and Hettche's imaginaries of cultural identity in *Windows on the World* and *Woraus wir gemacht sind* may perhaps in itself be taken as an indication of the divisions within French and German society that have surfaced after the 2001 attacks. By not even registering Muslims as part of France's and Germany's cultural texture, both novels may be said to reaffirm the marginal status of Muslims in Western Europe and to implicitly reject the idea of France and Germany as multi-cultural societies. Moreover, while Beigbeder does not represent Muslims and Arabs as members of his own society in *Windows on the World*, they do feature repeatedly in the novel. They are, however, evoked only as a globalized, largely faceless threat from the outside of France and are thus used to "reconstruct [... the West] *ex negativo*."[28] Beigbeder's literary relegation of Muslims to a space outside of France suggests, once more, that he imagines France as a culturally homogeneous society.

---

[26] On Peters' novel see also Kaulen, "Vom Scheitern des Dialogs mit dem Täter: Überlegungen zu Christoph Peters' *Ein Zimmer im Haus des Krieges* (2006)," Gansel, "Von der Primärerfahrung zur medialen Konstruktion? 'Soldatisches Opfernarrativ,' 9/11 und Terrorismusdarstellung in der deutschen (Gegenwarts)Literatur," 172–174.

[27] In a highly negative appreciation of German post-9/11 or "terror" texts, Michael König has spoken of these four particular foci as "navel-gazing." "Most recent German 'terror' texts do not deal with non-Western cultures; they neither seek to understand the differences between 'us' and 'them' nor do they ask for reasons for the increasing number of terrorist attacks. In my view, such inquiries are missing as much from recent German literature as they are from politics" (König, "Literary Accounts," 171f.).

[28] Versluys, "9/11 as a European Event," 74.

Context II: The National Other: Anti-Americanism

The second decisive context that Porra cites for French 9/11 novels is the "critical discourse about the contemporary US which is particularly pronounced [in France] and often grows into an unrestrained anti-Americanism."[29] Here Porra implicitly makes an important distinction: that between a well-informed, well-argued, and thus legitimate criticism of past or present US politics, culture, or military actions and anti-Americanism, which is characterized by the irrational rejection of all things American. Anti-American discourse does not criticize specific actions or characteristics but argues largely ahistorically, targets an essentialized American "nature," and confers blanket judgements.[30] Because anti- and pro-Americanism express European sentiments rather than describe the United States in any accurate way, they say more about European than about American identity.[31] Or, as Oliver Simons, discussing images of America in German literature, states: "In descriptions of America, German hopes and ideas are reflected, be they attempts at self-determination by individual adventurers and emigrants or by an entire nation."[32]

Windows on the World and *11 septembre mon amour* serve Porra as examples of the two ways in which authors have taken up the issue of anti-Americanism in French society. Their novels "either become platforms to express a bad conscience and celebrate a renewed friendship and Western solidarity with the US or [they use 9/11] for further criticism of American values and projections of self"[33]: they decidedly reject or wholeheartedly embrace and elaborate on anti-American perspectives. The *ressentiment* against America is always the flipside of a similarly undifferentiated love-relationship with America, and as stereotyped,

---

[29] Porra, "Risse in der Mimesis," 174; my translation.

[30] Cf. Gulddal, *Anti-Americanism in European Literature* or Dehez, "Anti-Amerikanismus," 151f.

[31] This has famously been noted by Hannah Arendt in her 1954 essay "Dream and Nightmare," and "Europa und Amerika." Cf. also, for instance, Dehez, "Anti-Amerikanismus," 155; Diner, *America in the Eyes of the Germans: An Essay on Anti-Americanism*, 108; Gassert, *Amerika im Dritten Reich: Ideologie, Propaganda und Volksmeinung, 1933–1945*, 370; Markovits, "Anti-Americanism and the Struggle for a West German Identity," 37; Schwaabe, *Antiamerikanismus: Wandlungen eines Feindbildes*, 9.

[32] Simons, "'Amerika gibt es nicht': On the Semiotics of Literary America in the Twentieth Century," 197.

[33] Porra, "Risse in der Mimesis," 174; my translation.

one-dimensional images can easily be viewed as either wholly positive or negative, anti-Americanism always exists in a dialectical relationship with Americanophilia. This split between a "good" and a "bad" America in the eyes of its national Others has frequently been described as a "Janus figure."[34]

European anti-Americanism is generally played out in three interconnected arenas: culture, economics, and politics.[35] Cultural superiority vis-à-vis the United States is perhaps the sentiment that is most pervasive among the intellectual class, and a discussion of it is always present, too, in texts that primarily grapple with stereotypes of America as an economic predator and military aggressor. One might assume that after 9/11, and particularly in the context of the grassroots opposition against the Iraq War across Europe, sentiment against the American "aggressor" was used to construct a European identity rather than "monadic" national European identities. No less important

---

[34] Cf. Porra, "Risse in der Mimesis," 175; my translation. Donnerstag also uses the term "Janus-faced" ("The Documentaries of Michael Moore," 143), as do Gassert and Leggewie (Gassert, "Was meint Amerikanisierung?" 795f.; Leggewie, *Amerikas Welt: Die USA in unseren Köpfen*); examples of other scholars who characterize the relationship between Germany or Europe and the United States as a bi-polar love-hate-relationship are Fraenkel, one of the earliest students of anti-Americanism in the 1950s and 1960s (Fraenkel, *Ernst Fraenkel: Gesammelte Schriften Band 4, Amerikastudien*), Gienow-Hecht (Gienow-Hecht, "Europäischer Anti-Amerikanismus im 20. Jahrhundert," 33f.), Kreis, who speaks of the relationship as one oscillating between "rejection and fascination" (Kreis, *Anti-Amerikanismus. Zum europäisch-amerikanischen Verhältnis zwischen Ablehnung und Faszination*), and Schwark (Schwark, *Zur Genealogie des modernen Anti-Amerikanismus in Deutschland*). A volume by Lüdtke et al. borrows Hannah Arendt's similarly doubled figure of "Traum und Alptraum" ("Dream and Nightmare") to describe views of the phenomenon of "Americanization" in Germany, Lüdtke et al. (eds), *Amerikanisierung: Traum und Alptraum im Deutschland des 20. Jahrhunderts*; cf. Arendt, "Dream and Nightmare." For a related argument on the function of the figures of the "good" and the "bad" American in German news media, see also Christ, "Michelle Obama, the Good American and Icon of Global Power Femininity: Gender Politics and National Boundary-Making in German News Coverage."

[35] These arenas can be said to be interconnected because feelings of inferiority in one arena may be compensated by the need to prove superiority in another. For instance, as Fraenkel observes, the German relationship to the United States is characterized by a "strange mixture of an arrogant feeling of intellectual superiority [...] and an almost despondent sense of economic inferiority": in German constructions of national identity, the repeated affirmation of cultural or intellectual superiority serves as a compensation for economic inferiority, quoted in Buchstein and Kühn, "Vorwort," 18.

thinkers than Jacques Derrida and Jürgen Habermas saw the demonstrations against the impending US intervention in Iraq of February 15, 2003 as the "rebirth of Europe" and the "birth of a European public."[36] Yet the literary engagement with criticisms of American politics and with anti-Americanism, I would like to suggest, focuses on nationally specific attitudes towards the United States instead of positing a European sensibility against an American one. Beigbeder's and Hettche's novels can serve as examples of ways in which anti-Americanisms, and hence the ways in which authors work through them, are nationally inflected.

In Chap. "8:34" of *Windows on the World*, Beigbeder explicitly takes on anti-Americanism as the theme of one of the "mini-essays" that the narrators intersperse in their narratives.[37] While he speaks at times about the relationship of "Europe" towards "America" and even can be said to use an inclusive European "we" in this chapter, his engagement with anti-Americanism here and throughout the entire novel takes a specifically French perspective: Beigbeder's text is explicitly countering "l'anti-américanisme hexagonal" (*WW*, 29), that is *French* anti-Americanism, and not a general "bigoted anti-Americanism" (*WW-E*, 16–17), as the English translation, in an internationalizing move (or, in labelling French anti-Americanism as "bigoted," even in an implicitly Francophobe move?), has it.

This national inflection of the novel's take on anti-Americanism is manifest in at least two other ways. For one, Beigbeder engages the specific discourse that anti-Americanism in France is mainly nourished by that of the "French exception." He uses the term "l'exception culturelle française" only in the last paragraph of Chap. "8:34," yet his argument is a literary adaptation of Jean-François Revel's position on French cultural exceptionalism and anti-Americanism in *L'obsession anti-américaine*

---

[36] Borradori, *Philosophy in a Time of Terror*, 33; my translation.

[37] The English translation adds a reflection on this form of mini-essays or "diary jottings or journal entries" in the Chapter "10:12" (Versluys, *Out of the Blue*, 141); this chapter is also devoted to an explanation of anti-Americanism: Beigbeder dubs the core of these mini-essays "ITNNOTs": "It is at this point that I whip out another of my famous ITNNOTs (Instant Though Not Necessarily Original Theories)" (*WW-E*, 280).

(2002).³⁸ According to "Beigbeder," polemicizing Revel only slightly, "le reste du monde" rejects American culture and needs to denigrate it because, "[a]u fond," they sense American culture's superiority and are driven by "jalousie et d'amour déçu" (*WW*, 31).³⁹ In a quasi-protectionist move, then, Beigbeder uses French examples exclusively to illustrate the "rest of the world's" (*WW-E*, 18) inferiority complex.⁴⁰ He even integrates this "European" anti-Americanism into a model of cultural hierarchies that is particular to the centralized French nation state and cannot be transferred to localized identities within other countries: "La France aujourd'hui a le même rapport avec les États-Unis que la province avec Paris: mélange d'admiration et de rejet, désir d'en être, gloire d'y résister. On veut tout savoir sur ce pays pour pouvoir hausser les épaules d'un air dédaigneux" (*WW*, 32).⁴¹

Another moment where *Windows on the World*, while sometimes paying lip service to the opposition of *Europe* and America, focuses exclusively on *French*-American relations is "Beigbeder's" framing of the Paris demonstration of February 15, 2003. He views the conflict over the Iraq War as one played out between France and America exclusively: according to "Beigbeder," it is "[l]e Président de la France" who does not agree with "le Président de l'Amérique" in the UN Security Council (*WW*, 123). Instead of using the proper names of Jacques Chirac and George W. Bush, "Beigbeder" stresses the national opposition by

---

[38] On the concept of "French exceptionalism," see the collection by Emmanuel Godin and Tony Chafer (eds), *The French Exception*. Revel has noted that the discourse on "cultural exceptionalism" has been replaced by a discourse on "cultural diversity" in the late 1990s, but argues that it similarly reinforces French cultural protectionism, Revel, "The Anti-American Obsession," cf. also Revel, *L'obsession anti-américaine: Son fonctionnement, ses causes, ses inconséquences*. Beigbeder links his thinking explicitly to Revel's when he mentions him next to Huntington, Baudrillard, Adler, and Fukuyama as those theorists whom the reader may refer to in order to disentangle "le nœud géopolitique du terrorism"/ "the geopolitical tangle of terrorism" (*WW*, 145f./*WW-E*, 115).

[39] "Anti-Americanism is in large part jealousy and unrequited love. Deep down, the rest of the world admires American art [...]" (*WW-E*, 18).

[40] See his story about Bernard Pivot, host of the "Bouillon de Culture," that he uses as a "symbol éclatant"/"compelling example" of the French inferiority complex (*WW*, 31f./*WW-E*, 18).

[41] "France has the same relationship with the United States nowadays as the provinces do with Paris: a combination of admiration and contempt, a longing to be part of it and a pride at resisting. We want to know everything about them so that we can shrug our shoulders with a condescending air" (*WW-E*, 19).

speaking of the French and the American presidents and, in addition, elides other nations' opposition against the intervention, which was clearly voiced in the Security Council and was popularly expressed on the streets on February 15. For the narrator, the demonstrations do not mark a moment of European unity vis-à-vis the US—a reading quite different from that of Derrida and Habermas. Instead of mentioning marchers all over Europe and the world, "Beigbeder" only notes that "[l]e même jour, il y avait le même nombre de manifestants qui disaient la même chose dans les rues de New York" (*WW*, 123).[42] At this point, he divides America into an authentic, "good" and a compromised, "bad America" and aligns the French marchers with the first.

The issues that configure Germany's relationship with America in *Woraus wir gemacht sind* are different from the discourse on the "French exceptionalism" in *Windows on the World*. Hettche's novel counters an anti-American discourse that is still informed by the Frankfurt School's indictment of the culture industry of the 1930s and 1940s. The text evokes this context by stressing Kalf's pro-American embrace of Hollywood and his experience of the "reality" or "aura" of American art that engages the nature of "mechanical reproduction" as in Donald Judd's "100 Untitled Works in Mill Aluminum" (cf. *Wwgs*, 135f.). Kalf, moreover, acknowledges how his view of the world has been shaped by American literature, film, and TV and admits to his longing to be part of a reality that hitherto he only had access to in medialized form, yet which paradoxically has barred his access to his "real" life in Germany:

> Alles wurde mit seinen englischen Bezeichnungen endlich bei seinem wirklichen Namen genannt, und die Preise in Dollar gaben allem seinen wirklichen Wert. [...] Im Mittelpunkt der Welt angekommen zu sein, verstand Kalf, hieß, daß alle Versprechungen der Fernsehsehnsuchtswelt seiner Kindheit nun eingelöst wurden, und er begriff, wie entsetzlich es gewesen war, als Kind nichts aus der Welt der Serien in der eigenen wiederzufinden. (*Wwgs*, 79f.)[43]

---

[42] "On the same day, the same number of marchers are saying the same thing on the streets of New York" (*WW-E*, 96).

[43] "Everything, it seemed to him, was called by its proper name in English, and the prices in dollars gave everything its actual value. The police sirens and the car horns had the right sound, all lights their proper colours. Arriving at the center of the world, Kalf understood, meant that all the promises of the television world of his childhood longing were now redeemed, and he understood how terrible it had been as a child to find nothing of the world of the television series in his own world" (*WWAMO*, 73f.).

"Beigbeder" goes against dearly held anti-Americanist convictions of the French left intelligentsia by proclaiming US cultural superiority over France but eventually joins the left again by condemning military intervention in Iraq. Kalf, by contrast, is shown to go even further: he comes to see pacificism—a position that is held more dearly among German than French left-leaning intellectuals—as a stance of weakness. He openly admires the politics of the Bush administration in the aftermath of September 11 and thinks of the marchers of February 15 as "Idioten" (*Wwgs*, 283). Early in the novel, Al Snowe, who is clearly critical of the Bush administration (*Wwgs*, 48f.), notices this disposition in Kalf and states: "Sie sind sehr von den USA fasziniert" (*Wwgs*, 47).[44] Suggesting that, once in the US, it is as if he has woken up from a dream, faced the realities of the world, and begun to admire American *Realpolitik* and the use of imperial powers, Kalf answers: "Ja, sicher [bin ich fasziniert]. Als ich Bush heute vor den UN sah, nicht zeitversetzt oder in einer unwirklichen Nacht, sondern unter derselben Sonne, verstand ich ein wenig, was die Macht der Macht ist" (*Wwgs*, 48).[45]

Kalf's uncritical and naïve adoption of a pro-American stance takes place in desperate circumstances: on September 12, 2002, as Bush addresses the United Nations and Kalf's wife Liz has disappeared from their hotel room, the spectre of war and the loss of his intimate "Other" conjoin to make him realize his complete loss of self, his lack of identity—which must be read as the loss of self of an entire nation, of "us."[46] As Bush finishes his speech, this loss of self is finalized:

---

[44] Snowe's statement is wrongly translated in the English version. It reads "*They*'re absolutely fascinated by the States" (*WWAMO*, 42) instead of "*You* are absolutely fascinated by the States," thereby referring back to German immigrants of the early twentieth century who are mentioned in the previous passage. This interpretation of "Sie" does not make any sense either in the context of Snowe's looking at Kalf curiously when making this statement or in the context of the conversation that follows.

[45] "Yes, of course [I'm fascinated]. When I saw Bush speaking at the UN today, not with a time delay or on some unreal night, but under the same sun, I began to understand the power of power" (*WWAMO*, 42).

[46] I agree here with Gerrit Bartels who stresses in his review of the novel that Hettche is not only writing the history of a generation but of a nation: "The 'We' that Thomas Hettche uses is not the banal 'We' of generations: [...] No, this 'We' includes us all, not humanity in its entirety, but all of us who live in Germany in the 21st century," Bartels, "Amerika, Blicke," my translation; Rainer Moritz, however, implicitly disagrees and sees Kalf as trying to figure out "himself and his [...] generation," Moritz, "Marfa ist nicht Frankfurt am Main: Thomas Hettches Roman *Woraus wir gemacht sind*," my translation.

> Erst jetzt realisierte Niklas Kalf wirklich, daß Liz verschwunden war, und dieses Wissen durchflutete ihn, kalt und schwarz schäumte es durch all die Räume seiner Erinnerung und Selbstgewißheit, nichts als brackige, ölschlierige Angst, die ihn lähmte und in der er widerstandslos und still ertrank, bis noch jener feine, leuchtende Punkt an der Spitze der Zunge, mit der man ‚Ich' sagt, einfach verlosch. (*Wwgs*, 28)[47]

His attempt to (re)gain an identity leads to his passive and complete abandonment of himself to America, its culture, people, and landscape. While he, like "Beigbeder," is sometimes paying lip service to the idea that what is lost may be a European identity, his identitarian struggles betray a German rather than a broader European predicament. What he needs to come to terms with vis-à-vis the United States is the history of the Holocaust and, partly related, the history of German emigration. When Elsa Meerkaz demands of him: "You have to show me now what you are made of" (*Wwgs*, 294), Kalf answers by relating a seemingly unconnected story about his first visit to Auschwitz: a vendor of refreshments whom he is conversing with in German tells him that, in contrast to Kalf, most younger German visitors address her in English—the language in which Elsa, who otherwise speaks German to him, has addressed him in this instance, too. While it may be considered standard behaviour to use English as a lingua franca anywhere abroad, Kalf sees these German visitors' use of English as mirroring his own behaviour in the US: Germans in Auschwitz are attempting, via the English language, to do what Kalf does more extensively on his trip through the US: they are trying to take on a non-German identity and shun historical responsibility for the Holocaust. Kalf, one has to infer, admits to be "made" primarily of the guilt of the Holocaust.

As Jürgen Donnerstag has pointed out, US politics after the 9/11 attacks have generally prompted a new "attempt to escape the shadow of the Holocaust" in Germany, as "Europeans – the Germans in particular – are laying claim to a moral superiority to the United States on the basis

---

[47] "Only now did Niklas Kalf fully realize that Liz had disappeared, and that knowledge flooded through him, cold and black it foamed through all the spaces of his memory and self-certainty, nothing but brackish, oily fear which paralysed him, and in which he drowned unresisting and silent, until that fine, gleaming point at the tip of his tongue, the one with which we say 'I,' was finally extinguished" (*WWAMO*, 22).

of a generally pacifistic attitude."⁴⁸ This reading of national identitarian dynamics is also at the basis of Robert Kagan's Germany-centred argument that the US is paying the military price for Europe's self-fashioning as a peaceful continent.⁴⁹ In Hettche's novel, this argument is rehearsed by the figure of the devil whom Kalf encounters in a phantasmagoric Faustian episode in the Chapter "Who's who?": "Ihr müßt begreifen, dass wir euer Paradies bezahlen! Die USA, wie mein Freund Kagan es formuliert, patrouillieren vor euren Mauern" (*Wwgs*, 177).⁵⁰

Kalf attempts to escape the "shadow of the Holocaust" by reversing the manoeuvre described by Donnerstag. Instead of identifying with the legacy of the Holocaust and insisting on pacifism, Kalf tries to erase the Holocaust from his memory and to embrace US military power as desirable and unproblematic. He feels drawn to America and particularly the landscape of Southern Texas because, supposedly, this landscape does not signify anything beyond itself, because it has no history. When Frank Holdt, one of Kalf's Marfa friends and son of a German POW who got involved with Eugen Meerkaz, suggests that Kalf is addicted to the emptiness of the landscape and to the idea that in this historical vacuum, even "Auschwitz hätte hier nichts bedeutet" (*Wwgs*, 153),⁵¹ Kalf first denies this idea but secretly has to admit that Frank is right: "Es war immer, als fehle hier etwas. Sollten es die Augen der Toten sein?" (*Wwgs*, 153).⁵² Kalf's Americanophilia can thus be described as an attempt to escape into an American identity that does not have to deal with this specifically German historical guilt.

The centrality of the Holocaust in negotiations of German identity in relation to 9/11 can similarly be observed in Susanne Riedel's *Eine Frau aus Amerika* [A Woman from America] (2003) and Katharina Hacker's *Die Habenichtse*, published like *Woraus wir gemacht sind* in 2006 (and translated into English as *The Have-Nots* in 2008).⁵³ The Holocaust

---

⁴⁸ Donnerstag, "The Documentaries of Michael Moore," 143.

⁴⁹ Cf. Kagan, *Of Paradise and Power: America and Europe in the New World Order*.

⁵⁰ "You've got to understand that we're paying for your paradise! The United States, as my friend Kagan puts it, are patrolling outside your walls" (*WWAMO*, 170).

⁵¹ "Even Auschwitz wouldn't have meant anything here" (*WWAMO*, 147).

⁵² "It always seemed as if something was missing. Could it be the eyes of the dead?" (*WWAMO*, 147).

⁵³ Hubert Spiegel, in a slating review after Hacker had received the recently established German Book Prize, complained exactly about this compounding of 9/11 and the Holocaust: "Anything of shock value is thrown into the mix: September 11, child abuse,

and the history of World War II, of course, figure centrally in many American representations of the 9/11 attacks, for example, in Jonathan Safran Foer's *Extremely Loud and Incredibly Close* (2005). American texts use this history mainly by way of comparison and in order to grasp the meaning of 9/11 and debate or affirm the attack's singularity.[54] In German 9/11 texts, by contrast, the attacks of September 11 function as a trigger for the characters to confront the Holocaust as that event that shapes their identity in much more profound ways than—thus the implied argument goes—9/11 ever will. The continuing presence of the "shadow of the Holocaust" in the twenty-first century is stressed by incidental references to the Holocaust throughout Hettche's novel.[55]

Kalf can, second, be read as working through and partly re-enacting the history of emigration from Germany: In addition to writing the

---

drug abuse, Holocaust. Does the new boss of a latently homosexual and unhappily married young attorney, who is offered an attractive job in London only because a good friend of his dies in the World Trade Center, really have to be a homosexual Jew who was persecuted by the Nazis [...]?" Spiegel, "Achtung, Kurve!," my translation. One answer to Spiegel would be that the Holocaust *has* to figure in German 9/11 texts. While texts like Hettche's and Hacker's may thus at times seem to dwell on an excess of historical tragedies, it is the Holocaust that German literature needed to revisit after 9/11 to put an end to the supposed decade of the "holiday from history" in the wake of the end of the Cold War and, for Germans, in the wake of re-unification.

[54] *Windows on the World* also compares the attacks of September 11, 2001 to the Holocaust for a similar function, namely in order to—ironically—capture the event as one that defies representation or to "deny both events their respective singularity" (Clemente, "Beigbeder's Evil Personae," 113). Chapter "10:10," the one preceding the announcement of David Yorston's death, compares the restaurant "Windows on the World" directly to the gas chambers in Auschwitz, a comparison that is cut from the English translation. On the politics of such cuts, see Clemente, "Beigbeder's Evil Personae," 112f. More indirect comparisons, however, such as Beigbeder's claim that he is not editing out the terror of the events as Spielberg did according to some critics in *Schindler's List* (*WW*, 251), are present in the English translation.

[55] One example is Kalf spotting the headline of the *New York Times* announcing Imre Kertesz as the winner of the Nobel Prize for Literature. In this scene, the novel once more links 9/11 and its aftermath to the Holocaust and suggests that taking a position towards 9/11 means taking a position towards its own history: "NOBEL FOR HUNGARIAN WRITER WHO SURVIVED DEATH CAMPS. Vorsichtig beugte Kalf sich hinab und angelte sich die Zeitung mit den Fingerspitzen. New York, Friday, October 11, 2002. CONGRESS AUTHORIZES BUSH TO USE FORCE AGAINST IRAQ" (*Wwgs*, 111).

biography of a German Jew who was forced to emigrate, Kalf's itinerary follows in the footsteps of Germans in America, from his choice of the "Excelsior, ein altes Emigrantenhotel" (*Wwgs*, 22)[56] as his abode in New York City via Marfa, where German POWs where held after World War II, to Pacific Palisades, where German *litterati* settled to escape prosecution and instrumentalization by the Nazi regime. Kalf can even be said to become an emigrant, a refugee himself. After some days in Marfa, he has severed all of his ties to Germany: he has left messages for family and friends that he and Liz will be travelling for an unspecified period and switched off his mobile phone permanently. Kalf has erased Germany as a fall-back option.

As many reviewers have criticized, it is hardly plausible that friends and family find no ways to even inquire after Liz and Kalf—or, as Hettche might say referencing his 2005 manifesto, this detail is, if at all, plausible only "on the surface."[57] On closer scrutiny, then, the text does not cohere to a conspiracy thriller's demands of complete plausibility. This is precisely because the text, while serving some demands of the thriller genre, simultaneously insists on presenting Kalf and his issues of identity as analogous to those of Jewish refugees in the 1930s and 1940s. These identity issues are closely modelled on Hannah Arendt's characterizations in "We Refugees" (1943). Once in Marfa, Kalf behaves like Arendt's Mr. Cohn who not only assimilates but becomes a patriot in every country he is forced to live in—"a 150 percent German, a German superpatriot," "a convinced Czech patriot," "a definite Austrian patriot [...]," and a Frenchman who identifies with "'our' ancestor Vercingétorix."[58] Kalf tries to become a 150% patriotic *American*, an *American* superpatriot: he is more loyal to "his" government and

---

[56] "The Excelsior, an old immigrants' hotel" (*WWAMO*, 16).

[57] The reader might wonder why, for example, no worrying family members try to track Kalf down through his credit card payments, or why Kalf, a freelance writer in the year 2002, does not have an email address which family members would expect him to use to stay in contact. In a highly unlikely dialogue Kalf tells Lavinia Sims that he cannot access his email account in the US, and when Lavinia asks him to set up an account in order to forward him pictures of Liz that she has received from the kidnappers, she even asks whether he knows how to do that (*Wwgs*, 89). Compare Steinfeld who criticizes these and other implausibilities, Steinfeld, "Der deutsche Dichter und sein Satan. Ein Liebling der Kritik: Thomas Hettches Roman *Woraus wir gemacht sind*."

[58] Arendt, "We Refugees," 271.

thus more patriotic—in an obedient sense—than the Americans in the novel who maintain a critical distance to their country and its politics. The construction of Kalf's postmodern, post-9/11, navel-gazing, self-inflicted desperation in search of an identity as analogous to the situation of refugees (and especially to refugees from Nazi Germany), I would argue, constitutes a rather problematic trivialization of Hannah Arendt's conceptualization of the refugee and Giorgio Agamben's more recent reconsideration. Hettche's novel should perhaps be less criticized for its implausibility than for establishing this kind of parallel. Ultimately however, as I will show, the text is clever enough to debunk this analogy and to demonstrate that Kalf is misled and presumptuous in seeking his identity in America and that, as Arendt points out, "the recovery of a new personality is as difficult—and as hopeless—as a new creation of the world."[59]

CONTEXT III: FRENCH AND GERMAN NATIONAL LITERARY PARADIGMS

Porra's third context for specificities of French literary responses to 9/11 is that of literary form and literary traditions. There is general agreement among critics that Beigbeder's explicit, even "in-your-face" meta-textual reflections are in keeping with the French anti-mimetic, deconstructivist school around *Tel Quel*, even if "Beigbeder" may be said to complicate and update deconstructivist claims of the impossibility of realist representation, for example, when he states that "[l]'écriture de ce roman hyperréaliste est rendue difficile par la réalité elle-même" since "[d]espuis le 11 septembre 2001, non seulement la réalité dépasse la fiction mais elle la détruit" (*WW*, 20).[60] Porra finds comparable concerns and thus an engagement with by now "traditional" French literary concerns in Luc Lang's, Y.B.'s, or Maurice Dantec's novels.

Woraus wir gemacht sind engages German literary paradigms in different ways. The text does not engage *explicitly* in reflections about the possibility of writing and representation. Its backbone of intertextual collage and its surface realism simply exist alongside each other. The issue

---

[59] Ibid., 271.

[60] "Writing this hyperrealist novel is made more difficult by reality itself. Since September 11, 2001, reality has not only outstripped fiction, it's destroying it" (*WW-E*, 8).

that the text engages instead is what Porra calls the first, rather than the second, "link of the mimetic relation"—in other words, the question of "what *is* reality?" rather than "how can reality be represented?"[61] In doing so, Hettche's text follows an agenda that is similar to those European 9/11 texts that explore the validity of European media theory and semiotics in the context of 9/11, which are the focus of Part I in this volume. But moreover, by grappling with what constitutes the "real," Hettche places his novel in the tradition of the specifically German genre of the "Amerikaroman" ("America novel").

In the chapter "Who's who?," the devil claims that the reason for Kalf's confusion about his identity is his being in love with the idea that life might just be a dream: "Wenig hat euch [Europäer] so begeistert wie die Annahme, eigentlich sei nicht zu unterscheiden, was wirklich ist und was ausgedacht" (*Wwgs*, 174).[62] Kalf's inability to know who he is stems from his unwillingness to acknowledge reality: he does not know "was Traum ist und was wirklich" (*Wwgs*, 175).[63] But his "dreams" and his life in Marfa are also played out along the lines of movie scripts, as in this very meeting with the devil: the devil takes the shapes of various Hollywood actors in their different roles—and thus shapes which exhibit a double layer of signification in themselves. Kalf displays expert skills at recognizing both actors and roles, but does not recognize the shape-shifter as the devil. In other words, Kalf cannot see the referent, he only sees the references.

While the devil in this scene alludes to *La vida es sueño* and Calderón de la Barca as the father figure of a modern European sensibility that is epitomized in Baudrillard's notion of the simulacrum, the scene is rich in specifically German ways of engaging with the problems of this "European idea." In fact, with regard to the loss of "America" as referent, Hettche writes himself into a particularly rich genre of German literature: as Oliver Simons points out, "numerous America novels of German literary history deal very fundamentally with the loss of

---

[61] Porra, "Risse in der Mimesis," 172; my translation.

[62] "Few things have excited you so much as the supposition that you can't really tell what's real and what's imagined" (*WWAMO*, 167).

[63] "[…] he thought again of Dostoevsky and the fact that anything can happen when you don't know what's a dream and what's real" (*WWAMO*, 167).

referentiality,"[64] since their America is no more than "a textual construction."[65] The loss of the referent, of America as the entity in relation to which Kalf and so many travellers before him try to work out their own identity, renders the identification of the self impossible.

Yet more important with regard to specifically contemporary German concerns about literature is the way in which this chapter and the nod to *La vida es sueño* sets in motion a chain of intertextual referencing through which the novel suggests an answer to the question of the 2005 manifesto, "What Is the Novel Supposed to Do?" The chapter with its programmatic title "Who's who?" questions the way in which identities are made and whether they "are made of" reality or dreams. The chapter thus allows the novel's title to forcefully resonate with Prospero's lines "We are such stuff /As dreams are made on; and our little life / Is rounded with a sleep" and Hugo von Hofmannsthal's German appropriation "Wir sind aus solchem Zeug wie das zu Träumen" from *Terzinen*.[66] The next link in this intertextual chain, then, is Johannes Mario Simmel's 1971 espionage thriller *Der Stoff, aus dem die Träume sind* [The Stuff That Dreams Are Made Of]. Like Hettche's ahistorical insistence to cast Kalf as a "refugee," this link provides clues to turns of the plot that have been perceived as implausible or simply "too much"[67]: more often than not, seemingly ludicrous twists and details must be

---

[64] Simons, "'Amerika gibt es nicht,'" 197.

[65] Ibid., 196.

[66] Steffen Richter, in what I consider the most insightful review of the novel, notes that the title *Woraus wir gemacht sind* "sounds like Shakespeare's *The Tempest* – which is also a story of shipwreck in the new world, and where Prospero suggests that we are made of 'such stuff that dreams are made of,'" cf. "Utopie in der Prärie. Der Hauch des amerikanischen Imperiums: Thomas Hettches Roman *Woraus wir gemacht sind*," my translation. Without commenting, Auffermann entitles her review "Der Stoff, aus dem der Westen ist" [The stuff that the West is made of] and Brandt summarizes major plot lines of the novel by punning "Das ist der Stoff Woraus wir gemacht sind" [That is the stuff that we are made of], cf. Auffermann, "Der Stoff, aus dem der Westen ist," 50–52 and Brandt, "Ein Schlaukopf haut rein."

[67] Thomas Steinfeld criticizes "the permanent outdoing" that characterizes plot and style: "This outdoing begins with Kalf's partner, who is not only partner, but also pregnant. It continues in the representations of the United States […]," cf. Steinfeld, "Der deutsche Dichter," my translation.

attributed to Hettche's referencing of Simmel's bestseller.[68] Hettche thus inscribes his novel into both "high" and "low" literary traditions, which are cleverly brought together in its title. In doing so, he interprets "Relevant Realism's" task of combining "lived experience" and "virtuosity" as the task of overcoming the incommensurability of "high" and "low" forms of literature that is often seen as responsible for the contemporary German "serious" novel's perceived irrelevance and lack of a broader readership.[69]

The events of 9/11 have led literature in general to question the limits and ethics of representation anew, yet raising these universal issues has also become an occasion for revisiting, modifying, or challenging specifically national traditions of novelistic representation. The French and German relationship to the United States and its cultural productions, which is so central to both novels, may also play a part in both Beigbeder's and Hettche's negotiations of their own literary traditions. Beigbeder opines that "[l]a culture américaine n'écrase pas la planète pour des raisons économiques mais par son talent spécifique" (*WW*, 30)[70] and goes on to explain that "les artistes américains cherchent toujours la nouveauté, mais une nouveauté qui nous parle des nous-mêmes. Ils savent concilier l'invention avec l'accessibilité, la création originale avec l'envie de séduire" (*WW*, 31).[71] Beigbeder, in a gesture of self-effacement, claims that his own works do not achieve such a combination of

---

[68] Examples of how *Woraus wir gemacht sind* takes up motifs from Simmel include that Simmel's Roland, a journalist, wants to cover a story about a Czech refugee just like Kalf is covering the story of the refugee Eugen Meerkaz, he and his colleague Engelhardt witness how a pimp attempts to abduct a pregnant woman (and can, in contrast to Kalf, just prevent the abduction), that Engelhardt comes into the possession of sensitive material (which both CIA and KGB—rather than a Hollywood film producer, as in Hettche's novel—are after), and that Engelhardt's apartment is ransacked and he is killed, as Frank Holdt is for not delivering the sensitive material on Eugen Meerkaz.

[69] Steinfeld notes that Hettche tries to bridge the "high" and the "low" and is adamant about Hettche's failure to do so, cf. Steinfeld, "Der deutsche Dichter." For an ironic literary treatment of the expectation of the German novel to be as readable as the American model, cf. also Kristof Magnusson's novel *Das war ich nicht* (2010).

[70] "American culture dominates the planet not for economic reasons, but because of its quality" (*WW-E*, 17).

[71] "American artists are constantly searching for something new, but something new which speaks to us of ourselves. They know how to reconcile imagination and accessibility, originality with the desire to seduce" (*WW-E*, 17f.).

originality and popular success when he includes them "dans ce triste constat" (*WW*, 33) that is the "French cultural exception," but this gesture is a calculated one: The (international) success of *Windows on the World*—which, given Beigbeder's celebrity status and the taboo-breaking elements of the text, was not entirely surprising—in effect turns this gesture into an appraisal of Beigbeder's work. His novels have achieved exactly that which he sees as an American quality: critical acclaim due to their meta-reflexivity combined with popular success due to their shock value. Hettche's very similar attempt to unite intellectuality and entertainment can be read as a response to that same challenge that contemporary American literature may be said to constitute for the German novelist: the sales numbers of and enthusiasm for novels by Paul Auster, Dave Eggers, Jeffrey Eugenides, Jonathan Safran Foer, Philip Roth, or John Updike in Germany—considered "highbrow" yet with a broader appeal—have surpassed those by "serious" German contemporary writers during the last, if not during earlier decades.[72]

"French Fries": The US as Part of a Globalized France in *Windows on the World*

My argument that *Windows on the World* proclaims a pro-American stance different from widespread French intellectual attitudes, but uses it for the less altruistic purpose of constructing and affirming a positive French identity takes its lead from Birgit Däwes's observation that the novel "ends up confirming transatlantic hierarchies" and "eventually regresses to stereotypes and self-interest."[73] The text does so, I would like to show, in four interconnected ways: first, it turns appraisals of America into appraisals of France; second, it offers arguments why

---

[72] Cf. Martin, "Die unreifen Verehrer amerikanischer Helden." The picture is complicated by Martin's polemic contention that, with the exception of John Ford and Jonathan Franzen, the American authors that are embraced by the German public are those who represent a clichéd version of the United States that suits European tastes; however, this dynamic echoes the dynamic that I trace in Beigbeder's and Hettche's novels, namely that of using a specific image of the US for one's own, narcissist purposes, on the level of readers and the book market.

[73] Däwes, "On Contested Ground (Zero): Literature and the Transnational Challenge of Remembering 9/11," 528. Susana Araújo makes a similar point in passing, cf. "Images of Terror, Narratives of Captivity: The Visual Spectacle of 9/11 and Its Transatlantic Projections," 30f.

America actually is and has always already been French; third, Beigbeder betrays the same feelings of "jalousie et d'amour déçu" (*WW*, 31)[74] vis-à-vis the US that he diagnoses as the roots of anti-Americanism; and finally, he ridicules Americans and perpetuates negative stereotypes of America. These dynamics interact and are particularly interesting because the text does not render them transparent on the meta-textual level. This constitutes a striking exception to the way in which Beigbeder's explicitly addresses his other moves and motivations that may be criticized for their underlying narcissism. In the case of what can be read as his own anti-Americanism, Beigbeder does not set up a "paratonnerre" (*WW*, 12; 44)[75] to anticipate criticism of his use of the tragedy of 9/11 to affirm French greatness.[76]

Chapter "8:34" displays all of the above dynamics and thus invalidates the text's supposedly pro-American stance in a nutshell. As I have already discussed, when Beigbeder praises American artists for combining intellectual originality with popularity, this functions extra-textually to ultimately present the French author Beigbeder in a positive light. This dynamic is repeated intra-textually as well. Beigbeder's second major point of why American literature is superior to any other in "8:34" is that "[l]es auteurs américains croient être naturalistes mais sont tous marxistes! Ils sont très critiques avec leur propre nation. Aucune démocratie n'est plus contestée au monde par sa propre sphère littéraire" (*WW*, 31).[77] In one of the last chapters and at a moment in which Beigbeder questions his own motivations for writing "ce livre" most critically, he legitimates his writing about "les sujets tabous" by claiming for French literature that same tradition of rebellion in the name of true democracy: "La littérature française est une longue histoire de désobéisance [...] Le seul intérêt de vivre en démocratie, c'est de pouvoir la

---

[74] "jealousy and unrequited love" (*WW-E*, 18).

[75] "lightning rod" (*WW-E*, 28).

[76] On Beigbeder's technique of anticipating "accusations of self-indulgence, cynicism, narcissism, trivialization, bad taste or exploitation" to the extent that the novel seems "almost hermetically sealed and, thus, resistant to criticism," see Martin Randall's excellent chapter on Beigbeder's metafiction, cf. Randall, *9/11 and the Literature of Terror*, 69 and 70.

[77] "American authors think of themselves as realists when in fact they are all Marxists! They're hypercritical of their own country. No democracy in the world is as contested by its own literature" (*WW-E*, 18).

critiquer" (*WW*, 359).[78] Miraculously, at the end of the novel, not only does "Beigbeder" write as well and as successfully as the Americans, but the whole of French literary history, in fact, does and has always already been doing what supposedly makes for American literature's greatness.

Through Yorston's voice in the chapter preceding "8:34," *Windows on the World* also suggests that American democracy was made possible only because the French intervened in the War of Independence. In "9:04," Beigbeder admits that "Oncle Sam" has superseded France in everything but in age, yet as it turns out, the experience that comes with age is what prevents nations from engaging in dangerous follies—such as imperialist aspirations. In a patronizing move, which is announced by the use of the ambiguous moniker "Oncle Sam," Beigbeder states: "Tout ça, merci, on connaît: bon débarras, ça n'attire qu'emmerdes. Les États-Unis, eux, avec leur enthousiasme juvénile, ont encore envie d'être les patrons du globe" (*WW*, 144).[79] He concedes later that America has made a step forward in its development after 9/11, yet of course lags a good 400 years behind France: "L'Amérique est entré dans l'ère de Descartes" (*WW*, 327)—and thereby patronizes the US further.[80] The idea that democracy and liberty have been given to Americans by the French recurs over and over in the novel.

One might perhaps, as many critics have done, read what I consider French appropriations of "American" qualities and achievements more benevolently as Beigbeder's attempt to represent the cultural interconnectedness between France and the US. Sure enough, he does concede at times that the Americans also gave France a similar gift of liberty when they freed France from the Nazis (see *WW*, 26f. and 305) and that there is reciprocity in other fields as well. However, in conjunction with his feelings of being ignored by the Americans—his feelings of "jalousie et d'amour déçu" (*WW*, 31)—these repeated, almost droning declarations of how "French" the US supposedly is cannot but be interpreted as a "Frenchifying" of America, as claiming America as one's own.

---

[78] "French literature is a long history of disobedience [...] The singular interest of living in a democracy is to criticize it" (*WW-E*, 301).

[79] "We've all been there, thanks: good riddance, it only gets you into shit. America, with its youthful enthusiasm, still wants to see what it feels like to rule the world" (*WW-E*, 114).

[80] "America has entered the age of Descartes" (*WW-E*, 273).

Beigbeder betrays a sense of being underappreciated by the US, for instance, when he urges Americans to wake up to the fact that the US and France have an interconnected history and claims, in an almost desperate, pitiful move, vying for American attention:

> La France peut encore aider, pour une fois que mon pays servirait à quelque chose. La France n'est pas la mère de l'Amérique – c'est l'Angleterre – mais elle peut prétendre en être la marraine. Vous savez, cette vieille tante moustachue qu'on ne voit dans les grandes occasions, qui sent mauvais de la bouche, dont on a un peu honte et dont on oublie le plus souvent l'existence, mais qui se rappelle à vous de temps à autre en vous offrant un beau cadeau. (*WW*, 234)[81]

The fact notwithstanding that aged aunts and godmothers are stereotypically known to come up with gifts that are useless and tasteless, this image of an ailing, isolated France begging America to acknowledge it motivates many of "Beigbeder"'s reflections. Similarly, Beigbeder quotes from Whitman's poem "Salut au Monde!" and states: "Au XIXe siècle, les poètes américains parlaient français" (*WW*, 29),[82] implying—with a miffed undertone—that they no longer do. And, even more explicitly acknowledging his feelings of inferiority, he suggests that his motivation to become a famous writer was that New York women, when he visited the Windows on the World nightclub two decades earlier, were interested only in the wealthy stockbrokers, and not in him: "C'était sinistre d'avoir autant besoin d'être aimé. Je crois que c'est au *Windows on the World* que j'ai décidé de devenir célèbre" (*WW*, 107).[83] This statement, which sums up his personal relationship with the American women he meets in New York, can be seen to describe the libidinous, troubled relationship between France and America that permeates the novel—and in

---

[81] "France can still help, my country could be useful for something for once. France is not America's mother – that's England – but it could claim to be America's godmother. You know, the crusty old aunt with the facial-hair problem whom you only see on big family occasions, her breath stinks, you're a bit ashamed of her, more often than not you forget she exists but who reminds you of her existence from time to time by giving you a beautiful gift" (*WW-E*, 194).

[82] "In the nineteenth century, American poets spoke French" (*WW-E*, 16).

[83] "It was creepy, needing so desperately to be loved. It was at that moment, I think, that I decided to be famous" (*WW-E*, 83).

which France, in its insecurity, is permanently driven to prove its worth and attractiveness to the US.

Beigbeder's negative representations of American tourists are also shaped by this feeling of not being appreciated enough. He ridicules American tourists for their shallowness and sensationalism, because most are primarily interested in getting their picture taken in memory of Princess Diana at Pont de l'Alma. Instead, he suggests, they should visit 56, rue Jacob, where the Treaty of Paris was signed. They should, in other words, honour the birthplace of American independence and acknowledge that it was born out of French thought. And Beigbeder adds, again on a sour note: "Peut-être préfèrent-ils l'oublier?" (*WW*, 28).[84] In another instance, an American couple leaves Le Ciel de Paris when they discover that they cannot order ham and eggs for breakfast. Always a defender of consumerist pleasures, Beigbeder first seems to sympathize ("D'un strict point de vue commercial, ils n'ont pas tort") but then asks: "Mais pourquoi voyager si c'est pour manger la même chose que chez soi?" (*WW*, 69),[85] only to go on to demand that "les Américains devraient cesser de vouloir à tout prix exporter leur mode de vie sur toute la planète" (*WW*, 69f.).[86] It is particularly ironic, then, that "Beigbeder" acts in exactly the same way when he travels to New York: he frequents the Pastis, a French restaurant which is decorated like a French brasserie (see *WW*, 219) and stays at the Mercer Hotel, "décoré par un Français (Christian Liaigre)" (*WW*, 347).[87] He eventually does not leave the hotel, taking to an extreme the isolationism, parochialism, and exportation of lifestyles that he indicted American tourists for.

---

[84] "Perhaps they prefer to forget" (*WW-E*, 15).

[85] "From a strictly commercial viewpoint, they're not wrong. But what's the point in traveling if it's to eat the same things you eat at home?" (*WW-E*, 51).

[86] "And Americans should stop trying to export their lifestyle to the entire planet" (*WW-E*, 51). By contrast, earlier visitors to Paris, American expat artists and writers like Gertrude Stein, F. Scott Fitzgerald, or Ernest Hemingway, in whose footsteps Beigbeder rediscovers Paris, represent "good Americans" who do not export their lifestyle to France but appreciate Paris for what, in the eyes of Beigbeder, it really is and like the right things about it, which he identifies as "sexe, [...] littérature et [...] mort" (*WW*, 147); and Hemingway, though physically in Idaho, chooses to spend the last years of his life "mentalement" in Paris, writing *A Moveable Feast* (see *WW*, 168f.).

[87] "designed by a Frenchman (Christian Liaigre)" (*WW-E*, 289).

In *Windows on the World*, globalization, maybe even cultural colonization, seems to be legitimate, as long as it emanates from France: Beigbeder is "Frenchifying" New York. His New York city is all made and inhabited by Frenchmen, and even 9/11 is essentially a French event: Rodin sculptures were found in the debris of the World Trade Center site (*WW*, 330); the Naudet brothers made the only film of the attacks (*WW*, 317); Beigbeder fantasizes that it is in fact Des Esseintes, the protagonist of *À Rebours*, and thus French decadence that brought the Twin Towers down instead of bin Laden (*WW*, 83); within the North tower, a bottle of French wine brings some sort of desperate relief to those huddled with Carthew Yorston in front of the door to the roof, and this bottle figures at the same time as a catalyst that can overcome religious conflict and achieve a moment of peaceful globalization (*WW*, 181–183). And the list of Beigbeder's strategies to render France the better America could go on.

As much as I agree with critics like Kristiaan Verslyus or Martin Randall that *Windows on the World* is successful—perhaps more so than any other 9/11 novel—in finding a complex, challenging answer to the question of how literature can represent events such as the attacks of September 11, the text fails miserably as an attempt to construct a "joint Western episteme." Instead, *Windows on the World* re-establishes clear boundaries and a hierarchy between France and the US. It primarily does so by a particularly insidious move: by proclaiming America, and certainly the "good America," as always already French—a dynamic embodied by the epitome of American cuisine that Carthew Yorston's sons love: French fries (*WW*, 27).

"Waiting for Doomsday Conscious Unconscious": The Fallacy of Becoming American in *Woraus wir gemacht sind*

Beigbeder engages in an affirmation of French identity through an embrace of the US, which, however, ultimately amounts to an appropriation and even erasure of America. Such "identity politics" undermine the construction of a united West and a unified Europe, but are beneficial for the (re)construction of French self-esteem. Hettche's novel debunks exactly these politics of identity formation and argues that appropriating, even colonizing a national Other in order to construct a sense of self always eventually backfires. It demonstrates the self-destructive nature of this type of identity formation in at least three ways: first, it represents Kalf's search of identity through "becoming American" as a deformation of self; second, it shows that the American Other's supposed values and virtues that Kalf is trying to emulate do not exist (any more): they are nothing but his own (and Hollywood's long-gone) projections; and, third, it establishes a parallel between identity formation and empire building and shows empires to be inevitably declining towards their "doomsday" from their inception.

The notion that Kalf's attempt to take on an American self is a deformation becomes most obvious, once more, in the chapter "Who's who?" The devil not only engages Kalf in a conversation at a gas station but also—in the shape of Robert Duvall—takes him on a trip to the prairie to feed a calf. The calf, it turns out, is deformed, it has five legs: "Die linke Hinterhand schien verdoppelt, wobei das natürliche, etwas kürzere Bein aus dem anderen schräg herausgewachsen war" (*Wwgs*, 176).[88] It eagerly sucks at the devil's fingers, "als wären es Zitzen" (*Wwgs*, 176).[89] The analogy between "Kalf" and "calf" is linguistically more obvious in the English translation than in the German original, and is thus reinforced by dialogue in the latter. Kalf, incredulously realizing that the five-legged calf is supposed to tell him something about himself, inquires twice "Was soll das?" (*Wwgs*, 176).[90] He is disgusted by the deformation and by the calf's long tongue which has sucked the devil's fingers hungrily, yet in vain, and rejects the devil's comparison: "Kalf ist nicht Kalb" to which the devil replies: "Aber Kalf ist Calf, oder?"[91]

The reader is led to agree with the devil: Kalf, who is frequently described as almost transparent, a quality that he has maintained since

---

[88] "The left hindquarter seemed to be double, and the unnatural, slightly shorter leg had grown crookedly out of the other one" (*WWAMO*, 169).

[89] "as though there were teats" (*WWAMO*, 169).

[90] "Is that supposed to mean something? [...] What's that supposed to mean?" (*WWAMO*, 169).

[91] "But Kalf is Calf, right?" (my translation; not in the English translation by Shaun Whiteside). For the reader of the German original, the series of the words "Kalb-Kalf-Calf" immediately evokes "Calw," the birth place of Hermann Hesse, which is, moreover, pronounced "Kalb" in regional dialect. Hettche thus suggests that *Woraus wir gemacht sind* must also be read as a novel of growing up, a Bildungsroman of the twenty-first century which takes as its protagonist a 40-year-old "child."

his childhood (*Wwgs*, 8), is immature, naïve and—perhaps—dumb like a calf.[92] He lacks identity, and he eagerly licks up what America, and Hollywood in particular, seem to offer him for identification. Yet just like the devil's/Duvall's fingers do not provide any nourishment for the calf, American culture does not provide Kalf with the substance to become a mature individual. Instead, Kalf is represented as a monstrosity: his search for identity is not a process of growth, but one of deformation. This is stressed through Kalf's reading of *The Brothers Karamazov* and about Marfa Ignatyewna, after whom the Texas town where he spends three months was allegedly named. The novel quotes in detail from Marfa's story: She gives birth to a six-fingered boy—a parallel to the five-legged calf. The boy is rejected by his father Grigory, who calls him a "dragon" and a "confusion of nature" (*Wwgs*, 78). Likewise, the town of Marfa has given birth to Kalf as a monster. Marfa has made him contemplate becoming another and sacrificing his wife in the process: "Hierzubleiben, wußte er, wäre die Versuchung. Für immer Teil zu sein dieses Landes. Und er wußte, damit dies gelänge, bräuchte es nichts, als das Leben von Liz" (*Wwgs*, 180).[93] The thought that "nothing except Liz's life" is needed for him to become a different person is monstrous; yet this thought, *ex negativo*, also implies—and this is confirmed at the end of the novel—that the only thing that can give an individual a hold on life and on his own existence is the love of a human Other.

At the same time that the novel argues that appropriating another's identity as one's own is monstrous, it also distinguishes between the concepts of growth as transformation and as deformation. Transformation is seen as inevitable and even necessary to the integrity of the self over time. The novel achieves this by opposing the story of Marfa's six-fingered child with the story of Daphne in Ovid's *Metamorphoses*. In the first chapter, Al Snowe relates the case of a 15-year-old girl who killed a

---

[92] Shortly after the description of Kalf's childlike physicality, Liz also explains to Al Snowe that her husband is a biographer and thus writing about other people's lives because he is almost without agency with regard to his own: "Niklas ist etwas hilflos, was sein eigenes Leben angeht" (*Wwgs*, 10) / "Niklas is a bit awkward where his own life is concerned" (*WWAMO*, 4).

[93] "Staying here, he knew, would be the temptation. Always to be part of this country. And he knew that for that to happen, Liz's life was what it would take" (*WWAMO*, 173).

man in Central Park in 1997, called Daphne Abdela,[94] and thus prompts Kalf/the narrator to quote from Ovid: "*Keines, heißt es bei Ovid, verbleibt in derselben Gestalt und Veränderung liebend /Schafft die Natur stets neu aus anderen andere Formen. /In der Weite der Welt geht nichts, das glaubt mir, verloren*" (*Wwgs*, 21).[95] Daphne has to change physically in order to maintain her physical integrity that is assaulted by Apollon. By analogy, individuals—and by extension, nations—need to develop, change, and grow but must maintain their core. Giving up that core and exchanging it for another, as Kalf does in his attempt at becoming American, is, by contrast, a deformation.

A scene towards the end of the novel takes up the story of Daphne and moves from stressing the need to maintain one's true core to stressing its flipside: the fact that, ultimately, no individual can escape that core—or that "woraus wir gemacht sind." In this scene, Kalf confronts Elsa Meerkaz to find out about Liz's whereabouts. Elsa confesses that she was threatened by Jackson to hand over material about Parsons' and Meerkaz's secret development of a new rocket fuel. Her objective had been to preserve her husband's legacy, and if Jackson got hold of the documents that she knew must be somewhere, the documents would also inevitably give her husband away as a member of Ordo Templi Orientis and as a participant in rituals that involved sex magic—because the scientific experiments were conducted as a part of such secret rituals.[96] In order to diffuse attention from her person and to lead Jackson

---

[94] Daphne Abdela appears later in the novel and prompts Kalf's second recitation from Ovid in person; a discussion of her complicated role would be leading too far away from my argument here. What should be noted, though, is that the Ovidian intertext and the reflections on metamorphoses vs. monstrosities are lost in the English translation: presumably because of legal issues, the historical Daphne Abdela is replaced by the fictional character of Imogen Engel; the quotations from Ovid are replaced by quotations from the Gospel of John and Goethe's *Faust*, with rather different implications.

[95] "Nothing keeps its own shape, and Nature renews / By recycling one form into another. / Nothing dies, believe me, in the world as a whole / [But only changes its looks.]" Book XV, *The Teachings of Pythagoras*, l. 278–281. Not in the English translation by Shaun Whiteside; quoted from Ovid, *Metamorphoses*, 425. Hettche uses the classic translation by Johann Heinrich Voß.

[96] The novel suggests that as Parsons's wife and Elsa Meerkaz were involved in the rituals, Parsons, Meerkaz, "Pinky," and Hans Holdt engaged in heterosexual intercourse as part of the spiritual techniques of the higher orders Ordo Templi Orientis under Aleister Crowley.

astray, she had hired Kalf to write her husband's biography and thus used him as a decoy.[97]

During this scene of confrontation with Elsa, Kalf reads out loud—and in German—the story of Daphne's desperate flight from Apollon and her final transformation (*Wwgs*, 301f.). This second quotation from Ovid illustrates the consequences of the attempt to escape one's identity: Flight from that identity—just like Daphne's flight from Apollon—is exhausting and futile. An individual has to deal with the matter he or she is made out of and transform it, but not deform it, into something he or she can live with and maintain integrity. Kalf's reading of Ovid leads to a fundamental change in Elsa's attitude: "Elsa Meerkaz lächelte, als denke sie über eine Entscheidung nach, die ihr Freude mache" (*Wwgs*, 301).[98] It becomes evident that the decision that she is making here is, in terms of the thriller plot, to let Kalf go and hand the material over to Jackson. In terms of the identity plot, it is the decision to accept as part of her history that she and Eugen were members of a secret cult. The turn to Crowley's spiritual teachings (and away from Judaism) may be understood as a strategy of coping with their rootlessness and loss of identity as a result of the Holocaust. This, of course, is a parallel to Kalf's turn towards American and away from German culture. Both moves are represented as similarly absurd and futile. In the final analysis then, Elsa's need to accept her intermezzo with Ordo Templi Orientis means coming to terms with her history of persecution and identity as a Jew. It is no coincidence that this acceptance of "what she is made of" is triggered by a text that is being read to her in her

---

[97] While the role of conspiracies and conspiracy theorizing in the novel cannot be discussed here in detail, my brief sketch of the outrageous turns of the plot may at least suggest the following: By making the German emigrants part of a conspiratorial sect and drawing Kalf into a grotesque, outlandish conspiracy plot that he needs to solve, the novel further undergirds the identity issues that these Germans, who have "become American," are facing: they are lacking a stable core and pursue ways of drawing the boundaries of self that, from an outside perspective, must seem paranoid at best. On the function of conspiring and conspiracy theorizing as a strategy to deal with one's own perceived "powerlessness," which is one aspect of a lack of sense of self and identity, see Fenster, *Conspiracy Theories: Secrecy and Power in American Culture*, viii. For a comprehensive analysis of conspiracy theories in French and German culture and literature, cf. Jean-Philippe Mathy's chapter "Seeing is Disbelieving: The Contested Visibility of 9/11 in France" in this volume.

[98] "Elsa Meerkaz smiled as if she was contemplating a decision that gave her pleasure" (my translation; not in the English translation by Shaun Whiteside).

mother tongue: what she also has to come to terms with is her identity as a *German* Jew. For Kalf, the story signals that he has been in flight from himself, in particular in flight from the guilt of the Holocaust, and needs to confront his German identity and history, and thus become an agent of his own life.

Another of Kalf's ways of fleeing his own identity is to become an "American hero." Kalf finds models to emulate in Hollywood but also in George W. Bush whom—like the Hollywood heroes of his young adulthood—he sees on TV at the beginning and at the end of the novel: first, on September 12, 2002, when Bush gives his speech in front of the United Nations and Liz is abducted, and then on March 17, 2003, when Bush addresses the nation to announce his decision to go to war with Iraq. And indeed, like the rugged individualists of the Hollywood Western and like George W. Bush, Kalf shows grit and self-reliance: he eventually kills two people with his bare hands—a nameless intruder in Marfa and, in order to free Liz at the end of the novel, Jack Jackson. Jan Brandt has read this ending as representing Kalf unambiguously and unabashedly as a "hero"—and as thus celebrating macho individualism and aggression.[99] Such a reading, however, misses the way in which the novel links its debate of the US as an aggressive empire with its reflections on the role of Hollywood's images for Kalf's sense of self: both America as represented by Hollywood and America as a thriving empire are a thing of the past. When the devil shifts shapes to confront Kalf with his favourite Hollywood heroes, Kalf observes that the devil only assumes characters that appeared in movies of the 1980s: "Irgendwie bist du ein Mensch der achtziger Jahre, oder?" The devil replies: "Alles für dich! Ist alles nur für dich, mein Sohn" (*Wwgs*, 180).[100] Not only does Kalf take Hollywood projections for actual role models, but in doing so, he is also stuck in his young adulthood that is long over, yet that he is unable to leave behind and use as a basis for growth.

The showdown with Jackson, then, significantly takes place in the L.A. Theatre, an old cinema that has been abandoned for decades. Through heavy imagery, the novel drives home the fact that Kalf, in search of his identity, has clung to ghosts, has aspired to something that is already dead. Approaching the theatre, Kalf sees an old photograph

---

[99] Brandt, "Ein Schlaukopf haut rein."

[100] "You're somehow a person of the Eighties, aren't you? [...] All for you! It's just all for you, my son" (*WWAMO*, 173).

of Chaplin and Einstein in 1931 behind a rusty gate and fears that Liz, like those two, might already be dead (*Wwgs*, 303f.). His meeting with Gallagher and his freeing of Liz are represented as a trip into the past and, moreover, as a trip into the underworld. Just as "Hollywood heroism" is shown to be a thing of the past and the dead, so is the "American empire" that Kalf admires and that is epitomized by George W. Bush's unilateral decision to go to war with Iraq. At the beginning of the novel, Al Snowe suggests that Kalf's admiration for the US as an empire in all its glory might be misplaced. The US today might instead be an "Imperium der Spätzeit, als die Cäsaren wie die Wölfe die Grenzen entlangschnürten, in unentwegte Verteidigungsschlachten gegen die Barbaren verwickelt, geboren und gekrönt in Städten wie Trier oder Byzanz. Die kannten Rom nicht mehr" (*Wwgs*, 49).[101] At the end of the novel, Kalf agrees with Snowe that while the US might still be able to project itself as the world's only empire, it is already in decline and hollowed out at the core (*Wwgs*, 320). The novel establishes a clever parallel between the mechanisms of colonialism and imperialism—to make other nations one's own—and Kalf's attempts of identity formation through the appropriation of another culture as one's own. Both mechanisms are shown to be aggressive, as leading away from "what we are made of," and as eventually self-destructive.

Kalf signals his understanding of both these mechanisms and expresses his simultaneous inability to completely detach himself from his desire to "become American" by reciting lines from a late autograph by German dramatist Heiner Müller[102]: "*Die Bäume verneigen sich [...] Vor dem Wind vom Pazifik der Bescheid weiß /Über die Dauer der Millionenstadt /Waiting for doomsday conscious unconscious /Of its fate rising from past*

---

[101] "the late Empire, when the Caesars were roaming the borders like wolves, getting involved in persistent defensive battles against the barbarians, and being born and crowned in cities like Trier or Byzantium. They no longer knew Rome" (*WWAMO*, 43).

[102] The choice of this particular autograph that Müller composed during his stay at Villa Aurora in the hills of Pacific Palisades, as well as the text's double play with "Asia," the name of the woman Kalf is sexually drawn to at the same time that he is caught up and trying to escape Germany's "past," are as such highly evocative. Villa Aurora, today an artists' residence, is the former home of Lion and Marta Feuchtwanger and was one of the central places where German emigrant writers and artists met. Elsa Meerkaz' home is modelled after Villa Aurora where Hettche worked as a fellow in 2002, seven years after Heiner Müller.

and Asia."[103] The wind, the admiring trees, and by extension readers and reciters of these lines are conscious of the finiteness and the imminent destruction of the "Millionenstadt," the Western heart of the American empire, yet at the same time may let this knowledge recede into their unconscious as a way of not having to confront it, of living the fantasy instead. These lines are given special emphasis because Kalf recites them twice: once when Elsa Meerkaz comments on the precariousness of existence in America (*Wwgs*, 258f.), and once when he looks out at the Pacific with Liz and into their future at the end of the novel (*Wwgs*, 317). Moreover, *Woraus wir gemacht sind* slightly alters Müller's lines: the text adds the word "conscious" to Müller's original line "Waiting for doomsday unconscious."[104] Kalf's line "Waiting for doomsday conscious unconscious" grasps the ambivalence of (self-)knowledge and simultaneous denial of this knowledge; the addition of the word "conscious" signals that Kalf has indeed come to understand his struggle for identity through "becoming American," through becoming a "hero," and thus through becoming an aggressive "colonizer" to be fallacious.[105]

Both *Woraus wir gemacht sind* and *Windows on the World* are centrally concerned with the textures of national identity formation in the post-9/11-era, yet this larger issue is always linked with and explored through their protagonist's personal crises and searches for identity. In closing, I would like to comment on the "personal solutions"—indeed: happy endings—that the two texts offer their protagonists and point to ways in which these become problematic if they are read as part and parcel of the novels' constructions of national identities as well as national literary cultures.

---

[103] Müller's first lines are given in the German original in Shaun Whiteside's English translation, but may be paraphrased as follows: "The trees bow to / the wind from the Pacific that knows about / the permanence of the metropolis."

[104] Mayer and Müller, *Der Tod ist ein Irrtum. Bilder – Texte – Autografen*, 122f.

[105] Going beyond the idea that empires are always doomed to self-destruct, the novel also suggests that aspirations to empire can never be benevolent and innocent. It comments on the aggressive nature of imperial expansionism in the figure of Jack Jackson. The producer not only wants to get hold of the formula for a revolutionary kind of rocket fuel in order to win a ten million dollar prize for privately sending a space ship into orbit, but thereby he eventually wants to push the frontier of the American empire further out into space in order to save white civilization before its extermination on Earth. Notions of empire, the novel suggests, are always coupled with supremacist ideology, not unlike the fascist ideology that Kalf has to come to terms with in his own history.

While *Woraus wir gemacht sind* eventually rejects an identity politics that is founded on anti-Americanism and appropriations of "America" in the manner of Beigbeder in *Windows on the World*, with regard to their characters' individual searches for a sense of self, the two novels, nevertheless, suggest exactly the same panacea: love. In both novels, it is an individual other, rather than a national other, that ultimately makes an individual complete. Both protagonists emerge from their desperate searches for themselves revitalized and made complete through love. This happens rather abruptly on the last pages of the texts and without much, if any, actual development of their relationships to their respective partners: Liz remains almost silent and passive during her reunion with Niklas Kalf, while he internally, yet pompously, formulates a theory of love as the explanation of all things, and Beigbeder's nameless fiancée is across the Atlantic and ignorant of any change in their strained, on-and-off relationship when he is overtaken by renewed love for her in New York.

First, it might be argued that instead of offering intellectually and emotionally complex and satisfying reflections on what it means to be a mature, loving individual in a post-9/11 world, the texts become stuck in sentimentality and kitsch: if easy happy endings constitute the French "new new novel" or a German "relevant realism," their newness and relevance remain doubtful. The fact that both protagonists are shown to eventually experience themselves through what I have in the beginning called "relationalities among individuals," however, is problematic in two further respects. First, in the context of the attacks of September 11, 2001 and American military actions in their aftermath, the novels undertake a retreat from the political into the private. If the protagonists ultimately position themselves at all towards politics, and thus to the question of how human beings with very different identities—French, German, American, and others—can live together peacefully on this planet, they do so through positioning themselves towards an individual, a woman they love. While it may be true that one has to find one's identity and embrace it in order to be able to fully love another, and that love among two individuals may be the basic configuration that also makes peace among nations possible, the texts fall short of developing such implications and ultimately embrace wholly un-political standpoints.

Second, the inability of the protagonists—who are physically separated from their fiancée and wife throughout the whole or most of the text—to relate to their partners, or other women they engage with, as full human individuals leads the reader to wonder whether in returning to their partners they are perhaps again appropriating an Other to complete themselves. The women that Beigbeder relates to in *Windows on the World* are, with the exception of his absent fiancée, sexual objects such as the secretaries he/Yorston observes from above, Yorston's girlfriend Candace, a lingerie model, or strippers in a night club. In *Woraus wir gemacht sind*, women are either on the side of the kidnappers and killers, such as Elsa Meerkaz, Lavinia Sims, or Venus Smith who represents an African American, female menacing incarnation of (the German physicist) Dr. Strangelove, or they satisfy Kalf's extra-marital sexual urges—which are not very different from Beigbeder's indulgences—such as Asia and Daphne. While this leads away from my central concern in this chapter, the fact that Beigbeder and Kalf seem less to complete their selves through love of an equal other and more through making their fiancée and wife more fully their "own"—Kalf, by saving her from the kidnappers, Beigbeder by waving a Tiffany's ring (*WW*, 367)—may also suggest that their lack of self-confidence and desperate search for identity are bound up with anxiety about their masculinity—a type of anxiety that generally can be said to have intensified in the wake of September 11, 2001.[106]

In light of the protagonists' need to affirm a traditional version of white masculinity in their intimate relationships, the solutions that *Windows on the World* and *Woraus wir gemacht sind* offer in terms of transnational understanding and an understanding of one's national self in the post-9/11 era may hence be seen as even more problematic. The complex ways, however, in which both novels reflect on and wrestle with anti-Americanism and its flipside merit our attention. My discussion of *Windows on the World* and *Woraus wir gemacht sind* may also, I hope, help direct our gaze at other, less explicit "uses" of 9/11 for national identity-making in literature from outside the US.

Acknowledgements I would like to thank Michael Butter and our students at the German National Academic Foundation's summer academy in Greifswald in 2011 for the discussions of Beigbeder's *Windows on the World* and US American representations of 9/11, as well as Małgorzata Myk and our students for the

---

[106] On *Windows on the World* as a text that is dominated by fear of emasculation and struggles to defend "white middle-class masculinity," see Araújo, "Images of Terror," here 34; for a related consideration of masculinity after 9/11, see Christ, "Männer."

discussions of Polish and German representations of 9/11 in a joint course held in November 2011 at the University of Łódź and January 2012 at the University of Gießen. I am indebted to many of their insights on European treatments of 9/11. A special thanks goes to my student Bruno Gehrts who tackled *Woraus wir gemacht sind* in his independent project.

References

Araújo, Susana. "Images of Terror, Narratives of Capitivity: The Visual Spectacle of 9/11 and Its Transatlantic Projections," *Symbiosis*, vol. 11, no. 2 (2007), 27–46.
Arendt, Hannah. "Dream and Nightmare," in Jerome Kohn (ed.), *Essays in Understanding, 1930–1954* (New York: Harcourt, Brace & Company, 1994 [1954]), 409–417.
———. "Europa und Amerika," in *In der Gegenwart: Übungen im politischen Denken II*, transl. by Eike Geisel (München: Piper, 2000 [1954]), 238–257.
———. "We Refugees," in Jerome Kohn and Ron H. Feldman (eds.), *The Jewish Writings* (New York: Schocken Books, 2007 [1943]), 264–274.
Auffermann, Verena. "Der Stoff, aus dem der Westen ist," *Literaturen*, no. 9 (2006), 50–52.
Bartels, Gerrit. "Amerika, Blicke. Am Ende aller Gewissheiten und am Anfang der Liebe und der Diskurse: Thomas Hettches Roman *Woraus wir gemacht sind*," *taz*, September 16, 2006, available at http://www.taz.de/1/archiv/archiv/?dig=2006/09/16/a0058 (accessed 1.4.2015).
Bauder-Begerow, Irina, and Stefanie Schäfer (eds.). *Learning 9/11: Teaching for Key Competences in Literary and Cultural Studies* (Heidelberg: Winter, 2011).
Beigbeder, Frédéric. *Windows on the World* (Paris: Gallimard, 2003).
———. *Windows on the World*, trans. Frank Wynne (London: Harper, 2004).
———. "Pour un nouveau nouveau roman," *CRIN* 2008, 43–49.
Borradori, Giovanna. *Philosophy in a Time of Terror. Dialogues with Jürgen Habermas and Jacques Derrida* (Chicago/London: Chicago University Press, 2003).
Brandt, Jan. "Ein Schlaukopf haut rein." *Spiegel online*, September 15, 2006, available at http://www.spiegel.de/kultur/literatur/roman-woraus-wir-gemacht-sind-ein-schlaukopf-haut-rein-a-436472.html (accessed 1.4. 2015).
Buchstein, Hubertus, and Rainer Kühn, "Vorwort," in Alexander von Brünneck and Hubertus Buchstein (eds.), *Ernst Fraenkel*, 7–48, here 18.
Christ, Birte. "Männer," in Michael Butter, Birte Christ, and Patrick Keller (eds.), *9/11. Kein Tag, der die Welt veränderte* (Paderborn et al.: Schöningh, 2011), 90–105.
———. "Michelle Obama, the Good American and Icon of Global Power Femininity: Gender Politics and National Boundary-Making in German News Coverage," in Birte Christ and Greta Olson (eds), *Obama and the Paradigm Shift—Measuring Change* (Heidelberg: Winter, 2012), 167–195.

Cilano, Cara (ed.). *From Solidarity to Schisms: 9/11 and After in Fiction and Film from Outside the US* (Amsterdam/New York: Rodopi, 2009).

Clemente, Marie Christine. "Beigbeder's Evil Personae in *Windows on the World*: Authorial Ethics and 9/11," in Scott M. Powers (ed.), *Evil in Contemporary French and Francophone Literature* (Cambridge: Cambridge Scholars Publishing, 2011), 109–135.

Däwes, Birgit. "On Contested Ground (Zero): Literature and the Transnational Challenge of Remembering 9/11," *Amerikastudien/American Studies*, vol. 52, no. 4 (2007), 517–543.

———. *Ground Zero Fiction: History, Memory, and Representation in the American 9/11 Novel* (Heidelberg: Winter, 2011).

Dean, Martin R., Thomas Hettche, Matthias Politycki, and Michael Schindhelm. "Was soll der Roman?" in *Zeit online*, June 23, 2006, available at http://www.zeit.de/2005/26/Debatte_1 (accessed 1.4.2015).

Dehez, Dustin. "Anti-Amerikanismus," in Michael Butter, Birte Christ, and Patrick Keller (eds.), *9/11. Kein Tag, der die Welt veränderte* (Paderborn: Ferdinand Schöningh, 2011), 150–165.

Diner, Dan. *America in the Eyes of the Germans: An Essay on Anti-Americanism* (Princeton: Markus Wiener Publishers, 1996).

Donnerstag, Jürgen. "The Documentaries of Michael Moore and Their German Reception: Anti-Americanism and Intercultural Learning," in Gisela Hermann-Brennecke and Wolf Kindermann (eds.), *Anglo-American Awareness: Arpeggios in Aesthetics* (Münster: LIT, 2005), 142–160.

Durham, Carolyn A. "Daring to Imagine: Frédéric Beigbeder's *Windows on the World* and Slimane Benaïssa's *La Dernière Nuit d'un damné*," in Cara Cilano (ed.), *From Solidarity to Schisms: 9/11 and After in Fiction and Film from Outside the US* (Amsterdam/New York: Rodopi, 2009), 165–182.

Fenster, Mark. *Conspiracy Theories: Secrecy and Power in American Culture* (Minneapolis: University of Minnesota Press, 2008).

Fraenkel, Ernst. *Gesammelte Schriften Band 4, Amerikastudien*, eds. by Alexander von Brünneck and Hubertus Buchstein (Baden-Baden: Nomos, 2000).

Gansel, Carsten. "Von der Primärerfahrung zur medialen Konstruktion? 'Soldatisches Opfernarrativ,' 9/11 und Terrorismusdarstellung in der deutschen (Gegenwarts) Literatur," in Hennigfeld (ed.), *Poetiken des Terrors*.

Gassert, Philipp. *Amerika im Dritten Reich: Ideologie, Propaganda und Volksmeinung, 1933–1945* (Stuttgart: Steiner, 1997).

———. "Was meint Amerikanisierung?" *Merkur*, vol. 617, no. 8 [2000], 785-796.

Gienow-Hecht, Jessica. "Europäischer Anti-Amerikanismus im 20. Jahrhundert," *Aus Politik und Zeitgeschichte*, vol. 5–6 (2008), 33–38.

Godin, Emmanuel, and Tony Chafer (eds.), *The French Exception* (New York/Oxford: Berghahn Books, 2005).

Greiner, Bernd. *9/11. Der Tag, die Angst, die Folgen* (München: C.H. Beck, 2011).
Gulddal, Jesper. *Anti-Americanism in European Literature* (New York: Palgrave Macmillan, 2011).
Harper, Mihaela P. "Turning to Debris: Ethics of Violence in Wilkomirski's *Fragments* and Beigbeder's *Windows on the World*," *symploke*, vol. 20, no. 1–2 (2012), 227–240.
Hennigfeld, Ursula (ed.). *Poetiken des Terrors: Narrative des 11. September 2001 im interkulturellen Vergleich* (Heidelberg: Winter 2014).
———. "Vorwort," in Ursula Hennigfeld (ed.), *Poetiken des Terrors: Narrative des 11. September 2001 im interkulturellen Vergleich* (Heidelberg: Winter 2014), 7–17.
Hettche, Thomas. *Woraus wir gemacht sind* (Köln: Kiepenheuer & Witsch, 2006).
———. *What We Are Made Of*, trans. Shaun Whiteside (London: Picador, 2008).
Hicks, Gavin. "My Roommate the Terrorist: The Political Burden of September 11 in Elmar Fischer's *The Friend*," in Cara Cilano (ed.), *From Solidarity to Schisms: 9/11 and After in Fiction and Film from Outside the US* (Amsterdam/New York: Rodopi, 2009), 131–144.
Irsigler, Ingo, and Christoph Jürgensen (eds.). *Nine Eleven: Ästhetische Verarbeitungen des 11. September 2001* (Heidelberg: Winter, 2008).
Kagan, Robert. *Of Paradise and Power: America and Europe in the New World Order* (New York: Knopf, 2003).
Kaulen, Heinrich. "Vom Scheitern des Dialogs mit dem Täter: Überlegungen zu Christoph Peters' *Ein Zimmer im Haus des Krieges* (2006)," in Ursula Hennigfeld (ed.), *Poetiken des Terrors*, 137–157.
Klohs, Kathrin. "Frédéric Beigbeder," in Fernand Hörner, Harald Neumeyer, and Bernd Stiegler (eds.), *Praktizierte Intermedialität: Deutsch-französische Porträts von Schiller bis Goscinny/Uderzo* (Bielefeld: transcript, 2010), 303–318.
König, Michael. "Literary Accounts of Terrorism in Recent German Literature: An Attempt at Marginalization?" in Michael C. Frank and Eva Gruber (eds.), *Literature and Terrorism: Comparative Perspectives* (Amsterdam: Rodopi, 2012), 155–172.
Kozlowski, Timo. "Thomas Hettche," in Heinz Ludwig Arnold (ed.), *Kritisches Lexikon zur deutschsprachigen Gegenwartsliteratur* (München: Text + Kritik, 2007), no pag.
Kreis, Georg. *Anti-Amerikanismus. Zum europäisch-amerikanischen Verhältnis zwischen Ablehnung und Faszination* (Basel: Schwabe, 2007).
Leggewie, Claus. *Amerikas Welt: Die USA in unseren Köpfen* (Hamburg: Hoffmann und Campe, 2000).

Lehngut, Henrike. "Sleepers, Informants, and the Everyday: Theorizing Terror and Ambiguity in Benjamin Heisenberg's *Schläfer*" in Sandra Poppe, Thorsten Schüller, and Sascha Seiler (eds.), *9/11 als kulturelle Zäsur. Repräsentationen des 11. September 2001 in kulturellen Diskursen, Literatur und visuellen Medien* (Bielefeld: transcript, 2009), 115–130.

Lüdtke, Alf, Inge Marßolek, and Adelheid von Saldern (eds.), *Amerikanisierung: Traum und Alptraum im Deutschland des 20. Jahrhunderts* (Stuttgart: Steiner, 1996).

Markovitz, Andrei S. "Anti-Americanism and the Struggle for a West German Identity," in Peter H. Merkl (ed.), *The Federal Republic at Forty* (London/ New York: New York University Press, 1989).

Martin, Ralph. "Die unreifen Verehrer amerikanischer Helden," transl. Michael Bischoff, *Frankfurter Allgemeine Zeitung*, October 8, 2007.

Mayer, Brigitte Maria, and Heiner Müller, *Der Tod ist ein Irrtum. Bilder – Texte – Autografen* (Frankfurt: Suhrkamp, 2005).

Mergenthaler, Volker. "Warum die Frage 'Wie reagieren Schriftsteller auf die Terroranschläge?' auf dem Feld der deutschsprachigen Literatur die falsche Frage ist," in Ursula Hennigfeld, *Poetiken des Terrors*, 179–196.

Mohr, Dunja M., and Sylvia Mayer (eds.). *9/11 as Catalyst—American and British Cultural Responses*, Special Issue *ZAA*, vol. 58, no. 1 (2010).

Moritz, Rainer. "Marfa ist nicht Frankfurt am Main: Thomas Hettches Roman *Woraus wir gemacht sind*," *Stuttgarter Zeitung*, October 4, 2006.

National Commission on Terrorist Attacks upon the United States. *9/11 Commission Report* (National Commission on Terrorist Attacks upon the United States, 2004).

Ovidius Naso, Publius, *Metamorphoses*, trans. by Stanley Lombardo (Indianapolis: Hacket Publishing Company, 2010).

Poppe, Sandra, Thorsten Schüller, and Sascha Seiler (eds.). *9/11 als kulturelle Zäsur. Repräsentationen des 11. September 2001 in kulturellen Diskursen, Literatur und visuellen Medien* (Bielefeld: transcript, 2009).

Porra, Véronique. "Risse in der Mimesis – Bemerkungen zur romanesken Darstellung des 11. September 2001 in der französischen Literatur," in Sandra Poppe, Thorsten Schüller, and Sascha Seiler (eds.), *9/11 als kulturelle Zäsur. Repräsentationen des 11. September 2001 in kulturellen Diskursen, Literatur und visuellen Medien* (Bielefeld: transcript, 2009), 163–181.

Randall, Martin. *9/11 and the Literature of Terror* (Edinburgh: Edinburgh University Press, 2012).

Reinhäckel, Heide. *Traumatische Texturen: Der 11. September in der deutschen Gegenwartsliteratur* (Bielefeld: transcript, 2012), 137–144.

———. "Literarische Schauplätze deutscher 9/11-Romane" Sandra Poppe, Thorsten Schüller, and Sascha Seiler (eds.), *9/11 als kulturelle Zäsur. Repräsentationen des 11. September 2001 in kulturellen Diskursen, Literatur und visuellen Medien* (Bielefeld: transcript, 2009), 121–138.

Revel, Jean-François. *L'obsession anti-américaine: Son fonctionnement, ses causes, ses inconséquences* (Paris: Plon, 2002).

———. "The anti-American obsession," *The New Criterion*, vol. 22, no. 2 (2003), 12–19.

Richter, Steffen. "Utopie in der Prärie. Der Hauch des amerikanischen Imperiums: Thomas Hettches Roman *Woraus wir gemacht sind*," *Der Tagesspiegel*, August 28, 2006.

Schwaabe, Christian. *Antiamerikanismus: Wandlungen eines Feindbildes* (München: Wilhelm Fink Verlag, 2003).

Schwark, Sebastian. *Zur Genealogie des modernen Anti-Amerikanismus in Deutschland* (Baden-Baden: Nomos, 2008).

Schehr, Lawrence R. "*Éffondrements*: Frédéric Beigbeder's *Windows on the World*," *French Cultural Studies*, vol. 21, no. 2 (2010), 131–141.

Simons, Oliver. "'Amerika gibt es nicht': On the Semiotics of Literary America in the Twentieth Century," *The German Quarterly*, vol. 82, no. 2 (2009), 196–211.

Spiegel, Hubert. "Achtung, Kurve!," *Frankfurter Allgemeine Zeitung*, October 4, 2006.

Steinfeld, Thomas. "Der deutsche Dichter und sein Satan. Ein Liebling der Kritik: Thomas Hettches Roman *Woraus wir gemacht sind*, ein Produkt der Schwerarbeit an der Leichtigkeit," *Süddeutsche Zeitung*, September 14, 2006.

Verslyus, Kristiaan. "9/11 as a European Event: the Novels," *European Review*, vol. 15, no. 2 (2007), 65–79.

———. *Out of the Blue: September 11 and the Novel* (New York: Columbia University Press, 2009).

Author Biography

Birte Christ is Assistant Professor of American Literature and Culture at Gießen University, Germany. She is the author of *Modern Domestic Fiction* (2012) and has co-edited the volumes *American Studies/Shifting Gears* (2010), *9/11. Kein Tag, der die Welt veränderte* (2011), and *Obama and the Paradigm Shift: Measuring Change* (2012). Her interest in contemporary European literature dates back to her studies at Freiburg University and to her teaching of German at Yale University, USA. She has co-edited two student editions of contemporary German novels for Yale University Press [Barbara Honigmann: *Eine Liebe aus nichts* (2008) and Caroline Link: *Jenseits der Stille* (2011)].

The Mimicry of Dialogue: Thomas Lehr's *September. Fata Morgana* (2010)

Svenja Frank

Rather than establishing a unilateral image of the West set against the religious and cultural Islamic "Other," post-9/11 literary discourse in Europe tends to put forth an alternative model. European identity is negotiated through a double Othering of both Muslim communities within Europe and Islamic nations, on the one hand, and of the US, on the other. The 9/11 novel *September. Fata Morgana* (2010) (English translation *September. Mirage*, 2013)[1] by German author Thomas Lehr (*1957) is a prime example of this tendency yet at the same time transcends simple us-versus-them-dichotomies and instead confronts its readers in a highly complex way with their own Eurocentric perspective. The aim of this chapter is to reveal a hitherto neglected double structure of

---

[1] Page numbers henceforth quoted in brackets refer to Thomas Lehr, *September. Fata Morgana* (Munich: Carl Hanser, 2010). All English translations are taken from Mike Mitchell's translation of the novel, *September: Mirage* (London: Seagull, 2013).

S. Frank (✉)
Göttingen University, Göttingen, Germany

© The Author(s) 2017
S. Frank (ed.), *9/11 in European Literature*,
DOI 10.1007/978-3-319-64209-3_10

the novel: in contrast to the prevalent reading of *September* as a utopian dialogue of cultures, the present interpretation discloses how this initial notion is undermined and, on the contrary, reveals the idea of intercultural dialogue in the novel as an act of self-deception. I argue that the novel should not be read as an intercultural dialogue but as the 'mimicry' of an intercultural dialogue. I am deliberately evoking Homi Bhabha's use of the term here as his description of how the dominant culture is being subverted by a colonial subject which is "almost the same, but not quite"[2] can be fruitfully applied to the novel.

September is a quintessential 9/11 novel as it is centred entirely around the 9/11 attacks, the subsequent wars in Afghanistan and Iraq, and their long-term causes and consequences. The novel parallelises its two plotlines through a double father-daughter narrative: one set in New York at the time of the terrorist attacks and one in Baghdad during the second Iraq War. The novel renders the events through four alternating narrator-protagonists: The US plotline is narrated by the German Professor of German Literature, Martin, and his daughter Sabrina, who live in New York. The dramatic effect of the Saddam regime and US military retaliation in Baghdad are narrated by the Iraqi physician Tarik and his younger daughter Muna. Through its multiperspectival narration *September* strongly encourages the reader to identify with both the Western and Eastern perspectives: Martin's loss of his ex-wife Amanda and his daughter Sabrina in the attacks on the World Trade Center are mirrored in the strong suggestion that Tarik's wife and Muna or his older daughter Jasmin die during a bomb attack on a market square in Baghdad. The novel thus gestures not only towards the global interrelatedness of terrorism and state violence but also to the similarities between their atrocities.[3]

Through realistic depiction[4] and internal focalization, both victim narratives equally invite the readers' sympathy: in contrast to the official line in US discourse which had ample reason to hinder such identification, Iraqi casualties are represented as "grievable lives," to use

---

[2] Bhabha, *The Location of Culture*, 127.

[3] For the equal validity of victim perspectives, cf. also Zimmer, "Abschied von typischen 9/11- (Satz-)Zeichen," 95.

[4] Böttiger, "Zeitschmetterlinge."

Butler's words,[5] i.e. as fully appreciated subjects, through the psychological realism of the text's interior monologues. Apparently the German reader is invited to relate to the cultural Other throughout the novel. It seems, then, that *September* meets the task that the post-9/11 social novel allegedly has: that it should open up a dialogical space between different cultures.[6]

The immediate critical acclaim that the novel received, its shortlisting for the German Book Prize (2010) and Lehr's subsequent invitation to the Freie Universität as Heiner-Müller Visiting Professor for German poetics (2011), however, are probably not only a result of this humanist idea of dialogue that the parallel plot structure suggests but just as much of its elaborate stylistic form. The intricate narrative structure and the experimental style have already raised considerable scholarly interest within German Studies and the translation into English will certainly spur further critical attention in the field of 9/11 literature. Lehr, who studied biochemistry at the Freie Universität in West Berlin and worked as a programmer for the university library prior to becoming a writer, is a versatile author whose novels not only cover a range of genres, including autobiographical and historical texts as well as science fiction, but who has also written various essays, a novella, and most recently a collection of aphorisms. Certainly, this diverse artistic output can be attributed to Lehr's ambition to give each subject matter its own specific formal structure, style and tone.[7] It is likely then that the images of the attack on the Twin Towers in New York—their shocking hyperrealistic and fictional quality, as well as the victims' inability to comprehend the act of violence—correlated on a thematic level with Lehr's formal interests at the time. The style of broken syntax, which he had already started to develop before the attacks in his novella *Frühling* [Spring] (2001), pushed to its limits here in a stream of consciousness, seems to have offered an

---

[5] Butler, *Frames of War: When is Life Grievable?* Christoph Deupmann mentions *September. Fata Morgana* as one example of how literature can bring in the perspective of the Other widely excluded by the discourse of mass media, Deupmann, "Erzählweisen vom 11. September 2001".

[6] Nelson, "You Can't Write a Social Novel After September 11," 59.

[7] Böttiger, "Zeitschmetterlinge," 279 and also Thomas Lehr himself in an interview, Rohde et al., "In der Werkstatt der Gegenwart oder Über das Romaneschreiben. Carsten Rohde und Hansgeorg Schmidt-Bergmann im Gespräch mit Thomas Lehr, Sibylle Lewitscharoff und Peter Stamm," 356.

appropriate literary form for the catastrophic events. Through its complete eschewal of punctuation and choice of line breaks and enjambments, *September* creates syntactic and hence semantic polyvalences that make for a challenging reading. On a formal level, the immediacy of this poetic flow communicates something of the speed, chaos and panic during the attack on the Twin Towers and the military action on Iraqi soil to the reader.

This stream of consciousness continues through the four narrative perspectives, blending memories and present experiences,[8] associating seemingly different times and places and merging fictional and factual elements, thus creating a dreamlike effect in the narrative. Among the many literary references, the marked allusions to the collection of stories *One Thousand and One Nights* (e.g. 11, 172, 341) with its fantastic incidents, can be seen as increasingly aligned with the depiction of the surreal architectural proportions of the modern metropolis and New York as a variously coded cinematic space. Skilfully, the novel re-enacts the global mediascape[9] created by the 9/11 footage through its very own medial conditions, showing a Hollywood-like scenario of two airplanes crashing into the Twin Towers before an artificially blue sky. The novel propagates a constant shifting between simulation and elemental reality as a predominant mode of perception catalysed by the iconic images of 9/11. As has repeatedly been pointed out, the novel's subtitle *Fata Morgana*[10] should hence be read as a genre definition.[11] The author also described the very typographical appearance of the text as a Fata Morgana, with its ragged margins and short lines due to the incessant enjambments.[12] Yet critics have neglected to explore this cue in detail; here, it is central to the discussion of mimicry in the text.

---

[8] This broken syntax and the juxtaposition of chronological succession are also typical of other works by Thomas Lehr, as Meike Herrmann has shown for the novella *Frühling* [Spring] (2001), with the backdrop of the Holocaust, "Erinnerungsliteratur ohne sich erinnernde Subjekte oder Wie die Zeitgeschichte in den Roman kommt. Zu Erzähltexten von Katharina Hacker, Thomas Lehr, Tanja Dückers und Marcel Beyer," 254–259.

[9] Appadurai, "Disjuncture and Difference in the Global Cultural Economy," 299.

[10] Alexander Osang and Anja Reich also employ the image of "Fata Morgana" to describe the tower in *Wo warst du? Ein Septembertag in New York*, 127.

[11] Schuster, "Luftspiegelungen," and Krekeler, "Die Ilias aus dem Hinterhof".

[12] Krekeler, "Die Ilias aus dem Hinterhof".

The Novel's Eurocentricism

Even before a closer textual analysis, a latent Eurocentricism is noticeable in the novel's largely clichéd portrayal of US citizens. This is in opposition to the claim that Lehr's novel forms part of a phase in German 9/11 literature, which, for the first time, overrides solely German or European perspectives of earlier texts.[13] Rather, I agree with the claim that these more recent texts bring out the specifically German context even more by including long-term-expat protagonists placed in non-European settings.[14] Hence, in Lehr's novel the German perspective of Martin, who holds an exposed position in as much as he might also be read as the fictional author of the novel, sheds more light on his national identity than on that of his chosen home country.

By negotiating a European identity which, although also Western, is clearly distinct from the US, the true Other, according to a first reading, seems to be not the Eastern but the American Other. This initial construction is evident from Lehr's use of stock stereotypes in the representation of the two central US-American characters.[15] Martin's blonder-than-life Californian ex-wife Amanda is a businesswoman who worked at the World Trade Center, i.e. at the very centre of global capitalism and commerce, before she was killed in the attacks. Her new partner, the American Seymour, is a high-flying executive in an oil company. Despite his sympathetic depiction—united in their grief for Amanda and Sabrina, Seymour and Martin become close friends—the novel's two US protagonists thus stand in for materialism and military aggression as well as the ruthless exploitation of the planet's resources. They are clearly juxtaposed to the literary scholar Martin: as the professional warrantor of

---

[13] Reinhäckel, *Traumatische Texturen*, 223. Heike Reinhäckel analyses the German literary adaptations of 9/11 between 2001 and 2011 in her doctoral thesis and places Lehr's novel in the third phase of the decade (2007–2010) which she claims is dominated by the political, international novel (ibid., 212).

[14] König,"'Alles wird anders'—Der 11. September in deutscher Literatur," 830.

[15] For the ambivalent negotiations of European identity between Americaphilia and anti-Americanism in 9/11 novels, cf. also Birte Christ's Chapter "National Identity and Literary Culture after 9/11: Pro- and Anti-Americanism in Frédéric Beigbeder's *Windows on the World* (2003) and Thomas Hettche's *Woraus wir gemacht sind* (2006)" in this volume. The easily recognisable dichotomy between the US and Germany, in contrast to Anna Zimmer's conclusion, is only a token approach to the Eastern Other, as will be argued here, cf. Zimmer, "Abschied von typischen 9/11- (Satz-)Zeichen," 96f.

literature and culture and an enthusiast of poetry, as the perhaps most self-reflexive of all literary genres, he represents a non-utilitarian self-sufficiency and pure aesthetic appreciation. Furthermore, Martin's research concentrates on intercultural relations in literature, while Amanda and Seymour are stereotypical representatives of an imperialistic, unilateral system. The German's overly symbolic divorce from his American wife equates anti-Americanism with anti-capitalism and anti-globalisation and thereby takes up a topos of European self-representation which was reinforced in post-9/11 discourse.[16] While the US-German marriage fails, Martin is tellingly shown later on with his new partner Luisa, a woman of Spanish descent, travelling Europe's cultural Christian-Islamic heritage in Andalusia (416f.).

This largely clichéd Othering of the US is confirmed throughout the novel. The novel's US setting, New York, for example is established as a quintessential cinematic space. With its leitmotif of the gleaming mirage (think "fata morgana"), the novel gestures towards the make-believe of films and also offers a representation of the US through Hollywood images. The repeated farcical denotation of George W. Bush as a "COWBOY GOTTES" (323, see also 60, GOD'S COWBOY, 275) or "Avatar" references a long-standing history of US cinema from Western to science-fiction movies. *September* much like several other German 9/11 texts, thus relies on a European association of the US with the dream factory.[17] The strong presence of Hollywood as an instance of popular culture sets the US further apart from the high-brow culture and canonical literature represented by the German protagonist and stereotypically establishes European cultural superiority, a familiar staple of US-European antagonisms.

It has been argued that one function of this striking Othering of the US lies in the hybridization of the West in order to dissolve the West-East binary, and use this foil to make the kinship of the German protagonist and reader to the Iraqi Tarik and his family, as the seemingly much more obvious cultural and religious Other, appear even closer. Indeed, *September* has been interpreted and celebrated as a critique of

---

[16] For a general account of this topos cf. Cvek, "Good Mourning, America: Genealogies of Loss in *Against the Day*," here especially 50.

[17] Cf. especially the analysis of Thomas Hettche's *Woraus wir gemacht sind* [What We Are Made Of] in Birte Christ's Chapter "National Identity and Literary Culture after 9/11: Pro- and Anti-Americanism in Frédéric Beigbeder's *Windows on the World* (2003) and Thomas Hettche's *Woraus wir gemacht sind* (2006)" in this volume.

the dichotomy between the Western and the Islamic worlds[18] and as a poetic counter-model to the clash of civilizations,[19] supported by claims to its pronouncedly anti-ideological experimental form.[20]

Intercultural Dialogue as an Illusion

In the reception of the novel as a "literary east-west-symbiosis" which "is not about the clash of civilisations" but about how "closely Western and Eastern culture are interlinked one to another,"[21] writing and especially literature play a pivotal role. As the cultural space that is capable of unifying thoughts, emotions, and viewpoints of people who have never met,[22] literary history is employed to demonstrate that communication between cultures is possible.[23] This reading is endorsed by the author's own comments who describes the six years he spent working on the novel as a dream of a dialogue of cultures[24] and declares that his ethical and aesthetic intention was to enter into a dialogue with the Other and to understand the Other.[25]

To an educated German readership such an interpretation would strongly suggest itself by the novel's substantial references to another West-Eastern literary dialogue, Goethe's extensive collection of lyrical poems, his *West-östlicher Divan* [West-Eastern Divan] (1819).[26] Inspired by an 1812 German translation of a collection of poems, the fourteenth-century Persian poet Hafis's divan, Goethe here enters into an imaginary

---

[18] Zimmer, "Abschied von typischen 9/11- (Satz-)Zeichen," 93, for a reading as a dialogue between East and West, cf. Reinhäckel, *Traumatische Texturen*, 194f.

[19] Zimmer, "Abschied von typischen- 9/11 (Satz-)Zeichen," 94.

[20] Ibid.

[21] My translations, cf. the review of *September. Fata Morgana* by Böttiger, "Das Geflecht zweier Kulturen," for his reading of the novel as a utopian interrelation of Occident and Orient, cf. also Böttiger, "Zeitschmetterlinge," 285, and along the same lines Reinhäckel, *Traumatische Texturen*, 195.

[22] Cf. Beatrix Langner's review of Thomas Lehr's book, "Märchen gegen Bomben".

[23] Krekeler, "Die Ilias aus dem Hinterhof".

[24] Ibid. More concretely, Lehr also speaks of a dialogue between the fathers, Lehr, Rohde et al., "In der Werkstatt der Gegenwart," 356.

[25] Thomas Lehr in an interview with Jürgen König, "Ein doppelt kritischer Blick".

[26] For intertextual references to Goethe's *West-östlicher Divan* and structural homologies between the two texts, cf. also Herrmann, "Die Wiederentdeckung des Kreises am Ende der Ironie," especially 50–53.

dialogue with his Oriental counterpart. These intertextual foils, quoted throughout the novel, are also integrated as plot-elements. Martin has a professional interest in both collections: he is writing a monograph on Goethe's lovers and the *West-östlicher Divan* is tangential to this project as it was largely based on Goethe's correspondence with his late love, the much younger Marianne von Willemer. Martin's daughter Sabrina (cf. 58) and the Iraqi Tarik (cf. 47, 96) also know and read Hafis's divan and Goethe's collection. Doubtless, the reference to Goethe's poetic dialogue contributed to the dominant interpretation of *September* as a celebration of intercultural understanding between the Orient and the Occident through shared cultural-literary ground.

On the level of plot, the two cultures are interlinked by both physical and intellectual border-crossings towards the hemisphere of the other. While Martin's research and visits to Andalusian Moorish architecture and to Amman clearly demonstrate a cultivated appreciation of the Other, Tarik had immersed himself in a European lifestyle while he studied and lived with his wife and eldest daughter in Paris. From this point on, he and his wife engage with Western European philosophical discourse and it seems no coincidence that existentialism in particular is mentioned: more than other traditions, it stands in for those secular and social-democratic roots that define core Europe, according to German philosopher Jürgen Habermas's account in the wake of the anti-Iraq invasion.[27]

Beyond the elaborate motivic, symbolic and intertextual inter-weavings between the Eastern and Western narratives,[28] the four protagonists in some instances of the dreamlike stream-of-consciousness appear to almost be able to touch each other through a mirror or seemingly to address each other across temporal and spatial distances.[29] This notion

---

[27] Jürgen Habermas, together with his nominal co-author Jacques Derrida, mentions secularism, the welfare-state, anti-capitalist tendencies and a certain scepticism about unlimited technological progress in their definition of "core Europe," cf. Habermas and Derrida, "February 15, Or, What Bind Europeans Together," here especially 9.

[28] Jennifer Clare theorises these various intratextual associations creating continuities of time and place beyond factual relations as a form of mythical narration, "'Es ist die leichte Begehbarkeit von so vielen Epochen und Kulturräumen' '9/11' als vielstimmige mythische Episode in Thomas Lehrs Roman *September. Fata Morgana*," 109–132.

[29] Cf. the review of *September. Fata Morgana* by Krekeler, "Die Ilias aus dem Hinterhof," similarly Schuster claims that they enter into dialogue with one another, cf. "Luftspiegelungen," the dialogical structure in itself of the novel, however, is undoubted, cf. also Graf, "Es gibt keinen Sieger außer Gott. Goethe und der 11. September," 130.

is brought about by the narrators' occasional use of the second person singular and reinforced by the instrument of the two plots' apparent permeability, the "mirror," which references the leitmotif of the mirage-effect,[30] as an optical phenomenon reproducing displaced images of sky, water or objects.

This intercultural approximation finds symbolic expression when the novel's epilogue dramatises an instance of eye contact between Martin's daughter Sabrina on a journey to Paris and a girl who—so the text strongly suggests—is Tarik's daughter Muna, sitting with her father and older sister in a street café (cf. 472). In the blink of an eye, the otherwise separate plotlines seem to cross and the encounter with the "sister," as repeatedly imagined by the two female narrators, becomes real in this apparent West-East encounter.

This optimistic reading of the novel as an intercultural dialogue is, I would argue, radically called into question by the novel's epilogue which jeopardises the preceding text entirely as it contains what I consider a key scene of the novel. After the first suggestion of an intersection of the novel's separate plotlines through the two daughters' eye contact in Paris, a second intersection appears to build on it. While on a journey to Amman with his new partner Luisa, Martin engages in a conversation with an Iraqi and his daughter. As an actual intercultural dialogue, this encounter could clearly be read as an affirmation of the novel's motivic and intertextual implications, if it were not for the passage's irritating use of unreliable narration. The passage misleads the reader into believing that, in Amman, Martin meets the Iraqi protagonists.[31] Meticulous detail[32] about the father and daughter match earlier accounts about the Baghdad family and leave no doubt that at the end of the novel the Western and Eastern hemispheres metonymically and literally enter into dialogue. The Iraqi's fate—who has lost his wife and one daughter in

---

[30] As Tarik's, possibly addressing Martin, for instance (cf. 382).

[31] Stühring, "Unreliable Narration, Deception, and Fictional Facts".

[32] He presumably is a doctor (457) from Baghdad, speaks French, his younger daughter is likely to be pregnant, her lover Nabil killed by militia, and his only son has gone underground (476f.) while his wife and older daughter possibly have been killed in a terror attack. Even the minutiae about a climbing frame for children, a red elephant on a pedestal next to the Roman theatre in Amman and the favourite animal of his daughter, who baptised it "Hannibal" when a child (476), agrees with an earlier account of Tarik's daughter Muna.

a bomb attack—preoccupies Martin as he shares the story with Luisa back in the hotel room. Having suffered similar losses, Martin is shown to identify and sympathize with his cultural Other. In this respect, his reaction reflects that of the reader who is invited to identify with Tarik and Muna throughout the course of the novel. The idea of intercultural dialogue which has been built up so laboriously, however, collapses all of a sudden when Martin, in reply to Luisa's questions, states the names of the two Iraqis: "Fatima und Machmud" (477).[33] The detailed description of the father and daughter in Amman is but a reflection of Tarik and Muna. This abrupt disappointment of the readers' expectation and inferences as the novel ends calls into question not only the previous transitory intersection of plots in the Parisian street café but the reliability of the text as a whole. Through the use of unreliable narration, the epilogue demonstrates to the Western readers that their identification of the cultural Other was premature. This symbolically demonstrative gesture can be interpreted as a metonymy which applies to the novel as a whole: the erroneous familiarity with the epilogue's Iraqi and his daughter are a strong suggestion of an erroneous familiarity with the narrator-protagonists, Tarik and Muna. In the epilogue, the reader thinks he knows the Other but turns out to be mistaken: the father and daughter are—literally—someone else and thus, symbolically—always remain the Other. Worthy of its genre description "Fata Morgana," the novel reveals a deceptive structure and marks itself as a reflection or delusion rather than the real thing. The etymological origin of "Fata Morgana"—the Italian name for the legendary Arthurian sorceress Morgan le Fay plays into this idea of delusion.

The epilogue's use of unreliable narration reveals the Western projections at work. This is further supported by another narrative element. In contrast to the chapters, the epilogue is not attributed to one of the four narrator-protagonists through a respective chapter heading and the focalization is not limited to one of the four. Thus, the speaker of the epilogue appears to be situated on a higher narrative level than the four narrator-protagonists, thereby suggesting an author-figure. Whether we equate this author-figure with Martin (as has been convincingly

---

[33] Possible alternative interpretations such as Martin's incorrect recollection ("Fatima und Machmud / glaube ich" (477); "Fatima and Mahmud / I think" (S, 418)) or the adoption of new names in the face of death threats (477) are unlikely as the name "Fatima" (476) is also used in the Iraqi father's internal focalization.

argued)³⁴ or with Lehr as the real author, the presence of an author-figure in the epilogue self-consciously discloses that the apparently multi-perspectival novel is narrated from a single, Western European viewpoint. This is at odds with the dialogic quality that has been ascribed to *September*. Lehr himself states that the novel's invisible utopia is its dialogic quality and sets the polyphony of literature against the hysteria of official discourse.³⁵ This assessment was readily taken up by the initial critical reactions to the text. It is strongly suggestive of Bakhtin's theory of the novel. Along the lines of Bakhtin's concept of polyphony and the dialogic, *September* indeed brings together independent ideological positions and involves hugely heterogeneous material.³⁶ However, the stylistic consistency of the novel's poetic stream of consciousness that runs through all four narrative voices interfuses them. According to Bakhtin, however, "the essence of polyphony lies precisely in the fact that the voices remain independent and, as such, are combined in a unity of a higher order than in homophony."³⁷ In contrast to Bakhtin's idea of "coexisting consciousnesses"³⁸ indicative of the "freedom and independence characters possess,"³⁹ Lehr's four narrator-protagonists reflect each other's intellectual horizons and eventually merge indistinguishably in the epilogue. The author-narrator which is established in the epilogue, jeopardises the independence of the novel's four different perspectives as it acknowledges their ultimate origin in one single individual's consciousness: the author's.⁴⁰ Due to the epilogue's convergence of the four narrative voices as well as the presence of an author-figure, the novel should not be attributed an unambiguous dialogical quality.

---

³⁴ Cf. Horstkotte, "Transcending Trauma," 44.

³⁵ Haas, "Es ist gut, wenn starke Symbole fallen. Ein Gespräch mit dem Schriftsteller Thomas Lehr".

³⁶ Bakhtin, *Problems of Dostoevsky's Poetics*, 18.

³⁷ Ibid., 21.

³⁸ Ibid., 32.

³⁹ Ibid., 13.

⁴⁰ That Martin should be this author figure (Graf, "Es gibt keinen Sieger außer Gott," 124, Horstkotte, "Transcending Trauma," 43f.) might be possible even if it has not been argued in an entirely satisfactory way and probably cannot be narratologically justified through the epilogue alone.

Mimicry as a Leitmotif

The final twist in the narrative jeopardises the reader's supposed identification with the Muslim Other. Yet, the ending not only shares its illusionary effect with the titular "Fata Morgana". After reading the epilogue, the mirage and the closely connected mirror motif which are deployed throughout the novel also have to be re-evaluated. Since the novel acknowledges the origin of its various narrative perspectives in one authorial Western European viewpoint, it can be argued that the apparent approximation of the cultural Other is but a reflection of the Western self. *September*, rather than celebrating the understanding of the Other, self-critically reveals a deeply Eurocentric perspective. At the core of the novel, seems to lie not the 'Orientalization' of the Other, as has been argued, but rather its Europeanization.[41] The novel indicates that the European reader identifies so effortlessly with the Iraqi characters, Tarik and his family, precisely because they share his values of secularity, democracy and gender equality as well as his literary, philosophical and cultural frames of reference.

Following this line of argument, the unsettling doubling of Tarik and Muna in the Iraqi doctor and his daughter, whom Martin meets in Amman, can be instructively connected to Homi Bhabha's concept of "mimicry." According to Bhabha, the subversive force of the "mimic man," the colonial subject who has assimilated to the coloniser, comes from the fact that he is "almost the same, but not quite."[42] It is this perplexing similarity from which the novel derives its most decisively subversive element—the epilogue's unreliability with the *doppelgängers* of Muna and Tarik. As it turns out that Martin is not talking to whom the reader thought he was talking, his Eastern counterpart Tarik and the man he meets can be understood as a mimicry of each other.

The reader's misidentification of Tarik and the Iraqi described in the epilogue unsettles the assumption they knew who the characters were. The reader's projection in the epilogue seems to open up the possibility that we might also be mistaken in knowing Tarik. Indeed, as has been shown, the reader's identification with the Iraqi protagonists can be read as a European appropriation of the Other. Comparable to Bhabha's concept, this novelistic mimicry questions the dominant—here

---

[41] Horstkotte, "Transcending Trauma," 44.
[42] Bhabha, *The Location of Culture*, 127.

European—discourse and lays bare its inner contradictions: In this case, it reveals the Eurocentric gaze which is at work in the discourse of tolerance and Enlightenment and which—blind to differences—does not try to understand the radical Other but appropriates it.

Such a reading of the text as mimicry of dialogue is consolidated by a key plot element which marks writing, and written dialogue in particular, as manipulative: The relationship between the Iraqi daughter Muna and her lover Nabil is brought to a tragic end when Tarik's only son, Sami, in his increasing religious fundamentalism and radicalization, uses his interest in and talent for calligraphy, that is stressed throughout the novel, to trap his sister's lover and, together with his associates, to kill him.[43] It is by mimicking his sister's and her lover's hand in letters (462f.) that he can execute his plot. While Sami sends a forged letter to his sister in which her lover Nabil supposedly breaks up with her, he sends another one to Nabil in which Muna supposedly asks him to meet up in her grandparents' house where Nabil is eventually killed. This literal 'mimicry of dialogue' can be read as a mise-en-abyme of the novel as a whole foreshadowing the feigned dialogue between the representatives of West and East in the epilogue. In the novel, writing is given a manipulative quality: the deception of the reader reflects the deception of the lovers. This interpretation of the forged letters as a mise-en-abyme of the novel is supported by the etymological origins of the protagonists' names: "Martin," a derivation of Mars and "Tarik," an Arabic translation of Venus, point to the godly lovers of antiquity and are thus symbolically aligned with the young couple.

This in turn also deconstructs the apparent function of Goethe's *West-östlicher Divan* as a guarantor of intercultural approximation: the reference to the imagined literary dialogue forms a further analogy to the fateful written conversation between the lovers. In fact, in relation to Lehr's novel, it has already been pointed out that the *Divan* in its orientalizing tendency might not ideally serve as an unambiguous emblem of intercultural understanding,[44] a reservation which is confirmed by the textual evidence laid bare here. The link between the *Divan* and the

---

[43] Contrary to Herrmann's claim, Muna's lover does not leave her because she is a Shiite, the couple fall victim to her brother's murderous intrigue, cf. Herrmann, "Die Wiederentdeckung des Kreises am Ende der Ironie," 47.

[44] Eke, "'Es gibt keinen Sieger außer Gott'. Dialog im Raum der Schrift: Thomas Lehrs Roman *September. Fata Morgana*," 212.

forged letter exchange on the plot level is further strengthened through the biographical context in which Goethe wrote his imaginary dialogue. Martin's research points to the relevance of this context: his book project, *Goethe lieben* (loving Goethe) involves another correspondence between lovers which formed the very basis of the *Divan*: that of Goethe and Marianne von Willemer which, since they never saw each other after their first encounter, continued until his death. This correspondence is crucial to the textual genesis of Goethe's *Divan*: it inspired his dialogue poems between the fictional Oriental lovers Hatem and Suleika—Goethe dedicated the "Buch Suleika" [Book of Suleika] in the *Divan* to his muse Marianne—and she also co-authored several parts.

In addition to this formation on the basis of a letter exchange between lovers, Goethe's *Divan* is also associated with the fateful mimicry of letters in Lehr's novel through the aspect of calligraphy: in *September*, Sami's training and accomplishment in calligraphy enable him to mimic a written dialogue. The *Divan*, in turn, is one of the rare Goethe texts that the writer himself transferred into a clean copy by his own hand (rather than having it delegated to scribes), i.e. which he wrote in calligraphy. Furthermore, the composition of the *Divan* coincides with Goethe's keen interest in Arabic calligraphy as part of his engagement with the literature and culture of the Middle East.[45] Decisively, his own serious efforts in calligraphy, copying from manuscripts he bought for the Weimar Hofbibliothek (today the Anna-Amalia-library), are an entirely formal external imitation because he was fully ignorant of the language. Thus, we are, in this superficial imitation again directed towards the idea of mimicry.

This threefold association of mimicry with written dialogue—on the level of plot, intertextual reference and narrative technique—is supported by the novel's intricate motivic network. An example of how the text is repeatedly marked as unreliable can be found in the incident when the drunken Tarik, in an Old Testament allusion sees 'Writing on the Wall' (138), only visible to him, entailing a warning only he can read, thus linking in a self-reflexive manner writing and illusion once again in this unreal mirage-like apparition.

The unreliability of writing is also implied by the novel's continuous reflection of its fictionality. As mentioned above, Lehr tries and finds

---

[45] Bosse, "Magische Präsenz. Zur Funktion von Schrift und Ornament in Goethes 'Westöstlichem *Divan*,'" 317.

new forms for each of his literary subjects. The metafictional and surreal nature of *September* explores a narrative form that is adequate to the attacks in Manhattan and its medial representation. Certainly, the novel as a whole gestures towards its own textuality, narrativity and fictionality through various techniques. Opening with a reference to the frame narrative of *One Thousand and One Nights*, the novel positions itself within fictional markers from the very beginning: Muna poetically imagines herself and her sister as the Persian Scheherazade (56) who tells her husband King Shahryār the fantastic stories of *One Thousand and One Nights* while her sister Dinarasad hides under their bed.[46] The allusion to *One Thousand and One Nights* in the novel's first two lines point towards its narratedness:

Unsere Geschichte
hängt in der Luft in der Nacht (11)
Our story
is hanging in the air in the night (3)

More importantly, the image links the story to the mirage effect: reinforced by the line-break as its typographic reproduction it implies that the novelistic text to follow is a "Fata Morgana." Both the reference to the novel's title and to the nocturnal frame narrative of *One Thousand and One Nights* put an emphasis on the illusory character of what is about to be told.

Given that references to the frame narrative weave throughout Lehr's entire novel, it is worthwhile showing how it more specifically touches on the theme of mimicry. In *One Thousand and One Nights* Scheherazade—prompted by her sister hiding under the bed—each night tells her husband, King Shahryār, a story in order not to be killed the following morning.[47] As a consequence of his first wife's adultery, Shahryār had killed all her successors after the wedding night to take revenge on womanhood. What is important for my line of argument is that the adultery scene, which provoked this cruel ritual, crucially involves cultural-racial mimicry: to conceal her erotic encounters, the queen has black slaves dress up as maids so that they can accompany her and her white maids without suspicion into the palace garden where they then throw off their clothes and reveal themselves before all joining the queen, who

---

[46] For an explicit statement cf. 90.
[47] There are several references to this violent ritual, cf. 462.

also conducts her affair.[48] This links the queen's betrayal of her husband to a betrayal—both gendered and more importantly for the present context, pronouncedly racially encoded through the inter-racial affair—which, as a further example of delusion and camouflage clearly points to the context of mimicry and its motivic importance in the text.

Not only is this episode implicit in Lehr's text through allusions to the frame narrative but also through a number of specific references. Besides the recurrent motifs of adultery[49] and the conjunction of sexuality and violence (cf. e.g. 61), the scene in the palace garden is significantly associated with the novel's major plot element, the attacks on the World Trade Center. Even without reminding ourselves that Bhabha explicitly associated his post-colonial concept of "mimicry" with camouflage as a military strategy, *September* clearly exploits this connection.

September draws the September 11 attacks as its major theme even closer together with the adultery scene in *One Thousand and One Nights* and thus with the idea of racial-cultural mimicry. The deception of the reader through the epilogue's mimic doubling of Tarik and Muna is linked to the attacks through the unreal footage and through the twin motif embodied by the buildings themselves and stressed throughout the novel. More specifically, the phallic symbolism of the Twin Towers and their demolition as an act of castration[50] lend itself to a literary association with Shahryār's figurative unmanning by his adulterous first wife. In *September*, the American president George W. Bush takes the role of the emasculated king. Lehr reinforces the link between the September attacks and the adultery scene in *One Thousand and One Nights* in an equally subtle and creative way. He employs the dual reference of the German "Türme," i.e. to the "towers" of the World Trade Center and the "rooks"[51] in chess to associate the board game, as the ubiquitous

---

[48] Ott, *Tausendundeine Nacht*.

[49] Cf. Martin's implied adultery with the nurse as well as his new partner Luisa's affair with a historian in Amherst and Jasmin's, Muna's sister (367).

[50] This association has been explored by cultural studies from the beginning and forms a prominent part of 9/11 imagery. The World Trade Center alternatively appears as the double phallus or as the female body being penetrated by the phallic airliners, cf. Elisabeth Bronfen, quoting Klaus Theweleit, *Der Knall: 11. September, das Verschwinden der Realität und ein Kriegsmodell*, 142.

[51] For some of the repeated linking of chess and the towers of the World Trade Center, cf. 189, 201, 305. The double meaning of "rook," linking it back to an act of betrayal is only implied by the English translation and might overstretch the argument in relation to the German original. A more likely association, however, can be found in the shared

symbol of military strategy and combat, to the September attacks. The adultery scene again is explicitly linked to chess pieces by the same colour contrast between the white queen and her maids, on the one side, and the black slaves, on the other.[52]

The intricate motivic association exemplifies how the novel explores the connection between the September 11 attacks and the theme of mimicry. This interpretation can be further supported by the fact that cultural-racial deception is an essential aspect in 9/11 discourse. The idea of camouflage through assimilation which is brought up in *One Thousand and One Nights* by the cross-dressing of the black slaves also doubly characterises the historic circumstances of the attacks: the cultural and religious Other, the Islamic terrorists, who were apparently assimilated into the majority culture, employed the Trojan horses of an American Airlines and United Airlines jet[53] to attack the US homeland. Thus, 9/11 can be read as a real symbol of cultural mimicry: the very mechanisms of the attacks stand in for the "mimic man," who apparently adapts the dominant culture, and for the subversive effect of this process which brings out the inner contradictions of the imperial power.

MIMICRY IN GERMAN AND EUROPEAN 9/11 DISCOURSE

This association of mimicry and the attacks has also been put forward through the initial philosophical discussion of 9/11 in Europe. One of Germany's most eminent living poets and political intellectuals, Hans Magnus Enzensberger, for example, linked the terrorists with the idea of the "stranger within" in his comment-piece "Die Wiederkehr des Menschenopfers" [The return of the human sacrifice] (2001), published

---

etymological origin of "betrayal" and "trade" in the Latin "tradere" (i.e. "to hand over," betrayal as one form of a deal) as the English word would be used for the World Trade Center. For references to chess, cf. 189, 201, 305.

[52] Cf. 189. The comparison to the chess game is possibly inspired by the repeated stress on the black-and-white colour contrast in the original, cf. Ott, *Tausendundeine Nacht*, 12.

[53] Cf. also Beigbeder's protagonist Yorsten's reflection in the burning North Tower on the changed world picture after the end of the Cold War when Russia was lost as an Other against which the US could clearly define itself and instead the enemy now is within "L'Amérique est devenue son propre ennemi." Beigbeder, *Windows on the World*, 151—note the ambivalence of "propre," meaning as in English that the major enemy comes from within.

in the national daily newspaper *Frankfurter Allgemeine Zeitung* only a week after the events. For Enzensberger, apparently under the influence of Kristeva's psychoanalytical theory, the terrorists' camouflage and assimilation into the dominant culture symbolise the West's internal contradictions, that it is a "stranger to itself." He argues that the act as well as the means of terrorism are part of the global power structure itself and that its perception as an attack from outside is illusory.[54] The parallels with the instance of cultural mimicry in Lehr's novel become apparent in Enzensberger's biological metaphors, describing the terrorists as "pathological copies, similar to the retrovirus of an affected cell." According to his article, the 9/11 attackers instrumentalize the system for their own purposes not only by hijacking the planes but also by factoring in the effect of the iconic images of the atrocious act on a globalised media community. While Enzensberger's essay explains how the globalisation of terrorism propagates the very system it is attacking, *September* pursues this idea in its imagery, continuously joining state violence and terrorism. This is also true of Lehr's depiction of the attacks on the Twin Towers themselves when the distinct emphasis on the kerosene-induced flames (cf. 168) joins the terrorist plot to the oil consumption of the West and its aggression to sustain that supply, represented as elaborated above, by the American Seymour.

Along similar lines albeit with a perspective more explicitly indebted to both psychoanalytical and post-structural theory, Žižek and Baudrillard prominently conceptionalized 9/11 as the decay of the West's own structures and as an effect of the Other within the hegemonic discourse. Žižek describes the terrorist as Other within capitalism,[55] and Baudrillard expands on the nature of the event as demonstrating internal difference.[56] In his essays collected in *L'ésprit de terrorisme*, by now a constituent of 9/11 discourse, like Enzensberger, Baudrillard

---

[54] Enzensberger, "Die Wiederkehr des Menschenopfers".

[55] Cf. Žižek's rhetorical questions: "[…] are not 'international terrorist organizations' the obscene double of the big multinational corporations—the ultimate rhizomatic machine, omnipresent, albeit with no clear territorial base? Are they not the form in which nationalist and/or religious 'fundamentalism' accommodated itself to global capitalism? Do they not embody the ultimate contradiction, with their particular exclusive content and their global dynamic functioning?," "Welcome to the Desert of the Real," 38.

[56] Baudrillard, "Hypotheses on Terrorism," 55.

argues that terrorism operates within the very mechanisms it attacks,[57] before building up the argument of terrorism as the expression of the Other within. Baudrillard claims that 9/11 is what the superpower secretly wished for, not only because the attacks provide it with the missing victim status that retrospectively legitimises the exercise of hegemonic power,[58] but also because this dialectic reversion lies in the nature of absolute power.[59]

European cultural theoretical analyses of the 9/11 attacks are thus preoccupied with the subversive potential of the cultural and religious Other that lays bare inner contradictions of the dominant culture through assimilation. *September* invites the reader to draw parallels from these forms of camouflage to Bhabha's concept of cultural mimicry.[60] The epilogue's deceptive mimicry brings out the inner contradictions of the novel questioning its discourse of Enlightenment, pacifism and tolerance and deconstructing the assumed European cultural and moral superiority.

The idea of the terrorist as a clandestine danger is moreover particularly pronounced in the German context. The jihadists around Mohammed Atta who coordinated the four September 11 hijackings from their Hamburg terror cell were inconspicuous students in Germany well acquainted with a Western lifestyle. They can thus be said to have used assimilation as a camouflage. The Hamburg terror cell is Germany's major link to 9/11. It is not surprising then that the sleeper figure plays a prominent role in the German cultural responses to the

---

[57] Baudrillard, "The Spirit of Terrorism," 19.

[58] Ibid., 5; cf. also Baudrillard, "Hypotheses," 61f.

[59] Baudrillard, "The Spirit of Terrorism," 5. To him, the Twin Towers were the most powerful symbol of hegemonic power because of their double nature. Whereas all other Manhattan skyscrapers competed in height and with their individual façades, the two identical monoliths were an architectural manifestation of a power that has risen above competition. According to Baudrillard's interpretation, the collapse of the towers was not primarily a consequence of the plane's actual impact, but also a symbolic reaction to the total order that wishes for its own destruction, a suicide, responding to and mirroring that of the suicide terrorists, ibid., 7.

[60] After all, despite the different context and mechanisms, Bhabha is heavily indebted to Kristeva's reading of Freud, according to which individual identity is always already split within and integrates the Other within themselves, cf. Kristeva, *Etrangers à nous-mêmes* (1988).

attacks.[61] It features in a number of German films,[62] while several novels engage with the radicalised cultural Other, such as the protagonist in Sherko Fatah's *Das dunkle Schiff* (2008, trans. by Martin Chalmers, *The Dark Ship*, 2015). The novel tells the story of the Iraqi Kerim whose isolated life in Berlin reminds him of the attraction of the jihadists from whom he had originally fled. Christoph Peters' *Ein Zimmer im Haus des Krieges* (A Room in the House of War) (2006) explores the "Other within" from a different angle. Set in pre-9/11 Berlin, it describes how the young German Jochen Sawatzky converts to Islam, is radicalised and joins a group of terrorists who plan an attack on the Luxor temples in Egypt. Similar themes appear in non-fiction books, such as journalist Elmar Theveßen's paperback *Schläfer mitten unter uns* (Sleepers in Our Very Midst) (2002), published soon after the events, which further demonstrate the presence of the sleeper figure in German discourse. Furthermore, Hamburg, as the home of the 9/11 terror cell, is a recurrent setting of German novels with a 9/11 tangent,[63] even if the terrorist cell itself does not feature—and it does come up in *September* as the residence of Martin's demented mother who confuses the attacks with the Hamburg air raids. Arguably, Lehr's novel with its themes of simulation and its narrative deception, making the reader take the cultural Other for someone that he is not, thereby also continues a strand which is characteristic of German 9/11-literature. Before locating this line of argument also within a wider context of post-9/11 literature in Europe, I will draw attention to the historical pessimism weaving throughout *September*. This overlooked aspect shows that the disillusioned reading of the novel as a mimicry of cultural dialogue can be aligned with a global interpretation of the text.

---

[61] This does not mean that the sleeper figure is limited to the German context, as John Le Carré's espionage thriller *A Most Wanted Man* (2008) demonstrates, as well as the film adaptation of the same name (2014).

[62] Cf. also Birte Christ's Chapter "National Identity and Literary Culture after 9/11: Pro- and Anti-Americanism in Frédéric Beigbeder's *Windows on the World* (2003) and Thomas Hettche's *Woraus wir gemacht sind* (2006)" in this volume.

[63] Cf. Kristof Magnusson's new economy novel *Das war ich nicht* [It Wasn't Me] (2010) or Thomas Pletzinger's *Bestattung eines Hundes* (2008, trans. by Ross Benjamin, *Funeral for a Dog*, 2011).

The Novel's Historical Pessimism

So far, only some scholarly discussions of Lehr's text have started to put the reading of the novel as a hopeful vision into perspective.[64] The epilogue's mirage-like doubling of the Iraqi father and his daughter like the novel as a whole has so far often been interpreted in a more positive light, where the marking of the text as unreal supposedly places the peaceful interculturalism in the realm of utopia. However, in addition to the irritating effect of its unreliable narration frustrating readers' expectations, the novel's themes of war, terrorism and atrocious violence, its pronounced dystopian framing and ongoing infusion with motifs of historical pessimism concur with the alternative disillusionary interpretation of *September* put forward here.

With its two plotlines of the New York attacks and the Iraq War, the novel is centred on terrorism and state violence and—as a 500-page-long epic poem—pays formal homage to the much earlier war narrative of Homer's *Iliad*. One or two of the four narrator-protagonists die during the events of the novel and the emotional devastation of the others is paramount. Given, in particular, Martin's mourning for his daughter, echoed in the repeated quotations from Friedrich Rückert's (1788–1866) song cycle *Kindertotenlieder* (Songs of the Death of Children), *September* is also very much an elegy. Though the two father-daughter plots have been unanimously read as a symbolic fulfilment of intercultural dialogue, the novel's movement from utopia to dystopia in the light of atrocious reality has also been noted.[65] Indeed, when towards the conclusion of the novel, for instance, Tarik compares the terror of the dictatorship under Saddam before the war to the new regime of democracy in Iraq after the war, the novel gestures towards an inevitable continuity of violence (cf. 461). This historical pessimism is consolidated throughout the novel. One example is the repeated comparison of the Twin Towers to the Old Testament Tower of Babel as a stock image of 9/11 literature. The story of the Tower of Babel in the Book of Genesis provides a mythical explanation for the existence of different languages. According to this biblical story, the people of Babel spoke one

---

[64] Cf. Herrmann, "Die Wiederentdeckung des Kreises am Ende der Ironie" and Horstkotte, "Transcending Trauma".

[65] Graf, "Es gibt keinen Sieger außer Gott," 120f., Herrmann, similarly calls it dystopian, "Die Wiederentdeckung des Kreises am Ende der Ironie," 54.

single language until they started to build a tower high enough to touch the heavens. It is transparent how the sheer doubled size of the World Trade Center—according to some—a provocative emblem of globalisation, came to be likened to the Biblical Tower. God punishes the hubris of their endeavour by afflicting mankind with the Babylonian confusion. Unable to communicate with each other, humans are dispersed throughout the entire world. With *September*'s emphasis on cultural conflict, it seems to take up the negative connotation of the biblical Tower of Babel where the diversity of languages and cultures are conceived of as a godly punishment. Along the same lines, the novel also suggests that the major reason for the violent ending of Muna and Nabil's love lies not primarily with the pre-marital romantic relationship which in itself would be deemed inappropriate in a traditional Islamic context: rather, the forged letters insinuate that the major provocation to Muna's radicalised brother are cultural-religious differences, i.e. the fact that Muna, a "SuSchi" (219, 397), descending from a Sunni father and a Shiite mother, loves a Shiite man.

Further to this marked emphasis on intercultural clashes, Lehr embeds 9/11 into a *longue durée* of violence stretching back to the beginnings of mankind through an explicit intermedial reference to Stanley Kubrick's science-fiction cult film *2001 A Space Odyssey* (1968). While references to the film are also found in several pop-cultural reactions to 9/11, Lehr moves beyond the titular date and establishes a graphic link between Kubrick's motif of a monolith block to the World Trade Center Twin Towers.[66] Of its four appearances in Kubrick's film, the monolith most famously features in the opening scene "The Dawn of Man," where a group of curious ape-men gather around it. As the intersecting shots of the monolith clearly signals, it inspires them to use bones as weapons. Eventually, a bone is thrown into the air and substituted by a satellite circling the earth, a foundation of modern warfare, thereby short-circuiting the history of humankind as a history of violence and significantly linking it to the notion of technical progress.

The historical pessimism of this intermedial reference is consolidated by the very parenthesis of the novel. The paratextual motto "Die

---

[66] Cf. also Frédéric Beigbeder's 9/11 novel *Windows on the World* where the narrator compares Kubrick's monolith block to the Parisian skyscraper Tour Montparnasse, the place where he tries to imagine how the victims felt during the attacks on the Twin Towers; ibid. 44.

Geschichte ist der Irrgarten der Gewalt" (7) ("History is the labyrinth of violence", n. p.),[67] an idea which is taken up again in a variation towards the end of the novel (cf. 442), positions the text as a whole under the signs of continual and inevitable violence. With poetic licence, Lehr attributes the words to Goethe, presumably an adapted quotation from Goethe's late collection of aphorisms *Zahme Xenien* (Tame Xenia, here no. 9).[68] This attribution is ironic, if not cynical, in the way it undermines the putative warrantor of poetic intercultural dialogue and further demonstrates that the *West-östlicher Divan* as a major intertextual foil of the novel cannot be taken unambiguously for a belief in a peaceful coexistence of East and West.

Given its prominent position at the beginning of the text, the force of this motto is perhaps only exceeded by the final frame in its effectiveness to signpost historical pessimism. The novel ends with Martin's and his new partner's, Luisa's, trip to her native country, Spain, specifically to Granada in the southernmost province of Andalusia where they visit the UNESCO World Heritage Site Alhambra. The current form of this Moorish palace was built under the last Muslim emperors in Spain before the Reconquista and the Nasrid dynasty who ruled over the Emirate of Granada from 1232 until 1492. Though the stunning beauty of the influence of Arabic culture on the European mainland manifest in the Alhambra is explicitly denoted as a dialogue of cultures earlier in the novel (cf. 208), this is reversed into its opposite as the novel closes, just as suddenly as the expectations of an encounter between Martin and Tarik were disappointed only a page earlier: when the couple enters the heart of the Alhambra an architectural image of paradise known as the Court of the Lions, its central fountain fills with oil and enflames everything around it.

---

[67] That Lehr sees war and its literary representations in a great historical continuity is also demonstrated in his article on Alfred Döblin's *Wallenstein*-novel which was published at the time of writing *September. Fata Morgana*, and where in the Introduction he draws a direct comparison from the Thirty Years' War (1618–1648) to the War on Terror in Afghanistan, Lehr, "'In Tod und Trümmern—finde' Alfred Döblins *Wallenstein*-Roman als Glanzpunkt der literarischen Kriegsberichterstattung," 112.

[68] Cf. "Es ist die ganze Kirchengeschichte / Mischmasch von Irrtum und von Gewalt" (The entire church history is a mishmash of error and violence, my translation), Goethe, *Berliner Ausgabe*, 381.

Very much the antipode of the hopeful picture alleged by several critics,[69] the novel dissolves into an apocalyptic final frame which makes it all the more surprising that *September. Fata Morgana* has so often been interpreted in a culturally optimistic light. An emphatic image of violent destruction, the ending actually points to the continuation of cultural conflict from the Moorish invasions of Spain up to the present-day oil wars and even to Islamic terrorism, if we consider that 11-M, the 2004 al-Qaeda attacks on several Madrid urban trains, according to the Islamist ideology is understood as part of recapturing territory lost during the Christian Reconquista.[70]

Conclusion

The wealth of evidence for historical pessimism and the focus on cultural conflict gravely challenge the celebration of Thomas Lehr's 9/11 novel *September. Fata Morgana* as a poetic intercultural dialogue. This chapter has revealed a hitherto neglected double structure in the novel, and proposed to read the novel instead as a mimicry of dialogue. This line of argument thus subscribes to the more recent strand of scholarship that has seen Lehr's novel in a less optimistic, even a dystopian light.

As has been shown, the rich intertextuality of *September* supposedly exhibiting a long tradition of shared cultural heritage between the Orient and the Occident is jeopardised crucially within the text. While its major reference texts are already heavily charged with Eurocentrism as they stand, the Arabic collection of stories *One Thousand and One Nights* has for most of its translation and editing history been distorted by European Orientalism, while Goethe's imaginary dialogue with

---

[69] Though Leonhard Herrmann notes that Granada is the location of the Reconquista and thus the violent conflict between East and West, he interprets the architecture solely as the "hoffungsvolles Zeichen der Möglichkeit friedlicher Koexistenz," (hopeful sign of possible peaceful coexistence, my translation), Herrmann, "Die Wiederentdeckung des Kreises am Ende der Ironie," 48, and does not mention the final images. Neither does Eke but sees in it a hopeful ending, see Eke, "'Es gibt keinen Sieger außer Gott,'" 219.

[70] Cf. Henningfeld, "Zäsur oder Wiederkehr des Immergleichen," 179, with reference to Reinares, *Terrorismus Global. Aktionsfeld Europa*. For the populist agitation of Spain's former Prime Minister José María Aznar of the conservative party Partido Popular (PP), the Madrid train bombings insinuating their understanding within the context of the Reconquista by Islamic radicals, cf. also Tremlett, "Foreword. 'Welcome to Moorishland'," especially xvii–xviii.

Hafis in the poems of the *West-östlicher Divan* is not only interspersed with Orientalist imagery, but rather becomes entangled in Lehr's novel with the murder of Muna's lover. In contrast to Scheherazade's nocturnal cliff-hangers, poetry in *September. Fata Morgana* does not prevent violence.

The narrative twist in the novel's epilogue demonstrates that the Muslim Other, as the object of identification, remains quite literally an Other. Lehr thus confronts the educated and literary refined German or European readers of this aesthetically highly complex text with their own Eurocentrism. The jarring mimicry of Tarik and his daughter at the end of the novel causes the readers to realise that their identification with the characters over the preceding almost 500 pages was based on a delusory Eurocentric projection. Tarik is portrayed as the oriental Other which the German or European reader desires: democratic, secular,[71] and well versed in Western European philosophy and literature and with respect for gender equality.[72] It is this appropriation of the cultural Other in the tradition of the European Enlightenment, the assimilation to what the culturally refined, educated and tolerant reader takes for his own European identity, that makes entering into dialogue seem possible, not because the exchange with the genuine Other is embraced. Rather, according to this reading, the novel could be seen as an illustration of how the West wants to erase differences, as the cultural critiques of Baudrillard and Terry Eagleton posit.[73] In fact, the process at work in Lehr's *September. Fata Morgana* is comparable to that in Frédéric Beigbeder's *Windows on the World*, where as Birte Christ astutely observes in chapter "National Identity and Literary Culture after 9/11: Pro- and Anti-Americanism in Frédéric Beigbeder's *Windows on the World* (2003) and Thomas Hettche's *Woraus wir gemacht sind* (2006)" in this volume, Americaphilia is really based on Frenchifying the US. It does not seem, then, as if Lehr's account oversteps its national or European perspective towards an international novel, as has been claimed. On the contrary, it negotiates European identity first through the explicit Othering of the American, claiming cultural superiority.

---

[71] Cf. 372.

[72] It becomes clear, for example, that he allows his daughters a largely emancipated lifestyle, they both study and travel and it is said explicitly of Jasmin that she never wears the *abaya* and her wedding followed a Western style, cf. 136.

[73] Eagleton, *After Theory*, 160.

This is, however, put into question by the second implicit Othering of the Iraqi. The epilogue's unreliable narration disappoints the supposed approximation—the Eastern Other remains an Other. In his mimicry, the Europeanized Iraqi—just like Bhabha's Anglicized Indian—discloses the inner contradictions of a European discursive identity. In this alternative reading set against the author's intention of a utopian dream of intercultural dialogue, the text perhaps then turns into a dialogical and anti-ideological novel in Bakhtin's sense, even if polyphony is not executed on the level of the narrator-character. In its ambivalences it opposes the mono-directional ideology of Islamic terrorism as well as the official discourse of national trauma and mourning in the US or the European claim to cultural superiority. In its unveiling of Eurocentrism, *September. Fata Morgana* also forms part of a wider context of emerging post-9/11 self-critical strands of the European novel that have been most conclusively exemplified with regard to Dutch literature.[74] Lehr's novel thereby also tends to locate violence within the European context, not only in the American or Islamic Other.[75] In fact, the stress on the analogies and shared imagery between the September 11 attacks on the World Trade Center and cultural mimicry in the novel almost seem to point to the similarities between the violent structures, comparing the terrorist act to the Eurocentric appropriation.

The forms of violence attributed to Europe are subtler than the military imperialism or terrorist atrocity, and are often embedded in assumedly ethical ideas. In the dialogue with the cultural Other, the novel consciously positions itself in a humanistic tradition of understanding and tolerance, while at the same time stressing its cultural superiority and refinement over and above the US. With the literary heritage integrated into the highly intertextual novel, this seems to provide a basis for cultural understanding that brings Germany, or Europe, in fact closer to its cultural counterpart of the Islamic Other than to the US as its more obvious ally. Thus, for most of the text, *September* seems to underline the

---

[74] Cf. Chapter "Europe and Its Discontents: Intra-European Violence in Dutch Literature after 9/11" in this volume by Maria Boletsi as well as her article "Cannibalism and Literary Indigestibility".

[75] With the example of the violence against migrants in particular, cf. Maria Boletsi's analysis of Bart Koubaa's novel *De leraar* and the Dutch context, "Cannibalism and Literary Indigestibility," here especially 40 and her Chapter "Europe and Its Discontents: Intra-European Violence in Dutch Literature after 9/11" in this volume.

transatlantic rift within the West. It is only towards the end of the novel that it becomes clear that this supposedly virtuous idea of tolerance is not only inherently hierarchical but also an expression of power relations.[76] In fact "know-it-all [...] Europe,"[77] as German writer Peter Schneider criticised with respect to its stance towards the US and its claims to the tradition of the Enlightenment, is deconstructed as ideological and, in the end, it is Europe which appears to be the true aggressor. Where US historian and expert on foreign policy Robert Kagan used the godly lovers of antiquity Mars and Venus as a dichotomous image to describe warmongering US and peace-loving Europe,[78] these roles are shared out differently in Lehr's novel. While Venus is assumed by the East, in its Arabic translation "Tarik," the role of Mars, the god of war, is tellingly given to the German aesthete Martin.

References

Appadurai, Arjun. "Disjuncture and Difference in the Global Cultural Economy," *Theory Culture Society*, vol. 7, no. 2 (1990), 295–310.

Bakhtin, Mikhail. *Problems of Dostoevsky's Poetics*, ed. and transl. by Caryl Emerson, Introduction by Wayne C. Booth (Manchester: Manchester University Press, 1984).

Baudrillard, Jean. "Hypotheses on Terrorism," in Jean Baudrillard, *The Spirit of Terrorism and Other Essays*, transl. by Chris Turner (London/New York: Verso, 2002), 49–83.

———. "The Spirit of Terrorism," in Jean Baudrillard, *The Spirit of Terrorism and Other Essays*, transl. by Chris Turner (London/New York: Verso, 2002), 1–34.

Beigbeder, Frédéric. *Windows on the World* (Paris: Gallimard, 2003).

Bhabha, Homi K. *The Location of Culture* (London/New York: Routledge, 1994).

Boletsi, Maria. "Cannibalism and Literary Indigestibility: Figurations of Violence in Bart Koubaa's *De leraar*," *Journal of Dutch Literature*, vol. 3, no. 2 (2012), 39–67.

Bosse, Anke. "Magische Präsenz. Zur Funktion von Schrift und Ornament in Goethes 'West-östlichem Divan,' *Arcadia*, vol. 33, no. 2 (1998), 314–336.

---

[76] Boletsi, "Cannibalism," 53.

[77] Schneider, "The Day of the Know-it-Alls," first published in *Der Spiegel*, 23 June 2003.

[78] Kagan, *Of Paradise and Power: America and Europe in the New World Order*.

Böttiger, Helmut. "Zeitschmetterlinge. Laudatio auf Thomas Lehr zum Berliner Literaturpreis," *Akzente*, vol. 58, no. 3 (2011).
Butler, Judith. *Frames of War. When is Life Grievable?* (London/New York: Verso, 2009).
Clare, Jennifer. "'Es ist die leichte Begehbarkeit von so vielen Epochen und Kulturräumen.' '9/11' als vielstimmige mythische Episode in Thomas Lehrs Roman *September. Fata Morgana*," in Ursula Hennigfeld and Stephan Packard (eds.), *Abschied von 9/11?—Distanznahmen zur Katastrophe* (Berlin: Frank & Timme, 2013), 109–132.
Cvek, Sven. "Good Mourning, America: Genealogies of Loss in *Against the Day*," in Sylvie Mathé and Sophie Vallas (eds.), *European Perspectives on the Literature of 9/11* (Paris: Michel Houdiard Éditeur, 2014), 48–58.
Deupmann, Christoph. "'das hättest du sehen müssen, how das ding collapsed' Erzählweisen vom 11. September 2001," *literaturkritik.de*, vol. 9 (2011).
Eagleton, Terry. *After Theory* (London: Penguin Books, 2004).
Eke, Norbert Otto. "'Es gibt keinen Sieger außer Gott'. Dialog im Raum der Schrift: Thomas Lehrs Roman *September. Fata Morgana*," in Axel Dunker and Michael Hofmann (eds.), *Morgenland und Moderne. Orient-Diskurse in der deutschsprachigen Literatur von 1890 bis zur Gegenwart* (Frankfurt a. M.: Peter Lang, 2014), 205–220.
Enzensberger, Hans Magnus. "Die Wiederkehr des Menschenopfers. Der Angriff kam nicht von außen und nicht aus dem Islam," in Hilmar Hoffmann and Wilfried F. Schoeller (eds.), *Wendepunkt 11. September 2001. Terror, Islam und Demokratie* (Cologne: DuMont Literatur und Kunst Verlag, 2001), 116–121.
Goethe, Johann Wolfgang von. *Berliner Ausgabe*, 16 vols., *Poetische Werke*, vol. 2 (Berlin: Aufbau-Verlag, 1966).
Graf, Guido. "Es gibt keinen Sieger außer Gott. Goethe und der 11. September," in Toni Tholen (ed), *Literatur und Religion* (Hildesheim: Universitäts-Verlag, 2012), 117–133.
Haas, Daniel. "Es ist gut, wenn starke Symbole fallen. Ein Gespräch mit dem Schriftsteller Thomas Lehr," *Frankfurter Allgemeine Zeitung*, May 2, 2011.
Habermas, Jürgen, and Jacques Derrida. "February 15, Or, What Bind Europeans Together: Plea for a Common Foreign Policy, Beginning in Core Europe," in Daniel Levy, Max Pensky, and John Torpey (eds.), *Old Europe, New Europe, Core Europe. Transatlantic Relations After the Iraq War* (London/New York: Verso, 2005), 3–13.
Henningfeld, Ursula. "Zäsur oder Wiederkehr des Immergleichen," in Thorsten Schüller and Sascha Seiler (eds.), *Von Zäsuren und Ereignissen. Historische Einschnitte und ihre mediale Verarbeitung* (Bielefeld: transcript, 2010), 177–197.

Herrmann, Leonhard. "Die Wiederentdeckung des Kreises am Ende der Ironie. Thomas Lehrs Roman *September. Fata Morgana* als Reenactment eines zyklischen Geschichtsbewusstseins nach 9/11," *Germanisik in Ireland. Jahrbuch der/Yearbook of the Association of Third-Level Teachers of German in Ireland*, vol. 6 (2011), 41–54.

Herrmann, Meike. "Erinnerungsliteratur ohne sich erinnernde Subjekte oder Wie die Zeitgeschichte in den Roman kommt. Zu Erzähltexten von Katharina Hacker, Thomas Lehr, Tanja Dückers und Marcel Beyer," in Erhard Schütz and Wolfgang Hardtwig (eds.), *Keiner kommt davon. Zeitgeschichte in der Literatur nach 1945* (Göttingen: Vandenhoeck und Ruprecht, 2008), 251–265.

Horstkotte, Silke. "Transcending Trauma. Thomas Lehr's 9/11 Novel *September. Fata Morgana*," *Image & Narrative*, vol. 14, no. 1 (2013), 35–46.

Kagan, Robert. *Of Paradise and Power. America and Europe in the New World Order* (New York: Alfred A. Knopf, 2003).

König, Michael. "'Alles wird anders' – Der 11. September in deutscher Literatur," in Thomas Jäger (ed.), *Die Welt nach 9/11. Auswirkungen des Terrorismus auf Staatenwelt und Gesellschaft* (Zeitschrift für Außen- und Sicherheitspolitik, Sonderheft, vol. 2 (2011)), 819–841.

Krekeler, Elmar. "Die Ilias aus dem Hinterhof," *Die Welt*, October 4, 2010, https://www.welt.de/welt_print/kultur/article10062354/Die-Ilias-aus-dem-Hinterhof.html (accessed 1.11.2016).

Langner, Beatrix. "Märchen gegen Bomben," *Neue Zürcher Zeitung*, October 5, 2010, http://www.nzz.ch/maerchen-gegen-bomben-1.7822843 (accessed 1.11.2016).

Lehr, Thomas. *September. Mirage*, transl. by Mike Mitchell (London: Seagull, 2013).

———. *September. Fata Morgana* (Munich: Carl Hanser, 2010).

———. "'In Tod und Trümmern—finde' Alfred Döblins *Wallenstein*-Roman als Glanzpunkt der literarischen Kriegsberichterstattung," *Neue Rundschau*, vol. 120, no. 1 (2009), 112–121.

Lehr, Thomas, and Jürgen König, "Ein doppelt kritischer Blick," *Deutschlandradio Kultur Radiofeuilleton*, August 18, 2010, available at http://www.dradio.de/dkultur/sendungen/thema/1251128/ (accessed 17.2.2015).

Mergenthaler, Volker. "Warum die Frage 'Wie reagieren Schriftsteller auf die Terroranschläge?' auf dem Feld der deutschsprachigen Literatur die falsche Frage ist," in Ursula Hennigfeld (ed.), *Poetiken des Terrors. Narrative des 11. September 2001 im interkulturellen Vergleich* (Heidelberg: Winter, 2014), 179–196.

Nelson, Camilla. "You Can't Write a Social Novel After September 11," *New Writing*, vol. 5, no. 1 (2008), 50–64.

Osang, Alexander, and Anja Reich. *Wo warst du? Ein Septembertag in New York*. (München/Zürich: Piper, 2011).

Reinhäckel, Heike. *Traumatische Texturen. Der 11. September in der deutschen Gegenwartsliteratur* (Bielefeld: transcript, 2012).

Rohde, Carsten et al. "In der Werkstatt der Gegenwart oder Über das Romaneschreiben. Carsten Rohde und Hansgeorg Schmidt-Bergmann im Gespräch mit Thomas Lehr, Sibylle Lewitscharoff und Peter Stamm," in Carsten Rohde and Hansgeorg Schmidt-Bergmann (eds.), *Die Unendlichkeit des Erzählens. Der Roman in der deutschsprachigen Gegenwartsliteratur seit 1989* (Bielefeld: Aisthesis Verlag, 2013), 347–374.

Ott, Claudia. *Tausendundeine Nacht* (München: Beck, [10]2009).

Schneider, Peter. "The Day of the Know-it-Alls," in Daniel Levy, Max Pensky, and John Torpey (eds.), *Old Europe, New Europe, Core Europe. Transatlantic Relations After the Iraq War* (London/New York: Verso, 2005), 107–113.

Schuster, Karin. "Luftspiegelungen," *Der Freitag*, August 21, 2010.

Stühring, Jan. "Unreliability, Deception, and Fictional Facts," *Journal of Literary Theory*, vol. 5, no. 1 (2011), 95–108.

Theweleit, Klaus. *Der Knall: 11. September, das Verschwinden der Realität und ein Kriegsmodell* (Frankfurt a. M./Basel: Stroemfeld/Roter Stern, 2002).

Tremlett, Giles. "Forword. 'Welcome to Moorishland'," in Simon R. Doubleday and David Coleman (eds.), *In the Light of Medieval Spain. Islam, The West, and the Relevance of the Past* (New York: Palgrave Macmillan, 2008), xi–xx.

Zimmer, Anna. "Abschied von typischen 9/11- (Satz-)Zeichen. Multidirektionale Erinnerungen aus New York und Bagdad in Thomas Lehrs *September. Fata Morgana*," in Ursula Hennigfeld and Stephan Packard (eds.), *Abschied von 9/11?—Distanznahmen zur Katastrophe* (Berlin: Frank & Timme, 2013), 87–107.

Žižek, Slavoj. *Welcome to the Desert of the Real! Five Essays on September 11 and Related Dates* (London/New York: Verso, 2002).

Author Biography

Svenja Frank is a member of the Ph.D. programme "Text Studies" at Göttingen University, Germany, and works on the reflection of literary criticism in fictional texts. After completing her studies in European Culture, English and German Literature, she has taught Modern and Contemporary German literature at Freiburg University, the University of Latvia and Oxford University. Among her research interests are German and comparative contemporary literature, intermediality and literary theory.

Europe and Its Discontents: Intra-European Violence in Dutch Literature After 9/11

Maria Boletsi

The terrorist attacks in the United States on September 11, 2001, already seem distant in time. For many of my students in Holland, they are an indistinct childhood memory. That may be less the case in the US, where practices of commemoration keep the collective memory of these events alive. But even though in Europe direct references to what has been named "9/11" grow scarcer, life in many European societies is still dominated by discursive frameworks and sociopolitical practices in which the events of 9/11 and their aftermath have left a distinctive mark.

9/11 brought an abrupt end to the optimism that many liberal thinkers expressed in the 1990s, after the end of the Cold War and the fall of Eastern-bloc communism. As the hegemony of Western neo-liberalism, led by the US, was left unchallenged, many liberal political theorists heralded this professed post-political era in celebratory tones, epitomized by Francis Fukuyama's proclamation of the "end of history."[1] Western

---

[1] I refer here to Francis Fukuyama's book *The End of History and the Last Man* (1992).

M. Boletsi (✉)
Leiden University, Leiden, The Netherlands

politics welcomed the inauguration of a post-political world, in which violence and passions would have no place in a political life dominated by reason and consensus.[2]

Since 9/11, the confident declarations of the 1990s have been turned on their head. The fear of others—terrorists, Muslim fundamentalists, ethnic minorities, migrants, refugees—has been an animating force in politics, in both the US and Europe. After the 9/11 attacks on US soil and the subsequent attacks in Europe (such as those in London in 2003, in Paris in 2015 and 2016, in Brussels in 2016, in Manchester and in Barcelona in 2017), the fear of a violent disruption of the Western way of life produced a sense of crisis that served to support stringent anti-immigration policies and practices of biopolitical control. This politics of fear led to significant shifts in the European political landscape, that included the increased popularity of anti-immigrant populist parties and the intensification of nationalism in a time of waning nation-state sovereignty.[3]

The sense of living in perpetual crisis has been enhanced as a result of the global financial crisis of 2007–2008 and the Eurozone crisis since 2009. Eruptions of violence against the state, such as the 2005 Paris riots, the riots in Athens in December 2008, and those in London in the summer of 2011, projected an image of Europe in turmoil and drew attention to the inability of European states to achieve socio-economic stability in the face of global forces of finance capitalism. In 2015, the near break-up of the Eurozone due to the Greek debt crisis underscored Europe's internal rift between North and South and the hierarchies of power between strong and weak European states. To this landscape, one may also add the ongoing refugee crisis since the summer of 2015, which, according to Salil Shetty, Amnesty International's Secretary General, is "the worst refugee crisis of our era."[4] With millions of people primarily from Syria, but also Afghanistan, Iraq, and Sub-Saharan Africa having to flee their countries and arriving on a daily basis at Greek coasts,

---

[2] Mouffe, *On the Political*, 28, 31.

[3] For an outline of these rearrangements, see Žižek, "Liberal Multiculturalism Masks an Old Barbarism with a Human Face."

[4] Shetty's statement is quoted in an article from June 15, 2015 on the website of Amnesty International, entitled "World leaders' neglect of refugees condemns millions to death and despair," available at https://www.amnesty.org/en/latest/news/2015/06/world-leaders-neglect-of-refugees-condemns-millions-to-death-and-despair/ (accessed 10.11.2016).

current public rhetoric in Europe does not shy away from rekindling the trope of the "barbarian invasions" to refer to those "others" storming the "gates" of Fortress Europe.

Of course, the complex forces that generated these shifts in the European socio-political landscape cannot all be linked to 9/11. Nevertheless, the discourses that framed 9/11 and the politics that ensued in response to these events—particularly, the rhetoric of crisis and fear of others and the rhetoric of civilization against barbarism—have left clear imprints on current European public discourses. In the fear-driven politics of many European countries, violence is assumed to stem mainly from external others, against which Western societies try to barricade themselves.

Several novels from Europe and the US address this climate of fear and the relation between self and other in the post-9/11 era. Viken Berberian's *The Cyclist* (2003), Mohsin Hamid's *The Reluctant Fundamentalist* (2007), Salman Rushdie's *Salimar the Clown* (2005), John Updike's *Terrorist* (2006), Maurice Dantek's *Cosmos Incorporated* (2007), François Vallejo's *Métamorphoses* (2012) and Michel Houellebecq's *Soumission* [Submission] (2015) are among the novels that explore terrorism or Muslim fundamentalism after 9/11. Even in the novels that critically interrogate the climate of Islamophobia or the "civilization versus barbarism" rhetoric, the agents of violence often remain (semi-)external to the West. Violence either stems from an outside terrorist threat, confirming a divide between the forces of "good" and "evil," or from Muslims raised in Western societies (as in Updike's *Terrorist*), or it is partly linked with American politics and global capitalism (as in Hamid's *The Reluctant Fundamentalist*). But even when the implication of the US in fundamentalist violence is foregrounded, as in Hamid's novel, fundamentalism still represents a threat materialized by non-Western others.

The issue of violence in the post-9/11 *European* space has preoccupied several novels by Dutch and Flemish authors.[5] If in so-called "9/11

---

[5] Under "Dutch literature," I include novels written in Dutch by Dutch and Belgian authors. Some of the ideas, theoretical framing, and literary analyses in this chapter are drawn from two previous publications of mine (my article "Cannibalism and Literary Indigestibility: Figurations of Violence in Bart Koubaa's *De leraar*" and the book chapter "Literatuur tussen cynisme en geloof: Hedendaagse kannibalen of boze blanke mannen in *De leraar* en *De maagd Marino*"). My article "Cannibalism and Literary Indigestibility"

novels," the violent agents are usually non-Western others living within or outside Western societies,[6] recent Dutch literature addresses forms of violence that are endemic in European societies or performed by Western European subjects. In this chapter, I probe this engagement with *intra-European* violence in Dutch literature: a tendency to deflect attention away from the other as violent agent (the terrorist, the fundamentalist, the migrant) and redirect it to Europe itself as a space that generates violence. In the novels discussed in this chapter, violence is exercised by European subjects, and primarily frustrated, disillusioned white men who experience a loss of power and control. Many of these characters share a cynical attitude and an inability to believe in something: be it an ideal, worldview, religion, ideology or literature itself. Violence is for them a way of reasserting power or experiencing the intensity of the 'real' as an antidote to cynical distancing. Their violence is directed against others—especially migrants, Muslims, refugees—and in some cases against themselves.

This chapter centres on intra-European violence in five Dutch novels against the backdrop of the aforementioned climate of crisis in Europe and of recent Dutch rhetoric on migration and multiculturalism: Elvis Peeters' *De ontelbaren* [The Uncountables] (2005), Arnon Grunberg's *Tirza* (2006), Robert Anker's *Oorlogshond* [War Dog] (2011), Yves Petry's *De Maagd Marino* [The Virgin Marino] (2010), and Bart Koubaa's *De leraar* [The Teacher] (2009). In referring to forms of violence, I take up a distinction Slavoj Žižek makes between *subjective* violence, which is visible and performed by a "clearly identifiable agent"; *symbolic* violence, which is inscribed in language; and *systemic* violence, which is embedded in economic and political structures.[7] I use the term *intra-European* either for forms of subjective violence exercised

---

(2012) contains a more extensive analysis of Bart Koubaa's novel *De leraar* [The Teacher]. My chapter "Literatuur tussen cynisme en geloof" in *De lichtheid van literatuur* [The Lightness of Literature] (2015), published in Dutch, contains an extensive comparative analysis of Koubaa's novel and Yves Petry's *De maagd Marino* [The Virgin Marino].

[6]The category "9/11 novel" refers to novels "that deal directly or indirectly with the events of 9/11" (Versluys, "9/11 as a European Event: The Novels," 65). It is, however, a rather loosely defined generic category that has not received rigorous theoretical delineation.

[7]Žižek, *Violence*, 1.

by European subjects or for systemic and symbolic forms of violence, inscribed in the conceptual, cultural, political, and economic construct of Europe and its value system, which is largely indebted to Enlightenment thought. The term, however, deserves elucidation, as it contains certain problematic implications. To suggest that it is possible to clearly distinguish internal from external forms of violence in Europe would be naïve, to say the least. Such a distinction would presuppose a homogeneous European subject and could end up reinforcing an oppositional "we" versus "them" logic. Nevertheless, the qualification *intra-European*, catachrestic as it may be, can be strategically useful when theorizing a tendency in Dutch novels to foreground the violent underside of European liberal discourse and subjectivity. The novels under discussion, of course, not only address European-wide discourses that have been shaped or intensified in the aftermath of 9/11. They also respond to the particularities of the Dutch and Belgian contexts, which I also discuss.

By engaging with current European realities, the novels in this chapter also raise the question of literature's function in present-day Europe. The role of literature in the so-called post-9/11 era has been an object of heated debate, especially in the American context. As Richard Gray argues in an article on American prose after 9/11, "Open Doors, Closed Minds: American Prose Writing at a Time of Crisis," literary responses to 9/11 generally acknowledge that the "old mindset has been destroyed or at least seriously challenged," but "[w]e are still, perhaps, waiting for a fictional measure of the new world view" (132). If fiction assumes the task of expressing this new vision, Gray diagnoses the failure of many novels written soon after 9/11 to deal with new dilemmas and challenges. Although many novels recognize the need for new "imaginative structures" that can "register the contemporary crisis," they do no really "act on that recognition" and fail to move beyond the "preliminary stages of trauma" (130, 134). Gray calls for a fiction of "critical multiculturalism" that would grasp the internal differences of American culture and open up "the territory of American writing by radical deterritorialisation" (146).[8]

---

[8] "Critical multiculturalism" is a term Michael Rothberg uses to describe Gray's proposal (Rothberg, "A Failure of the Imagination: Diagnosing the Post-9/11 Novel, A Response to Richard Gray," 153). The other quoted phrases in this sentence are Gray's. Lucy Bond shares Gray's critical view of 9/11 novels. In her view, American literature approached 9/11 not as an event of global historical magnitude, but as a catalyst for private events

How do these Dutch novels, then, envision literature's role in post-9/11 Holland, Belgium, and Europe? Do they offer a European version of Gray's "critical multiculturalism" and do they devise new "imaginative structures" for capturing the challenges and contradictions of European realities? This chapter unravels their search for a renewed role for literature in the contemporary European context, in which the echoes of 9/11 are still at work.

The Rhetoric of Truth and Other Fictions

At the dawn of the new millennium, the image of Holland as a successful multicultural society gave way to a new image, reflected in a much-discussed article by Paul Scheffer in the Dutch newspaper *NRC Handelsblad* in January 2000, entitled "The multicultural drama." According to this new vision, Holland's preceding happy multiculturalist profile supposedly constituted a hypocritical covering of the truth about multiculturalism and the failed integration of migrants, which now had to be exposed. The Dutch philosopher Baukje Prins termed this rhetoric "new realism." In the rhetoric of new realism, which has been popular in Dutch public debates on integration and multiculturalism at least since the beginning of the twenty-first century, there is recourse to an undisputed notion of reality that people should dare to address 'as it is,' without hiding behind relativist approaches and nuanced arguments. The new 'truth' and 'ugly reality' about multiculturalism served as legitimation for the tightening of immigration laws and proposals for anti-immigration (and anti-Islamic) measures by right-wing politicians in Holland and Belgium.

The rhetoric that appeals to authenticity, directness, and a straightforward notion of reality and truth is certainly not exclusive to Holland. It has a wider reach in the current political climate in Western Europe and the US. It was reflected, for example, in Donald Trump's rhetoric during the American presidential election campaign: even when Trump's statements were contradictory or clashed with the facts, his appeal to

---

and personal traumas, to which the attacks formed a suitable background ("Compromised Critique: A Meta-critical Analysis of American Studies after 9/11," 750). Most works, Bond argues, shunned critical historical explorations and indulged in an "overpersonalization of history" (753).

supporters was based on the perception that he "tells it as it is." In these versions of the rhetoric of "new realism," controversial, morally disputable and even racist or discriminatory language enters mainstream politics under the guise of a supposed uncovering of an uncomfortable truth. This rhetoric also marked American responses to 9/11. Immediately after the attacks, many stressed the need, even the moral imperative, to acknowledge an uncontested notion of reality. Commentators proclaimed the end of the postmodern "age of irony," while relativism was considered morally reprehensible, certainly when it came to facing the reality of the attacks and the evil nature of the enemy.[9] The terrorist attacks on US and European soil, and the ensuing politics, unleashed a *desire* in the West for the false security of absolute truths—a desire that also underlies the Dutch rhetoric of new realism.

This rhetoric tends to rely on familiar and simplistic narratives that produce certain realities as self-evident. One of these narratives is that of civilization versus barbarism, which was pivotal in the rhetoric of the Bush administration after 9/11, but has also been popular in Europe. Civilizational rhetoric since 9/11 constructs a series of metonymical associations, through which civilization is identified with the West or with Europe and its values, and barbarism with terrorism, Muslim fundamentalism, or non-liberal societies. This narrative, combined with explicit references to 9/11, was used, for example, to frame the shootings in the satirical newspaper *Charlie Hebdo* in Paris by two members of an Islamist terrorist group on January 7, 2015. Although many rushed to denounce an "us" versus "them" rhetoric that would enhance anti-Muslim sentiments in France and Europe, the civilization versus barbarism narrative and the trauma discourse that framed 9/11 were immediately mobilized for this event. The following article headings are telling: "Will Charlie Hebdo Become the French 9/11?"; "Paris Attack is Europe's 9/11"; "Charlie Hebdo Attack: Refining the Post-9/11 Model"; "Why Paris is Calling the Charlie Hebdo Attack France's 9/11."[10] In official reactions to the shooting by governments worldwide, the term "barbaric" is by far the most popular qualifier for the

---

[9] See also Boletsi, *Barbarism and Its Discontents*, 48, "Still Waiting for Barbarians after 9/11? Cavafy's Reluctant Irony and the Language of the Future," 65, and Vaessens, *De revanche van de roman: Literatuur, autoriteit en engagement*, 69.

[10] See Platov, Yetkin, Dorsey, and Massi respectively.

event.[11] The term also regularly pops up as a self-evident characterization of the event in the international press. Remarkably, however, the same term scarcely comes up in responses to other violent incidents in Europe that are unrelated to Muslim fundamentalism, such as the bloodbath in Norway on July 2011, during which Anders Breivik killed 77 people to call attention to his view that Muslim immigration should stop.[12] The narrative of civilized Europe versus barbaric others seems less suitable to frame such cases. Such discrepancies suggest a reluctance to face barbaric violence as endemic to Europe.

Even thinkers who are critical of fear-driven politics in Europe often endorse the identification of Europe with civilization. In *The Fear of Barbarians* (2010), philosopher Tzvetan Todorov, for example, draws attention to the violence generated by our fear of others in the West since 9/11. His central thesis is that our fear of barbarians threatens to turn us into barbarians. The military interventions in Afghanistan, Iraq, and elsewhere under the banner of the War on Terror demonstrate the dangers of giving in to this fear. Anti-immigration policies and xenophobia in Europe after 9/11 are manifestations of the same fear. When "we" (by "we," Todorov refers to Europe) set out to defend democratic and humanist values, we end up betraying them (106).

For Todorov, such instances of violence are contrary to the spirit of Europe itself. Todorov locates European identity in a non-hierarchical, non-hegemonic plurality: the way Europe accommodates "regional, national, religious and cultural identities" and allows the coexistence of different perspectives forms the basis for European unity (174). In his vision, "the idea of civilization merges into that of Europe" (195). When Europe deviates from these values by exercising violence, this is undoubtedly barbaric. But in Todorov's vision, instances of intra-European violence constitute exceptions in a narrative of Europe as synonymous with civilization.[13]

---

[11] Based on the responses listed in the Wikipedia article entitled "International Reactions to the Charlie Hebdo Shooting," available at https://en.wikipedia.org/wiki/International_reactions_to_the_Charlie_Hebdo_shooting (accessed 10.11.2016).

[12] This observation is based on a rudimentary Internet search I have conducted.

[13] For a more extensive discussion of Todorov's argument, see Boletsi, *Barbarism and Its Discontents*, 52–55.

The novels I discuss in the following intervene in the above debates on the present and future of Europe and test Europe's image as plural, rational, self-critical, and open to otherness by juxtaposing it with different narratives.

From Genocide to Cannibalism: Dutch Novels and the Other Europe

De Ontelbaren [The Uncountables]

De ontelbaren [The Uncountables] by Flemish author Elvis Peeters materializes a scenario that underlies the rhetoric of fear of others since 9/11: endless streams of refugees enter Europe. The novel zooms in on the repercussions of this 'invasion' in a small Belgian village. The anxiety these others raise in the local inhabitants eventually leads to unspeakable genocidal violence against them.

The novel comprises three parts. The first and third short parts are narrated by an unidentified male refugee. In the first part, this narrator recounts parts of his risky journey as he tries to enter Europe. The narration unravels in a flat, unemotional tone, despite the chilling violence his narrative involves. In the second and main part we are transferred to a peaceful Flemish village, in which one day groups of refugees appear in the streets in search of shelter. An external narrator takes over in this part, but there is a constant switch of perspectives, as various villagers focalize different parts of the narrative. As Liesbeth Minnaard notes in her analysis of the novel, the switch from the cruel, lawless world of the first part to the familiar landscape of the Flemish countryside in the second part has a reassuring function—a reassurance, however, that evaporates as soon as the world of the refugees penetrates the "safe haven" of this prosperous European community.[14] As the numbers of refugees gradually grow out of control, so do problems and tensions in the local society. With countless people seeking shelter, food, and the satisfaction of basic needs, the local authorities and inhabitants find themselves at a loss. All standards of normality and familiar social structures disintegrate. Prosperity gives way to subhuman living conditions. Life in the village reverts to a quasi-primitive state, until the last bastions of tolerance and humanity break down and violence aimed at eradicating the refugee-problem becomes more and more severe.

---

[14] Minnaard, "Wij, zij, jullie…Over de grenzen van gastvrijheid in Elvis Peeters' roman *De ontelbaren*," 58.

The third part returns to the voice of the anonymous refugee, this time located in a post-apocalyptic landscape, as the Flemish village has now been razed to the ground, leaving "ashes everywhere, scorched earth, smoldering wreckage."[15] The novel can be read as a literary intervention to the rhetoric of fear of migrants, which has acquired new impetus due to the ongoing "refugee crisis" in Europe since 2015. Images showing crowds of newly arrived refugees in Greece under dreadful conditions almost tempt one to read Peeters's novel as prophetic. Many of the refugees from Syria and Africa who survive the boat trip and get through the borders try to continue their journey towards Western Europe. If readers in 2005 read the novel as an exaggerated scenario that will hopefully never come true, the inability of many European governments and institutions to deal with the current refugee crisis bears ominous signs for the future.[16] The cynicism in the responses of many European governments and part of the media to this crisis and the way the rhetoric of the "barbarian invasions" has been rekindled in some of these responses make Peeters's novel particularly topical. The controversial anti-immigration poster used by the United Kingdom Independence Party (UKIP) as part of their Brexit campaign for the referendum held in the UK in June 2016 on whether Great Britain should leave the European Union epitomizes this rhetoric visually. The poster shows thousands of Syrian refugees marching on their perilous journey towards Western Europe. The phrase "Breaking point" is printed with red letters on the image, which is captioned with the sentence "We must break free of the EU and take back control of our borders." *De ontelbaren* takes the violent implications of this rhetoric to an extreme and shows how thin the line is between tolerance and hostility in times of crisis.[17]

---

[15] Peeters, *De ontelbaren*, 173.

[16] An Amnesty International report refers to "the response of the international community" as "a shameful failure" (from an Amnesty International report entitled "The Global Refugee Crisis: A Conspiracy of Neglect," quoted in Shaheen, "World leaders accused of shameful failure over refugee crisis," n.p.).

[17] See also Minnaard, "Wij, zij, jullie...Over de grenzen van gastvrijheid in Elvis Peeters' roman *De ontelbaren*," 65. For an extensive analysis of the ways in which the novel magnifies and hyperbolizes the rhetoric of doom and fear of migrants, see Minnaard, "'Pas op, ze komen...' De uitvergroting van een publiek doemscenario in Elvis Peeters' roman *De ontelbaren*."

In the novel, a stark conceptual division is at work between the "autochthonous" population—those who see themselves as the rightful inhabitants of the country—and the "allochthonous" others, who, from the perspective of the former, have no legitimate share in European prosperity and disrupt the ethnic purity of the autochthonous group.[18] The "autochthonous" group, as Minnaard observes, is presented as heterogeneous, since the novel's main part presents us with the diverse, conflicting perspectives of various Flemish villagers.[19] The refugees, however, are presented as a homogeneous group, regardless of their points of origin: they are cast as groups or crowds, not individuals. The villagers often dismiss their voices as incomprehensible, as in the following example, in which Ward, a family man, tries to keep the intruders away from his home:

> They said something. Ward tried English, German, French, they just gestured, heavily, pointing inside, to the garden. [...] Ward could do nothing else but pretend that he didn't understand them. He closed the door. (Peeters 81)[20]

Ward does not engage with them, even though he understands what they want. His perception of their speech as noise, and thus as irrational and illegitimate, recalls the etymology of the word "barbarian" in ancient Greek, referring to someone whose speech sounds like an incomprehensible mumbling ("bar bar bar").

The reader may identify with the villagers' perspectives and experience their dilemmas and growing frustration. After all, many of them are cast as common, caring, reasonable people. However, as their tolerance runs out, the barbaric face of their liberal values manifests itself. As the 'state of exception' in which they find themselves becomes permanent, the villagers resort to extreme measures, legitimized by their construction of

---

[18] The distinction between *autochthonous* and *allochthonous* citizens (both words of Greek origin, which refer to people from the same and from another land, respectively) is a common distinction in the Dutch language, decisive for determining notions of national identity and belonging. In public rhetoric, the use of these categories suggests that autochthonous citizens have a birthright to the country as opposed to allochthonous citizens (even when the latter are second-generation immigrants).

[19] Minnaard, "Wij, zij, jullie…Over de grenzen van gastvrijheid in Elvis Peeters' roman *De ontelbaren*," 59.

[20] Throughout this chapter, all translations from the Dutch are mine. This quote is also discussed in Minnaard, "Wij, zij, jullie…Over de grenzen van gastvrijheid in Elvis Peeters' roman *De ontelbaren*," 64.

'the others' as barbarians, animals, insects.²¹ "We have come to delouse," says one of the men that knocks on someone else's door asking him to lead him to the refugees who live under his roof.²² Villagers decide to take matters into their own hands and "cleanse" the village of the invaders. The lack of empathy that results from the others' dehumanization triggers extreme violence.

But if the dehumanization of refugees in the novel seems extreme, one need only read the novel alongside callous attitudes to refugees in the current crisis. Such attitudes are exemplified in a May 27, 2015 article from the British newspaper *Daily Mail*, entitled "Holiday makers' misery as asylum seekers turn Kos into hellhole."²³ The article describes the situation on the Greek island of Kos—a popular tourist destination—on which thousands of refugees arrived in the summer of 2015. In the article, descriptions of the situation on the island as "disgusting" and "a nightmare" (for tourists and holiday makers) and of Kos as "paradise lost" betray an utter absence of empathy for the refugees' misery. The situation is viewed solely from the perspective of tourists and holiday makers. The perspectives both of the refugees and the local population are erased, trumped by the tourists' 'suffering.' Refugees are objectified as disgusting intruders who spoil the paradise-like island. A newspaper such as the *Daily Mail* may express only a particular portion of public opinion, yet the absence of empathy in this article is not an exception. The inaction of European governments and the disregard for human lives lost at sea during the refugee crisis are a manifestation of a comparable lack of empathy in politics.²⁴

Peeters's novel plays with the dangerous ramifications of giving in to fear and failing to relate to the other in times of crisis. The way the

---

²¹ A detailed analysis of the way the novel exemplifies Giorgio Agamben's notion of "state of exception" and shows that we are all potential *homines sacri*, see Minnaard, "Wij, zij, jullie…Over de grenzen van gastvrijheid in Elvis Peeters' roman *De ontelbaren*," 61–65.

²² Peeters, *De ontelbaren*, 146.

²³ At http://www.dailymail.co.uk/news/article-3099736/Holidaymakers-misery-boat-people-Syria-Afghanistan-seeking-asylum-set-migrant-camp-turn-popular-Greek-island-Kos-disgusting-hellhole.htmlx.

²⁴ See, for example, the article by Ignaas Devisch on the cynicism of Europeans and their disregard for refugee lives in the Belgian magazine *Knack*, characteristically entitled "The core of our cynicism: We don't give a damn about bodies washed up daily" (my translation from the Dutch).

book concretizes the violence generated from the 'reasonable' attitudes of civilized European citizens is likely to shock readers into imagining alternative ways of relating to others. This shock is enhanced by the novel's conjuration of historical spectres: that of the Holocaust and South-African apartheid. References, for example, to "clearance operations" evoke the raids of German troops looking for Jews or resistance fighters in World War II. Descriptions of the building of walls around European cities, which people without a special "pass" cannot go through without risking execution, allude to the internal passport system known as "pass laws" during apartheid.[25] The evocation of these violent historical chapters stirs the still waters of historical amnesia on which the contemporary benign image of Europe rests. "The romance of the European Union," Sadia Abbas writes, "was always to enable a certain amnesia," a selective suppression of Europe's past.[26] "When Europeans talk about the ideals of peace and prosperity, of forgetting the violence of the two world wars," Abbas continues, "it is hard not to see this as a remarkable exercise in the creation of a collective innocence fully dependent upon an erasure of the past" (n.p.). The historical memories with which the fictional scenario of *The Uncountables* is invested complicate this narrative of Europe's innocence and redirect attention from the threat of violence against Europe to the violence Europe itself can generate.

The novel presents Europe in a state of emergency, with democratic laws and human rights suspended. Its scenario may be hyperbolic, but it offers a glimpse of the possible implications of living in a state of unending crisis. As Agamben argues in a recent interview, the "concept 'crisis' has indeed become a motto of modern politics, and for a long time it has been part of normality in any segment of social life."[27] The threat of terrorism, the debt crisis, the Eurozone crisis, the refugee crisis in Europe are all symptomatic of the construction of *crisis* as a permanent state in present-day Europe. As Agamben notes, the idea of crisis is mobilized to legitimize "political and economic decisions that in fact

---

[25] Kaptein, *Elvis Peeters' roman* De ontelbaren *als kritiek op het (im)migratiedebat in Nederland en Vlaanderen*, 29.

[26] In her article, Abbas refers particularly to the past of European colonialism: this past, which lives on in contemporary neo-liberal practices of the European Union, is suppressed so that Europeans can maintain the fiction of a "benign Europe," she argues.

[27] Agamben, "The Endless Crisis as an Instrument of Power: In Conversation with Giorgio Agamben," n.p.

dispossess citizens and deprive them of any possibility of decision."[28] This state of "unending crisis," Agamben continues, "is incompatible with democracy." The novel's casting of Europe as a violent continent out of control materialises the destructive ramifications of this use of crisis. The novel, however, not only conveys gloomy prospects for Europe's future. Its rekindling of historical memories as disturbingly familiar motifs in the estranging European landscape it sketches serves not only as a warning, but also as a possible alternative to the scenario of doom: Europe might exit the state of crisis if it stays in critical dialogue with its own history, including the violent, disturbing chapters thereof. As Agamben also argues, such a dialogue with history is essential if Europe wants to become a kind of culture that stays "human and vital."[29]

Tirza

If violence in *De ontelbaren* takes the form of mass killings committed by European citizens, the other novels I discuss focus on individual agents of violence: middle-aged or older white men. In Arnon Grunberg's *Tirza*, the protagonist, Jörgen Hofmeester, is a middle-aged man who considers emotions "the curse of this time" and "a belief that has to be overcome" (37). He tries hard to maintain civil manners and socially acceptable behaviour—"[t]he eternal need to appear civilised under all circumstances," as he calls it (269).[30] Hofmeester works as an editor of translated fiction. Not long before his retirement, however, he is made redundant by his employer, who still pays him until his retirement age but dismisses him from all tasks. His redundancy is amplified by an intense sense of emptiness when his youngest daughter Tirza is about to leave the house after graduating from high school in order to travel to Africa with her Moroccan boyfriend, Choukri. Hofmeester is fixated on Tirza, who fulfils the role of a wife and a daughter at the same time, even though he has no sexual relations with her. She is Hofmeester's project

---

[28] Ibid.

[29] Ibid.

[30] *Tirza* is the only Dutch novel discussed in this article that has been published in English translation (by Sam Garrett). Translations from the book in this chapter are, however, mine.

and endows his life with meaning. Having heard nothing from her for a few weeks after her departure, he heads to Africa in search of her. As he wanders in Africa, the reader suspects that he may be involved in the couple's disappearance. The suspicion is confirmed: Tirza and Choukri never made it to Africa. During their stay in Hofmeester's cottage just before he was to take them to the airport, he brutally murdered Tirza and Choukri, whom he hated for taking his daughter away from him.

Hofmeester's life revolves around power and control. He does his best to repress emotions and maintain the semblance of civilized behaviour, terrified at the thought that others may judge him. Since the narrative unravels from his perspective—there is a third-person narrator, but Hofmeester is the focalizer—the reader gets a glimpse of his inner world, where aggression, rage, and a racist mind-set form the undercurrent of a civilized and modest exterior. His violent instincts and drive for power only find a symbolic outlet through fantasy and role-play.[31] A few violent outbursts, such as the beating of his tenant when he catches him and his oldest daughter having sex, betray his repressed rage, enhancing the reader's sense of foreboding that a worst outburst is still to come.

His sense of loss of control takes a turn for the worst after the life savings he invested in a hedge fund to secure his daughters' future evaporate as a result of the turmoil of the global economy after 9/11. The "world economy" is an abstract "enemy without face and without name" (175), an enemy Hofmeester cannot fight or control (176). Having no means of countering the elusive forces of finance capitalism, he has to hypostatize the enemy by giving him a face and a name: that name is Mohammed Atta, hijacker-pilot and ringleader of the 9/11 attacks. Just as the Bush administration after 9/11 turned Osama Bin Laden into a synecdoche for an ungraspable new enemy—global terrorism—Hofmeester substitutes the "world economy" with "Atta": "The anonymous world economy acquired a face, a body, a name. Mohammed Atta: he deprived Hofmeester of his money, his financial independence, the freedom for his children which was so close, so terribly close. Mohammed Atta was behind this, Atta decapitated Hofmeester's hedge fund."[32]

---

[31] In a game he used to play with his wife, for example, he was the rapist in the park and she the victim (e.g., 364).

[32] Grunberg, *Tirza*, 176.

He goes further in his metonymic substitutions: when he meets Tirza's Muslim boyfriend, he sees him as the spitting image of Atta, a "doppelgänger" (202). This (pseudo)-identification turns Choukri into his arch-enemy: the one who took his life away (his life savings) and has now returned to steal his daughter. Hofmeester refers to Choukri as "Atta" throughout the narrative: he refuses to see him as an individual. Choukri's attempts to dissociate himself from the stereotype of the Muslim other, which determines Hofmeester's gaze, falls on deaf ears: "'I determine who I am,' *Atta* says. 'I am Choukri. I play guitar. I love your daughter. This is who I am. The 'other' has nothing to do with it'" (296, emphasis added). In a series of absurd synecdochic substitutions, the original enemy—global economy—becomes 9/11, then Mohammed Atta, then every Muslim, then Tirza's Moroccan boyfriend. Although all indications point to Choukri as a caring, respectful, kind man who deviates from stereotypes attached to Muslims after 9/11—for example, he is not religious—Hofmeester only sees him as a type: the Muslim terrorist. Even in the moments before Hofmeester kills him with a chainsaw, he ignores Choukri's cry that he is not Mohammed Atta and mocks his supposed faith, even though Choukri has stated he is agnostic (299):

> "Atta, who do you think is stronger, Allah or the MS 170? Pray to Allah, perhaps he will come to help you. Or to the prophet, maybe he will come to your help, Atta." But he didn't want to pray. He refused to pray. Can you imagine that? I tore a page from the Koran and said: "If you don't want to pray, you will eat, Atta." I shoved the page in his mouth. (404)[33]

Perceiving the situation as a hunting game, Hofmeester has to dehumanize Choukri in order to treat him like a beast. His words to Choukri are surrounded by the signifier "Atta," which emphatically form the beginning and the end of his address to him, as this signifier filters his perception of the 'enemy.' Choukri's reaction—his refusal to pray, and, soon after, his denial of Hofmeester's appellation ("I am not Mohamed Atta. I am not Mohammed Atta," 405)—underscores the discrepancy between Hofmeester's and Choukri's perspectives. The colonially inflected narrative of the white father trying to save his talented daughter who is seduced by a brown Muslim is so intensely experienced by Hofmeester

---

[33] Hofmeester speaks here to a little girl, Kaisa, who accompanies him in his journey in Africa.

that it becomes his only reality. The associations that shape Hofmeester's reality mimic the absurd game of metonymical substitutions in Western rhetoric after 9/11 that turned each Muslim into a (potential) terrorist. However, the actual enemy at the origin of Hofmeester's metonymical associations remains ungraspable and uninhibited in its workings: the world economy.

Hofmeester's actions, behaviour, and inner life are cast through a vocabulary of pathology and decay. He refers to himself as a "wreck" and a "broken" man who "has to learn to die" (e.g., 287, 304); he talks about the "curse" he has been carrying his whole life (e.g., 152) and the "sickness" that he is (e.g., 236). His pathological love for Tirza whom he keeps under constant watch, leads to her developing an eating disorder: starving herself almost to death is her attempt to disengage herself from her father's clutches and regain control of her life. Hofmeester comes to see himself as the source of her sickness: "I am what made Tirza sick, I am the sickness of the white middle class" (377). Hofmeester signifies the malaise and dark side of the white middle class: "Happiness is a pose, a myth, a form of politeness, in parties, during dinners. I am unhappy, but not unhappier than others [...] My unhappiness was average. I have two children. A nice house. A very nice house" (354). The designation "average" casts him as the rule, not the exception of his class. The average bourgeois dream of a nice home and family reveals itself as a sugar-coated nightmare.

Hofmeester correlates his unhappiness with a loss of faith. Having lost his personal ambition, which used to be his faith, he can no longer believe in anything. This condition is not only his own; it is the predicament of the "we" he belongs to, that of the white European middle class: "Look at us, Kaisa. What are we? People without faith" [...] I wander through space. I am not attached to anyone" (365). The lack of a convincing narrative to live by and a certain feebleness of faith have often been diagnosed as the predicament of the Western liberal subject, especially in the context of so-called postmodern relativism. The need for, and inability to construct, a new narrative were intensified after 9/11.[34] Eruptions of fundamentalist violence in the West since

---

[34] In the US, attacks against postmodern irony and relativism as weakening the nation's ability to show faith and commitment to a cause were already underway before 9/11 (see, for example, Purdy, *For Common Things: Irony, Trust, and Commitment in America Today*). But such critiques of postmodernism acquired new impetus after 9/11 (see Roger

9/11, Terry Eagleton contends, confront the West with a contradiction: "the West's own need to believe and its chronic incapacity to do so".³⁵ While for the fundamentalist 'enemy' commitment, dogmatism, and absolute truths are a given, Eagleton argues, Western subjects have abandoned grand narratives and metaphysical foundations for scepticism and irony (141f.). According to Eagleton, this "liberal lukewarmness about belief may turn into a predicament at times of crisis" (145).³⁶ Hofmeester's rage against Choukri, whom he unjustly constructs as a full-blooded metaphysical enemy—a non-liberal other with a blind belief in the Koran—may be read as a desperate attempt to compensate for his own lack of faith through excessive violence: "Atta, who do you think is stronger, Allah or the MS 170?" (404). This question, moments before he murders Choukri, confronts divine power with that of technology (the chainsaw). Here, Western modernity and technological progress, which have killed and replaced God, unleash destructive violence merely aimed at a display of power.

Hofmeester's journey through Africa is an attempted escape from the constraints of a civilization that yields unhappiness. His travel companion is a little Namibian girl named Kaisa, who approaches him and follows him everywhere. Although he knows that his appearance with this girl in public may raise eyebrows, his obsession with societal judgement evaporates outside European space: "What they think of him is unimportant. Here in Namibia they can think anything" (367).

If Choukri's protests did not impede Hofmeester's construction of him as an evil Muslim, Kaisa's silence—which Hofmeester interprets as acceptance—also turns her into a blank slate on which Hofmeester inscribes his own story. If the "Muslim" represents for him the *threatening* other *to European civilization, Africa, in his vision, is the outside* of this civilization. Hofmeester's self-image is premised on a racist deprecation of Europe's others, typecast as either the 'dangerous Muslim enemy'

Rosenblatt's denunciation of "the age of irony" after 9/11, "The Age of Irony Comes to an End," and Stanley Fish's defense of postmodern relativism against such attacks, "Don't Blame Relativism").

³⁵ Eagleton, *Reason, Faith, and Revolution*, 141.

³⁶ The age-old religiously invested narrative of "good versus evil," popular in the rhetoric of the Bush administration after 9/11, was a problematic attempt to adapt an old narrative to a new situation. This rhetoric, however, found less fertile ground in Europe, where political rhetoric tends to be less receptive to a religious vocabulary than in the US.

or the 'silent African other' devoid of culture, history, and humanity. The following address to Kaisa is telling in that respect: "You are nothing. Even if someone would end your life, it would not hurt you. In fact, you are already dead" (385). But just as his construction of Choukri as an "evil Muslim" fails to convince the reader, his Western construction of Africa also cannot hold up. The image of an old, defeated white man next to a silent African girl becomes a confrontation of the European man of progress next to the Eurocentric image of Africa as the childhood of humanity—an image that found one of its most memorable expressions in Hegel.[37] Contrary to the European narrative of progress, however, here both figures emerge as futureless: the homeless girl who grows dependent on Hofmeester and follows him around in silence; and Hofmeester who has killed not only his supposed Muslim enemy but also his daughter, and thereby his own future. As a European man, Hofmeester proves unable to represent the 'adulthood' of humanity. As he comes to realize, "he was never, in fact, anything else than a nine-year-old [...] approximately as old as Kaisa" (421): "the adult Hofmeester, the editor of translated fiction" was "a role" that this nine-year-old perfected in the course of his life (420). Africa may appear as an empty space outside civilization (the desert, the silence of Kaisa) on which Hofmeester can freely re-narrate his life-story and then disappear. But Africa does not fully succumb to his wishes. Kaisa is unresponsive and therefore neither validates nor disproves his projections. Through her silence, she refuses to grant him access to her inner self. And despite her silence, her role is not solely passive: when he tries to disappear, she comes after him and drags him back from the desert. Africa does not allow him to vanish, drown his guilt in oblivion, and die in the desert, as he planned. In the end, he has to return to Holland.

Hofmeester's self-descriptions throughout the narrative seem contradictory: his self-identity as "civilized" sits alongside references to himself

---

[37] Hegel writes in his Introduction to *The Philosophy of History*: "Africa proper, as far as History goes back, has remained—for all purposes of connection with the rest of the World—shut up. It is the Gold-land compressed within itself—the land of *childhood*, which, lying beyond the day of self-conscious history, is enveloped in the dark mantle of Night" (91, emphasis added). And later on: "At this point we leave Africa, not to mention it again. For it is no historical part of the World; it has no movement or development to exhibit. Historical movements in it—that is in its northern part—belong to the Asiatic or European World" (99).

as a "beast," a "sickness," a "curse," and a "monster" (e.g., 152, 236, 254, 407). These contradictions typify the European civilization as such rather than cast Hofmeester as a deviation from it. "I am a product of civilisation," the protagonist exclaims as he tries to disappear in the desert (410). Significantly, he identifies himself not as "sick" but as an embodiment of "the sickness" itself: "That is the difference between the adjective and the noun. The sickness has to remain sickness. I am the noun" (388). A sick person can be cured, while the locus of the sickness is outside the patient. As sickness personified, however, Hofmeester hints at European civilization's inherent disease. Rather than the victim of an external disease that contaminates this civilization, Hofmeester casts the civilization that produced him as the source of a sickness that destroys not only others but itself, like an autoimmune disease.

Oorlogshond [War Dog]

In Robert Anker's *Oorlogshond* [War Dog], we come across another white male protagonist who finds a source of energy and power in violence. The protagonist is a tough, virile man who works as a high school teacher of classical languages and literature. His real name is not revealed but he is referred to as "Michiel de Ruyter"—a Dutch admiral and hero in Dutch history, who scored several victories against the French and particularly the English during the Anglo-Dutch wars in the seventeenth century. Michiel's life story is narrated by his biographer, who follows him around. He employs controversial teaching methods: he believes that students do not need empathetic or lenient teachers, but authoritative figures they can look up to. Driven by a Nietzschean worldview, he tries to train his students into becoming an intellectual elite so that they can be leaders rather than followers. A firm believer in a life of freedom without taboos, he regularly engages in fighting, drug use, and orgies with students. In the second part of the novel, he leaves Holland to fight as a mercenary in Africa, where he becomes part of a commando group and gets involved in barbaric acts of violence. Upon his return to Holland, his addiction to violence leads him to join the separatist fight of the fictive province of Saumerland who wants to gain independence from Holland. He shaves his head in imitation of Pim Fortuyn, the controversial anti-Muslim right-wing Dutch politician who was assassinated in 2002 and is one of Michiel's idols. Like another Pim Fortuyn, he taps into his charismatic qualities in order to lead the local population in their revolt.

Michiel's life-story comprises many inconsistent chapters. The red thread in his actions is his unstoppable fury. Rage is for him a source of happiness that helps him move forward.[38] Subscribing to a Nietzschean philosophy that distrusts reason, he sees rage as the driving force of European civilization. The following excerpt from one of his lessons to his students epitomizes his view on European progress and modernity:

> Jesus preached forgiveness instead of revenge, love instead of hatred, humility instead of pride. But our Western culture would have never moved a step further if we had kept to that. Not the monk but the knight has brought us further. Ambition, self-assertion, the deep need for recognition, haughtiness even, and pride—all that, let's say "the fury of Achilles," the battle, that has brought the world forward, also in the negative sense of course, think of the fury of Hitler, Mao, Stalin. This has baffled us because after the Enlightenment we thought reason would keep barbarism at bay, but, guess what, it didn't. Hitler's fury [...] was, by the way, quite rationally organised.[39]

Michiel recaps a narrative of European modernity that debunks Christian morality and Enlightenment values. Barbarism, rage, violence, are neither external to the European project nor the opposites of reason, love, and humility. Rather, they are constitutive of European progress. Hitler's barbarism was a product of European reason. Enlightenment values and Christian morality may be the means for the self-legitimation of European civilization, but its actual mobilizing force is rage; a drive to unrestricted violence. Given that rage also runs Michiel's life, he emerges as a prototypical figure of (the other face of) Western civilization.

But is he a hero or an anti-hero? Even though he calls himself after a Dutch hero, his actions, instead of glorifying his heroism, are more likely to 'contaminate' the Dutch heroic narrative of Michiel de Ruyter with suggestions of illegitimate violence and questionable motives. A 2015

---

[38] Discussing the rage of Achilles in Homer's *Iliad*, he tells his students: "Rage [in the *Iliad*] is considered as a positive force, not as something to be ashamed of because you couldn't restrain yourself, but as a primordial force that brings happiness" (Anker, *Oorlogshond*, 22).

[39] Anker, *Oorlogshond*, 23.

Dutch film on Michiel de Ruyter, largely successful in Holland, sought to consolidate his positive image as a Dutch national icon.[40] By appropriating de Ruyter's name, the protagonist of *Oorlogshond* invites a revisiting of Dutch nationalism through Holland's colonial past. The Dutch naval hero could also be read as a ruthless colonialist, a racist, and a key figure in the consolidation of the Dutch slave trade. European progress and heroism, it seems, are built on a system of exploitation.

Is Michiel then projected as a figure the reader should identify with, just as Michiel expects his own students to do? Does Michiel invite readers to follow his musings or to challenge his authority? His status remains ambivalent: some readers might find him fascinating, while others will find him arrogant, appalling, dangerous. Either way, Michiel's attitudes and views in the novel are not particularly original. He joins a series of European thinkers who have questioned European progress. He adopts Nietzsche's perspective on the Greek classics. He quotes and discusses Euripides, Plato, Dante, Martin Heidegger, Joseph Conrad, and a wide array of thinkers and literary authors from the Western (and Dutch) canon. He is in fact a composite of certain bits and pieces of the European tradition, which highlight its discontents.

His actions and statements do not always add up and do not seem to rest on a firm faith in an ideal. His fury is the *source* of his actions, not the *means* to a (noble or ignoble) goal. His deeds are often inconsistent with the Western philosophies he privileges in his teachings. For example, while he trains his students to become an elite that masters others, in the last part he becomes a fervent defender of the rights of the 'people' of the province of Saumerland. As Anker himself remarks in an interview about his protagonist, "[i]n fact, he does not give a damn [what the goal of his actions is], as long as he is in motion."[41]

Just as the protagonist in *Tirza* associates his sickness with a loss of faith, Michiel, though in a different way, also projects the Western subject's inability to construct a convincing new narrative after the postmodern debunking of metaphysical foundations. Michiel's controversial response to this predicament—suggesting that underneath all actions, fights, and revolutionary projects there is no faith or project but the energy of violence for violence's sake—is hardly promising.

---

[40] The film was directed by Roel Reiné and was a big success with Dutch audiences.

[41] Anker in Velzen, "De wereld wordt te veel versimpeld" (Interview with Robert Anker), n.p.; my translation.

De Maagd Marino [The Virgin Marino]

Yves Petry's *De Maagd Marino* [The Virgin Marino] tackles the same predicament through a different protagonist. Just like Michiel in *Oorlogshond*, the main character in *De Maagd Marino* teaches literature. Bruno is a university lecturer in literature, who quits his job after growing disillusioned with the academic world and the diminished relevance of literature in society. Disenchanted and unable to feel connected to others, he makes a suicide pact with his lover, Marino: a shy computer nerd, pathologically attached to his mother. The opening scene describes the execution of this pact: Marino drugs and ties up Bruno, cuts off his penis, and when the pain gets unbearable, he kills him by cutting his throat. Afterwards, Marino cuts off parts of Bruno's body, which he consumes in the following weeks.[42] In the present of the novel, Marino is imprisoned for his act, while the dead Bruno—the narrator—speaks to the reader through Marino's pen as a ghost that enters Marino's mind. The novel explores the past and the state of mind of both Marino and Bruno through the narrative voice of Bruno, who controls the narrative.

In many respects, Bruno is the reverse character of Michiel in *Oorlogshond*. What they share is a sense of disillusionment with the present, an inability to believe strongly in something, and a loss of privilege and authority. But their responses to this experience are starkly distinct. While Michiel does his best to assert his authority as a teacher, Bruno decides to abandon the ivory tower. In contrast with Michiel's positive energy, Bruno is overcome by resignation; while Michiel shows aggression against others, Bruno engages in self-inflicted pain and violence (a suicide pact); contrary to Michiel's drive to move forward, Bruno develops a death-wish.

In his early days, Bruno is a prime specimen of the traditional humanist intellectual in his ivory tower—or a "hopeless romantic" as a colleague calls him (95). The way he talks about the magic of literature is fraught with religious overtones. As a humanist, he teaches the canon of Western white male and primarily modernist authors, including "Musil, Kafka, Beckett, Nabokov, Roth, Amis, Sebald" (101). Good literature, he believes, shakes the ground under our feet, it is "a crocodile's mouth that grabs you unexpectedly" (103).

---

[42] Petry's source of inspiration was a well-known murder case in Germany: that of a man who asked his lover to castrate him, kill him, and eat parts of his body.

The magic of literature turns into empty words, however, as he grows disillusioned with the declining role of the humanities and literature. "Literature as a crocodile's mouth? What nonsense had I been selling all this time. Who would let himself be devoured by a book?" (110). The fact that his favourite metaphor ceases to make sense signifies his turn from the metaphorical world of literary language to the material world, to which he now ascribes a form of authenticity. His disillusionment with the world of the spirit and his longing for the materiality of experience are not unrelated to the way he decides to die. The horrific manner of his death is an attempt to momentarily experience the physicality of his own flesh. His suicide pact aims at an overcoming of a Cartesian subjectivity, premised on the devaluation of the body and the privileging of the mind. His wish to have his penis cut off is significant in this respect. Traditionally, castration signifies loss of virility and power. His castration is an act of *submitting* to another person's violence. The autonomous Cartesian subject becomes vulnerable: a body in pain, dependent on somebody else's actions. Although Bruno's castration remains a self-chosen act, it is a partial giving up of this autonomy in his search for another mode of self-definition, through the body.

Although Marino's violence is mainly directed against himself, the 'others' of Western liberalism still haunt the narrative: for both Bruno and Marino, the others they cannot tolerate are those who show faith in a transcendent truth and endorse a collective identity. Bruno's and Marino's inability to believe in something raises their intolerance (and possibly concealed envy) against those others—religious people, Muslim migrants, people with collective identifications—who have something they do not: faith. Both characters are products of a Western liberal thought-system that privileges rational self-doubt over irrational faith and collective identifications.

Marino, for example, shows utter contempt for the Christian religious group his mother becomes part of. Bruno's intolerance is directed towards Muslims, as his brief encounter with a Muslim passer-by showcases. Bruno and this "brown-colored, bearded young man" exchange contemptuous looks before continuing their walks. The man does not look like a bum or criminal and thus does not pose a physical threat to him. So "what was the problem?" Bruno asks himself (195). Bruno's anxious reaction stems from the Muslim's refusal to succumb to his gaze:

We piercingly looked at each other in the eyes for a few anxious seconds. We did not speak a word. We silently gauged the potential depth, the possible heat of the conflict. My aura against his. What had I done to him? Where did this conceited smug think he got the right to push me intentionally? Surely not from that pathetic little book of his? But my aura succumbed remarkably fast, shamefully fast, humiliatingly fast actually, under the pressure of his contempt. (195)

When Muslims living in Western societies are deemed objects of tolerance, a hierarchy of power is at work, producing the generous tolerator as superior and the tolerated as inferior. This safeguards the position of the Western white tolerator as the norm. When the Muslim casts his intolerant gaze back at Bruno, Bruno cannot fathom that this other would not tolerate *him*. The normative status of Bruno's position is threatened by the other's defiant gaze.

In Bruno's eyes, the Muslim represents a complete identification with a culture that absorbs the individual into a collective: "They who hate individual thinking because they mean nothing as individuals, I who hated their collective consciousness because I did not belong to any group. Me, me, me" (197). This assumption enacts a binary that found fertile ground after 9/11: that between "those who are ruled by culture" and "those who merely 'enjoy' their culture" and are free to choose it.[43] The Western liberal subject, as Žižek argues in *Violence*, perceives itself "as capable of stepping outside his particular cultural roots and asserting his full autonomy and universality," whereas non-liberal subjects are believed to *embody* a culture inextricable from their being (142).

Bruno's self-image rests on the assumed universality and cultural neutrality of his position as a Western white male. Becoming the *object* of the Muslim's gaze, however, makes him conscious of the particularity of this position: "From then on it occurred to me more and more often that in the image of the street I was roughly the only representative of the white, urban, highly educated middle class, which I tried to despise as deeply as possible" (196f.). The other's gaze is disruptive for Bruno not because it triggers Bruno's need to defend his own class, but because it makes him conscious of *his unwillingness* to defend it. This *lack* of conviction, thought to typify postmodern liberal subjectivity, is why Bruno

---

[43] Žižek, *Violence*, 120.

loses the staring contest: he cannot counter the Muslim's stare by posing a convincing alternative to (what he perceives as) the Muslim's faith.

Bruno's shifts in the novel can also be viewed in this light: from the idealist humanism of a literature lover to disillusionment and cynicism, until he succumbs to a self-destructive desire for the intensity of physical pain. Lacking an alternative narrative, Bruno stages a central predicament of the post-9/11 liberal subject.

But why does literature lose its capacity to provide meaning for Bruno? Bruno's disillusionment may not reflect the failure of literature as such, but of the way Western liberal readers have conceptualized its function. Reading literature, according to Catherine Gallagher, presupposes a loose attitude to belief.[44] We may identify with characters or lose ourselves in a novel's world, but we also read knowing that this is fiction. Thus, "the story becomes a kind of speculative venture in which one does not invest too quickly, keeping one's options open and remaining alert to other possibilities" (147). Such mental flexibility is a prerequisite of modern liberal subjectivity (147). This function of literature—fictional, disconnected from truth claims—showcases the liberal postmodern subject's inability to believe. Viewed as such, literature's function in Western (post)modernity is opposed to full-blown commitment to a cause: the kind of faith ascribed to non-liberal others. As fiction, literature is often not taken seriously, as a form of truth, and it is this realization that troubles Bruno: "I could not any more take my favourite authors altogether as seriously as before as producers of reality."[45]

Bruno's former belief in literary autonomy as producing a reality superior to real life rests on an elitist attitude that finds little resonance in today's world. His new sceptical attitude to literature is marked by the kind of "lukewarmness" to belief that, following Gallagher and Eagleton, typifies the liberal reader. This attitude does not offer Bruno a satisfactory alternative either. These attitudes, which, following Thomas Vaessens, can be identified as "humanistic modernism" and "relativist postmodernism" respectively, have grown less convincing after 9/11.[46]

---

[44] Gallagher in Eagleton, *Reason, Faith, and Revolution: Reflections on the God Debate*, 146.

[45] Petry, *De maagd Marino*, 200.

[46] In his study of recent Dutch literature, Vaessens traces a new "late postmodern poetics" on the rise today: overcoming a rigid adherence to literary autonomy, contemporary Dutch authors today seek to re-establish literature's power to interfere in the social

The novel neither suggests that the West needs to return to metaphysical truths to save itself nor that we should read literature for its truth-value. However, it does not give up the quest for alternative functions for literature after 9/11. In this context, it is worth looking at a striking paradox in the novel: Bruno's declaration of literature's death, sealed by his own death, takes place within a literary work that still seems to believe in the power of literary language. Bruno may denounce a life of the intellect, but literature's ghost keeps haunting him beyond his grave. And a ghost can have a more pervasive impact than a living entity: The ghost of dead Bruno, after all, is the narrative's animating force: Marino from his prison cell writes down what this ghost dictates.

The novel's final lines are a desperate plea by the ghost-Bruno to Marino not to destroy the literary Bruno: "I beg you: don't succumb to the compulsion to erase these pages. I am more fond of this Bruno than the Bruno I was playing when I was still Bruno [...] He is the best that could be made of me. Please, do not destroy him."[47] Bruno, who chose to die, is now terrified at the thought of the destruction of his literary self. But why is Bruno's ghost, and the ghost of literature, worth saving?

The ghost may of course be seen as a figure of the Cartesian subject, which Bruno epitomized as an intellectual: the triumph of the spirit over the body. The ghost, however, is also a transgressive figure that defies oppositions: it hovers between presence and absence, life and death.[48] It confuses the neat division between past, present, and future, as it is marked by a perpetual, unpredictable coming-back.[49] The ghost enables the coexistence of contradictory states. The visible and the invisible, presence and absence, the knowable and the unknowable, come together in this in-between figure.

As such, the ghost constitutes a symbolic overcoming of the dilemmas that Bruno experienced as either/or choices: either belief or cynicism; either literature or the authenticity of life; either individualism or collective identifications. As a ghost, then, literature invites readers to face

---

sphere. Without denouncing the postmodern scepticism towards 'truths,' they abandon the "cynical relativism" ascribed (not always rightfully, in my view) to postmodern poetics (*De revanche van de roman: Literatuur, autoriteit en engagement*, 13).

[47] Petry, *De maagd Marino*, 284.

[48] Davis, "États présent: Hauntology, Spectres and Phantoms," 373.

[49] Derrida, *Specters of Marx*, 11.

contradictions as impossible possibilities through which new configurations can emerge. How could we *only* opt for the rational when listening to a ghost-narrator presupposes a form of irrational belief? How can we stick to a univocal notion of reality when the ghost upsets the self-evidence of clear-cut distinctions?

Thus, the novel's narrative situation hints at an alternative worldview, in-between cynicism and belief, even if Bruno did not succeed in finding that during his life. If the novel-as-ghost calls for the reader's willing suspension of disbelief—we do, after all, have to accept a supernatural narrative situation—this suspension does not necessarily presuppose an act of ironic distancing, but can be seen as a *leap of faith*.

De Leraar [The Teacher]

De Maagd Marino is not the only recent Dutch novel that thematizes cannibalism. In Flemish author Bart Koubaa's *De leraar* [The Teacher], the reader enters the mind of a disillusioned fifty-five-year-old teacher in a Flemish technical high school, in which most students come from underprivileged migrant families. In 120 short chapters, the protagonist, nicknamed "the Crow," narrates early memories and incidents from his life as a schoolteacher. As readers eventually find out, the protagonist is a cannibal, who has murdered and consumed thirteen people, most of whom belong to ethnic minorities, including one of his students.

As a teacher, his task is to improve his students' language skills and teach them to name car parts in correct Dutch. In the first pages, the Crow traces a recent change in the way he and his colleagues talk: they miss no chance to speak the 'truth' about the deplorable state of the students and of an educational system foreign to their needs. Now "we are not any more ashamed of what we think, we do not withhold our opinions any more" (11). This shift exemplifies the aforementioned rhetoric of the new realism, marked by disdain for political correctness. The Crow is convinced that his students lack the skills to escape their grim fate. According to the official education plans sent from Brussels, the objective of his teaching should be that students "develop skills and attitudes that will allow them to function in an adequate and meaningful way as adults in society" (12). For the Crow, however, these teenagers from underprivileged families, who cannot even utter a sentence in correct Dutch, have no future.

Readers who have internalized the new realist rhetoric may applaud his refreshing truthfulness about the predicament of these teenagers. But the novel gradually inserts elements that make the reader's potential identification with the Crow disturbing. His 'reasonable' speech is interspersed with markers of violence, both subjective (physical) and symbolic (linguistic). Thus, he makes a Moroccan student write the sentence "I am a monkey" a hundred times. He has violent fantasies about beating his students, which materialize when he gets into a fight with them during the rehearsal of a school play (54f., 163). He likens their broken Dutch to animal sounds (79). "The more pitiful their Dutch is," he remarks, "the stronger their body language, their deaf and dumb slapstick" (119). His migrant students are cast as primitive creatures acting upon instinct—the opposite of the rational, eloquent European subject.

Sympathy and cynicism, paternal understanding and condescension, create a strange mixture in his narrative, in which these students are subjectivized as lesser citizens. Having no other narrative authority to rely on, the reader is forced to follow the Teacher's perspective: a perspective that confronts us with the symbolic violence (the racism, the patronizing stance, the violent fantasies) implicit in popular 'reasonable' views towards migrants in Belgian society.

The Crow's narrative is a battlefield in which different discourses and ideological perspectives reinforce or undermine each other. Extreme-right and racist convictions are often undercut by an ironic mimicking of right-wing liberal discourse:

> Of course it would be easy and unethical to say that the weak are weak because they are unlucky, genetically and in terms of environment; it is indeed their own fault if they do not jump at the chances that are offered to them to step out of the vicious circle; especially the chances that our school offers them. (134)

The Crow's ironic statement confronts a liberal discourse that holds the weak responsible for their condition with an implied Marxist viewpoint that holds the violence of the system responsible for the plight of the lower classes. His ironizing of several viewpoints invites a critical reading of both right-wing and left-wing discourses and the versions of subjectivity they (re)produce through language. The Crow recounts a series of stereotypes about migrants in Dutch and Flemish societies, and concludes:

> My students know very well how people think about them and their family, how their faith is considered as the root of all evil, how they are branded as the cause for lack of safety. The language I teach is an instrument to say something about ourselves and our surroundings, every word draws a boundary and gets in the way of nuancing, my students feel that, just as the whole world population feels what love and hate is but has no words for them; which does not mean that they are stupid or insensitive, it is the language, our language, that makes sure that we get this impression […]. (121)

The inability of his students to form a counter-discourse to social prejudice is here not only attributed to their poor Dutch, but to the ideologies inscribed in this language. Language subjectivizes them as stupid, or, worse, dangerous citizens, potential criminals or terrorists, the "root of all evil." This exclusionary violence of language remains invisible, so that, as the Teacher says, we get the impression that these boundaries are natural. Even if his students were to speak perfect Dutch, they would still not be able to posit a legitimate self in a language in which they are abjects.

Nevertheless, there is an instance in which his students' linguistic deficiency becomes an instrument of resistance. The Teacher gives them an exercise: he divides a series of Dutch proverbs into two parts, placing each part in two columns. The students are asked to match each half of every proverb with its other half. One of the students makes the following mismatch: "Oost, West, tikt het nergens" (96). This erroneous proverb is a merging of two synonymous Dutch proverbs:

> "Zoals het klokje thuis tikt / tikt het nergens."

> "Oost West / thuis best."

Both correspond to the expression "there is no place like home." Both contain the word "home" (*thuis*). But the student joins precisely those parts from which "home" is missing. A literal translation of his mismatched proverb would read: "East, West, it ticks nowhere." The connecting lines in the exercise—allegorizing perhaps the longed-for connection with the host culture—turn into lines of exclusion in the resulting proverb: the society in which some feel "at home" makes the concept of "home" alien to others. The verb "ticks" metonymically evokes bombs and terrorism: this connotation turns the homely, safe content of these proverbs into something uncanny and violent: a bomb ticks, as it were, inside this home. The evocation of terrorism here suggests that the violent agent is the one *without* a home: the migrant. This could give credence to the popular association of migrants with the threat of violence since 9/11. However, in the novel, the actual violent agent is the one "at home": the Teacher. If the power of proverbs resides in their naturalization by convention, which makes us accept their meaning as self-evident, the student's erratic rewriting defamiliarizes these proverbs, drawing attention to their exclusionary underpinnings.

The Teacher's language stages the contradictions within foundational categories of liberal discourse, particularly those of tolerance and hospitality—two central concepts in debates on multiculturalism and integration in Europe. Tolerance, Jacques Derrida argues, implies a paternalistic gesture and a hierarchical relationship: the other is accepted as subordinate and inferior. The tolerant subject always represents the "reason of the stronger."[50] In Western liberal discourse since the mid-1980s, and especially at the turn of the twenty-first century, Wendy Brown argues, the liberal subject poses as having a unique capacity for tolerance—a capacity identified with civilization. Western societies pose as the generous "tolerator" of minorities (166).

Derrida considers hospitality the opposite of tolerance.[51] In *Of Hospitality* (2000), he makes a distinction between "absolute" and "conditional" hospitality. Absolute hospitality requires the opening of the host's home to "the absolute, unknown, anonymous other."[52] It is hospitality offered without any demand from the host.[53] In conditional hospitality, on the other hand, the host exercises sovereignty over the guest, who submits to the host's laws.[54] The guest is tolerated as long as he complies with the host's Law. Tolerance for Derrida describes precisely this conditional hospitality.

In the novel, the violence of tolerance as (conditional) hospitality becomes manifest in the Teacher's relationship with a migrant student.

---

[50] Derrida, "Autoimmunity: Real and Symbolic Suicides," 127.
[51] Ibid.
[52] Derrida, *Of Hospitality*, 25.
[53] Ibid., 83.
[54] Ibid., 27, 55.

Early in the narrative there are references to "*his* student," whom he appears to have taken under his care. Hints of violence and sexual abuse make us sense something fishy in their relationship. Towards the end things clear up: this student, Mustafa S., was involved in an incident, during which some students pulled down the Crow's trousers and underwear and uploaded the scene on YouTube. The Crow kidnaps Mustafa S. and keeps him in his basement, where he subjects him to an "educational process" involving repeated raping, drugging, and torture. Eventually, the student is ritualistically murdered and his body is consumed by the Teacher.

Following his humiliation during the "incident," kidnapping one of the students involved is the Crow's way of resuming power: "I will teach him to speak with two words, to bow and show respect for what we have realised, for our culture and our property. This is my task" (113). His task is to impose the host's law upon the other and remind him that this home will always remain the host's property. The liberal tolerance-talk shows its nasty face as the Crow assumes power of life and death over the boy. "Without me you do not exist," he remarks (105).

Nevertheless, the Crow's treatment of his student is enveloped in a vocabulary of love, care, self-sacrifice, and forgiveness. If he beats his student, it is for his own good; if he bleeds, he takes care of his wounds (54). The drugs he gives him are referred to as "medication." He wants to "save" the boy, whom he declares he treats as a son. When he rapes him, he presents it as fair punishment. Healing and hurting, discipline and rape, fair punishment and torture, medication and drugging, the loving father and the ruthless torturer: these emerge as sides of the same coin. The Crow exemplifies an over-identification with the power system: the system's values are drawn to their extreme implications, revealing their obscene side. Power, Žižek argues, generates its own excess. As an embodiment of the system's excess, the Teacher is the "obscene underside of the Law," which the Law tries to hide in order to sustain its credibility and authority.[55] In Western politics after 9/11, such excesses are often dismissed as exceptions. President G. W. Bush, for instance, stated that the "abhorrent" torture practices in Abu Ghraib "don't represent our America" and do not reflect "the nature of the men and women who

---

[55] Žižek, *Welcome to the Desert of the Real*, 29.

serve our country."[56] The novel forces us to see such excesses as endemic in Europe. The Teacher is the system's abject, and, simultaneously, he *is* the system itself: a modern Frankenstein, whose body stitches together the paradoxes of liberalism.

In the last twenty pages of *De leraar*, a new narrative voice takes over—probably a journalist who investigates the Crow's case, probes different explanatory frameworks, and compares him with other modern Western cannibals. At first sight, the journalist's narrative serves to 'close' the Teacher's case by establishing his insanity through a pseudo-scientific discourse that places him in a genealogy of Western cannibals—a few other anomalies in Western civilization. The report of his arrest and confinement in a psychiatric institution also has a reassuring function: he is withdrawn from society. Through medical, journalistic, psychological, anthropological, and legal discourses, the journalist tries to make the Crow 'digestible,' categorizable.

Suddenly, in the book's last paragraph, a remark about the Crow's anthropophagy disrupts the journalist's rationalist account: "Incomprehensible, because any of us who has ever tasted human brains will agree with me: raw or fried, they hardly differ from the taste of sheep brains" (283). This unexpected comment, which casts anthropophagic practices as a generalized phenomenon, hints at a perverse subtext to the journalist's rational discourse. The reassuring function of his report thus turns upside down: all narrative voices in the novel are equally disturbing.

In the book's final sentence, the journalist draws a parallel between cannibalism and terrorism. Neither of these acts, the journalist remarks, can be accommodated within existing linguistic structures: "every situation is unique and our language is too poor to fully account for cannibalism. Just as terrorism is a deep human predisposition, on which the last word has not been written yet" (283). This parallelism—the novel's only explicit reference to terrorism—conjoins the Teacher's violence (the system's own excess) and terrorism (associated with non-Western others). Neither this European cannibal nor the terrorist are absolute others—both are symptomatic of the Western system's internal contradictions.

---

[56] The quote is from an interview with *Al Arabiya*, May 5, 2004, available at http://abcnews.go.com/Politics/story?id=120660&page=1 (accessed 10.2.2011).

An allegorical reading of the book can follow different directions. Does the West's fear of losing global power push it to violence against others? Is the integration of migrants in European societies a form of cannibalism—a strategy of accepting others into the body of Europe by devouring the threatening aspects of their difference? Does Europe prosper by 'eating' (exploiting, appropriating) its others, just like the Crow's fatal cancer disappears through the consumption of his victims' flesh? Does Europe destroy the 'evil enemy' by becoming evil itself? The enigmatic elements in the Teacher's and the journalist's narratives forestall a univocal interpretation. The novel makes sure it produces its own semantic excess, which stalls the reader's attempt to consume it in the same cannibalistic fashion.

LITERATURE IN EUROPE'S MURKY WATERS

The main characters in these novels embody distorted versions of the European liberal subject that expose the discontents of liberal discourse, especially as it is mobilized in debates on European identity, multiculturalism, and the relation between self and other after 9/11. *De ontelbaren* and *De leraar* literalize violent desires embedded in public rhetoric about migrants and refugees. Many Belgian characters in *De ontelbaren* are kind, tolerant, family people. Their human face, however, presupposes conditions of Western prosperity; when forced to give this prosperity up, they turn into a paranoid, violent multitude. When the plight of poorer parts of the world literally knocks on their doors and ceases to be an issue they deal with through charity donations, the violent undercurrent in their liberal values surfaces. Koubaa's protagonist in *De leraar* is also a paradoxical embodiment of liberal subjectivity and its excesses: a vocabulary of love, paternal care, and hospitality co-exists with punitive acts, torture, and anthropophagy. In *De Maagd Marino*, Bruno fails to successfully embody the type of the elitist humanist intellectual. But he is also unable to lead a satisfying life as a liberal cynic who turns his back on belief. His double failure hints at the exclusionary character of both attitudes: his elitist humanism excludes the 'others' of the Western canon: the Muslim with his Koran, women, people outside the ivory tower. His cynicism is also an impediment: it prevents him from connecting to others and to himself.

Hofmeester, the protagonist in *Tirza*, is obsessively attached to propriety and civilized manners. His violent outburst is the product of a rationalist liberal attitude that suppresses affects. If irrational faith-holding, which is usually ascribed to non-liberal others, can lead to fanaticism, fundamentalism, and blind violence, then so can rationalism when it leaves no place for affect.[57] Unlike Hofmeester, Michiel in *Oorlogshond*, makes no secret of his inability to show restraint and follows a path driven by desire and aggression. If Hofmeester's violence springs from an overblown superego and a severely repressed 'id,' typical of the structures of (European) civilization according to Freud,[58] Michiel's violence reflects an unwillingness to comply with the superego's demands. Nevertheless, as an erudite teacher, he is also the product of a European tradition of thought, inspired by the Greek classics and Nietzsche. His controversial persona hints at the problematic aspects of this tradition too.

These characters embody and simultaneously dispossess several European traditions—humanism, anti-humanism, rationalism, positivism, liberalism, secularism. The novels hint at the limitations or perverse underside of these traditions that constitute European culture. It is no coincidence that most of these characters exercise a profession related to literature or education: Michiel is a teacher of classics, Bruno, a literature lecturer, the Crow, a language teacher, and Hofmeester is an editor of translated fiction. Their estrangement from others, their redundancy, their wish to reclaim their waning authority, are projected as challenges that literature itself faces today, as it searches, to quote Gray, new "imaginative structures" to "register the contemporary crisis" (134). Through and against the examples of these characters, the novels invite us to imagine new modes of speaking or relating to others, beyond the concepts we keep recycling without questioning—tolerance, human rights, hospitality, education, humanism.

These characters' failure as teachers or authority figures suggests that literature cannot exercise a prescriptive function or show readers the 'reality' under supposedly hypocritical representations, in the mode of the new realist rhetoric. What these novels do is tease out the affects and

---

[57] For the way rationalism and fideism (as irrational faith-holding) are both interrelated as the negative sides of reason and faith respectively, see Eagleton, *Reason, Faith, and Revolution: Reflections on the God Debate*, 148.

[58] In *Civilization and Its Discontents* (1962), Freud sees a progression of humans from an unrestricted satisfaction of instincts (a primitive state) to a repression of instincts, which is the precondition for a civilized society.

irrational dimensions involved in public rhetoric in post-9/11 Europe. They offer imaginative structures through which the fantasies, anxieties, and fears ingrained in this rhetoric can be inflated, exposed, and renegotiated.

The novels do not leave much ground on which to sustain the image of Europe's identity as non-violent, open to otherness and plurality. Europe emerges as a space that harbours far-reaching forms of violence. In *De Maagd Marino*, the narrator's final thoughts sketch Europe as a sick body: "The Maas, the Rhine, the Scheldt, have grown frighteningly broad. Clearly, something is really going on. Holland trembles and shakes. The Danube has turned into an inland sea, not beautiful and blue anymore."[59] These words signal a pathology in the heart of Europe. This Europe, then, could use literature's haunting—a literature that does not look at the world from a safe promontory, but dives in the murky waters of the Danube or the Maas.

After 9/11, Gray argues, America was "faced with the challenge of new forms of otherness that are at best virulently critical and at worst obscenely violent".[60] Novelists, Gray writes, should "dramatise the contradictions that conflict engenders".[61] By inserting themselves into different perspectives, "they can represent the reality of their culture as multiple, complex, and internally antagonistic".[62] The novels presented here do not directly delve into these new "violent" "forms of otherness"—by which Gray probably hints at (Muslim) fundamentalism and terrorism. Instead, they stage the "internally antagonistic" nature of European cultures by probing forms of violence within liberal discourse. In so doing, they invite us to relate this violence to the "new forms of [external] violence" Gray alludes to. These novels may not yield an optimistic image of Europe's present. But their bold engagement with the ugly sides of European realities suggests that imagining new, better narratives after 9/11 may not work without facing the contradictions within the self-image of Europe and the liberal subject.

---

[59] Petry, *De maagd Marino*, 284.
[60] Gray, "Open Doors, Closed Minds: American Prose Writing at a Time of Crisis," 147.
[61] Ibid.
[62] Ibid.

References

Abbas, Sadia. "Neoliberal Moralism and the Fiction of Europe: A Postcolonial Perspective," *Open Democracy* website, July 16, 2015, available at https://www.opendemocracy.net/5050/sadia-abbas/neoliberal-moralism-and-fiction-of-europe-postcolonial-perspective (accessed 25.8.2015).

Agamben, Giorgio. "The Endless Crisis as an Instrument of Power: In Conversation with Giorgio Agamben," *Verso Blog*, June 4, 2013; trans. from the German article in *Frankfurter Allgemeine Zeitung*, May 24, 2013, available at http://www.versobooks.com/blogs/1318-the-endless-crisis-as-an-instrument-of-power-in-conversation-with-giorgio-agamben (accessed 10.11.2016).

Anker, Robert. *Oorlogshond* (Amsterdam/Antwerp: Querido, 2011).

Boletsi, Maria. "Cannibalism and Literary Indigestibility: Figurations of Violence in Bart Koubaa's *De leraar*," *Journal of Dutch Literature*, vol. 3, no. 2 (2012), 38–67.

———. *Barbarism and Its Discontents* (Stanford: Stanford University Press, 2013).

———. "Still Waiting for Barbarians after 9/11? Cavafy's Reluctant Irony and the Language of the Future," *The Journal of Modern Greek Studi*es, vol. 32, no. 1 (2014), 55–80.

———. "Literatuur tussen cynisme en geloof: Hedendaagse kannibalen of boze blanke mannen in *De leraar* en *De maagd Marino*," in Maria Boletsi, Sarah de Mul, Isabel Hoving, and Liesbeth Minnaard, *De lichtheid van literatuur: Engagement in de multiculturele samenleving* [The lightness of literature: Engagement in the multicultural society] (Leuven: Acco, 2015).

Bond, Lucy. "Compromised Critique: A Meta-critical Analysis of American Studies after 9/11," *Journal of American Studies*, vol. 45, no. 4 (2011), 733–756.

Brown, Wendy. *Regulating Aversion: Tolerance in the Age of Identity and Empire*. (Princeton/Oxford: Princeton University Press, 2006).

Davis, Colin. "États présent: Hauntology, Spectres and Phantoms," *French Studies*, vol. 59, no. 3 (2005), 373–79.

Derrida, Jacques. *Specters of Marx: The State of the Debt, the Work of Mourning, and the New International*, trans. Peggy Kamuf (London: Routledge, 1994).

———. *Of Hospitality (Anne Dufourmantelle Invites Jacques Derrida to Respond)*, trans. R. Bowlby (Stanford: Stanford University Press, 2000).

———. "Autoimmunity: Real and Symbolic Suicides—A Dialogue with Jacques Derrida," in Giovanna Borradori, *Philosophy in a Time of Terror: Dialogues with Jürgen Habermas and Jacques Derrida* (Chicago/ London: The University of Chicago Press, 2003), 85–136.

Devisch, Ignaas. "De kern van ons cynisme: dagelijks aanspoelende lijken maken ons geen flikker uit," *Knack*, July 21, 2015, available at http://www.knack.be/nieuws/wereld/de-kern-van-ons-cynisme-dagelijks-aanspoelende-lijken-maken-ons-geen-flikker-uit/article-opinion-574627.html (accessed 10.11.2016).

Dorsey, James. "Charlie Hebdo Attack: Refining the Post-9/11 Model," *Fair Observer*, January 9, 2015, available at http://www.fairobserver.com/region/europe/charlie-hebdo-attack-refining-the-post-model-01448/ (accessed 10.11.2016).
Eagleton, Terry. *Reason, Faith, and Revolution: Reflections on the God Debate* (New Haven/London: Yale University Press, 2009).
Fish, Stanley. "Don't Blame Relativism," *The Responsive Community*, vol. 12, no. 3 (2002), 27–31.
Freud, Sigmund. *Civilization and Its Discontents*, trans. James Strachey (New York: Norton, 1962 [1930]).
Fukuyama, Francis. *The End of History and the Last Man* (New York: Free Press, 1992).
Gray, Richard. "Open Doors, Closed Minds: American Prose Writing at a Time of Crisis," *American Literary History*, vol. 21, no. 1 (2009), 128–148.
Grunberg, Arnon. *Tirza* (Amsterdam: Nijgh & Van Ditmar, 2006).
Hegel, Georg Wilhelm Friedrich. *The Philosophy of History*, trans. J. Sibree (New York: Dover Publications, 2004 [1821]).
Kaptein, Yumke. *Elvis Peeters' roman* De ontelbaren *als kritiek op het (im)migratiedebat in Nederland en Vlaanderen* (Bachelor thesis, Leiden University, 2014).
Koubaa, Bart. *De leraar* (Amsterdam/Antwerpen: Querido, 2009).
Massi, Alessandria. "Why Paris is Calling the Charlie Hebdo Attack France's 9/11," *International Business Observer*, January 15, 2015, available at http://www.ibtimes.com/why-paris-calling-charlie-hebdo-attack-frances-911-1784830 (accessed 10.11.2016).
Minnaard, Liesbeth. "'Pas op, ze komen...' De uitvergroting van een publiek doemscenario in Elvis Peeters' roman *De ontelbaren*," *Nederlandse Letterkunde*, vol. 18, no. 1 (2013), 60–77.
———. "Wij, zij, jullie...Over de grenzen van gastvrijheid in Elvis Peeters' roman *De ontelbaren*," in Maria Boletsi, Sarah de Mul, Isabel Hoving and Liesbeth Minnaard, *De lichtheid van literatuur: Engagement in de multiculturele samenleving* (Leuven: Acco, 2015).
Mouffe, Chantal. *On the Political* (Abingdon/New York: Routledge, 2005).
Peeters, Elvis. *De ontelbaren* (Amsterdam: Podium, 2005).
Petry, Yves. *De maagd Marino* (Amsterdam: De Bezige Bij, 2011).
Platov, Vladimir. "Will Charlie Hebdo Become the French 9/11?", *NEO (New Eastern Outlook)*, January 26, 2015, available at http://journal-neo.org/2015/01/26/rus-charlie-hebdo-i-posledstviya/ (accessed 10.11.2016).
Prins, Baukje. *Voorbij de onschuld. Het debat over integratie in Nederland* (Amsterdam: Van Gennep, 2004).
Purdy, Jedediah. *For Common Things: Irony, Trust, and Commitment in America Today* (New York: Vintage Books, 1999), 9–37.
Rosenblatt, Roger. "The Age of Irony Comes to an End," *Time*, September 24, 2001, 79.

Rothberg, Michael. "A Failure of the Imagination: Diagnosing the Post-9/11 Novel, A Response to Richard Gray," *American Literary History*, vol. 21, no. 1 (2009), 152–158.
Todorov, Tzvetan. *The Fear of Barbarians: Beyond the Clash of Civilizations*, trans. Andrew Brown (Cambridge: Polity Press, 2010).
Shaheen, Kareem. "World leaders accused of shameful failure over refugee crisis," *The Guardian*, June 15, 2015, available at http://www.theguardian.com/world/2015/jun/15/worst-refugee-crisis-since-second-world-war-report-middle-east-africa-syria (accessed 10.11.2016).
Vaessens, Thomas. *De revanche van de roman: Literatuur, autoriteit en engagement* (Nijmegen: Vantilt, 2009).
Velzen, Joost van. "De wereld wordt te veel versimpeld" (Interview with Robert Anker), *Trouw*, July 15, 2011, available at http://www.trouw.nl/tr/nl/4468/Schrijf/article/detail/2806663/2011/07/15/De-wereld-wordt-te-veel-versimpeld.dhtml (accessed 10.11.2016).
Versluys, Kristiaan. "9/11 as a European Event: The Novels," *European Review*, vol. 15, no. 1 (2007), 65–79.
Yetkin, Murat. "Paris Attack is Europe's 9/11," *Hurriyet Daily News*, January 8, 2015, available at http://www.hurriyetdailynews.com/paris-attack-is-europes-911.aspx?PageID=238&NID=76639&NewsCatID=409 (accessed 10.11.2016).
Žižek, Slavoj. *Welcome to the Desert of the Real* (London/New York: Verso, 2002), 29.
———. *Violence* (London: Profile Books, 2008).
———. "Liberal multiculturalism masks an old barbarism with a human face," *The Guardian*, October 3, 2010, available at http://www.theguardian.com/commentisfree/2010/oct/03/immigration-policy-roma-rightwing-europe (accessed 10.11.2016).

Author Biography

Maria Boletsi is Assistant Professor in the Film and Comparative Literature Department of Leiden University, the Netherlands. She has been a Stanley Seeger Research Fellow at Princeton University (2016) and a visiting scholar at Columbia University (2008–09) and the University of Geneva (2016). She has published on various topics, including the cultural history of barbarism; post-9/11 literature; and Greek literature, street art and subjectivity in the context of the Greek crisis. Her recent books include *Barbarism and Its Discontents* (Stanford University Press, 2013) and the co-edited volumes *Barbarism Revisited: New Perspectives on an Old Concept* (Brill, 2015) and *Subjects Barbarian, Monstrous, and Wild: Encounters in the Arts and Contemporary Politics* (Brill, forthcoming in 2017).

Tourist/Terrorist: Narrating Uncertainty in Early European Literature on Guantánamo

Philipp Hubmann

Degrading Pictures and the Problem of Representation

The world was stirred with confusion and indignation when pictures of prisoners held in the US military camp in Cuba's Guantánamo Bay were published. Along with the adverse sanitary conditions which the occupants of Camp "X-Ray" had to suffer, the US Department of Defense appeared to communicate that the overt display of such degrading pictures was a necessary foreign policy move, suggesting that the ruthless treatment of mostly Muslim prisoners was the new status quo military rule of action in the so-called "War on Terror." While claiming to reveal the camp to the international community, the pictures taken by US Navy photographer Shane T. McCoy on 11 January 2002 "work to ensure the

P. Hubmann (✉)
University of Zurich, Zurich, Switzerland

invisibility of the camp, the radical silencing and isolation of the occupants, and the concomitant suspension of Guantánamo Bay prison from the regime of international law."[1] Ever since the US government boasted that it was to create the "most transparent" prison on earth,[2] numerous statesmen, journalists, scientists, artists, and intellectuals—such as Nobel Prize laureate C.M. Coetzee and philosopher Judith Butler—have taken a stand against the policy of the Bush administration, which, after the attacks on the World Trade Center, developed an expanding international network to identify and arrest so-called "terror suspects." The estimated number of Guantánamo-prisoners amounts to 779. However, these detainees remained faceless and nameless figures for the public.

The uncertain factual situation surrounding the naval base camp led to a relatively subdued and aesthetic treatment of the occurrences in Guantánamo. In 2004, German writer Dorothea Dieckmann, competing for the Ingeborg Bachmann literary award in Klagenfurt, Austria, a talent contest for young authors of high renown, read out loud from a manuscript in which she describes the camp from the perspective of the protagonist of the Muslim Guantánamo detainee, Rashid Bakhrani. The live broadcast event made her the first person in German-speaking countries to address the issue poetically. At the same time, however, she encountered incomprehension and denial on behalf of a jury largely consisting of literary theorists, critics, and authors. Iris Radisch, jury chairperson and one of Germany's most eminent feuilleton critics, referred to the excerpt from Dieckmann's novel *Guantánamo* (2004), published only a few months later, as a "borrowed tragedy" that assumes an insider's narrative perspective while lacking much actual empirical material.[3] The same year, London's Tricycle Theatre[4] staged a play

---

[1] Bennett, "X-Ray Visions: Photography, Propaganda and Guantánamo Bay," 69.

[2] Cf. Smith, *Eight O'Clock Ferry to the Windward Side. Seeking Justice in Guantánamo Bay*, XII.

[3] Cf. Iris Radisch, ORF, 11.2.2004, Broadcast Bachmann Award.

[4] Since in 1994, the London Tricycle Theatre staged the so-called "tribunal plays" based on the reconstruction of public inquiries, it has become a central place for political theatre in Great Britain. During Nicolas Kent's tenure as Artistic Director, the Tricycle presented, for instance, dramatizations of the Nuremberg trials against the Nazi regime (*Nuremberg*, 1996) as well as a piece on the Genocide of Srebrenica, which occurred in 1995 during the Bosnian War (*Srebrenica*, 1997). See Stoller, *Tales of the Tricycle Theatre*.

entitled *Guantanamo: Honor Bound to Defend Freedom* (2004), which was co-written by Victoria Brittain and Gillian Slovo and is based on interviews with detainees, their friends, family members and experts in law.⁵

Since the publication of the early attempts at literary approaches to Guantánamo, this subject has experienced a boom within the arts. In 2008, *New York Times* reporter William Glaberson summarized the "globalization" and popularization of recent literary and cinematographic productions about Guantánamo as follows:

> But Guantánamo is no longer just a naval station or even just a detention center. It is an idea in worldwide culture—in more than 20 books and half a dozen movies and plays, with more coming out every month. It has become shorthand for hopeless imprisonment and sweltering isolation. "The strange new Alcatraz", one writer calls it, "the gulag of our times."⁶

Besides the wealth of fictional novels and thrillers,⁷ even children's books⁸ and gothic novels addressing the topic have found their way into bookstores. Early scholarship examining this artwork mainly dealt with Michael Winterbottom's documentary *The Road to Guantánamo*

---

⁵ The journalist and writer Victoria Brittain worked as a correspondent for *The Guardian* and various French magazines in Asia, Africa, and the Middle East. In her writing, she is mainly concerned with issues of human rights. Brittain counselled the UN on "The Impact of Conflict on Women" and has published several books such as *Death of Dignity: Angola's Civil* War (1997) and *Shadow Lives: The Forgotten Women of the War on Terror* (2013). Gillian Slovo, born in South Africa, is a novelist, playwright, and memoirist, who in her early career wrote almost only thrillers and crime fiction. The daughter of Joe Slovo and Ruth First, two major figures in the anti-apartheid struggle, published the memoir, *Every Secret Thing: My Family, My Country* as well as the critical plays *Guantanamo. Honor Bound to Defend Freedom* (with Victoria Brittain, 2005) and *The Riots* (2011).

⁶ Glaberson, "Guantánamo, Evil and Zany in Pop Culture." Concerning the commercialization of the camp, cf. also Hickman, *Selling Guantánamo: Exploding the Propaganda Surrounding America's Most Notorious Military Prison.*

⁷ Begley, *Why the Dreyfus Affair Matters*; Fesperman, *The Prisoner of Guantanamo*; Smith, *Guantanamo*; Whyman, *Inside the Cage.*

⁸ Perera, *Guantanamo Boy.*

(2006)[9] as well as an anthology of lyric poetry, featuring poems written by prisoners.[10]

At the same time, the lack of authentic material prior to the publications of the first autobiographical reports by former Guantánamo prisoners from 2006[11] onwards, and the almost scientific approach to the topic initiated in 2007,[12] have created uncertainty among artists and intellectuals as to whether the information available up until that time had been indeed representative and valid.[13] The present chapter therefore aims at exploring the question of how, in this early phase of literary review of events, the obvious knowledge gaps were dealt with and in which aporias such dedicated works of art may have become entangled.

---

[9] Haschemi Yekani, "The Politics of (Social) Death and Rebirth in 'The Road to Guantánamo' and 'Taxi to the Dark Side'." Gibbons, "Representing the Real on The Road to Guantánamo"; Bennett, "Cinematic Perspectives on the 'War on Terror': 'The Road to Guantánamo' (2006) and Activist Cinema."

[10] Falkoff, et al. (eds), *Poems from Guantánamo: The Detainees Speak*; Trapp, "The Enemy Combatant as Poet: The Politics of Writing in Poems from Guantanamo"; Weber, "Literary Justice? Poems from Guantánamo Bay Prison Camp", 417–434; Griswold, "'To Be Free from This Cage': The Poetry of Guantánamo Bay Detainees."

[11] For example, Kurnaz, *Fünf Jahre meines Lebens. Ein Bericht aus Guantánamo*; Begg, *Enemy Combatant: A British Muslim's Journey to Guantánamo and Back*; Pastouna, *Guantanamo Bay. Gefangen im rechtsfreien Raum*; Willemsen, *Hier spricht Guantánamo. Interviews mit Ex-Häftlingen*; Slahi, *Guántanamo Diary*. See also the analysis by Harlow, "Resistance Literature Revisited: From Basra to Guantánamo."

[12] Cf. Smith, *The Prison and the American Imagination*; Honigsberg, *Our Nation Unhinged: The Human Consequences of the War on Terror*; Silkenat and Shulman (eds), *The Imperial Presidency and the Consequences of 9/11. Lawyers react to the Global War on Terrorism*; Irving/Schwab (eds.), *Guantánamo, USA: The Untold History of America's Cuban Outpost*; J. Margulies, *Guantánamo and the Abuse of the Presidential Power*.

[13] With the title "Guantánamo Initiative," the artists Christoph Büchel and Gianni Motti published documentary material about the history of the camp in a touring exhibition. In 2005, they presented their project at the 51st Venice Biennale and petitioned the Cuban government to transform the detention centre into a cultural centre, cf. the program, www.hauserwirth.com/artists/3/christoph-buchel/images-clips/15/ (accessed 1.5.2015). Amnesty International also staged a performance called a "dissent event" in several cities, cf. Scalmer, *Dissent Events: Protest, the Media and the Political Gimmick in Australia*.

Dorothea Dieckmann's "Borrowed Tragedy," *Guantánamo*

As author and literary critic Dorothea Dieckmann[14] read out excerpts from her novel *Guantánamo* in front of the jury of the Bachmann literary award on 24 June 2004, her text encountered vast incomprehension. One of the most pronounced responses came from literary critic, Iris Radisch, who called the text a "borrowed tragedy"[15] that remained problematic because it only minimally relied on "real-life" facts and was thus forced to "infer about the soul [of the detainee, P.H.] through material gathered from the internet."[16] Journalist Martin Ebel expressed confusion caused by this first work of fiction on the military camp, as Dieckmann takes advantage of her character Rashid's alterity and thus maintains a distance from "the Other." Nevertheless, Ebel, similar to the Swiss writer of Hungarian-Slovakian descent, Ilma Rakusa, who was mostly unsettled by the lack of attention to the factual gaps surrounding the circumstances of Rashid's imprisonment, supports the claim that the text would not be representative of the experiences of detainees and militaries, and therefore seems to regard it as fiction in its own right.[17]

It was only after the event's live broadcast that a certain attempt to rehabilitate the text was made in the German press, the feuilleton in particular. Following Leipzig-based author Uwe Tellkamp's reception of the Bachmann award, Richard Kämmerlings, editor-in-chief of the daily *Frankfurter Allgemeine Zeitung* (FAZ), expressed dissatisfaction with the jury's inability to differentiate. The debates among literary theorists, critics, and authors had reductively treated Dieckmann's "far more complex text" within the frame of "trivial debates" involving components such as "witnessing," "authenticity," and the traces of "Holocaust literature." In this manner, Kämmerlings reminded his readers, one lost sight of the incoherence of the jury's decisions, as it declared "the description

---

[14] The author Dorothea Dieckmann, born in 1957 in Freiburg, graduated in Literature and Philosophy. Her oeuvre includes literary essays and novels such as *Kinder greifen zur Gewalt. Essay* (Children Take Up Violence) (1994) and *Die schwere und die leichte Liebe* (The Heavy and the Easy Love) (1996).

[15] Radisch, ORF, 11.2.2004, Broadcast Bachmann Award, my translation.

[16] Ibid.

[17] Ibid.

of a detainee's inner perspective" impossible, but at the same time praised texts which emphatically probed into the worlds of "the mentally insane," "the demented," and "the senile."[18] Kämmerlings' critique implicitly evokes this strange unease surrounding the Guantánamo camp that compels the reader to reconstruct it as an indescribable locus which hypothetically evades any claim to full comprehension.

In fact, the American military camp has largely withdrawn itself from public perception ever since its establishment in February 1903. Neither President Theodore Roosevelt nor Cuba's first president, Tomás Estrada Palma, provided specifications regarding the contract that was to determine whether US or Cuban law were to apply on the territory in question. Since the place had already been used as a site for the interrogation and detention of Cubans and Haitians seeking entry to the United States at the time, this juridical uncertainty was a deliberate political arrangement serving US interests. For more than 100 years now, the naval base has served various strategic purposes. During the Cold War, for instance, it was an important strategic point against the communist Cuban government of Fidel Castro. Along with the establishment of Camp X-Ray, it also became one of the crucial interrogation centres in the War on Terror. Historicists Stephen Irving und Max Schwab discuss this politico-historical switch of functions in their study *Guantánamo, USA: The Untold History of America's Cuban Outpost* (2009): "During the past century the significance of Guantánamo has changed from being central to peripheral. Ironically, it is at this periphery that Guantánamo has achieved its greatest notoriety as a prison/interrogation center for the detention of suspected international terrorists."[19] This marginalized position of the camp causes—as the discussions on the arrested terror suspects manifest—severe problems in the actual juristic qualification of the detention center, especially concerning the possibility of applying the Geneva Convention as well as *habeas corpus*.[20]

---

[18] Kämmerlings, "Was zählt ist auf dem Blatt," my translation.

[19] Irving and Schwab (eds), *Guantánamo, USA: The Untold History of America's Cuban Outpost*, 2f.

[20] The social, political, and juristic dilemma of "Guantánamo" is based on (1) the categorization of the detainees as "unlawful combatants," which excludes them *inter alia* from Article 5 of the Geneva Convention on the "Treatment of Prisoners of War"; and (2) the evaluation of the legal status of the lease agreement between Cuba and the United States, as the decisions of the Supreme Court on the cases *Rasul vs. Bush* and *Hamid vs. Rumsfeld* demonstrate: The first case ensures every detainee has the right to defend himself in the sense of the Habeas Corpus. As experts highlight the "decision radically breaks down the distinctions of citizens versus alien and inside versus outside," because even detainees in

Images and reports from the US camp have remained rare over the years. A document dating back to 1926 and written by navy officer K.C. McIntosh devotes a paragraph to it.[21] In 1972, producer Mike Wallace was allowed to film some material for his news magazine *60 min*, which was broadcast the same year under the title *A Place in the Sun* and later was used by the cinematographer Robert Richardson in his film *A Few Good Men* (1992), a production that evokes an image of the naval base as a place with its own laws, thus perpetuating its factual juridical and political status. Information about Guantánamo has been reduced to a minimum from the very beginning, and, according to Irving and Schwab, has not been investigated from an academic perspective up to the present day: "Much of the explanation for the lack of scholarly attention to Guantánamo is attributed to the difficulty of finding primary source documents in various archives."[22]

As one of the first European writers about this topic, Dieckmann meets this uncertainty about life in a detention camp by developing her story from the perspective of a German-Indian tourist called Rashid. Having been informed about Rashid's cultural roots, the reader is stopped from hastily distancing from the protagonist, whose subalterity becomes manifest as a result of institutional alienation. After a hike in the

---

Afghanistan and Iraq get the right to petition US courts. "On the other hand, the controlling [...] opinion in *Hamid v. Rumsfeld* [...] the Bush administration won the important right to categorize captured persons as 'enemy combatants.' As noted earlier, the administration's position is that there are no legal combatants at all in the war on terror." Michaelsen and Shershow, "Beyond and Before the Law at Guantánamo," 301f. Judith Butler highlights that the Geneva Convention itself provided the US strategy by its difference legal and illegal combatants. "The Geneva Conventions," Butler argues, "have already regarded 'terrorists' as 'outside the protocols' and even 'outside the law' by extending 'universal' rights only to those imprisoned combatants who belong to 'recognizable' nation-states, but not to all people." Aradau, "Law Transformed: Guantánamo and the 'Other' Exception," 490.

[21] K.C. McIntosh writes: "On the step shores of a ragged inket, cut through the mangroves, is the naval station, and storeshouse, Along the cliff-top the low green bungalows of the quarters nestle in a tangle of palms and trumpet vines, a flowery oasis in a desert of scrub and thorn... Then the fleet comes streaming in, a long gray line. The stolid battleships drop ponderous anchors near the naval station. Trim, lean cruisers in double row take position just beyond, and then come the clumsy, squat vessels of the train: store ships, repair ships, and tankers, their gray formation broken by the startling white of the droning wakes of a hundred busy motorboat gigs and barges sped back and forth carrying seniors on official visits... "Bong! Bong! That's all we'll hear between now and April," yelps a turret officer. "Come on gang, let's go!" K.C. McIntosh, "Guantánamo Bay," 109.

[22] Irving and Schwab, *Guantánamo, USA*, 7.

Himalayas, the German-Indian tourist Rashid, who lives in Hamburg—the city of the so-called "Hamburg cell" around Mohamed Atta, Ramzi bin al-Shibh and Marwan al-Shehhi—is arrested in Pakistan, his grandmother's country, and transferred to the US camp.[23] Instead of focusing on the camp's techniques, its rites, and procedures (about which sufficient material was already available in 2004), Dieckmann draws attention to the protagonist's inner drama as he is spatially and emotionally isolated from the other detainees in a cage within Camp X-Ray. Rashid displays psychological states verging on the autistic and suffers through a psychotic attack in which he seems to lose his ability to differentiate between dreams and waking life. Having lost sight even of major autobiographical facts, he ultimately begins to question whether he might not be a terrorist after all. Eberhard Falcke, who reviewed the book for the German weekly *Die Zeit*, praised the narrative form of the text, and the poetic quality of Dieckmann's language in particular:

> Es gibt einiges zu staunen, wie einfalls- und nuancenreich, wie makroskopisch genau hier das Innenleben der Gefangenenqual erforscht wird; in welch treibendem Rhythmus die Sätze Schlag auf Schlag den Gefangenen in seine Einzelteile zerlegen, um dem geringsten Empfindungsdetail die literarische Ehre zu erweisen [...].[24]

More questionably, the journalist detected something in Dieckmann's text which he called a "narrative colonisation" of a politically central

---

[23] As chapters "National Identity and Literary Culture after 9/11: Pro- and Anti-Americanism in Frédéric Beigbeder's *Windows on the World* (2003) and Thomas Hettche's *Woraus wir gemacht sind* (2006)" and "The Mimicry of Dialogue: Thomas Lehr's *September. Fata Morgana* (2010)" by Christ and Frank in this volume highlight, Hamburg, as the root of the terroristic cell, became a crucial point of reference in imaginations of 9/11.

[24] "It is astonishing to what extent the inner life of the detainee has been studied, how imaginative and rich in nuances and how microscopically exact the descriptions of the agonies of imprisonment are. In which pushing rhythm the sentences deconstruct the detainee in his individual parts in order to poetically honour every single detail of his sentiment [...]." My translation of Falcke, "Dorothea Dieckmann sucht einen Weg in das Innerste der Gefangenen von Guantánamo."

space, a procedure and an attitude he deemed to be symptomatic of some of the Western world's reception of Guantánamo.[25]

> Dieser Roman verrät manches über die Kehrseiten des Erste-Welt-Mitgefühls-Kultes zugunsten der Verdammten dieser Erde. Mit tausend Empfindungsdetails wirbt die Erzählerin um Mitgefühl für den armen Rashid, sie nimmt ihn vollständig auseinander, damit wir nur ja ganz bei ihm sein können. Sie weiß mehr, als er über sich selbst wissen könnte. Sie viviseziert ihn im Namen der Empathie. Zur Kolonialisierung des fremden Leidens ist es da nicht mehr weit.[26]

One of the most complicated and controversial, but also "classical" theoretical positions on the War on Terror is Italian philosopher Giorgio Agamben's concept of the *Homo sacer*, named after an outsider figure in late Roman law. In ancient times a *homo sacer* was a banned and outlawed person, who could be killed by anybody and in any way except as a religious sacrifice. In Agamben's view—despite all claims of cultural progress—the stigmatization of certain groups and individuals deprived of humanity experiences great continuity. For him the "homo sacer" functions even in present days as a special kind of renegade who is not worth more than his biological substance ("bios").[27] His position is neither that of a total stranger nor that of an accepted member of the community. In

---

[25] On the colonizing view in the European literature on 9/11, see chapters "National Identity and Literary Culture after 9/11: Pro- and Anti-Americanism in Frédéric Beigbeder's *Windows on the World* (2003) and Thomas Hettche's *Woraus wir gemacht sind* (2006)" and "The Mimicry of Dialogue: Thomas Lehr's *September. Fata Morgana* (2010)" in this volume.

[26] "This novel has a lot to say about the downside of the First World's cult of compassion in support of the wretched of this earth. With a myriad of details about his sensations, the narrator pleads for sympathy for poor Rashid; she takes his personality apart completely, in order for us to relate to him. She knows him better than he would ever know himself. She performs a vivisection on him, in the name of empathy. It is all not very far from colonising alien suffering." Ibid.

[27] Anthony Downey connects Agamben's "theory of marginalization" with the context of the War on Terror, which affects even daily life. "Under the latter conditions, the spectre of terrorism has increasingly promulgated 'states of exception' whereby the sovereign state can usher in laws to curtail, contain and monitor its own citizens. In the eyes of a sovereign power that has effectively usurped the legislative branch of the state is a move that renders us all potentially *homines sacri*." Downey, "Zones of Indistinction. Giorgio Agamben's 'Bare Life' and the Politics of Aesthetics," 112.

addition, he is denied both the positions of victim and perpetrator, and can only exist as an exceptional case. Following Agamben, Guantánamo can be seen as the current link in an ongoing chain in the history of civilization, which creates spaces of discriminating repression and discipline. In this perspective, the camp does not appear as a historical exception but as the "biopolitical paradigm of the modern."[28] Or, to put it more pointedly: The "state of exception" is not an exception, but constitutive of societies, which stabilize their order by stigmatizing people as "homines sacri" and deport them to zones of "irreducible indistinction"[29]:

> [T]he decisive fact in that, together with the process by which originally situated at the margins of the political order—gradually begins to coincide with the political realm, and exclusion and inclusion, outside and inside, *bios* and *zoé*, right and fact, enter into a zone of *irreducible indistinction*.[30]

Just as the "homo sacer" internalizes the lawlessness and emptiness of his political status in the camp, Rashid has to accept his "indefinite detention" and is stylized as a lonesome madman unable to integrate himself into the society of Guantánamo detainees. At the same time, he—deprived of any kind of agency—feels reduced to the status of a "heavy clump" (German: "schwerer Klumpen") or, in Agamben's terms, degraded to "bare life."[31] Rashid, son of a German shopkeeper, arrested, in a small cage on Cuban soil, has to suffer torture by American soldiers and also remains a foreign body in the community of the other detainees.

> Schon die erste Wiederholung erfaßte den ganzen Block. Auf einmal sprachen alle dieselbe Sprache, Allahs Sprache. Allahs Ah war Beschimpfung, Schlachtruf, Parole. Bei jeder Nennung wurde sein Name

---

[28] Peters, "Giorgio Agamben's Homo Sacer Project," 330.

[29] As Paul Hegarty argues, not only the "homo sacer" but also the sovereign, who punishes him, resides in the "state of exception" outside the order. "Both the ones who can be killed and the sovereign are outside the Law just as they are at its very core. The sovereign, in the form of the king, for example, is outside and beyond the Law. Agamben identifies this situation as the 'exception'—and from which the 'state of exception' can emerge—that is, the suspension of Law. The exception, the suspension of Law, is the moment Law is founded, which is itself neither legitimate nor illegitimate, but violent." Hegarty, "Giorgio Agamben", here 21.

[30] Agamben, *Homo Sacer. Sovereign Power and Bare Life*, 9.

[31] Dieckmann, *Guantánamo*, 13.

größer, lauter und höher, er wuchs über die Dächer, und über die Dächer kam er zurück. Das ganze Lager echote, wurde ein Volk, ein Volksfest.[32]

Rashid's experience of the detainees' religious vigour is a traumatic one, causing almost pathological symptoms: "[E]r preßte die Lippen zusammen, er knurrte wie ein Tier, er rüttelte wie verrückt an den Stangen von Tür und Türeinfassung, die er im ersten Moment umklammert hatte."[33] Meanwhile, he observes "the show" that surrounds him with the smugness of an amused ethnologist or a European tourist, remaining unmoved by the emotional evocations of Allah.[34] "Allahs Stimme hat keinen Hall, sie schraubt sich mühsam hoch und windet sich über die Wellblechdächer, sinkt, fängt sich, hebt sich wieder."[35] As Kristin Rebein argues, by sketching the protagonist as an outsider and tourist to the camp, his story shows more about the postmodern condition of an atomistic global world than the concrete description on the living and surviving in "Gitmo." Feeling foreign to his home as well as to India and Guantánamo, there seems to be "an underlying, fundamental symmetry between the two narratives [travel and arrest, P.H.]. They mirror each other in portraying a transnationalism that Rashid perceives first and foremost as disorienting."[36]

And, most importantly, he finds himself once again in a multilingual environment composed of languages he does not understand: English, Urdu, Pashto, Uzbek, and Arabic. Both in his travels and at Guantánamo, Rashid longs for a sense of cosmopolitanism, for the ability to integrate the distant

---

[32] Ibid., 47. "The first repetition was joined by the entire block. Suddenly, they all spoke the same language, the language of Allah. The 'ah' of Allah was a curse, a call to arms, a coded slogan. With each chant it grew bigger, louder, higher in pitch, rising above the roofs and swooping back down again. The entire camp echoed with it and became one people." Dieckmann, *Guantánamo: A Novel*, 39.

[33] Ibid.: "He pressed his lips together, he growled like an animal, he shook like mad at the bars of the gate and the doorframe."

[34] Ibid., 37.

[35] Ibid., 45f. "Allah's voice doesn't have any resonance. It winds laboriously up and swirls around the corrugated iron roofs, sinks, recovers, rises again."

[36] Rebien, "Cosmopolitan Perspectives. Globalization and Transnationalization in Contemporary Literature," 127.

with the familiar, and to inhabit different worlds simultaneously, but it remains a desire beyond his reach.[37]

Already in the Foreword to her novel, Dorothea Dieckmann stresses that her fictional text should not be perceived as bearing any topographical or historic reference. Rather, it should be seen as an "invention," even when her descriptions lean on material such as photographs and reports from journalists, the military, and former prisoners. Such material had, to a certain extent, already become available in 2003, the year she wrote the novel.[38] Since the text only loosely hinges on marginal reports, and avoids marking the transitions from factual knowledge to invention, it would perhaps be misleading to use Alexander Kluges' terms "facts and fiction" in relation to *Guantánamo*.[39] Dieckmann rather crudely sketches the tripartite schema of Rashid's detention in Pakistan, his placement in an interim camp after Kandahar, and later in Guantánamo (Chapter I "Down" and II "Food"), although details of the procedure (Chapter III "Kill") are found in many detainees' biographies. Also, the transfer from Camp X-Ray to Camp Delta (Chapter VI), following the closing of the former in April 2002, is described as a result of Rashid's failed suicide attempt (Chapter IV "Death"), which causes a traumatic coma and brings him to the hospital (Chapter V).

The Genre of "Institutionenroman" and the Ego-Documents of Former Detainees

As Rüdiger Campe, Professor of German at Yale University, suggests, two main types of German novels can be observed in modernity. The "Bildungsroman" in the tradition of Goethe's *Wilhelm Meister* (1776/1807), which follows the *vita* of the protagonist through different stages of his moral development, and the so-called "Institutionenroman," which originated in the literary discourse of the early twentieth century; examples of the latter type would be Robert Musil's *Die Verwirrungen des Zöglings Törleß* [The Confusions

---

[37] Ibid., 128.

[38] Ibid., author's note.

[39] Cf. Sombroek, *Eine Poetik des Dazwischen. Zur Intermedialität und Intertextualität bei Alexander Kluge.*

of Young Törless] (1906), Robert Walser's *Jakob von Gunten* (1909) and Franz Kafka's *Der Proceß* [The Trial] (1915).[40] In opposition to the "Bildungsroman," the protagonist of the "Institutionenroman" is not able to overcome a certain official facility such as a (boarding) school or a court, which dominates and absorbs his entire life and does not make the individual a result of his own will and talent (like the "Bildungsroman"), but an effect of the institution, which regulates his thinking, feelings, and dreams.

Bearing this difference in mind, there are many aspects that qualify Dieckmann's novel as an "Institutionenroman." First, all information the reader receives from the narrator about Rashid derives from the situation of his arrest. As a consequence, the recipient solely gets in touch with the protagonist under the conditions of his experiences in the camp, which effectively shape his mental state of mind. Rashid, affected by his isolation and the infusion of pharmaceutical substances, continually fails to accept his own discrepant cultural identity: "Er [Rashid] will sich nicht erinnern [...] Erinnerungen sind gefährlich. Sie bringen die Zeit in den Käfig, und dafür ist der Käfig zu klein."[41] In contrast to the teleological structure of the "Bildungsroman," Rashid does not reflect on his position in a chronological, linear manner. Stepping into the prison allows Rashid to enter a state of oblivion, slowly consolidating into a psychological vanishing point in which temporal and spatial boundaries are permanently erased. It is precisely this loss of identity that

---

[40] See Campe, "Robert Walsers Institutionenroman *Jakob von Gunten*," or "Kafkas Institutionenroman—*Der Proceß, Das Schloß*." About 50 years before Campe contoured the concept of "Institutionenroman," Hiram J. Friedsam published an article with the title "Bureaucrats as Heroes". Here the author discribed the conjuncture of so-called "bureaucratic novels", such as Churchill's *A far country*, Lewis' *Arrowsmith* and Dos Passos *The Big Money*. Similar to Campe Friedsam describes the "bureaucratic novel" as a narrative, which contrasts plots with 'strong' heroes like "entrepreneurs", who - in Friedam's view- were popular in American literature for quite a long time. In opposition to this main focus on agency, the "bureaucratic novel is one in which plot development is centered on the web of bureaucratic relationships, in which the hero is involved. It is not enough that the hero be identified as a bureaucrat; it is necessary that what does and what is done to him derive from the fact that he is a bureaucrat." Other than Campe Friedsams model of the "bureaucratic novel" is strictly limited on bureaucrats as central character. Friedsam, "Bureaucrats as Heroes," 270.

[41] Ibid., 35. "He doesn't want to remember [...] Memories are dangerous. They bring time into the cage, and the cage is too small for that. As soon as time has the chance to stretch out it pulls him off in every direction," ibid., 26.

offers a reading of the novel as a quest for identity, but in the way of the "Institutionenroman," which dictates the protagonist, his sorrows and hopes. Rashid, blindfolded and deafened by earflaps, a person who had travelled for adventure across the globe only to be brought to an unknown place, simultaneously fantasizing about mountaineering and the "carnival crowd" anti-American demonstration in Peshawar, where his detention took place, manages to rediscover himself only after this break within the coherent narrative of his self-perception as a civilized human being. Rashid's imprisonment has an existential dimension, in which the relationship between subject and object is inverted: within the cage of the prison cell, the human being with an actual biography is annihilated; instead, a new and anchorless shape emerges that does not seem to have anything in common with the 20-year-old German tourist, who wanted to meet his Indian grandmother in Delhi and made the acquaintance of young Mirgul Shinwari, who invited him to his family in Pakistan. Still, Dieckmann's protagonist is well aware that within the camp, the boundaries between the self and the world disappear. As a consequence, the protagonist's identity has to be recreated out of this state of chaos. The last sentence of the novel's first chapter traces the stages of Rashid's individuation from his arrival in the no man's land, to the detention, the creation of an I, and his initiation-like giving of a name, which is a kind of re-birth in his new environment: "Da ist er. Endlich angekommen. Irgendwo auf der Erde, ein Gefangener, ich, Rashid."[42]

At a later stage in the text, the responsive identity structure of Dieckmann's novel becomes even more pronounced, particularly when the protagonist declares that he only reaches himself through the camp's interrogation procedures: "Only when he's being interrogated does he feel whole. The questions and the fear of beatings permeate his body and concentrate all the loose fibers of his being into one, compressing in his strength and all the time into it as well."[43] Rashid is thus constructed as a weak hero, who needs the military's attention in order to find himself. His madness, the result of the camp's conditions and medication abuse, intensifies his behaviour in a manner which makes him an "unreliable narrator," only partially in a position to provide an account of his own inner life and the events outside his cell.[44] Even if we are to keep in mind

---

[42] Ibid., 31. "He is here. He's arrived at last. Somewhere on earth, a prisoner, I, Rashid," ibid., 23.

[43] Ibid., 91.

[44] Booth, *The Rhetoric of Fiction*.

the "factual uncertainty" that the jury of the Bachmann award criticized, on the narrative's technical level it is precisely this feature that is given particular attention and is deliberately extrapolated as the novel processes the experiences of its protagonist as the absolute Other, remaining inaccessible even to himself, and ultimately perceiving himself as a stranger. As Michel Faber for *The Guardian* states, during the interrogation,

> the hazy naivity of his [Rashid's] agenda in Pakistan seems less and less credible to him; his story disintegrates, reassembles, incorporates feeble lies, half-remarked impressions, guilty dreams. At no stage is the outside world permitted to restore some semblance of an objective perspective: we are trapped inside Rashid's increasingly diminished consciousness.[45]

Thus, Dieckmann's novel conducts what can be called "double othering." The narrative does not stop with the description of the life of a stranger, but it also documents his inner drama, which leads to a distrust in his own reliability. As an intermediate result it can therefore be concluded that Dieckmann does not solve the lack of reliable information about Guantánamo by a dubious claim of telling unknown truths. Instead, Rashid challenges himself and it is left to the reader to decide whether he is guilty or not. Through this strategy of "narrating uncertainty" the fiction unfolds its own poetic quality in initiating a reflection on the situation of the detainees before the first autobiographical reports were published.

A comparison with ego-documents about Guantánamo in Germany allows us to recognize which differences one could detect between the experiences of actual detainees and those of Rashid. One significant discrepancy that needs to be commented on is the insurmountable outsider position assumed by Rashid, as well as the inevitable lack of any bond between the military guards and the prisoners, which is propagated in *Guantánamo*. Similar to Giorgio Agamben's genealogical positioning of *homo sacer* as an ultimate victim, unable to defend himself in the face of the circumstances which have robbed him of his rights, Rashid is excluded from the group that would have the potential for protest and reconciliation. A helpless figure in every way, besides his juridical status as "bare life" (*à la* Agamben), he is also confronted with all the consequences of identity loss. Rashid sees himself through the eyes of the military.

---

[45] Faber, "Guantánamo. A Novel."

As the loss of personal rights and identity mutually condition one another, the state of exception creates a blueprint of the mental and somatic perception of one's own personality—an effect which Rashid experiences through the involuntary disinhibition of his bodily reactions.[46]

The information gathered from former prisoners' reports by German journalist Roger Willemsen, collected in the volume *Hier spricht Guantánamo* [Here Speaks Guantánamo] (2006), as well as the biography *Fünf Jahre meines Lebens. Ein Bericht aus Guantánamo* (English translation edition: *Five Years of My Life: An Innocent Man in Guantánamo*, 2007) by German-born Murat Kurnaz, who was kept at Kandahar and later in the Cuban US camp, report a sense of community among the prisoners and their relationship with the military guards that not only confirm the rigid adherence to the rules of the camp, but also allude to communicational and social liberties, which Dieckmann's self-absorbed protagonist is denied. Murat Kurnaz describes soldiers who exhibit a certain amount of solidarity with the detainees, or at least some compassion: "Ich hatte das Gefühl, manche Wärter hätten gern mit mir oder den anderen Gefangenen geredet. Aber sie sagten immer wieder: »Sorry, I can't talk to you, they're watching me«. Sie standen selbst unter Beobachtung." Kurnaz, whose autobiographical report caused much critique in Germany after its release, recalls another soldier, who always kept apart and publicly insulted his institution in front of both prisoners and military guards on the very last day of his service at the camp:

> An seinem letzten Tag [anonymous member of the Military Police] hatte er in meinem Block Dienst. Er kam zu mir und sagte: „Murat, ich habe nur noch zwei Stunden." Er war ganz aufgeregt. Dann kam er wieder und sagte: „Nur noch eine Stunde. „Als die Zeit fast um war, tauchte er wieder auf, stellte sich vor meine Käfigtür und sah auf seine Uhr. Einige andere Wärter standen etwas abseits. Er rief sie. „Hey, seht mal her, was ich jetzt mache!" Die Wärter kamen näher, er blickte auf seine Uhr und begann zu zählen. „Fünf, vier, drei, zwei …" Bei null nahm er die Armbinde ab. Er führte sie zu seinem Gesäß und machte zum Entsetzen der Wärter eine Bewegung, als wollte er sich damit den Hintern abwischen. Dann warf

---

[46] Cf. e.g. Dieckmann, *Guantánamo: A Novel*, 39, "He pressed his lips together, he growled like an animal, he shook like mad at the bars of the gate and the doorframe. So alone, so narrow, so alone was the moment when all the other prisoners had the same words on their tongues that he felt he could beat down the walls of his cage under cover of their anger. But the cage was stronger than his despair."

er die Binde auf den Boden und trat drauf. „Ich bin kein MP mehr!" Er trampelte darauf herum wie die Wärter auf dem Koran. „Seht ihr? So!"⁴⁷

Kurnaz also describes how the prisoners secretly organized themselves, selecting leaders, and appointing dates for hunger strikes,⁴⁸ aiming to secure temporary relief. In particular, commandant Michael Dunlavey and Rick Baccus, who both remained in the camp from January to November 2002, exhibited a greater willingness to compromise, according to both Kurnaz' and Willemsen's material, thus perpetuating a belief among the prisoners that their position was not completely hopeless: "We were not entirely helpless. We could bring them to their knees if we hunger-striked together!"⁴⁹ Nevertheless, all sources unanimously

---

⁴⁷ "On his last day he had to work in my block. Came to me and said: 'Murat, I only have two hours left.' Was so excited. Then he came again saying: 'Just one more hour.' Once the time was almost over, he reappeared in front of my cell and looked at his watch. The other guards were some distance away. He yelled at them: 'Hey, watch me as I do this!' The guards came closer, he looked at his watch and started to count. 'Five, four, three, two...' As he came to zero he took his wrist band, flapped it at his hind parts, and, to the horror of the remaining guards, made a gesture as if he was to wipe his ass with it. Then he threw the band on the floor and trampled over it. 'I'm no MP anymore!' He stamped on it like the guards would do with the Qur'an. 'You're watching? So!'" My translation, ibid., 208f.

⁴⁸ Kurnaz says: "We appointed a leader after the Qur'an assault. Each prisoner had to pick a candidate. The voting was kept in secret; the Americans knew nothing about it. It took many weeks, because it had to be done from mouth to mouth, from cell to cell. Out of 500 detainees ten were chosen to collect and sort out the votes. These ten picked out three men, and the three then agreed on one single person who would become a leader. This man we called Emir. Nobody except from the three, which had chosen him, knew who it was. This man was not to be known as our official leader. He picked a further person who was to speak with the Americans and make appearances as our Emir so that the real Emir could stay in the background." Kurnaz, *Fünf Jahre meines Lebens*, 152.

⁴⁹ Kurnaz, *Fünf Jahre meines Lebens*, 150. The combatant Khalid Mahmoud al-Asmar interviewed by Roger Willemsen draws a pronouncedly negative picture of the effectiveness of the detainees' protests: "The strikes and all other sorts of protest that took place in Guantánamo were only a reaction to the desecration of our faith and our religious rituals [...] We have often initiated strikes because of the desecration of the Qur'an. Then there always were negotiations and promises that this will be put to an end. But they also showed that the ones who were doing this were just stupid, and that these individual perpetrators had to be punished. Two days after we had ended a hunger strike, another desecration of an Afghani Qur'an took place [...] As we started a hunger strike all across the camp, a General came to us and said: 'Earlier, this was a cemetery for the Spanish, now it will be yours'." Khalid Mahmoud al-Asmar, quoted from Willemsen, *Hier spricht Guantánamo. Interviews mit Häftlingen*, 69f.

confirm that this readiness to cooperate on behalf of the military guards was put to an end as the camp was taken over by General Geoffrey Miller.[50]

All differences aside, a comparison between the biographical data and Dieckmann's novel still exhibits some overlaps: the tortures, the deliberate use of medical substances, suicide attempts, the interrogations in which the respondents were automatically assigned the roles of perpetrators, as well as the promises of early release which were to—at least formally—secure the silence and the consent of the combatants. Notwithstanding these apparent similarities with the ad hoc camp reports, the literary text, also according to Dieckmann's own estimate, portrays a picture of the camp that drastically deviates from the descriptions given by former prisoners.

Rashid's weapon against the insecurity caused by his imprisonment and the permanent threat that his position entails is imagination. It is this imagination, after all, that is triggered by ephemeral impressions and which, in the course of time, becomes a self-absorbing and compensatory fantasy. While Murat Kurnaz recalls that wild animals would occasionally come to the cages, making life in the camp a bit more diverse, Dieckmann's protagonist speaks of the spiders, tarantulas, iguanas, colibris, land crabs, and crabs that he has observed[51]: "Charly-Charly war einer der äußeren Verschläge, und wir waren der Natur am nächsten. Ich habe später nie mehr so viel Besuch bekommen. Einmal war eine Boa bei mir, sehr lang und schlank, ich dachte, sie wächst bestimmt noch."[52] The former prisoner Khalid Mahmoud al-Asmar, who was interviewed by the famous German journalist Roger Willemsen, also remembers visits by animals, which he, however, perceived as a major threat: "There were rats, snakes, and scorpions. Nobody was ever bitten by a snake, but many were attacked by scorpions. Animals from the woods came as well."[53]

---

[50] Cf. Worthington, *The Guantánamo Files: The Stories of the 774 Detainees in America's Illegal Prison*, 191.

[51] Kurnaz, *Fünf Jahre meines Lebens*, 112f. or rather 200.

[52] "Charly-Charly was one of the outer crates and we were very close to nature. I never had so many visitors later. Once there was this boa that came to me, very long and thin, I thought it could grow even more." (translation), Kurnaz, *Fünf Jahre meines Lebens*, 112.

[53] al-Asmar in Willemsen, *Hier spricht Guantánamo*, 68.

Besides these exotic aspects of daily life in the camp, Dieckmann's novel includes descriptions of torture methods such as the "eagle" during the interrogations,[54] the dispensing of pharmaceutical substances, the confinement in cooling chambers ("Eisschrank"[55]) and the methodical disruption of recreation periods by violent wakening. Murat Kurnaz confirms in his autobiography what the philosopher Giorgio Agamben would call the "state of exception" and what Rashid suffers in the camp as a concerted suspension of order. "Nobody found out anything about the secret law, which is the law to always break all laws."[56] The temporary and systematic breaking of routines is the task of the so-called "Extreme Reaction Force," a special commando team responsible for sprinkling the prisoners' cells with pepper spray, as well as for dog-hunting and beating up the "hors de combat" detainees.[57]

---

[54] "*Okay, you don't want to*, sagt der Offizier, *let's make an eagle, quick*, Rashid wird von der Pritsche gestoßen, wirbelt herum und klatscht dem Boden, auf den Bauch, den Stoffhaufen, vor dem Gesicht, einer kniet auf seinem Rücken, ein anderer schiebt mit den Stiefeln seine Beine auseinander, seine Arme werden über den Kopf geschoben und die Handflächen nach oben gewendet, *don't move*, brüllt der Offizier. Rashid rührt sich nicht, er schmiegt den kalten Körper an das kalte Linoleum. Er hört das Klappern und Trampeln und Scharren, er hechelt unter dem Druck auf seinem Brustkorb und zuckt erst, als zwei harte Stempel auf seine Fußsohle drücken, und wieder, als dasselbe mit den Händen geschieht, und hält still und schreit erst, als die stumpfen Druckstellen zu Stielen werden, die sich schlagartig in die Sohlen bohren, dann nageln sie die Hände fest, und er zwingt den Kopf in den Nacken und erkennt das Stuhlbein auf der Handfläche und die Stiefel und die gefleckten Hosenbeine davor. You say you know English, nazi = Der Offizier spricht von hinten, sein Stuhl steht auf Rashids Füßen." Dieckmann, *Guantánamo*, 80. "*Okay, you don't want to*, says the officer, *let's make an eagle, quick*. Rashid is pushed from the gurney, spun around, and smacks the floor on his stomach with the heap of clothes right in front of his face. One of them is kneeling on his back, another kicks his feet apart. His hands are pulled above his head, palms up. *Don't move*, growls the officer. Rashid doesn't squirm, he presses his cold body against the cold linoleum. He hears his teeth chattering, footsteps and scraping noises. He wheezes from the pressure on his rib cage and finally jerks when something is pressed into the soles of his feet and then into the palms of his hands. He only starts to scream when the bruised pressure points start to bore into his feet like broom handles and seem to drill his hands into place. He manages to crane his head and sees the legs of a chair on his hands, and the boots and camo pants of someone sitting on it. *You say you know English, nazi?* The officer's voice comes from behind him – he's sitting on the chair on Rashid's feet." Dieckmann, *Guantanamo. A Novel*, 73 (italics in the original).

[55] Dieckmann, *Guantánamo*, 77.

[56] Kurnaz, *Fünf Jahre meines Lebens*, 99.

[57] Ibid.

Dieckmann's *Guantánamo* also depicts appropriately the differences between the living conditions in Camp "X-Ray" and Camp "Delta," where Rashid, "Detainee JJJ A 204,"[58] was granted better accommodation which comprises a cabin within a stable house as well as access to books, the possibility of corresponding with family members ("cleared by U.S. Forces"[59]) on a regular basis and culinary rewards like "twinkies" and from time to time a "Happy Meal" with Coke from McDonald's.[60] Nonetheless, this information about Rashid's situation depends on his subjective perception of the camp, which cannot take a bird's eye view of the institution and the system "Guantánamo," and therefore fails—despite its profound poetic reconstruction—to supply the reader with more than just fictitious and selective impressions.

"No Man Is an Island"[61]: Brittain and Slovo's Biographic Montage

London's Tricycle Theatre—recently celebrated as the "most valuable home of political theatre in Britain"[62]—saw *Guantanamo* premiere in 2003. With the play, journalist Victoria Brittain and author Gillian Slovo started an early attempt to poetically include the camp into critical discourse. The title of the play alone suggests that the boundaries between narrated and 'real' worlds are to be suspended. Ursula Canton, for instance, suggests that the audience of the play by Brittain and Slovos first of all has to refer back to its "knowledge and hypothesizing" about Guantánamo, which is strongly tied to the representations of mass media.[63]

> The continuous presence of Camp Delta in the newspapers, both in reports and in commentaries means that for most of the audience a direct reference will evoke more than just a place name. [...] *Guantanamo* [italics

---

[58] Dieckmann, *Guantánamo*, 92.

[59] Ibid., 97.

[60] Ibid. 150 and 152.

[61] The play quotes John Donne's famous lines, ibid.

[62] Quoted from the theatre's homepage: www.tricycle.co.uk/home/about-the-tricycle-pages/about-us-tab-menu/archive/archived-theatre-production/guantanamo-honor-bound-to-defend-freedom/ (accessed 1.5. 2015).

[63] Canton, "Guantánamo. Documenting a Real Space?" 90.

P.H.] goes further than merely taking it for granted that the audience will complement the information given in the performance text: By using a proper noun for an entity in the world outside the theatre, it gives the audience a clear indication that the world presented in the play depends on the world outside it to a higher degree than in many other plays.[64]

Brittain's and Slovo's play *Guantanamo* is posited beyond any long-striding historical narrative, ultimately confining itself to the speech of politicians, lawyers, prisoners, their relatives, and various persons directly related to the case. The tripartite division of the play itself encompasses the detention's pre-story, the actual life in the camp, and the experiences which the three British detainees released in 2004 had to go through. In this manner the audience is able to trace individual and collective descriptions of impressions and evaluations. The audience is thus in a position to intellectually and emotionally relate to the situation of the detainees through the witness narratives and the stories told by family members. Direct speech plays a central role in *Guantanamo*, which is also why Lib Tayler classifies the play within "verbatim theatre," which experienced a boom after 9/11 in Europe and North America.[65]

> First, verbatim theatre, like *Black Watch* (2007) and *Guantanamo* (2004), is based in the representation of the actual words of real people collected through, for example, interviews or letters. Second, tribunal theatre, like *The Colour of Justice* (1999) and *Justifying War* (2003), is based on court and public enquiry transcripts and also uses actual words, but they are collected from formal documents and court records. Third, documentary

---

[64] Ibid., 89f.

[65] According to Mary Luckhurst, "Verbatim theatre has proliferated in Europe and North America since the 1990s, and post-9/11 has become increasingly visible on both mainstream and fringe stages." Based on the "German documentary tradition," practised by (among others) Erwin Piscator, Ralf Hochhuth, Heinar Kipphardt and Peter Weiß, the concept of "verbatim theatre" has established itself above all in Great Britain in recent decades. "The use of the term 'verbatim theatre' is specific to the UK, suggesting that particular political and cultural factors are in operation which make it important to distinguish the working method of this form of documentary theatre from others. As the Latin root of 'verbatim' suggests, the moment of utterance is privileged, and 'verbatim theatre', in its purest sense, is understood as a theatre whose practitioners, if called to account, could provide interviewed sources for its dialogue, in the manner that a journalist must, according to the code of ethics, have sources for a story. The term originated in England and was first coined in an article by Derek Paget in 1987 called '"Verbatim Theatre": Oral Techniques and Documentary Techniques', and it makes for intriguing study." Luckhurst, ibid., 200f.

plays, such as David Hare's *The Power of Yes* (2009) and *The Permanent Way* (2003) and Robin Soan's *Talking to Terrorists* (2005), juxtapose key historical turning points or situations.[66]

The authors' special creative achievement "was in the selection and editing."[67] Besides personalization and testimony, which enable the play to be lifted to a biographic sphere of reality, it is especially the procurement of detailed knowledge and associative leaps, by means of which the play manages to provide contrast to conventional media reporting at that time. One learns, for instance, that the prisoners communicated with their friends and relatives through letters. Moreover, the influence of political organizations on the camp is emphasized. While the Red Cross functions as a mediator between prisoners and their families, the pressure of other involved countries' ministries is able to force the early release of prisoners. The plight of the character and witness Moazzam Begg, who outstays the remaining protagonists in the military prison, enjoys strong audience impact, as the portrayal of his on-going imprisonment is meant to encourage the audience to commit to his case. The play gains an almost didactic character through the reproduction of the "real" into the literary world, a move effected by the introduction of politically responsible figures (e.g. Donald Rumsfeld) and concerned parties (i.e. Clive Stafford Smith.) It confronts the audience with the actual names of detainees' representatives, meanwhile abstaining from constructing the exotic utopia of Guantanamo, which contrasts with Donald Rumsfeld's vision of a compulsive tourist destination. "To be in an eight-by-eight cell," Rumsfeld said, "in beautiful sunny Guantánamo Bay, Cuba is not an inhumane treatment."[68] The anonymous Other is given a name and a face, speaking to the audience through the authenticated stage masque of a relative, politician, helper, or a former classmate.

This presence, however, hardly redeems the prisoner as an expressive subject of political discourse. Rather, the deprivation of rights becomes evident in the protagonists' speech, as, for example, when Bisher, a prisoner, reads aloud a letter to his mother, which adopts the whole range

---

[66] Taylor, "The Experience of Immediacy: Emotion and Enlistment in Fact-Based Theatre," 227.

[67] Gillian Slovo, symposium on 'Verbatim Practices in Contemporary Theatre,' July 13, 2006, cited by Luckhurst, "Verbatim Theatre, Media Relations and Ethics," 214.

[68] Brittain and Slovo, *Guantanamo*, 34.

of romanticization used by the US administration in order to soothe his relatives and obviate censorship. Bisher completely conceals his actual persona and experiences behind his disguised and restrained use of language.

> Bisher: Dear Mother, I'm writing this letter from the lovely mountains of Afghanistan at a US prison camp. I am very well. The conditions are excellent and everyone is very, very nice. I hope that you, my brother, my sister and all the family are well. Give my salaam to everyone and I hope we meet soon. P.S. Tell BISHER mouths a few names (to indicate censored words) that the food is very good and I can pray as much as I want. Your loving son.[69]

Brittain and Slovos's play engages in a documentary gesture which refuses to perpetuate the media images of Guantánamo. The investigation, extensive witness questioning and a mode of representation learned in the critical approaches of the *littérature engagée* of the 1970s fuse journalistic montage-like and essayistic components together, ensuring that *Guantanamo* still has evidence-informed status, and that the audience is given an unprecedented insider glimpse into the camp—one of the advantages of theatre's reality effect. Presenting the actual lives of Guantánamo prisoners on the stage of the Tricycle Theatre erases some of the distance between actual witnesses, and a witnessing and participating audience.

The production takes a postmodern turn by abstaining form creating a "grand narrative"[70] that would shove the presented content towards clear political ideology or convey meta-knowledge that exceeds individual impressions—all of which was still constitutive of classical documentary drama.

Unlike Dieckmann, Brittain and Slovo do not aim at vivisecting the prisoner's psyche through various empathy effects but evoke the difference between detainees and audience, then break it apart with the help of metaleptic elements to finally build up an open space on stage, and one that is marked by a polyphony of voices working against major US discourses. Along with a certain amount of doubt with regard to the prisoners' actual guilt, the play probes even further by presenting the figure of the well-informed citizen as an important representative of public opinion. Thus, the utterances of family members, victims, scientists, and non-profit organizations rub shoulders with those of politically significant individuals such as Donald Rumsfeld. Their 9/11 stories,

---

[69] Ibid., 25.
[70] Lyotard, *The postmodern condition*.

recollections or personal justification policies take place on equal grounds within a space of exchange, acceptance, mutual recognition, and influence. Guantánamo's detainees, and the figure of the terrorist in particular, are not perceived as they are in Dieckmann's novel, namely as exotic creatures conversing with snakes. *Guantánamo* sketches an image of the prisoners that does not radically depart from its societal context. As in Dieckmann's novel, the play does not declare the prisoners' innocence. Therefore, the motivations behind Rashid's and Moazzam's despondency-driven journeys from Germany to Pakistan and from England to Gambia respectively remain ambivalent.

Figures such as Bisher, a British citizen with an Iraqi background, complicate any sort of naïve solidarity with the prisoners. Bisher, who joins a friend in Gambia with the plan of establishing an oil company without any funds or previous knowledge on the subject, and who, as the owner of seven motorcycles, is described as a "speed freak" in the play by Mark Jennings, a British civil rights campaigner who was incorporated into Brittain and Slovo's play, fits well into the US stereotype of addictive behaviour. As owner of a licence permitting him to fly small helicopters, Bisher enters the US defence system's field of vision and through his characterization, the audience is confronted with its own fears and prejudices. His story is being sketched out in order to further throw light on publicly available facts. Finally, the play demonstrates consistency also on the level of its discursive-deconstructive agenda, which involves not only the arbitrariness of the main 9/11 metaphor of the "terrorist" through the representation of victims' and participants' perspectives, but also the portrayal of the topos Guantánamo and its one-sided instrumentalization as a place of justice/injustice. Responsibility is attributed not only to politically involved individuals, but Guantánamo is stylized into probing ground for an entire generation which perceives and reflects itself as "political," while having yet to determine in what ways it could prove its commitment under the modified societal conditions. Gareth Peirce, for instance, who likes to call himself an expert on law, states "Guantánamo [is …] an experiment" "in how you obtain information from people and it's an experiment in whether anyone is going to protest about that."[71] In Brittain and Slovo's play the aesthetic imagination functions as a resource of political self-discovery which continually engages in acts of experience transfer and responsibility transfer:

---

[71] Ibid., 51.

a father constantly thinking about his imprisoned son, a 9/11-affected person such as Tom Clark, who compares his private "hell" with the hypothetical misery of possibly innocent Guantánamo detainees anticipating their trials,[72] as well as major political actors, such as the British Minister of State for Foreign Affairs, who openly expresses his attitude towards the treatment of citizens of his country in the US camp and who, in July 2003, on the grounds of "some concerns about the Military Commission process," reclaims five British suspects of terrorism from Cuba. The play portrays personal commitment and political participation without discrediting any of the two. Where Dorothea Dieckmann's Robinsonade *Guantánamo* is emancipatory in its effort to offer a highly realistic scenario of communication breakdown, Brittain and Slovo's work complements the post-democratic dystopia of global isolation with a patchwork of factual material gathered from various interrelated realities set to activate audience participation. The status quo of the witness report does not confine itself to the past, but, in the postmodern vein of Brittain and Slovo's play, is confronted with a polyphonically staged space where contemporary voices are to be heard alongside prophetic ones. That way, seventeenth-century Londoner John Donne is used as a mobilizing force behind the various events:

> No man is an Island, entire of itself; every man is
> A piece of the Continent, a part of the main; ... any
> Man's death diminishes me, because I am involved in
> Mankind; and therefore never send to know for whom
> The bell tolls; it tolls for thee.[73]

Instead of evoking empathy by articulating the self-dissolution and nervous breakdown of a detainee, unlike Dieckmann's novel, Brittain and Slovo's *Guantánamo* focuses on the rehabilitation of witnesses

---

[72] Within the play, Clark utters the following summary: "If I had to sum up, it would be: I'm furious because those who are innocent have lost three years of their life, much as I lost, as I've been living in a sort of private hell since my sister was murdered, and although at least I've been able to recover and get over it and deal with, and still sort of have my life, they've had theirs taken away. And that's... and they'll never get it back and I'd buy them a drink if I met them, you know, if in truth they had done nothing wrong, I can't imagine a worse thing for any person, they deserve all of our sympathies and all of our efforts to sort of make sure they do actually get the justice they deserve." Brittain and Slovo, *Guantanamo*, 44.

[73] Donne, in Brittain and Slovo, *Guantanamo*, 59.

outside the camp. Following this move, the play not only activates a static and already exhausted journalistic and political representation agenda within its recipients, but also offers a re-contextualization of the events at hand. *Terra incognita*, the isolated island which the protagonist in Dieckmann's Robinsonade has to face, is no more. The suggestion and promise of Brittain and Slovo's play are that the destiny of the detainees of Guantánamo still lies in the hands of politicians and people who are able to have an impact on the lives of those who are forced to stay in the military prison where a legitimate trial is withheld.

Conclusion: Guantánamo—10 Years on

With the ten-year anniversary of the Guantánamo Bay camp in 2012, European and German media espoused different views. Following President Barack Obama's first unsuccessful attempt at closing the camp, a certain lethargy seemed to have crept into the public debate. The disillusionment was particularly visible with the online editions of the larger German newspapers. The *Frankfurter Allgemeine Zeitung*, for instance, instead of publishing extended political essays on the topic, offered a series of rare pictures from the camp as a sign of its silent protest. The *Süddeutsche Zeitung* issued the text "You only come out in a body bag" by Washington correspondent Reymer Klüver, which drew an unsettling picture of the developments after the years of the first wave of protest. In essence, the text traced phenomena following the waning international pressure on the US Democratic government and the subsequently dwindling numbers of releases from the naval base.

> Only the dead come out of Guantánamo. The last two prisoners that left the US detention camp took the journey to their home countries in body bags. Awal Gul from Afghanistan died last year of a heart attack at the age of 48. Three months later, Haji Nassim, a 37-year-old Afghani, hanged himself with his bed linen.[74]

Drawing a tentative conclusion after ten years, Human Rights Watch lists some figures which relativize the happenings after the opening of the camp in 2002: "600: Of the 779 detainees [...] were released without charges, many after being detained for years;" "149: Total number of

---

[74] Klüver, "Raus geht es nur noch im Leichensack" (My translation).

detainees remaining at Guantanamo;" while "15 [...] children under age of 18 who have been imprisoned at Guantanamo" and "9 [...] detainees [...] died while in custody, six by suspected suicide."⁷⁵ Far away from the hot spots of Western politics, for more than ten years an ethical drama seems to have taken place publicly. Germany, like other countries, got involved by refusing to accommodate a certain number out of 78 detainees, "who[m] the US ha[d] approved for transfer to home or third countries but remain at Guantanamo."⁷⁶

The situation of the detainees of Guantánamo has changed into an international problem which has not yet been solved and which still fills numerous people with both anger and despair. South African Nobel Prize laureate C.M. Coetzee, in his *Diary of a Bad Year* (2007), like other intellectuals,⁷⁷ spoke about the detention centre and sketched a project which he himself abstained from carrying any further. Coetzee's entry "On Guantánamo Bay" included the draft of a play entitled "Guantánamo! Guantánamo!," in which a "corps of prisoners, their ankles shackled together, thick felt mittens in their hands, muffs over their ears, black hoods over their heads" steps up, at which point "dances of the persecuted and desperate" begin.⁷⁸ Soldiers in olive-green overalls encircle the prisoners, beating them up, while a man bearing the masque of Donald Rumsfeld stands in the corner and "alternately writes at his lectern and dances ecstatic little jigs."⁷⁹ This "horror ballet," Coetzee's

---

⁷⁵ See http://www.hrw.org/features/guantanamo-facts-figures (accessed 1.5.2015).
⁷⁶ Ibid.
⁷⁷ In a radio interview broadcast the day before the election of Barack Obama as President of the United States, the Portuguese writer and Nobel Prize laureate José Saramago expressed his wish for the closing of Guantánamo as the first action of the new leader. For him, this step would not only have been an overdue procedure, that helps the detainees of the "concentration camp," but also progress for the relationship between the US and Cuba. Saramago, *Das Tagebuch*. In his book *American Vertigo* (English translation: *American Vertigo: In the Footsteps of Tocqueville*, 2006), the French philosopher Bernard-Henri Lévy especially criticizes the "intercultural comedy" by the US military, which, on one hand, serves eagerly to comply with religious rules—i.e. not wearing long shirts that could disturb the detained Muslims in their sense of shame—while, on the other hand, openly confesses to cudgelling prisoners, who show their reluctance by spitting at the guards or smudge walls of their prison cells with faeces. Lévy, *American Vertigo. Auf der Suche nach der Seele Amerikas*, 279. For the critique of American intellectuals, see, for example,. Chomsky, *Interventions* and Arnove (ed.), *The Essential Chomsky*.
⁷⁸ C.M. Coetzee, *Diary of a Bad Year*, 37.
⁷⁹ Ibid.

narrator assumes, would have had tremendous success in Berlin, London, and New York, and yet, the resonance created among intellectuals of the Western metropolises had to sadly remain without any consequence because "the people it targets [...] could not care less what ballet audiences think of them."[80]

This chapter has focused on the literary strategies employed in two rather divergent re-imaginations of terrorism suspects' identities. These two "horror ballets" have tried, beyond positing their effort as a mere gesture reminiscent of Coetzee's aestheticized thought experiment, to show the experiences of people whose physical and mental states had long remained unaccounted for. Within the context of this atmosphere of societal unwillingness, Dorothea Dieckmann's novel *Guantánamo* and Brittain and Slovo's play come across as literary sketches taking up the well-known media images of caged detainees seeking access to the inner worlds of the imprisoned individuals—be they guilty or not—who, arrested at airports, on the street, at their work places or during a fight, had been sent off on a journey whose purpose, length or stages remained entirely unknown to them. Dorothea Dieckmann's psychogram fleshes out the various ways in which this systematic "uprooting" blurs the boundary between the detainees' own perceptions and those of the people they confront at the camp, thus constituting a sadomasochistic bond between oppressed and oppressor in a gesture superseding the lack of human dignity. Due to its temporal proximity to the initial distribution of photographs taken at Guantánamo, Dieckmann's "Institutionenroman" comes with the immediate impression of a scenario, which, as Judith Butler notes, reminds one of a "Kafkan nightmare (or Sadean drama)."[81] Thus, in a way, the text sticks to "traumatic realism," which, as Glaberson from the *New York Times* analyses in his critique, imagines the camp as "strange new Alcatraz" and "gulag of our times," without, however, recontextualizing the newly emerging trauma. In fact, Dieckmann's novel runs the risk of operating an "activation of traumatic repetition."[82] By the biographical composition of Rashid's character, she is nonetheless capable of uncovering existential tragedies in the prisoners' fates. This chapter argues that Dieckmann establishes a distance between the protagonist and the reader to aesthetically include

---

[80] Ibid.

[81] Butler, *Precarious Life*, 80.

[82] Feldman, "The Actuarial Gaze: From 9/11 to Abu Ghraib," 15, quoted in Hesford, "Staging Terror," 32.

the social, political, and juridical uncertainty which characterized the camp at the time of the novel's publication. The "double-othering" of Rashid, who is presented in his traumatic isolation, gives the reader the possibility of stepping back from their own distress, although the trauma that Rashid experiences can nonetheless be transmitted to the recipient because the text does not create any kind of perspective for the imprisoned protagonist, who, in the end, seems to be far away from "Paradise," the prison section for those detainees, who face their release.

Unlike Dieckmann, Brittain and Slovo's play takes into account the personal stories of former detainees. Yet, instead of merging these utterances into a journalistic narrative, the authors use the method of the interview as the rationale of their emancipatory project and reconstruct the political world in which the prisoners are involved. Brittain and Slovo's play stages the trip to Guantánamo as a borderline experience for the terrorism suspects, marking the transition between a past gradually uncovered through interrogations and a future that is yet to be co-shaped with the help of the audience. Moazzam's release from the camp is not a final reconciliation following a political debacle; it is presented as the result of a process involving mostly British politicians and the pressure of non-governmental organizations on the US government. The protagonist is taken back to London while his Gambian friends remain in the camp. Brittain and Slovo's minimalist stage prose sets a puristic, simple piece of speech against the sheer emotive and traumatic force of the visual images circulating in the media. The authentic, biographic word, the act of fragmentary story-telling and listening, as well as the individual re-imaginations of the occurrences in Guantánamo build up the play's principal communicative structure, simultaneously opening up ground for responsible agency; from the words uttered on stage, recipients can then create their own imaginary pictures, thus gaining genuinely personal, emphatically substantialized access to the phenomenon called Guantánamo, while the protagonists themselves stagnate.

Guantánamo's straightforward exposition is a departure from the reproduction of spectacular victim narratives that dominate popular discourse. In the play, relationships between characters are not developed; instead, the characters' stories are presented to the audience in long, isolated stretches of verbatim readings from testimonies and letters.[83]

---

[83] Hesford, "Staging Terror," 35.

In this manner, the play succeeds in establishing an "imaginative zone," "in which the humanitarian appeal can be made without reproducing the spectacle."[84] With the ego-documents, Brittain and Slovo have material at their disposal, which helps them to dispel fundamental uncertainties surrounding the reality of the camp. Dieckmann, on the other hand, faces a dilemma: she has to create a text—without using authorized first-hand material—which has to shape and anticipate the interior space of the camp, to which the public has not had access at that point. Nonetheless, even the fact-based political writing of Brittain and Slovo refrains from simplified "truth telling" which would erase all "uncertainties" connected with the camp. Their play *Guantanamo* does not aim to give an answer to the question whether the terror suspects are "Taliban," "jihadist," or harmless tourists, who at the time of their arrest were just on a trip of self-discovery.

References

Agamben, Giorgio. *Homo Sacer. Sovereign Power and Bare Life* (Stanford: Stanford University Press, 1995).

Aradau, Claudia. "Law Transformed: Guantánamo and the 'other' exception," *Third World Quarterly*, vol. 28, no. 3 (2007), 489–501.

Arnove, Anthony (ed.), *The Essential Chomsky* (New York: Vintage, 2008).

Begg, Moazzam. *Enemy Combatant: A British Muslim's Journey to Guantánamo and Back* (London: Free Press, 2007).

Begley, Louis. *Why the Dreyfus Affair Matters* (New Haven, CT: Yale University Press, 2009).

Bennett, Bruce. "Cinematic Perspectives on the 'War on Terror': 'The Road to Guantánamo' (2006) and Activist Cinema," *New Cinemas: Journal of Contemporary Film*, vol. 6, no. 2 (2008), 111–126.

Brittain, Victoria, and Gillian Slovo. *Guantanamo. Honor Bound to Defend Freedom* (London: Oberon, 2004).

———. "X-Ray Visions: Photography, Propaganda and Guantánamo Bay," in Feona Attwood, Vincent Campbell, I. Q. Hunter, and Sharon Lockyer (eds.), *Controversial Images. Media Representations on the Edge* (New York: Palgrave Macmillan, 2013), 67–82.

Booth, Wayne. *The Rhetoric of Fiction* (Chicago: University of Chicago Press, 1961).

Campe, Rüdiger. "Kafkas Institutionenroman—*Der Proceß, Das Schloß*," in Rüdiger Campe (ed.), *Gesetz—Ironie. Festschrift für Manfred Schneider* (Heidelberg: Synchron, 2004).

---

[84] Ibid.

Campe, Rüdiger. "Robert Walsers Institutionenroman *Jakob von Gunten*," Rudolf Behrens and Jörn Steigerwald (eds.), *Die Macht und das Imaginäre* (Würzburg: Königshausen & Neumann, 2005).
Canton, Ursula. "Guantánamo. Documenting a Real Space?," in Thomas Rommel and Taylor, Lib, „The experience of immediacy: Emotion and enlistment in fact-based theatre," *Studies in Theatre & Performance*, vol. 31, no. 2, 223–237.
Chomsky, Noam. *Interventions* (San Francisco: City Lights Books, 2007).
Dieckmann, Dorothea. *Guantánamo*. Roman (Stuttgart: Klett-Cotta, 2004).
Dieckmann, Dorothea. *Guantánamo*. A Novel, translated by Tom Mohr (London: Duckworth Overlook, 2008).
Downey, Anthony. "Zones of Indistinction. Giorgio Agamben's 'Bare Life' and the Politics of Aesthetics," *Third Text*, vol. 23, no. 2, 109–125.
Faber, Michel. "Guantánamo. A Novel," *The Guardian*, June 21, 2008, available at, http://www.theguardian.com/books/2008/jun/21/saturdayreviewsfeatres.guardianreview4 (accessed 1.5.2015).
Falcke, Eberhard. "Dorothea Dieckmann sucht einen Weg in das Innerste der Gefangenen von Guantánamo," *Die Zeit*, September 2, 2004.
Falkoff, Marc et al. (eds.). *Poems from Guantánamo: The Detainees Speak* (Iowa City: University of Iowa Press, 2007).
Feldman, Allen. "The Actuarial Gaze: From 9/11 to Abu Ghraib," *Cultural Studies*, vol. 19, no. 2, 203–226.
Fesperman, Dan. *The Prisoner of Guantanamo* (New York: Vintage Books, 2007).
Friedsam, Hiram J. "Bureaucrats as Heroes", *Social Forces*, vol. 32, no. 3, 269–274.
Gibbons, Meghan. "Representing the Real on The Road to Guantánamo," in: Andrew Schopp et al (eds.), *The War on Terror and American Popular Culture—September 11 and Beyond* (Madison, NJ: Fairleigh Dickinson, 2009), 103–123.
Glaberson, William. "Guantánamo, Evil and Zany in Pop Culture", February 19, 2008, www.nytimes.com/2008/02/18/us/18gitmo.html?pagewanted=print&_r=0 (accessed 1.5.2015).
Griswold, Eliza. "'To Be Free from This Cage': The Poetry of Guantánamo Bay Detainees," *Book Forum: The Review for Art, Fiction, & Culture*, vol. 13, no. 2 (2006), 26f.
Harlow, Barbara. "Resistance Literature Revisited: From Basra to Guantánamo," *Alif: Journal of Comparative Poetics*, vol. 32 (2012), 20–29.
Haschemi Yekani, Elahi. "The Politics of (Social) Death and Rebirth in «The Road to Guantánamo» and «Taxi to the Dark Side»," in Anette Pankratz et al (eds.), *Birth and Death in British Culture—Liminality, Power, and Performance* (Cambridge: Cambridge Scholars, 2012), 67–80.
Hegarty, Paul. "Giorgio Agamben," in Jon Simons (ed.), *From Agamben to Žižek. Contemporary Critical Theorists* (Edinburgh: Edinburgh University Press, 2010), 14–28.
Hesford, Wendy S. "Staging Terror," *The Drama Review: A Journal of Performance Studies* 50, 2006, 29–41.

Hickman, John. *Selling Guantánamo: Exploding the Propaganda Surrounding America's Most Notorious Military Prison* (Gainesville, et al.: University Press of Florida, 2013).
Honigsberg, Peter Jan. *Our Nation Unhinged. The Human Consequences of the War on Terror* (Berkeley/Los Angeles/London: University of California Press, 2009).
Irving, Stephen, and Max Schwab (eds.). *Guantánamo, USA. The Untold History of America's Cuban Outpost* (Lawrence: University Press of Kansas, 2009).
Kämmerlings, Richard. "Was zählt ist auf dem Blatt," *Frankfurter Allgemeine Zeitung*, June 28, 2004.
Klüver, Reymer. "Raus geht es nur noch im Leichensack", sueddeutsche.de, 9.1.2012.
Kurnaz, Murat. *Fünf Jahre meines Lebens. Ein Bericht aus Guantánamo* (Berlin: Rowohlt, 2007).
Luckhurst, Mary. "Verbatim Theatre, Media Relations and Ethics," Nadine Holdsworth and Mary Luckhurst (eds.), *A Concise Companion to Contemporary British and Irish Drama* (Malden, et al.: Blackwell, 2008), 200–222.
Lyotard, Jean-François, *The postmodern condition: A report on knowledge.* (Minneapolis: University of Minnesota Press, 1984).
Margulies, Joseph. *Guantánamo. And the Abuse of the Presidential Power* (London et al: Simon & Schuster Paperbacks, 2007).
McIntosh, K.C. "Guantánamo Bay," *American Mercury* January 10, 1927, 106–112.
Michaelsen, Scott, and Scott Cutler Shershow. "Beyond and Before the Law at Guantánamo," *Peace Review*, vol. 16 no. 3 (2004), 293–303.
Pastouna, James. *Guantanamo Bay. Gefangen im rechtsfreien Raum* (München: Europäische Verlagsanstalt, 2005).
Peters, Michael A. "Giorgio Agamben's Homo Sacer Project," *Educational Philosophy and Theory*, vol. 46, no. 4 (2004), 327–333.
Radisch, Iris. ORF, 11.2.2004, Broadcast Bachmann Award.
Rebien, Kristin. "Cosmopolitan Perspectives. Globalization and Transnationalization in Contemporary Literature," in Irene Gilsenan Nordin, Julie Hansen, and Carmen Zamorano Llena (eds.), *Transcultural Identities in Contemporary German Literature* (Amsterdam: Rodopi, 2013), 113–136.
Lévy, Bernard-Henri. *American Vertigo. Auf der Suche nach der Seele Amerikas* (Frankfurt/New York: Campus, 2007).
Llena, Zamorano (eds.). *Transcultural Identities in Contemporary Literature* (Amsterdam/New York: Rodopi, 2013), 113–134.
Perera, Anna. *Guantanamo Boy* (London: Puffin Books, 2008).
Saramago, José. *Das Tagebuch. Mit einem Vorwort von Umberto Eco*, transl. by Marianne Gareis and Karin von Schweder-Schreiner (Hamburg: Campe, 2010).
Scalmer, Sean. *Dissent Events: Protest, the Media and the Political Gimmick in Australia* (Australia: University of New South Wales Press, 2002).

Schreiber, Mark, and Thomas Rommel (eds.). *Mapping Uncertain Territories—Space and Place in Contemporary Theatre and Drama*. Contemporary Drama in English, vol. 13, 87–101.
Silkenat, James R., and Mark R. Shulman (eds.). *The Imperial Presidency and the Consequences of 9/11. Lawyers react to the Global War on Terrorism*, vol. 1 and 2 (London: Preager Security International, 2007).
Slahi, Mohamedou Ould. *Guántanamo Diary*, ed. by Larry Siems (Edinburgh/London: Canongate, 2015).
Smith, Caleb. *The Prison and the American Imagination* (New Haven, London: Yale University Press, 2009).
Smith, Frank. *Guantanamo* (Paris: Seuil, 2010).
Sombroek, Andreas. *Eine Poetik des Dazwischen. Zur Intermedialität und Intertextualität bei Alexander Kluge* (Bielefeld: transcript, 2005).
Stafford Smith, Clive. *Eight o'clock Ferry to the windward side. Seeking Justice in Guantánamo Bay* (New York: Nation Books, 2007).
Stoller, Terry. *Tales of the Tricycle Theatre* (London/New York: Bloomsbury Methuen Drama, 2013).
Trapp, Erin. "The Enemy Combatant as Poet: The Politics of Writing in Poems from Guantanamo," *Postmodern Culture: An Electronic Journal of Interdisciplinary Criticism*, vol. 21, no. 3 (2011) [n. p.].
Weber, Elisabeth. "Literary Justice? Poems from Guantánamo Bay Prison Camp," *Comparative Literature Studies*, vol. 48, no. 3 (2001), 417–434.
Whyman, Matt. *Inside the Cage* (New York: Simon & Schuster, 2007).
Willemsen, Roger. *Hier spricht Guantánamo. Interviews mit Ex-Häftlingen* (Frankfurt a. M.: Fischer, 2006).
Worthington, Andi. *The Guantánamo Files The Stories of the 774 Detainees in America's Illegal Prison* (London: Pluto Press, 2007).

Author Biography

Philipp Hubmann undertakes research in German literature and film with special interests in political theory and the history of media. His publications are concerned with "political aporia" (*Politische Aporien*, 2016), issues of documentary narratives ("Dokumente des Amoks," 2012) and the relationship between literature and administration in the 19th century ("Verwaltete Not", 2016). From 2004–2009 he studied German literature, philosophy and rhetoric in Tübingen, Vienna and Paris with a grant from the German National Academic Foundation. From 2013–2015 he was coordinator of the Graduate School "Arts & Politics. Visual rhetoric and political language in historical perspective" at Innsbruck University, Austria. Currently he is member of research staff at the German Department of the University of Zurich (Chair: Prof. Dr. Davide Giuriato).

Appendix: Extract from Giovanna Capucci's *Twin Towers: poesie*, with Translations by Gillian Ania

Giovanna Capucci's Twin Towers: poesie: A Sequence of Poems Responding to the Tele-visions of 9/11

Gillian Ania

Gillian Ania has a Ph.D. in Italian (University of Hull, 2002). She has published books on Leonardo Sciascia (*Fortunes of the Firefly*, 1996) and Paola Capriolo (*Musica, Mitologia, Metamorfosi*, 2006), and essays on the nineteenth-century *Misteri* genre, contemporary apocalyptic, autobiographical and epistolary fiction, 9/11, and literary translation. She was Reader in Italian at the University of Salford, UK, until 2012, after which she held a research post at the University of Bangor, 2013–2014.

Abstract:

The attack on New York's World Trade Center by hijacked passenger airliners on September 11, 2001 provoked universal shock and dismay, yet also fascination. Giovanna Capucci's collection *Twin Towers: poesie* (2002), presented here in the original Italian and in English translation, 'documents' the tragedy, both as it unfolded and in its subsequent repercussions, particularly in the context of East-West relations. In her brief Introduction, Gillian Ania highlights the directness of Capucci's poems, the varying tones, moods, rhythms, religious imagery, the problematic nature of some of the concepts employed, and the collection's cumulative force. The attack on the Twin Towers was manna from heaven for all news media, an irony not lost on critics in their discussions of its real and symbolic effects.

Towers crumbling in clouds of smoke before the viewers' gaping eyes. Images of two planes plunging into adjacent towers, shocking images which are pored over, time and again, images which astound and compel. An aerial event which generates universal fascination and horror in equal measure.

Unsurprisingly, between individual quick-flash interpretations of the disaster and those arrived at through the hailstorm of mediated reports and repeated transmissions, a chasm opens up. And as the bigger picture gradually unfolds, we look beyond the smouldering waste-ground, the sirens, the frozen moment, to intuit acts of reprisal, of total war.

Accident turned into design.

As critics have pointed out, the attack on the Twin Towers was intended not only to shock and destroy, but to be *witnessed*, felt by the whole world. The East had apparently launched an attack against the West, against Western culture and its capitalist values, and yet the sensational nature of that attack boosted those very values in the West; it was manna from heaven for all news media, an irony that was not lost on critics such as Baudrillard or Žižek in their discussions of its real and symbolic effects.[1] A decade or so earlier, before the Internet and mobile phone technology allowed images to flash instantly across the globe, such an impact would have been unthinkable.

On September 11th, 2001, this reality was shown to be far more unbelievable than any dreamed-up fiction. Spectacularly so. And Giovanna Capucci was at once deeply moved by it and impelled to write.

Twin Towers: poesie, Capucci's second collection of poems, was published in January 2002.[2] The visions, re-visions and endless stream of accounts of the attack worked intensively on Capucci's subconscious mind over a very short span of time; the initial poems were composed within days, immediately following the tragedy, with a full draft of 39 poems and an epigraph completed just a few weeks later.[3]

---

[1] Baudrillard, *The Spirit of Terrorism*; Žižek, *Welcome to the Desert of the Real: Five Essays on September 11*.

[2] Capucci, *Twin Towers: poesie*.

[3] Interview with author, Università Cattolica del Sacro Cuore, Milan, April 29, 2010.

On first reading the work, I was attracted by the directness and simplicity of individual poems but also by their cumulative force, and was quickly inspired to read them with greater circumspection, and almost simultaneously to begin a translation, to experience Capucci's reactions through my own, English words. Twenty-five of the poems are presented below (in Italian and English), after a brief discussion of contexts and content, functions and purpose.[4]

Giovanna Capucci, from Faenza (Ravenna), was not, of course, alone in responding to 9/11 in Italy. The dailies, *Corriere della sera* and *La Repubblica*, quickly published the reactions and opinions of a number of Italian writers, including those of the noted poet, Valerio Magrelli; they also carried longer pieces by the controversial Oriana Fallaci (see chapter "The Islamic World as Other in Oriana Fallaci's 'Trilogy'" in this volume), and novelist-essayist, Alessandro Baricco. Subsequently, several poems drew on the theme, as did a handful of prose narratives either centrally (short stories) or peripherally (novels), to establish a post-9/11 aesthetic.[5]

Capucci has published six books of poems to date, the first in the wake of a personal tragedy, the loss of her son at the age of 28.[6] More realist than idealist, her subsequent collections touch frequently on the fragility of life, with individual poems feeling their way towards the meanings of love, loss, remembrance, being alone and 'different.' Most of her poems are short: spare, incisive reflections or dialogues with self, where judgements may be harsh or couched in a biting irony, and rhyme is minimal. At times, statements are beaten out, one after another, compelling the reader to seize on or infer connections. Elsewhere, the verse is more discursive, through sustained development of its theme. The collection *Effimera* (2007) is particularly fresh, with rhyme and assonance used sparingly, judiciously, as impressions, snapshots or stages

---

[4]Capucci has given permission for her poems to appear here. Translations of seven poems were published in 2013: Capucci and Ania, *Stand* 11 (3&4), 199/200 (2013), 38f. For a discussion of my working methods, see Ania, "Translating Giovanna Capucci's *Twin Towers: poesie*: Sound and Sense."

[5]Mario Luzi, Alda Merini, and Aldo Nove were among other poets who immediately responded to 9/11. See Arrigoni, "L'11 settembre nella poesia italiana." For discussion of the narrative response, see Ania, "11th September 2001: the Italian Writers' Response."

[6]*Occhi vivi occhi morti*.

of a relationship are subjected to the poet's microscopic scrutiny. In her most recent work, *Anima mia* (2011), the poems stretch across a wider thematic spectrum, with subjects receiving a lighter, more subtle or even whimsical treatment.[7]

The *Twin Towers* poems are to a great extent self-contained. For Italy, 9/11 was a distant tragedy, albeit one of global significance, and unlike some more socio-politically committed writers, Capucci draws little on aspects of shared Italian history and culture (other than, implicitly, the 'special relationship' between Italy and America); she works largely with religious metaphors and imagery, and visual parallels.[8] September 11th is imagined as a "Judgement Day" that "caught us all | unready" (poem 1, lines 1–3),[9] a "Holocaust" where "dreams and | desires | are embers spent" and the poet's heart "turned to ash" (poem 3, see lines 2–5), or an "Apocalypse" in which the perpetrators are given a Christian role, or persona, Muslim pilots as heralds of eschatological doom: "From the four compass points | Apocalypse flies. | Four Horsemen abroad | swoop down from the skies" (poem 7, lines 1–4).[10]

Not surprisingly, the use of end-of-the-world scenarios unleashes terror, agony, death and destruction, as well as anger, recrimination and hypocrisy. Frequently, a sense of vitality is transmitted in a few concentrated lines, through lexical crispness, some striking imagery and ambiguity, through varying tones, moods, rhythms and pace. There are visions of people falling, of towers burning, of day turning to night and the desperate search for survivors, conveying above all else the directly expressed view that after this fearful culture clash between East and West, "nothing will ever again | be the same" (poem 10, lines 12–13).[11]

---

[7]The collection includes some fine character sketches and reflections on our perceptions of others, on nature and existence. Capucci is still relatively unknown outside her region; Cinzia Sartini Blum and Lara Trubowitz do not include her in their collection of twenty-five women poets: *Contemporary Italian Women Poets: A Bilingual Anthology*. Capucci has also published narratives, including *L'ultimo ballo* and *Amore mio non piangere*.

[8]There is much political and superficial cultural overlap between Italy and America, in part owing to relations developed between the two countries in the post-war period.

[9]The poems are numbered here for ease of reference.

[10]One of Magrelli's poems, "11 settembre 2001," links the tragedy with a homework task for all, to keep the flame alive; see *Disturbi del sistema binario*, 15.

[11]In Magrelli's "12 settembre 2001," the heaviness of the previous night is lightened by the sight of a piece of white card, dove-like, on which the poet can write a grateful poem, "anche se nulla è finito e nulla finirà"; *Disturbi del sistema binario*, 16.

The reader of these poems encounters the opportunity—the obligation, even—to relive these events 'first-hand.'[12]

Where does the poet stand? Several poems conflate or co-mingle images, perhaps intentionally. Poem 9 announces that "Allah has killed God" who has "veiled | his face | with a black drape" (lines 1–2, 10–12)—as if the latter were donning a burka, from the grave. On the other hand, if God is deemed to be "the only God" (poem 16, line 6), who is Allah, "the Muslim God | thirsting for blood" (lines 3–4)—unless they are two faces of the same supraordinate being ("a two-faced God", poem 32, line 10)? In accusing the attackers of rape ("Raped | are the Towers of Manhattan | reaching for the skies"), poem 35 underlines the inherently Western perspective: an Arab might well view the towers as symbolic of the continual "rape" of his lands (for oil) by America, and the West at large (and see discussion of poem 4, below). The image of towers stretching heavenwards (note the ambiguity of the Italian "*cielo,*" line 3 [sky/heaven]) is significantly silent on whether this is a spiritual or a materialistic heaven they are aspiring to. The towers might even be standing for the Tower of Babel.

An irreparably deep gulf separates East from West ("A deep chasm | divides you | pitiless hate | defines you") (poem 32, lines 6–9), yet while there is a heavy bias in favour of Western cultural values, there is neither explicit espousal of such 'ideals' (poem 32, line 2) nor questioning of their precise nature, nor is there any sustained attempt at an understanding of the East: while the poet condemns the mistreatment of Islamic women by their co-religionists ("their faces obscured | their mouths sewn up | prisoners of a myth | denied all | even the right | to exist") (poem 29, lines 9–14), any fanaticism, or "fanatical intransigence" (poem 30, lines 10–11), belongs only to the Taliban and not the West. Poem 26 imagines Bin Laden as Aladdin, tinkering with his lamp, out of which (perhaps) this "Eastern Potentate" with "eyes metallic | cruel face", has already conjured up the Four Horsemen, a "lethal weapon | to deploy and take | us all | straight to hell" (lines 2–4, 9–12).

Yet the West is not above criticism. It is accused of complacency, of religious inobservance, of not being 'vigilant': 9/11 found America "unready"—for God (if the Apocalypse is God-driven), but also, and

---

[12]For a critical discussion of this point, see Breithaupt, "Rituals of Trauma: How the Media Fabricated September 11."

perhaps more pointedly, for attack. Furthermore, poem 35 closes with what might be an oblique concession to the attackers, whose patience had been tried for sixty years (following the carving out of Israel from their territory) and finally frayed to breaking point. They committed: "A violent rape | from too long lying | in wait" (lines 7–9).[13] But apart from this, there is no suggestion that the attack on New York was retaliatory, that American policy had (and still has) a case to answer so far as the Palestinian question is concerned.

In representing a reaction to visually transmitted stimuli and to the commentary coming with them, stimuli which are filtered entirely through Western and Christian sensibilities, Capucci's focus is inevitably on the effects of the specific moment in history, with causes and wider context (the twentieth-century history of East-West relations) undeveloped. Yet the destruction of the World Trade Center by hijacked passenger airliners was momentous, terrifying, 'experienced' all over the world, and the poems, short, sharp vignettes, stand as one individual's testimony. Capturing, by turns, the perspectives of spectator, TV viewer, commentator, perpetrator, victim, or (on one occasion) frustrated would-be tourist, they represent Capucci's own personal, verbal 'Ground Zero.'

Eight of these poems refer explicitly to the Twin Towers. Placed as they are at intervals throughout the collection, vertical pillars, huge structures that were once physical and are now (hugely) symbolic, these poems seem to remind us of the Twin Towers' continuing presence. The very fact of their 'symbolic' value for the Muslim perpetrators, indeed, underlines the huge gulf, culturally, between the two civilizations, Arabic culture being more deeply rooted in symbolic realities than are contemporary Western cultures.[14]

The opening poem, which sees us all falling "headlong | down from the towers" on Judgement Day (lines 7–8), underlines the problematic nature of some of the concepts employed. Scripturally, the Fall precedes the Judgement (and immediately invokes it), while here it is the result—suggestive, rather, of that first 'expulsion.'[15] Furthermore, who is

---

[13]A parallel can be found in poem 7: "They're come to strike blind | after long years in harness" (lines 5–6).

[14]See, for example, Barakat, *The Arab World: Society, Culture and State*, e.g. 25, 206.

[15]Yet Judgement Day can lead to "la seconda morte," as Dante has put it (*Inferno* I, 117): the death of the spirit or soul (after physical death) and its descent into hell.

judging whom? Has America's 'sleep of reason' ("Reason slept") (line 4) brought forth Islamic monsters? If the heart is seen as the seat of the emotions (as in the European cultural tradition), the choice of "*atrofizzato*" or atrophied ("hearts shrunk away") (line 5) takes the West to task for sealing off certain emotions, in its ruthless pursuit of commercial success.[16] Westerners have inhumanly averted their eyes from the damage their actions cause, both to themselves and to others, whether economically, socially or politically.

This theme recurs in poem 4, which raises, if incidentally, the question of the innocence of the victims, predominantly those working in the Twin Towers for private financial companies or governmental organizations involved in world trade. Perceived globally as the symbolic hub of the gigantic commercial wheel of American power, the Twin Towers were seen by the Arab world as the root of all the evil that had so humiliated and scarred millions of lives since 1945. Thus, all those "with appointments fixed | in those towers | gleaming in the sun" (lines 2–4), were fuelling an economy that was responsible for keeping the vast mass of people in the Middle East at poverty level. Were the towers' occupants complicit, complacent or simply 'guilty by association?' On a human level, and regardless of the numbers in question or the politics, of course, they are victims, their families and friends deserving of compassion—for their "appointments," that day, were not only with associates, but with death.

Such images are further developed in the taut verses of poem 8 where the towers are seen as a single entity, a blazing structure which suddenly implodes: "A monolith in flames | a visceral implosion | a menacing cloud…" (lines 1–3). The choice of "monolith" suggests the towers were a solid block, massive, immovable and unchanging, which is how America preferred to consider them, a symbol of America itself:

---

[16]The modern association of the heart and love has a long and continuous tradition in European literary culture. In Italy, it began with the poetry of the early fourteenth century—which Dante called the *dolce stil novo* [sweet new style]—but this was itself a particular development of the Troubadour tradition in Provence in the two proceeding centuries. Both, as Peter Dronke conclusively demonstrated (notably, in *The Medieval Lyric*) had their origins in the Arabic culture of Moorish Spain, going much further back in time than either. It should be remembered, too, that the heart and love featured in much medieval Latin poetry; see Helen Waddell's *The Wandering Scholars* (1927, reissued by rarebooks.com in 2012) and *Medieval Latin Lyrics* (1929, reissued by Four Courts Press in 2008).

the inviolate Superpower. Hence the profound shock occasioned by the attack: their implosion is described as "visceral," one that is felt deeply within. Dust-laden clouds billow up and hang suspended in the air, to be gradually dissipated into silence and the void of night. Speech is similarly suspended, frozen in our mouths: "Utter silence | now" (lines 4–5). The shock of the event has rendered words impotent.

The collection loosely follows the narrative of the event, from initial attack through to its immediate aftermath, with both snapshot and commentary. Several of the poems placed towards the middle of the volume refer to objects used symbolically in acts of remembrance: a photograph (poem 6), flowers (poem 11), candles (poem 14), and, rather less obviously—and consequently receiving a more inspired treatment—a shoe (poem 13): "I lost a shoe | falling from the tower, | a dainty little | summer shoe" (lines 1–4). Whoever finds it is entrusted with the preservation of the memory of a woman's life "since there's nothing left | of me" (lines 7–8).

Irony is a recurrent presence in the collection, frequently associated with ambiguity, as poem 23 demonstrates. "In a side street | beneath the Towers | a crooked sign | hangs above a door: | the 'Kabul Café'" (lines 1–5). This café is where "you," whether its proprietors, regular clients or passing visitors, had found "a safe haven," but, presumably, have now been discovered. Yet does the crooked sign suggest an air of abandon, a lack of care, even a place to avoid? Or has it simply been skewed by the impact of the crash? Are those hiding away in the café refugees from Afghan life? Do they too feel 'guilty by association,' and fear this very accusation?[17] Capucci's treatment highlights the irony of the situation whereby some Muslims had found safety and forged new lives for themselves in America while other Muslims sought to destroy that life.[18]

Rather different sentiments prevail in poem 36, where the voice of the disappointed tourist emerges: "I can't go now. | I'd planned | to go there | on Saturday. | The Twin Towers | have collapsed. Too bad" (lines 1–7). It's more 'a pity' than 'a sin' (the Italian use of "*peccato*" implies

---

[17]The attack on the Twin Towers subsequently generated such a thirst for revenge, especially within America, that it led the West into two wars, in Iraq and Afghanistan, in both of which it has been largely humiliated; and in this connection, see poem 38: "Poppies red: | chemical weapon | of the East" (lines 1–3).

[18]See also poem 31: "in the pyre of Manhattan | I lost my identity | and my life" (lines 3–5).

a decidedly plaintive tone; lines 7, 14, 15): all sense of horror at their destruction by an international Muslim organization, at the loss of life, or what terrors might ensue, has been brushed aside, obliterated by the personal inconvenience. Of far more importance were *my* plans to ascend to the 110th storey of a tower. An "act of madness | has swept them away" (lines 12–13), however, and prevented my visit, my panoramic viewing of the city. "Too bad | I can't see them" (lines 15–16). Yet as well as showing up the ugliness of egotism, can we discern in the poem a rather late association between this individual's reaction and America's blinkered pursuit of its own goals worldwide?

Giovanna Capucci erects her poetic memorial primarily to the victims of the immediate event, both collectively and, in some cases, individually. The poems commemorating individuals do so anonymously, highlighting the understandable sense of anger or bitterness at sudden, premature death, and the all-too-human need to be remembered (see poems 6, 13, 31). Otherwise the victims are captured essentially as a number, as: "a thousand | silent voices" (poem 3, lines 8–9), or "Thousands of victims | in the arms of Allah" (poem 16, lines 1–2), while the figure of "six thousand" recurs three times, signalling the enormity of the crime committed on that day—as was initially reported.[19] All the individuals "with appointments fixed | in those towers | gleaming in the sun" (poem 4, lines 2–4), were transformed into "falling stars | in a black-brimmed sky" (poem 17, lines 2–3), to lie, finally, "dead | in the wracked | cathedral" (poem 39, lines 3–5).

Occasionally, the poems question (Western) 'received wisdom' or censure moral and intellectual apathy, but more frequently, as in the concluding verses, the poet gives voice to a shudder of despair, the hopelessness of there ever being a world at peace with itself: "Two worlds | in collision – | endless division."

The Poems

1.

Il giorno del giudizio
universale
ci ha colto impreparati.

---

[19] Capucci seeks to preserve a sense of scenes as they were 'played out.'

La ragione era in sonno
il cuore atrofizzato.
Ma dopo lo schianto
verticale
dalle due torri
siamo caduti in tanti.

Judgement Day
caught us all
unready.
Reason slept,
hearts shrunk away.
Yet after the smash
headlong
down from the towers
so many of us fell.

3.
Olocausto del 2001.
Cenere è diventato
il cuore mio
tizzoni spenti
i sogni
le passioni.
Una montagna grigia
polverosa
di mille voci mute
imprigionate
nell'attimo fuggente.

Holocaust 2001.
My heart
has turned to ash,
dreams and
desires
are embers spent.
A mountainous mass
greyed by a thousand
silent voices,
immured
in a moment's passing.

4.
*In seimila
vi siete dati appuntamento
su quelle torri
luccicanti al sole.
Era l'alba
di un giorno come tanti
avvolta
ben presto
nel buio della sera.*

Six thousand of you
with appointments fixed
in those towers
gleaming in the sun.
Daybreak,
just another day
soon to be
shrouded
in evening darkness.

6.
*Portavo una foto
nel taschino
La foto
del mio piccolo bambino.
Ora sarà lui
a sorridere d'amore
a una mia foto
che ingiallirà
col tempo.*

I had a photo
in my pocket,
a photo
of my little son.
Now it will be he
who smiles lovingly
at a photo of me
that will yellow
with age.

7.
I cavalieri dell'Apocalisse
sono venuti dal cielo.
Quattro
dai quattro punti cardinali,
per colpire alla cieca
dopo un lungo allenamento.
Hanno colto in flagrante
colpendo al cuore
un mondo disattento.

From the four compass points
Apocalypse flies.
Four Horsemen abroad
swoop down from the skies.
They're come to strike blind
after long years in harness,
to strike at the heart
of a world all unready
and catch folk *in flagrante*.

8.
Un monolito in fiamme
un'implosione viscerale
una nube minacciosa
poi
un silenzio totale.

A monolith in flames
a visceral implosion
a menacing cloud…
Utter silence
now.

9.
Allah ha ucciso
Dio.
Un Dio lontano
senza gioia.
Allah è arrabbiato
potente
fa harakiri

*nel nome
dell'idea vincente.
Dio ha nascosto
il volto
con un drappo nero
Allah ha sfoderato
una spada rosso sangue.*

Allah has killed
God.
An unhappy
distant God.
Allah is angry
all powerful
his hara-kiri
reveres
one all-consuming idea.
God has veiled
his face
with a black drape
Allah has unsheathed
his blood-red sword.

10.
*Quando la nube nera
sarà dissolta
e lo strato di polvere
spazzato via,
quando l'ultima pietra
sarà rimossa
e ogni brandello di carne
raccolto,
quando saranno spenti
i lumi di preghiera
e ogni lacrima asciugata
niente
sarà più come prima.*

When the black cloud
has dissolved

and the layer of dust
been swept away,
when the last stone
is removed
and each scrap of flesh
is gathered,
when the prayer lamps
have guttered
and all tears dried
nothing will ever again
be the same.

11.
*Scavano
con le mani
i pompieri di New York.
Raccolgono
i fiori recisi
caduti nella polvere.
Suda sangue
la fronte
come quella del Cristo
sulla croce.*

Fire-fighters dig
with their hands
in New York.
They gather
cut flowers
fallen into dust.
Foreheads
sweat blood
like Christ's
on the Cross.

12.
*Un tuono
un lampo
una lacerazione.
Urla*

grida
maledizioni.

A thunder clap
a lightning flash
a laceration.
Screams
shouts
and damnation.

13.
Ho perduto una scarpa
nel volo dalla torre,
una scarpa leggera
ancora estiva.
Abbiatene cura
se la troverete
perché di me
non è rimasto niente.

I lost a shoe
falling from the tower,
a dainty little
summer shoe.
Take care of it
if you find it
since there's nothing left
of me.

14.
Un milione
di candele accese
per illuminare
i volti in cornice.
Basteranno
per illuminare
le nostre coscienze?

A million
candle flames
to illuminate

faces in their frames.
Will they suffice
to illuminate
our minds?

16.
Migliaia di vittime
fra le braccia di Allah
Dio musulmano
assetato di sangue.
Ma Dio pietoso
unico Dio
visto da un'altra
prospettiva.

Thousands of victims
in the arms of Allah
the Muslim God
thirsting for blood.
Yet a God of compassion
the only God
seen in
another light.

17.
Seimila stelle cadenti
in un cielo
listato a lutto.
Non è la notte
di San Lorenzo
ma l'11 settembre
del 2001.

Six thousand
falling stars
in a black-brimmed sky.
Not a starburst
heaven
but the morning
of 9/11.

21.
*Il cinismo
di chi non vuol vedere
di chi fa la somma
dei morti
di chi soppesa
colpe ed omissioni
e non è sfiorato
dall'orrore.
Vuol vivere tranquillo
il proprio tempo
senza un lutto
da portarsi dentro.*

The hypocrisy
of those who will not see,
who count up
the dead
or failings and faults
in their heads
and are untouched
by the horror.
They want to live
untroubled lives
not carrying
a loss inside.

23.
*Sotto le due Torri
in una via laterale
un'insegna sbilenca
sporge sopra la vetrina:
"Caffè Kabul".
Pace a voi,
che proprio qui,
fra polvere d'amianto
e sangue coagulato,
avevate trovato
un angolo sicuro
in cui sostare.*

In a side street
beneath the Towers
a crooked sign
hangs above a door:
the "Kabul Café."
Peace be unto you
who, in this very spot,
with congealed blood
and asbestos dust
all around,
a safe haven
had found.

26.
Bin Laden
principe orientale
sguardo metallico
volto crudele:
CI HAI FATTO PAURA!
La lampada di Aladino
con cui ti balocchi
non è un gioco
ma un'arma micidiale
che può portarci
dritti all'inferno
tutti quanti.

Bin Laden
Eastern Potentate
eyes metallic
cruel face:
YOU SCARED US!
This Aladdin's lamp
you tinker with
is no toy
but a lethal weapon
to deploy and take
us all
straight to hell.

29.
Inquieta
lo sguardo prigioniero
fra i graticci del burqa.
Il sole del meriggio
non indora la fronte
non illumina
il sorriso.
Donne afghane
dai volti oscuri
dalle bocche cucite,
prigioniere di un mito
negate a tutto
anche al diritto
di esistere.

Disquieting
the imprisoned gaze
through the burka's mesh.
Noonday sun
sheds no gold on temples,
illuminates
no smile.
Afghan women
their faces obscured
their mouths sewn up,
prisoners of a myth
denied all
even the right
to exist.

30.
Alì Babà
de "Le mille e una notte"
Talebani
dalle barbe nere
dai turbanti bianchi.
Il popolo dolente
non può consolarsi
con le gesta eroiche

di qualche Saladino.
Impresse sul volto
porta le stigmate
del vostro fanatismo
intransigente.

Ali Babas
from the *Arabian Nights*
the Taliban
with beards black
and turbans white.
A sorrowing race
no solace takes
in some Saladin's
heroic acts.
Your fanatical
intransigence:
stigmata marking
each harrowed face.

31.
Quel paese non è il mio paese
quella gente non è la mia gente.
Nel rogo di Manhattan
ho perso l'identità
e la vita.

This country is not my country.
These people are not my people.
Yet in the pyre of Manhattan
I lost my identity
and my life.

32.
Occidentali
dagli ideali infranti
pagani
dagli idoli dormienti,
mai capirete!
Un baratro profondo
vi divide

un odio senza amore
vi accompagna
un Dio bifronte
sfida se stesso
e spacca
il mondo in due.

Westerners
your ideals in pieces
pagans
with your sleeping idols,
you'll never understand!
A deep chasm
divides you
pitiless hate
defines you
a two-faced God
defies himself
and splits
the world in two.

35.
Stuprati
i grattacieli di Manhattan
rampicanti al cielo.
Stuprati
da lupi solitari
usciti dalla tana
con la forza crudele
di chi da troppo tempo
pativa l'astinenza.

Raped
are the Towers of Manhattan
reaching for the skies.
Raped
by lone wolves
unleashed from their lairs.
A violent rape
from too long lying
in wait.

36.
Non posso partire.
Avevo programmato
il viaggio
nel fine settimana.
Le Twin Towers
sono precipitate.
Peccato
non poterle vedere.
Volevo salire all'ultimo piano
affacciarmi dall'alto
salutare con la mano.
Una follia
le ha spazzate via.
Peccato.
Peccato
non poterle vedere.

I can't go now.
I'd planned
to go there
on Saturday.
The Twin Towers
have collapsed.
Too bad
I can't see them.
I wanted to go right to the top
look down from up there
and wave.
An act of madness
has swept them away.
Too bad.
Too bad
I can't see them.

38.
Papaveri rossi
arma chimica
d'Oriente
che sfalda i pensieri

e piega i ginocchi
a tutto l'Occidente.

Poppies red:
chemical weapon
of the East
that dissolves all thought
and bows every knee
in the West.

39.
Piange
il popolo decadente
i seimila morti
nella cattedrale
afflosciata.
Ride
il popolo medievale
per quei morti
di cui non gl'importa
niente.
Due mondi
uno scontro
nessun incontro.

The decadent state
weeps
for six thousand dead
in the wracked
cathedral.
The medieval state
laughs
at those dead
it cares not
one jot for.
Two worlds
in collision –
endless division.

REFERENCES

Ania, Gillian. "Translating Giovanna Capucci's *Twin Towers: poesie*: Sound and Sense," in Chris Conti and James Gourley (eds), *Translation as Literature / Literature as Translation* (Newcastle upon Tyne: Cambridge Scholars Publishing, 2014), 47–66.
———. "11th September 2001: The Italian Writers' Response," *Modern Italy*, vol. 17, no. 1 (2012), 119–37.
Arrigoni, Luigi Ernesto. "L'11 settembre nella poesia italiana," *Altre Modernità*, vol. 11 (2011), 162–72.
Barakat, Halim. *The Arab World: Society, Culture and State* (Berkeley/Oxford: University of California Press, 1993).
Baudrillard, Jean. *The Spirit of Terrorism*, trans. by C. Turner (London: Verso, 2002).
Blum, Cinzia Sartini, and Lara Trubowitz (eds.). *Contemporary Italian Women Poets: A Bilingual Anthology* (New York: Italica Press, 2010).
Breithaupt, Fritz. "Rituals of Trauma: How the Media Fabricated September 11," in Steven Chermak, Frankie Y. Bailey, and Michelle Brown (eds.), *Media Representations of September 11* (Westport, CR: Praeger, 2003), 67–81.
Capucci, Giovanna. *Amore mio non piangere* (Faenza: Società Editrice Il Ponte Vecchio, 2009).
———. *L'ultimo ballo* (Treviso: Edizioni Editing, 2003).
———. *Twin Towers: poesie* (Venice: Edizioni del Leone, 2002).
———. *Occhi vivi occhi morti* (Venice: Edizioni del Leone, 2000).
Capucci, Giovanna, and Gillian Ania, *Stand* 11 (3&4), 199/200 (2013), 38f.
Dronke, Peter. *The Medieval Lyric* (London: Hutchinson, 1978).
Magrelli, Valerio. *Disturbi del sistema binario* (Turin: Einaudi, 2006).

Waddell, Helen. *The Wandering Scholars* (London: Constable, 1966).
———. *Medieval Latin Lyrics* (Dublin: Four Courts Press, 2008).
Žižek, Slavoj. *Welcome to the Desert of the Real: Five essays on September 11* (London: Verso, 2002).

Index

A
Abu Ghraib, 314
Adorno, Theodor W., 54
Afghan, 40
Afghanistan, 5, 40, 41, 115
Agamben, Giorgio, 53, 295, 331, 332
Allievi, Stefano, 198
Al-Qaida attacks on European major capitals, 11
Americanophilia, 209, 211, 219, 225
Améry, Jean, 54
Amis, Martin, 25, 88
Anker, Robert, 302
Americanism
 -anti, 8, 10, 25, 26, 42, 106, 209, 218, 258
 -pro, 212, 218, 223
Apartheid, 295
Appadurai, Arjun, 5, 44, 45
Arendt, Hannah, 228
Art, 1, 39, 49, 51, 61, 70, 71, 73
Atlanticism, 10
Attacks in Europe, 5
 fictional, 21
Auster, Paul, 43

B
Babel, 361
Bali bombings, 5, 168
Barthes, Roland, 53
Baudrillard, Jean, 4, 42, 44–47, 49, 108, 111, 270
Beck, Ulrich, 7
Beigbeder, Frédéric, 17, 21, 112, 115, 172, 209, 211
Bhabha, Homi, 264, 271
Bin Laden, Osama, 37, 39, 48, 57, 361
Blurring boundaries of fact and fiction, 17, 45, 46
Bongartz, Barbara, 51
Britain, 41
Brittain, Victoria, 325, 342, 345
 Bryant Park, 54
Bush, George W., 40
Butler, Judith, 196, 198, 254

C
Capitalism, 5, 10, 52, 92, 95, 147, 257, 258, 270, 284, 297, 358
Capucci, Giovanna, 359

384 INDEX

Chomsky, Noam, 42, 43
Clash of civilizations, 24, 215
Clash of cultures, 43
Class, 23, 90, 97, 110, 131, 135, 139, 141–143, 155, 156, 219, 299, 307
Coalition of the willing, 9
Construction of the US, 10
Croatian, 7, 22
Cultural other, 15
Czech Republic, 9

D
DeLillo, Don, 55, 56, 62
Denmark, 9
Derrida, Jacques, 9, 45, 47, 91, 313
Dieckmann, Dorothea, 324, 329
Drama, 14, 153, 185, 188, 288, 330, 337, 342, 345, 349
Drew, Richard, 1, 52, 55, 57
The Falling Man, 1, 2, 53–55

E
Eastern Europe, 9, 10, 38
Emigrants, 214
Emigration, 224, 226
Enlightenment, 9, 13, 18, 19, 27, 43, 265, 271, 277, 279, 287, 303
Enzensberger, Hans Magnus, 269
Ethics, 69, 70, 83
Eurocentric, 264
Eurocentricism, 257, 276, 277
European identity, 9
European identity construction, 5
Europeanism, 10
Europeanization, 7, 19
European setting, 21

F
Fatah, Sherko, 25
Film, 1, 2, 49, 53, 163, 274
First World War. *See* World War I
Flusser, Vilém, 44
Foer, Jonathan Safran, 20
Functions of Literature, 288, 308

G
Globalization, 258, 270, 325
Goethe, Johann Wolfgang von, 259, 265
Grande, Edgar, 7
Grünbein, Durs, 62, 63
Grunberg, Arnon, 296
Guantánamo, 5, 26, 40, 332

H
Habermas, Jürgen, 9, 45
Herbst, Alban Nikolai, 51
Hettche, Thomas, 209, 213, 214
Holocaust, 54, 224, 225, 226, 295
Homo sacer, 331
Houellebecq, Michel, 12
Hungary, 9
Huntington, Samuel, 24, 186, 215

I
Immigration
  anti-immigration, 284
Immigrants, 216
Indistinguishability of fiction and reality, 4
Intermediality, 14, 55, 57, 61, 62
Iraq, 5, 9, 40, 41
Islam, 40, 188, 189
Islamists, 42

Islamophobia
  Islamophobic , 13, 25
Israel, 41, 42, 110, 169, 362
Italy, 9

J
Jünger, Ernst, 39, 51, 52

K
Kant, Immanuel, 72
Kertész, Imre, 12
Kling, Thomas, 64, 66

L
Lang, Luc, 21
Latvian, 21
Lehr, Thomas, 21, 253
Loss, 26, 44, 56, 89
Lyotard, François, 44

M
McCann, Colum, 86, 89
McEwan, Ian, 134, 143, 155
Media, 43–47
Media event, 14, 39
Medium: conditions of the medium, 75
Meyssan, Thierry, 119, 126
Migrant, 12, 191, 197, 284
Migration, 5, 286
Mimicry, 264, 266, 271
Motif
  shipwreck, 51
  Tower of Babel, 49
Muslim immigration, 5
Muslim other, 13, 25
Muslim population in Europe, 11

N
Narrative strategies, 17, 14, 54
National identity formation, 10
National context
  Britain, 135–137, 155
  Dutch, 302
  England, 41, 155
  France, 40, 106, 120, 215
  German, 40, 145, 146, 222
  Germany, 40, 42, 43, 153, 154, 215, 271
  Italy, 193–194
  Netherlands, 288
  Poland, 164
  US, 110
Nationalist parties, 12
National literatures, 8
National tragedy, 4, 5
Neo-cons. *See* Neo-conservative
Neo-conservative, 9, 40, 120

O
Obama, Barack, 40, 48
Other(s), 163, 196, 197, 210, 215, 219, 237, 255, 257–259, 262, 264, 269, 271, 272, 286, 294, 298, 300, 315, 337, 344
Othering, 208, 258, 277
Other within. *See* Stranger within

P
Palestine, 41
Palestinian, 362
Peeters, Elvis, 291, 292, 294
Peltzer, Ulrich, 54
Piaskowska, Ewa, 161
Petry, Yves, 286, 305
Poetry, 62, 64
Poland, 9
Portugal, 9

Postmodern, 64, 78, 88, 106, 154, 213, 228, 289, 299, 304, 307, 333, 345, 347
Postmodernism, 4, 308
Postmodernists, 118
Postmodernity, 109
Post-9/11 representation of terrorism, 5
Poststructuralism, 4, 25
Poststructuralist, 16
Proust, Marcel, 39

R
RAF. *See* Red Army Faction
Racism
  racist, 311
Realism, 14
Red Army Faction, 23, 131, 144, 145, 153
Refugees, 10, 25, 160, 227, 228, 230, 284, 286, 291–295, 316, 364
Representation (representation, questions of), 16, 18, 23
Richter, Gerhard, 61, 75–78
Right-wing, 12, 302, 311
Rushdie, Salman, 4

S
Schlink, Bernhard, 143, 155
Schmitt, Éric-Emmanuel, 25
Scottish, 21
Second World War. *See* World War II
Self-referentiality, 4, 14
Semiotics, 4, 83, 87, 218, 229
Shipwreck, 71, 72, 78
Skolimowski, Jerzy, 161
Sleeper(s), 146, 216, 272
Slovo, Gillian, 325, 342, 345
Sorrentino, Paolo, 1, 2, 21
Spain, 9
Spiegelman, Art, 49
State violence, 254
Stockhausen, Karlheinz, 4, 95
Stranger within, 24, 270
Sublime, 51, 67, 72–74, 78
Syrian refugees, 167, 292

T
Tochman, Wojciech, 165, 166, 172
Todorov, Tzvetan, 19, 26, 290
Tower of Babel, 49
Transatlantic, 5, 8, 10, 11, 26
Trauma, 16, 62, 63
Twin Towers, 4, 46, 49, 51, 62, 63, 68, 358

U
The United Kingdom, 9
US-European relations, 5, 38
US national identity, 20
Utopian, 96, 99

V
Victims, 365
Vietnam, 90, 92, 114

W
War on Terror, 26, 37, 40
Western lifestyle, 2
Windows on the World, 113
World Trade Center, 1, 4, 17, 50, 89, 95
World War I, 39, 41, 68, 133, 147
World War II, 9, 20, 39, 147, 160

Ž
Žižek, Slavoj, 46, 87, 107, 113, 114, 270, 286

Printed by Books on Demand, Germany